In Churchill's Shadow

30.00

~~20%~~

Purc   D0810124

In Churchill's Shadow

In Churchill's Shadow
Confronting the Past in Modern Britain

DAVID CANNADINE

OXFORD
UNIVERSITY PRESS
2003

OXFORD

UNIVERSITY PRESS

Oxford New York
Auckland Bangkok Buenos Aires
Cape Town Chennai Dar es Salaam Delhi Hong Kong Istanbul
Karachi Kolkata Kuala Lumpur Madrid Melbourne Mexico City Mumbai
Nairobi São Paulo Shanghai Taipei Tokyo Toronto

Published by Oxford University Press, Inc.
198 Madison Avenue, New York, New York 10016

Oxford is a registered trademark of Oxford University Press

Library of Congress Cataloging-in-Publication Data

Cannadine, David, 1950-
In Churchill's shadow : confronting the past in modern Britian / David Cannadine.
p. cm. Includes bibliographical references and index.
ISBN 0-19-521926-0
1. Great Britian--Politics and government--20th century. 2. Great Britian--Politics and
government--19th century. 3. Great Britian--Civilization--20th century. 4. Great
Britian--Civilization--19th century. 5. Churchill, Winston, Sir, 1874-1965. I. Title.
DA566.7.C293 2002
941.08--dc21
2002029345

1 3 5 7 9 10 8 6 4 2
Printed in the United States of America
on acid-free paper

In Memoriam

J. H. Plumb
Lawrence Stone

Contents

PART THREE:
VANISHING SUPREMACIES?

Preface

Historians write essays and articles for many specific and often unrelated reasons – to launch their careers, to establish a reputation, to keep their hand in; to please themselves, to impress their colleagues, to reach a broader audience; to sketch out a new idea, to anticipate a major work, to avoid writing a book; to take a break from a big project, to dabble but not delve too deeply, to revisit old friends and old haunts; to give as conference papers, to deliver as public lectures, to contribute to edited volumes; to indulge their scholarly curiosity, to make some (but not much) money, and (most recently and regrettably) to provide essential fodder for the Research Assessment Exercise. These one-by-one explanations are far from being exhaustive, but in varying combinations, and as explained more fully in the notes, they suffice for the essays which follow. Four of them (now chapters 4, 7, 11 and 12) were originally published more than a decade ago, and they have been thoroughly revised to take account of new material and interpretations; a further quartet (now chapters 2, 8, 9 and 10) were written during the 1990s, while I was living and working in the United States, and have been updated where appropriate; and the remainder (now chapters 1, 3, 5 and 6) have been composed since I returned to London in 1998 as Director of the Institute of Historical Research.

But however particular and personal their original circumstances of conception and composition, historical essays, regarded collectively, and undertaken interconnectedly, can also be the means of approaching one past period and problem by different but complementary routes, and so it is with the pieces gathered together here. In varied but related ways, they are all concerned with British history across the nineteenth and twentieth centuries – when the country reached its zenith, and when, by comparison, it began its long decline. More precisely, they investigate how the downside of that historical parabola, the relative sense of vanishing supremacies and diminishing possibilities, the feeling that things were no longer as great or as stable or as splendid as they had once been, was identified, dealt with and understood, or how it was ignored, regretted and denied, from the time of Joseph Chamberlain in the late nineteenth century to that of Margaret Thatcher in the late twentieth. And between them unfolded the extraordinary career of Winston Churchill, whose life was lived in a vainly magnificent attempt to preserve Britain's unrivalled Victorian inheritance in an increasingly hostile and post-Victorian world.

As such, Churchill is the dominant figure in this book: in part because of his many-splendoured character, astonishingly long public career, and remarkable range of activities and achievements; in part because he was so much a nineteenth-century personality living most of his life out of his own time; and in part because he touched Britain's twentieth century in so many ways and through so many people. Churchill was a child of the late-Victorian era, when the British parliamentary system seemed settled and secure (though not beyond criticism, some of it his); when monarchy was the conventional way in which most nations arranged their constitutions and social structures (ditto); when any aspiring politician needed to learn the craft of public-speaking and master the art of statesmanly oratory; when the Chamberlain family were establishing their dynastic dominance in Birmingham; when Stanley Baldwin, Josiah Wedgwood and G. M. Trevelyan were growing up in Worcestershire, Staffordshire and Northumberland; when Gilbert and Sullivan were pulling in the crowds at the Savoy Theatre; and when a few well-meaning and high-minded radicals were establishing a fledgling preservation society called the National Trust. As yet, Noël Coward, Ian Fleming and Margaret Hilda Roberts had not been heard of or from, but in each case it would only be a matter of time.

This was the world in which Churchill grew up, and the more it receded into the distance, the more appealing it retrospectively became. By the inter-war years, after the humiliation of the Dardanelles disaster, his prospects looked distinctly less promising than they had before 1914, and so did those of the wider world. He became disillusioned about a parliament elected on a mass franchise, he worried that the national will to rule was weakening, both at home and abroad, he looked back nostalgically to the settled social order and firmly grounded monarchies of his youth, and his elaborate, Victorian style of oratory seemed increasingly out of touch and out of date. In short, he did not adapt well to the changed circumstances of the twenties and thirties, and it pained him to see that there were others who did so much more easily. He lacked the sort of local power base that Austen and Neville Chamberlain were able to enjoy in Birmingham, he was out of sympathy with the eirenic, consensual brand of politics preached by Stanley Baldwin (and, in a different medium, by Francis Brett Young), and he scarcely subscribed to those 'spiritual values', associated with the countryside, the mountains and the big sky, that were proclaimed by the National Trust and celebrated in the writings of G. M. Trevelyan – who, like Neville Chamberlain, was also a supporter of the Munich agreement.

But everything changed in 1940, as Churchill rampaged his way towards the high peaks of historic destiny and national immortality, supported by the House of Commons (which now found his Victorian rhetoric much more to its taste), cheered on by as many monarchs as he could succour and support (from George VI in England to George II in Greece), admired by Wedgwood (on whom he conferred a peerage), and now also by Trevelyan (whom he appointed Master of Trinity College, Cambridge), flattered by Noël Coward (who sought with mixed success to transform himself from a playboy into a patriot), idolized by Ian Fleming (who had a good and proto-Bond war in naval intelligence), observed from afar by Margaret Roberts (en route from Grantham to Oxford University), and accompanied by Gilbert and Sullivan (who were played on the gramophone at Chequers to cheer everyone up). Meanwhile, the Chamberlain dynasty came to an abrupt end in Birmingham with the downfall and death of Neville, Stanley Baldwin was exiled to the countryside and derided as a 'guilty man', Francis Brett Young lost his touch and his audience as a Worcestershire storyteller, and the National Trust unexpectedly found a new purpose as a receiving agency for the houses of the once-dominant but now seemingly indigent aristocracy.

Throughout the Second World War, Churchill's defiance was magnificent – historically, militarily, politically and rhetorically. Yet he died a sad and disappointed man: for during his lifetime, and despite his heroic efforts to prevent it, Britain ceased to be a great power or a great empire, crowns vanished and thrones tottered in Europe and the Middle East, Parliament sank in the national estimation, and Chartwell was destined to go to the National Trust. These personal regrets were matched by a broader popular resentment at Britain's postwar decline, even when it was accompanied by unprecedented improvements in living standards – and from their Jamaican vantage point, Noël Coward and Ian Fleming shared and articulated these feelings, the former in his plays and musicals, the latter in his novels. Although they would not live to see it, Margaret Thatcher instinctively understood this national feeling of disillusion and annoyance, and during her long years of power she sought to halt decline, to win the Falklands back, to invoke 'Winston' at every possible opportunity, and to use an imagined version of the nineteenth-century past to reinvigorate, and in some senses re-Victorianize, late twentieth-century Britain.

Today, this all seems a long time ago, and a long way away, as Churchill's country (and, increasingly, Thatcher's too) becomes an ever more distant land. In a new century and a new millennium, and with the postwar generation of politicians now emphatically in power, Britain may finally be getting beyond the post-imperial trauma of disappointment and disillusion, resentment and regret, which lasted from Indian independence in 1947 to the Hong Kong handover fifty years later. But that process of recovery will not be complete until we can see the nineteenth and twentieth centuries – and their complex interconnections – more square-on than we yet do, and one of the essential ways of doing so is to recognize that many people in the twentieth century were trying – however inadequately and imperfectly – to come to terms with a world which was different from, and also seemed inferior to, the preceding century of unchallenged greatness which they had experienced or which they thought they knew. For most of the people discussed in the essays which follow, and for Winston Churchill above all, coping with the twentieth-century present also meant confronting the nineteenth-century past. Hence the sub-title of this book.

But as these pages also make plain, the nineteenth and twentieth centuries have left much unfinished business behind which carries over into our own time. The House of Commons that Churchill dominated and adorned is not the institution it was in his day and in his heyday: what is the future (and what should be the history) of the 'Mother of Parliaments' in the era of devolution and the Euro? The British monarchy that Churchill served and celebrated is visibly, belatedly and necessarily de-Victorianizing: how far can (and should) that process go? The sort of local power base that the Chamberlains built up in Birmingham has vanished from British provincial politics: would elected mayors for big cities restore it? The National Trust, one hundred years on, is actively (and rightly) reassessing its mission: but how should it redefine and conserve the national heritage in a new century? And so on. At varying levels of significance, all these questions – ostensibly about *escaping* the thraldom of the past – grow out of historic circumstances which need to be understood before they can be broken out from. For if post-imperial Britain is in the process of redefining itself, it needs to redefine its history, not reject it. Rule Britannia may have gone, but Cool Britannia is no substitute. We need to understand our recent history better, not disregard it. In the twenty-first century, as in the twentieth, coping with the present invariably involves confronting the past.

In revising these essays, and in gathering them together, I have incurred many general debts beyond those specifically acknowledged elsewhere: Cathy Pearson at the IHR managed my director's desk with her customary brilliance, efficiency and charm; Mike Shaw at Curtis Brown has provided much-needed encouragement, reassurance and support; Simon Winder at Penguin has been unfailingly helpful, wise and cheerful throughout; Monica Schmoller has turned a messy typescript into something the printers could read and recognize and handle; Joyce Horn has read the proofs with her inimitable accuracy and good grace; and once again, Linda Colley has made life worth living and history worth writing. But my final thanks, and with them the dedication, go to two great and remarkable historians whom I was lucky enough to encounter during the course of my career, and who died while I was working on this book: Jack Plumb and Lawrence Stone. They were not scholars to everybody's taste, they made many enemies and they courted (and relished) controversy. But they were creative, energizing, liberating figures who cared passionately about the past (and the present), and who brought it alive in ways that were unique and unforgettable. They taught me what history was about, and they taught me what historians should be about. I owe them much, mourn their passing and salute them both.

David Cannadine
Norfolk
18 November 2001

PART ONE

CHURCHILL IN HIS WORLD

I

Parliament: The Palace of Westminster
as the Palace of Varieties[1]

In the company of the Great Pyramid, St Peter's Cathedral, the Taj Mahal and the Eiffel Tower, the Palace of Westminster is one of the most famous and instantly recognizable buildings in the world. Its picturesque pinnacles and cloud capp'd towers create a Gothic-revival fantasy on London's sky-line, which is by turns, familiar, unique and much loved; and thanks to the ITN News and the BBC World Service, the chimes of Big Ben are broadcast across the nation and around the globe. But the Palace of Westminster is more than an unchanging architectural presence and a reassuringly robust clock: it is a building inside which history is constantly being made – and re-made. For it is also the place where national sovereignty is focused, embodied and asserted; where government and opposition confront each other; where laws are enacted by the Commons, the Lords and the Crown; where the legislature, the executive and the judiciary are mixed up together; and where important rituals of the state are regularly staged. It is, in short, the building where the British constitution is visibly displayed in both its efficient and dignified forms – not written down on paper, but physically expressed in masonry and mortar, sculpture and stained glass, frescos and furniture; and personally embodied in MPs and ministers, peers and prelates, politics and pageantry.[2]

This description of Barry and Pugin's palatial masterpiece, of the people who inhabit it, and of the things they do there, has held good throughout the entire century and a half of its existence. But it has held good only in the most general – and perhaps misleading – way. For while the Palace of Westminster has remained reassuringly constant in its inimitable physical form, the British constitution and British political life have been continually evolving and developing. This in turn means that perceptions of Parliament have themselves changed and altered as a result – and so have perceptions of the building that accommodates it. In order to appreciate these evolving images and protean identities, we must recognize that the history of the Palace of Westminster is as much about nation and empire, politics and ceremony, as it is about architecture and the decorative arts – and it is with the history of nation and empire, politics and ceremony, and their complex, contingent and changing relationship to architecture and the decorative arts, that this chapter is concerned.[3] As such, it seeks to explore and explain the Palace of Westminster, not only as a building which physically embodies a particular and time-bound version of the British constitution, but also as a theatre of state, where that same partial and anachronistic version of the constitution is annually performed as the 'traditional' ceremony of the state opening.

Thus contextualized and approached, the history of Parliament in its Barry-and-Pugin incarnation may best be described in terms of three separate but overlapping phases. As conceived and created in the 1840s and 1850s, the Palace of Westminster projected a backward-looking, conservative and exclusive image of the British constitution, in which greater importance attached to the monarchy and the House of Lords than to the Commons or the electorate. This vision, which was both powerful and limited, remained resonant until the late nineteenth century, albeit diminishingly so. From the 1880s until the Second World War, the British Parliament came to mean rather different things, as a result of the broadening of the franchise to full democracy, the expansion of imperial dominion and the raising of imperial consciousness, and the growing demands for Home Rule and schemes for devolution. Since then, the loss of empire, the erosion of national sover- eignty, and the creation of local assemblies for Scotland and Wales have once again drastically altered our sense of what 'Parliament' is and does. As a building, the Palace of Westminster would still today be instantly recognizable by the architect who designed it and the artist who decorated it; but the activities which go on inside it, the people who work there, and the meaning it has for us, would most likely leave them baffled, bewildered and dismayed. For their theatre of state has become our palace of varieties.

I

When fire destroyed much of the Old Palace of Westminster in October 1834, an event watched by a vast throng that included Turner and Constable as well as Barry and Pugin, contemporary reactions were mixed. For some shocked and grieving patriots, it seemed that the very heart of the nation had been torn out: 'I felt', noted a contributor to the *Gentleman's Magazine*, 'as if a link would be burst asunder in my national existence, and that the history of my native land was about to become, by the loss of this silent but existing witness, a dream of dimly shadowed actors and events.'[4] For those of a more robust inclination, it opened the way for the construction of a new legislature, fit for a reformed and imperial nation at the height of its international powers. For conservatives, it was proper punishment for a craven parliament which, in passing the Great Reform Act two years earlier, had surrendered to mob violence and middle-class pressure, and had grievously wounded the aristocracy and irretrievably damaged the hitherto perfect balance of the constitution. But for those of more progressive opinions, the fire was timely and opportune: for it swept away the ramshackle and inefficient buildings which were the physical embodiment of the world of 'old corruption', the end of which had already been portended in the legislation passed in 1832.[5]

These divisions of contemporary opinion, about the meaning and importance of events as they impinged on Parliament, and as Parliament impinged on events, continued throughout the remainder of the 1830s and on into the 1840s, the period when the New Palace of Westminster was commissioned and designed, and when its construction was begun. From one perspective, they were the most turbulent decades of the nineteenth century, as the nation-wide agitation for reform, followed by the abolition of so many rotten boroughs, the granting of representation to rapidly expanding industrial towns such as Birmingham and Sheffield, and the near-doubling of the franchise, were merely the prelude to further change and disruption: the Chartist outbursts in 1838, 1842 and 1848, the agitation of the Anti-Corn Law League, the 'Hungry Forties' in Britain, the Potato Famine in Ireland and the 'year of revolutions' in Europe. Yet these decades also witnessed unprecedented progress and improvement, in part symbolized by the opening of the Liverpool and Manchester Railway in 1830, in part as a consequence of the glut of reforming legislation: the Municipal Corporations Act, the New Poor Law, the repeal of the Corn Laws and the Factory Acts. Either way, these were indeed the 'iconoclastic years' in British government, politics and society, and it was against this unprecedentedly disrupted background that the rebuilding of the Houses of Parliament was debated and undertaken.[6]

Despite, or perhaps because of, this uncertainty, the image of the British nation, constitution and society which the new buildings set in stone was more concerned with stability and order than strife and dissent, and with tradition and continuity than progress and change. Like the Great Reform Act, the New Palace of Westminster was less of an abrupt break with the past than apocalyptic contemporary (or historical) accounts suggested. As with the Reform Act, those responsible for commissioning and designing the new legislature did not intend that it should be revolutionary. Far from recognizing 'the triumph of representative institutions over monarchical and tyrannical authority', it was meant to re-establish and reassert those visible ties to the nation's past which the fire had temporarily sundered.[7] Hence the decision of the House of Commons Select Committee appointed in March 1835 to report on plans 'for the permanent accommodation of the Houses of Parliament' that the new building must be in the 'national' style, which was deemed, rather implausibly, to be Gothic (or Elizabethan). As such, it would be an 'icon of hierarchy', stressing venerable authority, providential subordination and true conservative principles, and it would be the very antithesis of the classical style which, since 1789, had become associated in the popular patriotic mind with the rootless anarchy and national enmity of revolutionary France.[8] Hence, too, the formation of a Royal Commission to judge the competition, consisting of Charles Hanbury Tracey (later Lord Sudley), Sir Edward Cust (a courtier), the Hon. Thomas Liddell and George Vivian – all of them patrician amateurs with interests in the Gothic and the Picturesque.[9]

It was this essentially conservative committee which judged Charles Barry to have carried out this essentially conservative remit with matchless ingenuity and imagination. As the competition required, and as its name ('New Palace') implied, he designed a building which was a royal stronghold rather than a democratic legislature – instantly antique and self-consciously historical, richly ornamented, and full of allusions to the national past, to which (as if to console the writer in the Gentleman's Magazine) it provided a powerful reconnection and physical link. Like the Gothic-revival castles which had proliferated across the length and breadth of Britain since the turbulent 1790s, the New Palace of Westminster as conceived by the architect was no shrine to freedom or progress or public access: part club, part fortress, it was for the use of a tiny and privileged governing élite, and it was forbidding and unwelcoming to outsiders, with very limited accommodation for press or people. (The Times's call for 'amplitude of accommodation for the public as well as for the members themselves', had been completely disregarded.)[10] In all these ways, the New Palace had more in common with the building it replaced than is sometimes recognized, and this continuity was further reinforced by the decision to locate it on the same site as the old, and to incorporate into it the surviving, medieval Westminster Hall (hence, of course, the harmonizing attraction of the Gothic style). The result was a new-old building, proclaiming continuity rather than change: a display of 'national history', and 'national historicism'.[11]

As its name suggests, one of the architects' prime concerns was to create a palace which would enhance the position and assert the prestige of the monarch *vis-à-vis* the Lords, the Commons and the people. Hence the three hundred exterior statues with which the building was adorned, the majority of them depicting English kings and queens since the Saxon period, rather than politicians or peers.[12] Hence the Victoria Tower at the south-east corner, which on its completion in 1858 was the tallest secular construction in the world, and beneath which was placed the magnificent royal entrance, which was exclusively for the use of the sovereign. Hence the succession of state apartments of unparalleled splendour to which it led: the Royal Stair, the Robing Rooms, the Prince's Chamber and the Victoria Gallery.[13] These were the most opulently ornamented rooms in the palace, decorated with royal images, armorial bearings and heraldic devices, and with Arthurian frescos in the Royal Robing Room and Tudor portraits in the Prince's Chamber. Together, these right royal apartments proclaimed with over-powering visual force the idea of an ordered, rooted, hierarchical, venerable society; they paid homage to Sir John Soane, who had created a similar suite of rooms for King George IV in the Old Palace between 1822 and 1824; and they reasserted that Westminster was a royal palace, and that the monarchy was at the centre of British life and of British history.[14]

These elaborate decorations and imaginative embellishments were largely the work of Augustus Welby Northmore Pugin. He was a Catholic convert, and a passionate believer in precedent and scholarship, who thought the medieval world better than his own time. He delighted in aristocratic clients (such as Lord Shrewsbury, Charles Scarisbrick and Ambrose Phillipps de Lisle), and he specialized in designing Gothic churches and country houses. He believed hierarchy was the proper way of ordering society, and thought 'stage effect' and 'splendid mummery' were the appropriate means of articu-lating and safeguarding it. This profoundly conservative, anti-democratic, anti-utilitarian and anti-industrial vision was partly derived from such recent writers as Sir Walter Scott, Robert Southey and Sir Kenelm Digby, and it had much in common with the 'Young England' movement which was fashionable among some Tories during the 1840s.[15] Pugin's Gothic impulses reached their zenith in the House of Lords, which was concerned with celebrating the sovereign even more than the peers, and was 'fitted up for great pageants and state ceremonials, and not for the transaction of ordinary business'. It was regarded as 'a scene of royal magnificence', with its stained-glass windows portraying the monarchs of England and Scotland (replaced following the Second World War); with the fabulously embellished throne and sumptuous furnishings; and with frescoes depicting the religious and chivalric virtues of medieval sovereigns. By comparison, the Commons was a cramped and spartan house, there was insufficient seating for all the MPs, and it was difficult to make oneself heard.[16]

As conceived by Barry and Pugin, the Palace of Westminster was not so much a workaday legislature as a theatre of state, a building of uniquely dramatic intensity and potential, the setting for royal ceremonials which were more impressive than the somnolent debates in the Lords or the schoolboy-squabbles of the Commons.[17] Here too, the architects were following in the footsteps of Sir John Soane, who had been concerned to provide a fitting backdrop for King George IV when he visited Parliament to open it in state. Now Barry and Pugin in their turn had produced an even more splendid stage where the young Queen Victoria appeared as the centre of the annual pageant of the state opening – a festival of royal majesty and ordered hierarchy which may, without undue exaggeration, be described as a performance of the British constitution. There was a carriage procession from Buckingham Palace to the Victoria Tower; the queen entered the Royal Robing Room where she put on her crown and ceremonial costume; she walked through the Victoria Gallery to the House of Lords; and there she read the speech from the throne to the assembled peers and the Commons. The result was a living constitutional tableau, which put the three estates of the realm on parade, and which complemented those frescos that were being put on the walls of the palace, depicting the pageant of the nation's history. Throughout the 1850s, the Queen regularly opened Parliament in full state, accompanied by Prince Albert, and when the royal entrance was first used in 1852, she knighted Barry.[18]

Thus understood, as a building and as a theatre, the New Palace of Westminster embodied in stone and in ceremony a view of Britain's politics and society that was more Tory and backward looking than it was progressive and forward looking. According to this vision and version of things, the monarch was the most important personage in the nation and the legislature; the House of Lords was second in prestige and significance; the House of Commons came a distinct third; and the people as a whole scarcely mattered. Beyond any doubt, there was *some* truth in this vision. Victoria was no impartial constitutional monarch, but an opinionated and interfering sovereign, determined never to be queen of a 'democratic monarchy', and anxious to hand on her inherited powers, undiminished, to her successor.[19] Throughout most of the nineteenth century, the parliamentary peerage remained the richest, most powerful, most privileged group in the land, and they continued to veto bills sent up from the lower house (with the exception of those concerning finance), including Gladstone's second Home Rule Bill in 1893. As for the Commons: in terms of kinship and clientage, they remained subordinate to the Lords; their membership was overwhelmingly landed and leisured; and they were elected on a very narrow franchise. After 1832, scarcely one in five adult males had the vote, which meant Britain was arguably no more 'democratic' than it had been in the age of Queen Anne; and in 1865, the national franchise was one of the narrowest in Europe, behind Austria, France, Greece, Hungary, Portugal and Switzerland.[20]

The Palace of Westminster was also, and appropriately, a very *British* building – visibly embodying the sense of unitary statehood and national identity which had reached its culmination with the passing of the Act of Union with Ireland in 1801. In a legislature festooned with rich ornamentation, great attention was given to all three constituent kingdoms, and some to the Welsh principality. There were coats of arms of the English, Irish and Scottish royal houses, pictures and sculptures of monarchs from all three nations, and the insignia of the three great orders of chivalry: the Garter for England, the Thistle for Scotland, and also the Order of St Patrick, the motto of which, *Quis Separabit?* proclaimed the indissolubility of the Union with Ireland. And the four walls of the Central Lobby were to be decorated with mosaics of the patron saints of England, Ireland, Scotland and Wales.[21] When early and mid Victorians described the Palace of Westminster as the 'imperial parliament', they meant it in the sense that it was the 'four-kingdoms' legislature. Of course, MPs and peers spent time discussing Canada, South Africa, Australia and India; but there was no serious interest in any form of overseas representation, and apart from a single fresco depicting the embarkation of the Pilgrim Fathers for New England, there were no allusions to the colonies in the original decorative schemes.[22]

But while, in these ways, the Palace of Westminster embodied many truths about the Victorian constitution, politics and society, they were never more than a partial picture. Despite her strong views and imperious will, the queen did not govern, she could not veto bills, and she was less interfering than her predecessor, William IV. Her political power did not mirror or match her parliamentary pomp, and even that soon fell away: for after Albert died, she only opened Parliament in 1866, 1867, 1871, 1876, 1877, 1880 and 1886 – seven times in forty years. And she deliberately turned her back on those accoutrements of majesty for which Barry and Pugin had provided the backdrop: there were no trumpets, coaches or robes, she wore a widow's cap, a black dress and a long veil, and she left the reading of the speech to the Lord Chancellor. Nor were the Lords the omnipotent body suggested by Pugin's lavish decorations: they generally used their power of veto sparingly; they gave way over the repeal of the Corn Laws and the second and third Reform Acts; and their debates were somnolent. The best cure for believing in the upper house, Walter Bagehot once famously remarked, was to go and look at it.[23] Most serious debates took place in the Commons where, for all its cramped and austere plainness, politics really happened, and where ministries were made and unmade. Moreover, after the extension of the franchise under the second Reform Act, which roughly doubled the size of the electorate, the lower house came to possess a popular legitimacy which the Lords could not rival. And although the New Palace of Westminster was conceived and constructed as a *British* legislature, there were already demands, in the 1840s, that the recently enacted Union between Britain and Ireland should be repealed.[24]

The British constitution was not, then, in reality exactly as Barry and Pugin's palace suggested it was; and nor was Barry and Pugin's palace quite what it seemed, or what was intended. The building might be in traditional Gothic style, but its historical resonances were limited by the fact that construction continued until the 1870s – by which time both Pugin (1852) and Barry (1860) were dead, and their sons were publicly squabbling as to who had been responsible for what. Throughout this period, there was almost continual controversy – about the judges and the outcome of the original competition, about the endless delays and the ever-mounting costs, and about subsequent modifications to the original design.[25] The new Commons Chamber, first used in May 1850, was greatly disliked by MPs because of its poor acoustics and limited accommodation, and during Gladstone's first ministry of 1868–74, there were demands for it to be rebuilt; but they were rejected on the grounds of expense. By then, Victorian taste in Gothic had turned against the late perpendicular style, and the building was derided by many architectural critics as a stylistic travesty, and by Ruskin as 'empty filigree'.[26] As for the historical frescos that were the responsibility of a Royal Commission of Fine Arts, chaired by the Prince Consort: there was disagreement over the choice of artists and materials; many of the early commissions eventually went unexecuted; public access was so limited that they failed to fulfil the broader educational function originally intended for them; the whole initiative came to a standstill when Albert died in 1861; and the frescos have suffered as much from decay as from efforts at restoration.[27]

All of which is simply to say that during this first phase of commission, design, construction and function, the New Palace of Westminster presented a far from 'settled' image – of itself, or of the British constitution. On both counts, it was arguably as much about myth and make-believe as it was about truth and reality. Nor should this come as a surprise for, as Phoebe Stanton has pointed out, Pugin was a 'dreamer of dreams', who possessed a 'talent for creating architectural fiction' and 'majestic fantasy': romantic buildings which projected images of society and politics as they ought to be, that were in many ways at variance with the social and political realities of the time.[28] And it is scarcely coincidence that the politician from this period who relished similar illusions was Benjamin Disraeli. Like Pugin, he embraced the medieval revivalism of the 1840s, as a member of the Young England party, drawing on Bolingbroke, Digby and Scott for inspiration. Like Pugin, he disliked the Reformation, industrialism and utilitarianism, and in Coningsby (1844) he included portraits of two of Pugin's patrons, Lord Shrewsbury and Ambrose Phillipps de Lisle, in the figure of Eustace Lyle. Like Pugin, Disraeli possessed a powerful but idiosyncratic historical imagination, and he loved the 'aristocratic settlement', the peerage and (especially) the monarchy. Hence his flattery of Victoria later in his career as the 'faery queen' with her magic wand who, he artfully insisted, possessed greater powers than most people knew or would allow. There was about him, as about the Palace of Westminster, an unmistakable aura of Gothic enchantment, constitutional make-believe and political illusion.[29]

Like Disraeli, the Palace of Westminster projected an essentially Tory vision of the British constitution: but, in fact and in practice, it was increasingly the setting for a Whig narrative of British history – an unexpected but scarcely surprising trajectory since, for most of the period from 1835 to 1885, the Whigs and the Liberals were generally in power. Perhaps this was why, once the dark days of the 1840s were passed, and once complaints about the cost and the Commons chamber had largely died down, it became in the popular imagination more fairytale than foreboding – an identity which it retains in some quarters to this day. By the 1870s, it was commonplace to refer to it as a fairy palace, matching, as it were, Disraeli's fairy queen.[30] And it was this image which Gilbert and Sullivan caught and cultivated in Iolanthe, first performed in 1882. Act II opens with New Palace Yard bathed in pale, mellow moonlight: a romance of a romance. As her name implies, the Fairy Queen is as much a parody of Victoria as she is a Wagnerian caricature. The peers strut and process upon the stage in splendid style, but the Commons, the lower middle classes, the tradesmen and the masses, are nowhere to be seen. Although ostensibly irreverent and mocking, Iolanthe projects another essentially Tory vision of the British constitution, British politics and British society: it is Barry and Pugin, and the state opening, set to words and music.[31]

II

During the first phase of its existence, then, the New Palace of Westminster embodied and projected a more complex, more conservative and more ceremonial cluster of constitutional values, political assumptions and social attitudes than is now generally recognized. But these meanings and myths with which their building had originally been invested soon began to evolve and mutate in ways that neither Barry nor Pugin could have foreseen – or would have appreciated. Externally, their great architectural creation remained static, adamantine and immutable. But much else was changing in Victorian Britain, which meant the legislature was changing, too. In part this was because, during the last decades of the life of the 'faery queen', Westminster ceased to be the setting for the glittering theatre of state that had flourished during the earlier years of her reign. It bears repeating that after Victoria's non-majestic appearances in the 1870s, she scarcely visited Parliament again, leaving the grand royal rooms silent and uninhabited. Initially, this was because of her secluded grief, subsequently, on account of her incorrigible hostility to Gladstone, and lastly due to her age and infirmity, which meant the steps and the walk were beyond her. Meanwhile, the revived ceremonial of monarchy became more public and less parliamentary, centring on the queen's two Jubilees and on her funeral – popular pageants with vast crowds, for which the open streets of London, rather than the exclusive Palace of Westminster, served as the backdrop.[32]

At the same time, the balance of power between the three elements of the legislature shifted further away from the idealized model of the constitution proclaimed by the splendour of the royal rooms, the magnificence of the Lords, and the relative plainness of the Commons. From the later period of Queen Victoria's reign to that of King George VI, British monarchs interfered much less powerfully and opinionatedly in politics: the most they generally tried to do was to bring contending sides together, as in 1885 (the Third Reform Bill), 1910 (the Parliament Act) and 1931 (the formation of the National Government). But the earlier, assertive partisanship was largely given up; the abdication of Edward VIII showed that Parliament controlled the sovereign rather than the other way round; and most twentieth-century monarchs wisely settled for their three rights as defined by Walter Bagehot: to warn, to encourage and to be consulted.[33] At the same time, the might and prestige of the Lords were also dramatically lessened: with the passing of the Parliament Act in 1911, which reduced its powers of veto to two years' delay; with the scandals over the sale and purchase of peerages; with the gradual decline of the traditional aristocracy in cohesion and confidence; and with the broadening (or dilution) of the social base of the peerage.[34]

Part cause, part consequence of the decline in the relative powers of the monarchy and the Lords was that the Commons became ever more important – thereby rendering the original Barry–Pugin vision of the constitution even more anachronistic and illusionary than it had been during the mid-Victorian period. The third and fourth Reform Acts brought universal adult suffrage, which meant that by 1919 the lower house was representative of the entire British population for the first time in its history – though women between the ages of twenty-one and thirty had to wait until 1928.[35] As a result, the New Palace of Westminster, which had been conceived and constructed as a monument to monarchy and oligarchy, hierarchy and exclusiveness, ornament and decoration, had been transformed into a symbol of (and a shrine to) universal democracy and popular politics. The result was that, by the inter-war years, the Commons was dominated by middle- and working-class legislators, whose abundant presence within its hitherto-hallowed precincts would have been inconceivable in Barry and Pugin's day. Appropriately enough, the chimes of Big Ben were first broadcast by the BBC in 1923: parliamentary time was now everyone's time.[36]

But this was not the only way in which Parliament's meaning changed and evolved during these years. For during the late nineteenth century, the phrase 'imperial Parliament' increasingly came to describe the Palace of Westminster, not as the British legislature, but as the cynosure of a global Empire and earthly dominion on which the sun never set. One indication was the greater amount of time spent discussing imperial affairs: the establishment of the Australian Confederation in 1900; the granting of self-government to the former Boer republics in 1906; the creation of the Union of South Africa in 1910; the passing of the Statute of Westminster in 1931; and the lengthy debates over the Government of India Act of 1935. Another sign of the unprecedented importance of imperial business in the British Parliament was that by the inter-war years, there were three Secretaries of State dealing with India, the Dominions and the Colonies. Of course, much of this business was concerned with advancing the dominions further towards self-government; but the idea persisted until the Second World War that in some sense, albeit increasingly sentimental and metaphysical, the imperial legislature in Britain remained supreme: the 'Mother of Parliaments'. When the Lord Chancellor's Woolsack was restuffed in 1938, it was with a blend of wool from Britain and all the sheep-producing nations of the Empire.[37]

This growing belief that the British, four-nations legislature was (or should be) functioning as an imperial senate was reinforced by the increase in the number of MPs and (especially) peers with first-hand experience of governing the Empire: Curzon, Cromer, Lugard, Kitchener, Halifax, Lansdowne. Virtually all proconsuls were noblemen – many when they went out, most on their return – which meant that from the 1880s to the 1930s, the Empire was better represented in the British Parliament than it had been between the 1830s and the 1870s.[38] Moreover, the unprecedented ennoblement of such colonials as Lords Strathcona, Mount Stephen, Althostan, Beaverbrook, de Villiers, Sinha, Morris, Forest and Rutherford brought into the upper house peers who could genuinely claim to represent the furthest reaches of Empire. One such was Sir Gerald Strickland, a Maltese aristocrat who was also a protégé of Joseph Chamberlain, and had been governor of the Leeward Islands, Tasmania, Western Australia and New South Wales from 1903 to 1917. Between 1924 and 1927, Strickland was a member of the Maltese legislature, and he sat simultaneously in the British House of Commons as MP for Lancaster (or, his critics complained, 'for Malta'). Thereafter, he was elevated to the Lords, where he continued to represent the interests of the island and campaign for the award of life peerages to colonial premiers until his death in 1940.[39]

From the time Joseph Chamberlain had advocated it in the mid-1880s, there were many who urged a stronger overseas representation in what they hoped would become a fully fledged 'imperial' parliament. The most modest proposal was to recruit colonial premiers and Indian princes to the upper house, thereby consolidating its imperial function and personnel, and such reform schemes (to which Strickland remained abidingly loyal) were much discussed in the decades before the First World War.[40] But there were also more wide-ranging proposals, which envisaged transforming the second chamber from a domestic House of Lords into an authentically 'imperial Senate', 'reconstituted so as to comprise representatives from every British realm and colony'. All other second chambers in the Empire would be abolished; domestic issues would be discussed in what had previously been the local lower house; and imperial matters would be dealt with in the single surviving upper house in London. Yet a third suggestion was to extend the colonial and imperial conferences, which met intermittently in London, into permanent session, thereby making them into a new third chamber at Westminster.[41] Such imaginative schemes clearly envisaged a very different sort of 'imperial' parliament from the original four-kingdoms legislature Barry and Pugin had accommodated and designed.

It was in this much-changed context – national and imperial, political and constitutional – that the state opening of Parliament was revived by King Edward VII in February 1901, as one of the first public acts of his reign. In an increasingly democratic world, he thought it important that the sovereign should be seen with all the accoutrements of regal magnificence. And so, assisted by Lord Esher, he re-established the full dress ceremonial of constitutional performance, complete with the horse-drawn carriages, the glittering procession through the Palace of Westminster, and the reading of the speech from the throne in the House of Lords.[42] But this was more than the revival of a state theatre which had been virtually moribund since 1860: for Edward was Emperor of India and ruler of the British dominions beyond the seas, an imperial monarch in full finery in his imperial Parliament. And this new-old, popular-parliamentary spectacle was dutifully perpetuated by his successors down to the Second World War – except by Edward VIII who, on the one occasion he participated in the state opening, cancelled the horse-drawn procession on account of the weather.[43] At the same time, new royal 'traditions' were devised with close parliamentary association: on their deaths, both Edward VII and George V lay in state in Westminster Hall; and on his Silver Jubilee, George V received congratulations from the Lords and Commons in the same venerable building. As royal – and parliamentary – occasions, these were events without precedent.

While the full-scale ceremonial of the king-in-parliament was thus being reasserted in a more imperial and newly democratic context, renewed efforts were made to continue the wall-paintings which had largely been abandoned with the death of Prince Albert in 1861. Between 1908 and 1910, six pictures were completed in the East Corridor, devoted to the Tudor period; and from 1925 to 1927 eight panels were installed in St Stephen's Hall, originally entitled 'The Story of Our Liberties', but subsequently changed to 'The Building of Britain'. Their meanings were many and varied: more even than Barry and Pugin, they projected (and perpetuated) political and historical illusions. In a new era of democracy, they gave special prominence to monarchs, and they were paid for by individual peers. In a building that was a shrine to Tory constitutionalism, they presented the history of Britain as a Whiggish saga of freedom, extending from King Alfred the Great to the Union between England and Scotland in 1707. And in what had originally been a very 'British' legislature, they gave belated attention to the imperial theme, with pictures of Henry VII giving a charter to John Cabot to find new lands, and Queen Elizabeth commissioning Sir Walter Raleigh to sail for America. Here, for the restricted numbers who saw them, was the nation's history resumed as an unfolding pageant, with the monarch at the centre: just like the revived state opening that was now taking place again each year.[44]

At the same time that this visual narrative of Whig history was being added to the Palace of Westminster, there was a growing concern to investigate – and increasingly to praise – the unique continuity and slow, ordered evolution of the legislature itself. For this was the era of Stubbs and Maitland, with their pioneering work on the origins of medieval parliaments, and of A. F. Pollard, who insisted that 'parliamentary institutions have ... been incomparably the greatest gift of the English people to the civilisation of the world'. It was the era of G. M. Trevelyan, who saw the history of Parliament as the history of English liberties, and of Lewis Namier, who venerated it as an 'extraordinary club', a 'marvellous microcosmos of English social and political life'.[45] It was the era of Josiah Wedgwood, who sought to finance a full-scale history of the Commons and the Lords, so that MPs and peers would acquire some sense of the great tradition to which they belonged, and so that the people might learn from this matchless story of liberty and self-government. And it was the era of Stalin, Franco, Mussolini and Hitler: tyrants and dictators, who snuffed out the very freedoms for which the British Parliament now seemed, uniquely in Europe, to stand. As the young J. E. Neale put it in 1935, in a lecture celebrating the centenary of local government reform, 'particularly in these times of dictatorship abroad, we may thank God that we are not as other men are'.[46]

The result of these changes and developments, both inside the Palace of Westminster and outside, was that by the early decades of the twentieth century, and on into the inter-war years, there had gathered around Barry and Pugin's early Victorian Gothic extravaganza an accretion of sentiments, associations, ceremonies and histories which were significantly different from those with which it had originally been invested. Parliament was more democratic and more imperial, and these additional identities and extra layers of meaning were at their most resonant during and immediately after the Second World War. It was the House of Commons which brought down Neville Chamberlain in the spring of 1940; which was in the front line of battle and destroyed by Hitler's bombs; and which sustained and criticized Churchill and his wartime administration. Thus regarded, Britain's victory in the Second World War was a 'triumph of Parliamentary democracy', a parliament and a democracy symbolized by Barry and Pugin's unmistakable silhouette.[47] And it was a triumph for the British Parliament as the imperial Parliament. This, at least, was the message conveyed by the rebuilding of the House of Commons, which (like the Lord Chancellor's Woolsack a decade earlier) was reconstructed with materials donated by the dominions and colonies: the Speaker's chair from Australia, the central table from Canada, the two dispatch boxes from New Zealand, and the furniture for the division lobbies from Nigeria and Uganda.[48]

But as in the previous period, these new meanings and identities and associations which clustered around Barry and Pugin's building were not always as they seemed. The ceremonial of the state opening might be more splendid and imperial than ever but, as a performance of the British constitution, it concealed even more than it revealed. The monarch had never been so grandly displayed before the Lords and the Commons: yet he was far less influential than Victoria or William IV or George IV – as Edward VIII found out to his cost. The tableau in the House of Lords was unprecedentedly magnificent (Henry Channon thought it like 'a six no-trumper at bridge'): but the peerage was increasingly marginal to British political life.[49] As such, the whole pageant of the state opening presented a nostalgic, high-Tory picture of the British constitution, which had been partial and exaggerated in the 1850s, and which was by the 1930s even more anachronistic. Nor did the Palace of Westminster ever become a truly imperial parliament. Many inhabitants of the settler colonies did not like hereditary titles; the schemes for converting the upper house into an 'imperial senate' never materialized; and having won some measure of self-government, the dominions were unwilling to surrender it to what they rightly feared would remain a British-controlled legislature.[50] Not surprisingly, attempts to give the building an imperial face-lift also met with little success. In the 1890s and 1900s, there were proposals to attach to it a grand mausoleum where the heroes of Empire might be buried: but they were ruled out on account of their cost. And in the 1930s, Frank Brangwyn was commissioned to paint a new series of frescoes for the Lords which were to show the fruits and products of Empire. But they were deemed unsuitable, and were banished to Swansea Town Hall.[51]

Nor was the veneration for the British Parliament universally shared in these years. On the contrary, there was widespread criticism of the Westminster legislature, which came from a variety of groups, and was for a variety of reasons. The rise of Irish, Scottish and Welsh nationalism in the 1880s mounted an unprecedented challenge to the very idea of a unified 'British' parliament, and the vision the Palace of Westminster projected of four integrated kingdoms. Paradoxically, this view was also shared by many of those who supported the idea of an 'imperial' parliament, on the grounds that domestic business should be devolved to local legislatures, which would leave the Westminster Parliament free for bigger and broader matters. Schemes for separate assemblies for England, Ireland, Scotland and Wales were much discussed during the decade before 1914, when the phrase 'Home Rule All Round' became very popular, and again in the immediate aftermath of the First World War. They came to nothing.[52] But in December 1922, a separate parliament (and a separate nation) was created for Southern Ireland, and some powers were also devolved in Ulster on to a new legislature at Stormont. At the very time when the four-nations decorative scheme in the central lobby of the Palace of Westminster was completed (1923–4), with mosaics of St Andrew and St Patrick, the United Kingdom was itself being divided up again.[53]

There were other criticisms of Parliament, more explicitly directed at the Lords, the Commons and the electoral system. During the controversies over the Third Reform Bill in 1884–5, and over the 'People's Budget' in 1909–11, the House of Lords was regularly attacked for being (in Winston Churchill's words) 'one-sided, hereditary, unpurged, unrepresentative, irresponsible, absentee' and increasingly indefensible in a democratic world. Indeed, one reason there were proposals to reform it as an imperial senate was to give the upper house renewed purpose, power and legitimacy. Nor did the lower house escape censure: in the 1880s because the obstructive tactics of Irish nationalists regularly brought its proceedings to a standstill; and in the 1900s because the combined pressure of local, national and imperial business was becoming just too much.[54] Even in the 1930s, the veneration for Parliament as a bastion of freedom in an increasingly authoritarian world was not universally shared. From Winston Churchill to Oswald Mosley, there were those who contended that full adult suffrage had led to deteriorated democracy, with feeble and inept leadership, as exemplified by Baldwin and MacDonald. From this pessimistic perspective, Parliament's standing had entered a decline in the 1880s, from which it was only (and briefly?) rescued by and during the Second World War.[55]

Once again, then, albeit in rather different ways, there were elements of make-believe in the images and identities projected on to the British legislature in this post Pugin-and-Barry age of imperialism and democracy. The Palace of Westminster might have become the 'Mother of Parliaments', an imperial assemblage spawning new legislatures across and around the globe. But such emulation was constitutional rather than architectural. For in the era of Curzon and Milner, Lutyens and Baker, this later British imperial style was classical rather than Gothic: Admiralty Arch, County Hall, the Treasury Building and the Mall frontage of Buckingham Palace in London; and the legislatures and assemblies in South Africa, Australia and India. By the late nineteenth century, and on into the inter-war years, turrets and towers and pointed arches and buttresses were emphatically out: domes and columns and pediments were no less emphatically in. During the high-noon of the 'new imperialism', the Gothic style now seemed too English, and in the era of Lytton Strachey and the revolt against the nineteenth century, it also seemed too Victorian. By contrast, the classical style no longer seemed associated with the subversiveness of revolutionary France, but with the grandeur of imperial Rome.[56]

This shift in British stylistic sensibility away from the Gothic and towards the classical may help explain why the most resonant image of Barry and Pugin's Parliament in this period came from overseas: Monet's magnificent series of nineteen paintings of the Thames at Westminster, which he began in 1899 and first exhibited in 1904. Viewed through his eyes, the Houses of Parliament were neither an imperial senate, where great men made great history, nor a people's legislature, where democracy was inexorably advancing. For his concern was in capturing the varied effects on the building of light and colour, sunshine and smoke, sky and water, and changing atmospheric conditions. Thus depicted, the Palace of Westminster appeared as blurred, melancholic and insubstantial, constantly mutating with the weather and time of day, floating on the shimmering river, and melting into thin air – sometimes as an empurpled silhouette, going up in scorching sunset flames (shades of 1834?); sometimes peeping out from a vaporous Holmes-and-Watson fog. There was no drama, no history, no politician, no people in sight: only abstract shapes, dissolving evanescently into nothingness.[57]

III

Since the Second World War, the Palace of Westminster has continued its protean evolution as the fount and focus of different meanings and myths, images and illusions, which are both projected on to it, and derived from it. In the aftermath of the Second World War, Parliament's prestige was at its peak: Hitler and Hirohito had been defeated, democracy had been saved, and so it was scarcely surprising that the blitzed House of Commons was rebuilt as closely as possible to the original design. For much of the ensuing twenty years, its standing remained high, in large part because it shared in the Olympian fame of its greatest member: Winston Churchill.[58] Although past the peak of his powers, his greatest speeches, both as Leader of the Opposition from 1945–51, and as Prime Minister from 1951–5 were unforgettable parliamentary occasions. His eightieth birthday brought a unique tribute in Westminster Hall from both houses, and when he made a rare later appearance in the Commons in April 1958, one journalist observed that 'there is one glory of the sun and another of the moon, as we know, but there is also a glory of parliament'. When Churchill died in January

1965, his body lay in state in Westminster Hall for three days. 'He was in a very real sense a child of this House and a product of it,' Harold Wilson told the Commons, 'and equally, in every sense, its father.'[59]

As this suggests, Westminster Hall has remained the setting for great ceremonies of state but, as before, most of them have centred on the monarchy: the crown in Parliament. Thirteen years prior to Churchill, George VI had lain in state there; and Queen Elizabeth II's Silver Wedding and Silver Jubilee were both marked with loyal addresses from both houses. But the most visible affirmation of the continued link between the sovereign and the Palace of Westminster remains the state opening, and throughout her long reign, the present queen has been as attentive to this task as all but one of her twentieth-century predecessors. She first opened Parliament in state in November 1952, and she has scarcely missed a year since.[60] From October 1958, the ceremony has been broadcast live on television, so that what was previously a restricted group rite, confined to the members of both houses and some special guests, has now become a public pageant. The tone and treatment of this 'state occasion at its most magnificent' was established by the BBC's pre-eminent royal commentator, Richard Dimbleby, who depicted it in heightened and romanticized terms as a Puginesque tableau of hierarchy and history, with his dignified, reverential commentary, his silken descriptions of peers and judges, and his stress on the symbolism and splendour of the ceremonial.[61]

But just as the 'meaning' of the state opening – and of the parliament which was thus splendidly inaugurated – was different in Edward VII's day from what it had been in Victoria's, so it has become different again in the time of Queen Elizabeth II. For this is no longer an imperial occasion in an imperial legislature: by the time the House of Commons was rebuilt as a monument to imperial consciousness and concern, the Empire itself was already and rapidly and irreversibly on the wane. India became independent in 1947 and, during the next twenty years, most of the Empire in Africa followed suit. To be sure, parliaments modelled on Westminster were initially set up in the former colonies, but many of them soon became one-party states and dictatorships. There were suggestions that small nearby territories such as Malta and Gibraltar might send their own MPs to the British legislature, but they came to nothing.[62] Even the old dominions are less subservient to the 'Mother of Parliaments' than they used to be. South Africa became a republic in 1961, and in Canada and Australia the remaining vestiges of British parliamentary sovereignty have largely been removed. As a result, the British Parliament which the Queen opens is no longer an imperial legislature appropriately inaugurated by an imperial monarch; for she opens it, not as Empress of India and ruler of Britain's dominions beyond the seas, nor even as Head of the Commonwealth, but merely as a national sovereign.[63]

Such a diminished, post-imperial formulation of Westminster's range and reach also hints at a further diminution of power: for what does national sovereignty mean in the early twenty-first century, in terms of the British monarch and the British Parliament? The simple answer has to be that it means much less than it did even a generation ago. In part, this has been because of Britain's ever-closer ties with (and subordination to?) 'Europe', a new constitutional and political arrangement aptly symbolized by the construction of the millennium wheel on the south bank of the Thames, redolent of Harry Lime, the Prater in Vienna and 'the Continent', which seems to dwarf and diminish the more British Big Ben nearby. When it joined the European Economic Community in 1972, Parliament agreed that subsequent EEC legislation 'shall be recognized and available in law and be enforced, allowed and followed accordingly', an unprecedented diminution of its sovereignty. Since then, the adoption of the Single European Act of 1985 and the Maastricht Treaty of 1992 have further eroded Parliament's autonomy, and with the prospect of the single currency and full monetary union this trend seems likely to continue.[64]

In part, too, this erosion and diminution of the power of the British Parliament mirrors and replicates a broader, global trend. For national sovereignty is being undermined everywhere: the autonomous nation state, with its laws, its legislature and its law-makers, is no longer seen as something permanent, unchanging and immutable, as it was in the hundred years before the Second World War, but as something contingent, provisional and temporary, which rests on the relatively uncertain foundations of manu-factured myths and invented traditions. For in the brave new world of multi-national conglomerates, electronic information and instant commun-ication (even Parliament is now on the internet), more decisions are now taken about Britain's future in Tokyo and New York and Frankfurt than in London – or the Palace of Westminster. Only the fascination of the British media with British politics and British politicians perpetuates what is now the illusion that these are men (and, occasionally, women) of power in the way that their nineteenth-century predecessors were. They are not. For the reality, as Hugo Young has recently observed, is that 'the Queen in Parliament', and the whole accompanying paraphernalia of government and opposition, politicians and journalists, already looks like little more than 'a bejewelled dot on the ocean of the global economy'.[65]

But this is not the only way in which the sovereignty and autonomy of the British Parliament are being eroded – or eclipsed. By the early 1970s, the 'troubles' in Northern Ireland, and vigorous demands by Scottish and Welsh nationalists, led apocalyptic commentators to predict the 'break-up of Britain'.[66] These demands abated during the Thatcher years, but the recent creation of a Scottish Parliament and of a Welsh Assembly represents the greatest transfer of power away from the British legislature since the Irish legislation of 1919–21, and it has 'radically altered the role of Westminster'.[67] When the Queen opened the Welsh Assembly and the Scottish Parliament in person, this was rightly seen as an emphatic demonstration that the old, pan-British hegemony of the Palace of Westminster was over. And there may be more to come: probably not in the form of an elected assembly for England, but perhaps in the form of elected mayors of the great cities, who may turn out to be local figures of such stature that they can stand up to the Cabinet – and to Parliament. This is not to say that the break-up of Britain is nigh. But from below, no less than from above, the power of the British Parliament is being undermined: it is no longer the supreme legislative body for the unitary British nation state.

The meaning of Parliament has not only changed in terms of its external resonances and relations: there have also been many changes in terms of its functioning and personnel. The queen may continue to fulfil her ceremonial duties, but Westminster has ceased to be, in jurisdictional terms, the royal palace it has been throughout most of its history. Since 1965, the Lord Great Chamberlain has relinquished most of his rights and powers as the queen's representative, and today it is the Speaker, on behalf of Parliament, who is the prime custodian.[68] The House of Lords has been transformed by further reductions in its powers of delay, by the introduction of life peerages and by the expulsion of most hereditary peers, which means that it is no longer an aristocratic chamber, but is dominated for day-to-day business by nominated life senators, a substantial proportion of whom are now women.[69] And the House of Commons has seen similar if not greater changes: the introduction of new Select Committees in 1979, which offer a stronger check on the executive, and meet in the mornings; the live televising of debates, which enables everyone to see what goes on there; and since May 1997 the advent of an unprecedented number of women MPs.

To a considerable degree, these internal reforms have been in response to growing criticism, from both inside and outside. Even in the latter years of Churchillian apotheosis, Parliament was already coming under renewed scrutiny, and since the mid-1960s there has been a constant chorus of complaint, no doubt connected to the general decline of politicians in public esteem and estimation during these years. The continued existence of an unelected House of Lords aroused the ire of successive Labour governments; between 1968 and 1969 Harold Wilson tried to reform its composition and rethink its powers, and the Blair government has embarked on a more ambitious (but also more protracted) scheme of reform.[70] The House of Commons has been much criticized for its inability to fulfil its essential, historic function of checking and scrutinizing the executive – shortcomings which the introduction of the new Select Committees has not adequately eradicated.[71] There are also many who think the whole culture of Westminster is inappropriately anachronistic: too male, too blokeish, too clubby, and with indefensibly antisocial hours. And attention has repeatedly been drawn to the limitations and inadequacies of Barry and Pugin's palace: for the restricted office accommodation it provides for peers, MPs and committees, and for being more of a museum, weighed down by the deadening burdens of the past, than the home of what ought to be a modern, forward-looking, twenty-first-century legislature.[72]

These changes – imperial, national and internal – help explain two significant developments in popular perceptions across the postwar half-century. The first has been that as the power and esteem of Parliament as a legislature has declined, the veneration for Parliament as a building and as an historic national institution has significantly increased. This shift in taste was eloquently signalled in the 1950s by Nikolaus Pevsner's uncharacteristically effusive description of the Palace of Westminster as 'the most imaginatively planned and the most excellently executed major secular building of the Gothic Revival anywhere in the world'.[73] Since then, the paintings, drawings, sculptures and engravings in the palace have been authoritatively catalogued; the History of Parliament, covering the House of Commons from medieval times to 1832, has been almost completed; Pugin and Barry have been recognized for being the architectural and decorative geniuses that they undoubtedly were; and an extensive programme of refurbishment has been carried out, on the exterior in the 1980s, and the interior in the 1990s, restoring their masterpiece to its original early-Victorian grandeur.[74] Designated a World Heritage Site in 1987, the New Palace of Westminster has never been as well cared for and admired as it is now – and it cannot be coincidence that this unprecedented display of consciousness and concern has taken place during a period which has also witnessed the unprecedented diminution in Parliament's powers and autonomy.

The second development – which owes much to these same circumstances and changes, but tends in a rather different direction – has been the increasing criticism of the annual pageant of the state opening. Ever since Robin Day's 'rival' television commentary in 1958, which in contrast to Richard

Dimbleby's obsequiousness was brash, brisk and irreverent, those on the left have insisted that it is not so much a spectacle as a sham – part pantomime, part costume drama, projecting a dangerously deluded image of constitutional and national realities. Thus regarded, the state opening is excessively preoccupied with crowns and regalia, ermine and robes, protocol and precedence, and it presents a mistaken picture of Britain's current place in the world, of the relations between crown, Lords and Commons, and of the nation's social structure. For such critics, 'modern political reality' is more important than this 'ancient royal ceremony', and as national sovereignty and parliamentary power weaken and wane, this credibility gap between ritual and reality has widened still further.[75]

Of course, this is far from being a universally held view. The 'timeless ritual and splendour' of the 'traditional' state opening, and the picture of Britain it embodies and projects, retain their admirers and supporters.[76] It also bears repeating that the state opening is the very pageant that Barry and Pugin designed their palace to accommodate. But so much else has changed, both inside and outside that palace, that it may be pertinent to wonder how long that pageantry can, should or will be able (or allowed) to continue. For it is not just that Parliament's powers have been constrained, devolved and appropriated in unprecedented ways, or that the people who work in Parliament are very different from their early-Victorian forebears, or that the sort of work they do has changed so significantly – true though all of this undoubtedly is. It is also highly likely that the House of Lords will be even more drastically reformed in the near future, and that life peers may also be ejected from the Palace of Westminster. In such a reconstituted second chamber, inhabited by very different sorts of people, who would be chosen in very different sorts of ways, the Gilbert-and-Sullivan grandeur of the 'traditional' state opening may well come to seem at best unconvincing, at worst ridiculous.[77]

If this does indeed turn out to be the case, then one solution to the growing credibility gap which is opening up between parliamentary pageantry and parliamentary practice might be to adopt a more stripped-down royal ceremonial, harking back to the plainer style of Victoria's austere widow-hood, or of Edward VIII's single state opening. As usual, there are royal precedents for almost anything, although for obvious reasons neither of these is an altogether happy one, since both were the result of neglect of duty rather than fulfilment of it. A yet more radical alternative would be for the monarch's ceremonial participation in Parliament to be dispensed with altogether, and for the Prime Minister to deliver a more substantial and wide-ranging speech to a joint session of both houses at the beginning of the session, modelled on the American (or South African) President's State of the Union address. That may be taking innovation too far. But compared to the early-Victorian era, or the high imperial heyday, Britain is both a diminished and more democratic nation, with a diminished and more democratic Parliament, and it may well be that a new opening ceremony will have to be devised for the Palace of Westminster which recognizes these realities rather than continues to disguise them.

IV

These fanciful speculations carry us a long way from the burning of the Old Palace of Westminster in 1834 with which this chapter began. Of course, it is unwise and irresponsible for historians to try to predict the future. But whatever it may hold, the fact remains that our contemporary world is in many ways markedly different from the early-Victorian era when Pugin and Barry set out to create their Gothic-revival masterpiece. Put the other way, this means the New Palace of Westminster was very much a product of its time (not ours), and as such it projected a particular, powerful and partial vision of its time (not ours). Since then, the British nation and the British people, British politics and British politicians, have evolved and developed in ways that it has only been possible to sketch and summarize here. Yet the building itself has changed scarcely at all, thereby often disguising or concealing many of the variations in context and circumstance that have subsequently taken place – even as its own meaning has changed as a result of them. This is an extraordinary story about an extraordinary building – and about much more than an extraordinary building. Nor (unlike this chapter) is it over yet. Its future as the theatre of state may soon be put in doubt; but for as long as British parliamentary politics endure, the Palace of Westminster seems certain to remain what it has always been in its Barry and Pugin incarnation: the palace of varieties.

2

Statecraft: The Haunting Fear of National Decline[1]

There can be no doubt that since the last quarter of the nineteenth century, Britain has in many ways been a nation 'in decline'. The Empire on which the sun never set has become one with Nineveh and Tyre. The waves which Britannia once ruled so mightily have long since been subdued and sailed by other navies. The first industrial nation, the veritable workshop of the world, is seen by some as being little more than a de-industrialized theme park. Not surprisingly, God is no longer an Englishman but a multicultural deity of indeterminate gender. Of course, this is only part of the story. Much of Britain's international decline has been relative rather than absolute. It took – and is still taking – a long time, and it has been sometimes halted, though rarely reversed. Meanwhile, on the home front, changes have been in precisely the opposite direction: emphatically for the better rather than visibly for the worse. During the last hundred years, levels of output, income and national wealth have increased unprecedentedly. Today, for most people, life in Britain is more rich, prosperous, varied, abundant and secure than it was for their late-Victorian forebears over a hundred years ago.[2]

There is, then, only a part of our nation's recent historical experience which can be encompassed in such morbidly evocative phrases as 'the eclipse of a great power', the 'contraction of England' or 'Britannia overruled'.[3] The British Empire may have been won 'in a fit of absence of mind', but as far as the majority of the population seems to have been concerned, it was given away in a fit of collective indifference. Nor were Britain's governing classes and policy-makers as obsessed with 'the orderly management of decline' as the ample evidence for that decline suggests they should have been.[4] Gladstone regarded the rise of the United States with relative equanimity. Salisbury feared 'disintegration', but never enough to disturb his calm and imperturbable conduct of affairs. Asquith and Attlee were first and foremost domestic reformers, Baldwin was a domestic conciliator, Macmillan lacked the necessary crusading zeal, while Wilson vainly sought white-hot solace in the technological revolution. To be sure, all of them lived and ruled in an era of vanishing supremacies. But none had careers which could most appropriately be summed up by the phase 'a statesman in an age of decline'.[5]

Yet from the 1880s to the 1980s, there were three unusual, indeed extraordinary, figures in British politics who might best be described by this rather double-edged term, and who were in part so unusual and so extraordinary precisely because that label fits them so well. All three were heroic egotists, possessed of a powerful, obsessive, unreflective sense of messianic self-identity. Each developed a coherent, doom-laden and apocalyptic vision, part historical, part geopolitical, and part prescriptive. They were compulsively preoccupied by enemies without and by enemies within: internationally, they feared that Britain was being pushed to the margins of events by more vigorous overseas competitors; domestically they regretted what they saw as the moral decline in national character and national calibre. All of them looked back appreciatively (and selectively) to an earlier golden age of vigorous virtues, robust will, splendid endeavour and unchallenged supremacy. They advocated reform, renewal and regeneration as essential and imperative. And each one of them believed that they, and they alone, could lead the nation out of the abyss of despair and despondency into which it had sunk, towards the broad, sunlit uplands of rebirth and revival.[6]

The individuals in question were Joseph Chamberlain, Winston Churchill and Margaret Thatcher. All of them were members of Conservative administrations, yet their relations with the party were often difficult and acrimonious. They were regarded as outsiders, as social misfits, with excessively authoritarian attitudes and overbearing personalities. They were much disliked by traditional Tories from the shires, and that dislike was fully reciprocated. They were criticized for hijacking the party, for wrenching it out of its traditional trajectory, and for turning it in new and unwanted directions. But while they were much hated, they were also much admired: indeed, they were each made the centre of a personality cult in ways that have been true of no other twentieth-century British politicians. They all became obsessed with the problem of decline relatively late in their political careers, and there was nothing in their early years in public life to suggest that this would happen. And all three left office with a sense that their mission was incomplete, and with the fear, borne out by subsequent events, that their chosen successors would let them down. How, indeed, could it have been otherwise, given that their efforts to reverse Britain's twentieth-century decline were in no case lastingly successful?

I

Joseph Chamberlain has rightly been described as the first leading British politician 'to propose a drastic method of averting the sort of national decline which he saw as otherwise inevitable'.[7] Yet there was nothing about his boyhood, his business or his early career in local and national politics to suggest that 'messianic catastrophism' would become his creed, his cause, his crusade. For Chamberlain, born in 1836, had grown to maturity in the mid-Victorian era of liberalism and internationalism, when British industry and British power were both at their most pre-eminent. He was a Londoner by birth, but made his fortune in Birmingham as a manufacturer of screws. He retired from business in 1874, having already entered local politics as an advanced liberal. He was a legendary reforming Mayor of Birmingham, was elected one of the town's MPs in 1876, and within four years was a member of Gladstone's second administration as President of the Board of Trade. As the first self-made industrialist to reach the highest echelons of British public life, Chamberlain's career until the mid-1880s reads like something out of Samuel Smiles.

Thus described, he was the coming man in the new age of quasi-democratic politics: radical, nonconformist, undeferential. He had no time for the aristocracy, and precious little for Queen Victoria. He viewed Birmingham as a latter-day Venetian city state, proud, free and independent.[8] And he viewed the world beyond Britain as a market for exports rather than as regions ripe and ready for conquest. Not for nothing was he the political protégé and colleague of John Bright.[9] Yet this was the man who, in the ten years from 1886, was transformed from 'Radical Joe' into the 'First Minister of the British Empire'. He abandoned the Liberals and, from 1895 to 1903, served under Lord Salisbury and A. J. Balfour as Colonial Secretary, thereupon resigning to launch a national campaign for Tariff Reform. In and out of office, his all-consuming obsession remained the same: to alert the British people to their country's economic and international decline, and to urge them to accept his audacious programme for revival and renewal. Here is Chamberlain, in 1903, in full apocalyptic spate:

All history is the history of states once powerful and then decaying. Is Britain to be numbered among the decaying states: is all the glory of the past to be forgotten? ... Or are we to take up a new youth as members of a great Empire, which will continue for generation after generation the strength, the power and the glory of the British race?[10]

To Chamberlain, the evidence of British decline was as ample as it was alarming. The very year that he had retired from business had witnessed the end of the mid-Victorian boom, which was soon followed by the later Victorian 'great depression'. It was primarily a depression of prices, profits and interest rates, and the metal trades of Birmingham and the Black Country were especially hard hit.[11] But this first 'great depression' also coincided with the rise to industrial greatness of Germany and the United States – larger nations, with richer natural resources, bigger populations and greater markets. Gradually but inexorably, Britain's manufacturing supremacy was challenged, then overwhelmed: in output, in productivity, in investment, in innovation and in exports. To protect their own industries, other nations adopted tariffs, which made it even harder for Britain, stubbornly adhering to Free Trade, to compete. And the battle for overseas markets ushered in a new era of imperial rivalries. To be sure, Britain obtained the lion's share of the spoils in the 'Scramble for Africa'; but the increase in the amount of territory in the formal Empire was matched by a decline of informal control of a much larger area. In China, Latin America and the Middle East, the easy supremacy of an earlier era was gone. Everywhere, it seemed, the economic and imperial climate had turned harsh, cold and bleak.[12]

Thus were Britain's enemies massing without, and as befitted someone of his background, Chamberlain was the most significant politician to catch and share the resulting mood of domestic anxiety and unease. 'Our competitors', he warned, 'are gaining upon us in that which makes [for] national greatness.'[13] And there were also enemies within, who sought to weaken Britain at the very time when the country needed all its united strength to face and fight the world outside. To Chamberlain, these quislings came in two forms: Irish nationalists, who from 1880 made violence and subversion their stock-in-trade; and British Liberals, who showed every indication that they would give in to such threats. Here, indeed, was the great divide which opened up between Chamberlain and Gladstone. Gladstone regarded Home Rule as a legitimate concession, which would help to keep the Irish in the Empire. Chamberlain saw it as an unpatriotic policy of appeasement, which would lead to the break-up of the United Kingdom, and portend the dismemberment and dissolution of the Empire. Even worse, he feared that it would send an unmistakable signal to the world that Britain's will to rule had been mortally weakened, and that 'the sceptre of dominion' had 'passed from our grasp'.[14]

These anxieties, both economic and political, domestic and international, were rendered more credible and more urgent for Chamberlain by the writings of Sir John Seeley, whose book *The Expansion of England* he much admired. It is often read as a paean of praise to the British Empire, but in the context of its times, it was more apocalyptic than celebratory. The great empires of the past, Seeley argued, had been sea-borne: the Portuguese, the Spanish, the Dutch and the French. But they had all declined and, thanks to the steam engine and electricity, the great empires of the future were much more likely to be land based: in particular, the Russian and the American, with their huge populations and resources. As a result, Britain would soon be faced with an unprecedentedly severe challenge. Its greatness depended on the successful maintenance of the last surviving sea-borne empire. Without it, Seeley contended, Britain would decline into the ranks of a second-rate power – or worse. Accordingly, the most urgent and immediate task was to find a way of preserving and consolidating the British Empire so it could hold its own in this challenging era of changed geopolitics.[15]

From the mid-1880s until the end of his life, Chamberlain was haunted by these fears of national decline, and by the dread that the Empire was 'being attacked on all sides'. He felt 'great alarm at the prospect of the future', and saw Britain as 'the weary Titan, staggering beneath the too vast orb of his own fate'.[16] In industry after industry, Britain's manufacturing supremacy was being lost, and with it the strength Chamberlain regarded as essential for continued great power status. A nation with an economy increasingly dominated by bankers and brokers, rather than by entrepreneurs and innovators, was not going to last long in an ever more alien and hostile world. Such structural change – away from industrial production towards financial services – itself spelt economic decadence, and Chamberlain was appalled by the thought that Britain might become another Holland, 'an inconsiderable force in the world', a 'third-rate power', a 'fifth-rate nation'. As 'Brummagem Joe', he had been impressed by Venice in its prime; as Colonial Secretary, he was no less impressed by Venice in decline. 'The days', he believed, echoing Seeley, 'are for great empires and not for little states.'[17]

Having absorbed Seeley's analysis, Chamberlain sought to rise to Seeley's challenge: for his self-appointed task was to prevent Britain declining from a great empire into a little state by rousing the nation to the threats which it faced, and by implementing a practical and comprehensive policy of resistance and regeneration. Industry must be protected, the union preserved and the Empire consolidated. Yet despite the vigorous campaigns he waged, the powerful organization he created, the formidable array of academic advisers he assembled, and the confidence he felt in the appeal of his message, he actually accomplished very little. To be sure, he played a major part in defeating Gladstone's Irish Home Rule Bills of 1886 and 1893, and thus in wrecking the Liberal Party for a generation.[18] And with the House of Lords both able and willing to exercise its powers of veto, it looked as though the union was safe for the foreseeable future. But in 1911, the Liberal government passed the Parliament Act, and Chamberlain lived just long enough to experience the bitter defeat of knowing that a Home Rule Bill would finally make its way to the statute book in 1914.

As Colonial Secretary, his record was no less disappointing. He certainly raised Britain's imperial consciousness, with the Diamond Jubilee, the conferences of colonial premiers, the Boer War and the Australian federation.[19] But he signally failed to convert sentiment into structure: the formal unification of the Empire into one consolidated superpower eluded him. His preferred solution was some form of imperial federation, involving Britain, Canada, South Africa, Australia and New Zealand. But the colonists' growing sense of their own autonomy meant that this was never practical politics, even in the immediate aftermath of the Boer War.[20] Chamberlain's alternative approach, which kept the same ultimate end in view, was some form of trans-oceanic *Zollverein* – a massive imperial free-trade area, protected from the rest of the world by high tariff walls, within which the colonies would provide both the raw materials and the markets for the goods produced by revived British industry.[21] But the colonies were as jealous of their own infant industries as they were of their recently acquired sense of national identity, and Chamberlain's proposals were decisively rejected at the imperial conference of 1897.

Having failed to consolidate the Empire from within the government, Chamberlain took his greatest gamble, by resigning from the Cabinet in 1903 and carrying his campaign for Tariff Reform directly to the British people.[22] This time, his immediate aim was to overturn Free Trade in favour of imperial preference – an elaborate system of tariffs and duties which, while not creating a *Zollverein*, would promote greater trade within the Empire, would make possible the revival of British industry, and might be the prelude to imperial federation. But again, it did not work. The Conservative Party was deeply and bitterly divided, it went down to a massive electoral defeat in 1906, and did not recapture power in 1910, even though by then Tariff Reform had become its official policy. Four years previously, Chamberlain had himself been incapacitated by a stroke, and his eldest son and heir apparent, Austen, failed to obtain the leadership of the Tory Party on Balfour's resignation in 1911. Instead, the task fell to Bonar Law, who was himself sympathetic to Tariff Reform; but he in turn repudiated most of the programme in 1913. 'We are beaten,' Austen wrote to his wife, 'and the cause for which Father gave more than life itself is abandoned.'[23]

Chamberlain's last years were thus barren and unfulfilled. The self-appointed task to which he had devoted the second half of his career – the maintenance of 'Britain's position in the world' – had proved impossible, both for him and for his appointed successors.[24] Neither the electorate at home nor the colonies abroad could be persuaded to embrace his schemes for imperial unity. There were many parts of Britain beyond Birmingham which his vision did not encompass (especially the country and the City of London), and many parts of the Empire beyond the four great dominions (especially India) of which the same may be said. Moreover, there is no evidence that protective tariffs would have led to a revival of Britain's traditional manufacturing base, while Chamberlain seems to have had little interest in such new industries as chemicals or cars.[25] Above all, in the prosperous Edwardian years, there were many people who simply refused to accept his doom-laden analysis. He may have been correct in despising Balfour's languid and lethargic indifference to Britain's decline, and in so doing he certainly prefigured Margaret Thatcher's later hostility to the Tory 'wets', but his great schemes of national revival and imperial consolidation were simply beyond the bounds of practical politics.[26]

II

One relatively junior but excessively ambitious politician who shared neither Chamberlain's diagnosis of Britain's decline, nor his prescription for it, was Winston Churchill. Indeed, it was in part because young Winston believed in Free Trade and opposed Tariff Reform that he left the Conservatives and joined the Liberals in 1904. For him, as for many, Free Trade and British greatness were indissolubly linked: Tariff Reform would thus not be a cure for British decline, it would be the cause of it. For the world in which Churchill grew up – he was born in 1874 – was not for him the gloomy, battle-scarred landscape that it had seemed to Chamberlain. To be sure, it was an age of competition, of Darwinian struggle.[27] But it also seemed to be an age in which Britain's greatness was regularly and repeatedly reaffirmed. At the frontiers of Empire – in India, the Sudan and South Africa – Churchill saw and celebrated the extension of British rule. As a Liberal reformer, he sought to make life more stable and secure for ordinary men and women. And as First Lord of the Admiralty, he relished the challenge of creating the mightiest navy the world had ever seen. For him, as he later recalled, the nineteenth century ended amid 'the glories of the Victorian era, and we entered upon the dawn of the twentieth century in high hopes for our country, our Empire and the world'.[28]

The first forty years of Churchill's life were, as they had earlier been for Chamberlain, a time of hope, progress and improvement. But thereafter, as Chamberlain had also found, the skies suddenly and unexpectedly began to darken. In personal terms, Churchill's meteoric career crashed into ruins in 1915 in the aftermath of the Dardanelles fiasco, and rehabilitation was to prove a long, slow and painful process. And even someone as much in love with war as he had been was appalled by the cost – in men, in money and in materials – of fighting the Germans. Like so many members of his generation, the domestic and international landscape which Churchill surveyed in the aftermath of victory in 1918 was one he scarcely recognized. He was disturbed and disoriented by the collapse of settled values and ancient institutions, and saw contemporary Europe 'relapsing in hideous succession into bankruptcy, barbarism or anarchy'. And as he was to discover in his years as Chancellor of the Exchequer, even Free Trade, the very underpinning of British greatness, was no longer viable. 'The compass has been damaged,' he concluded. 'The charts are out of date.'[29]

Under these abruptly changed circumstances, Churchill's thoughts, writings and rhetoric became increasingly apocalyptic, as he became obsessed with what he saw as Britain's domestic and international decline from the golden era before 1914. On the home front, the man who had attacked the peerage with such glee in 1910 now lamented the demise of the great governing families of England. The one-time Liberal reformer, anxious to improve the condition of the working classes, pronounced the new Labour Party unfitted to rule. The restricted franchise that had existed before the Fourth Reform Act had been superseded by the 'universal mush and sloppiness' of mass democracy, with its rootless and ignorant electorate, its caucuses, wire-pullers and soap boxes, and with a parliament incapable of discharging its responsibilities.[30] The great men of his youth – Curzon, Morley, Asquith, Balfour, Rosebery – had been replaced by inter-war mediocrities such as Ramsay MacDonald ('the boneless wonder') and Stanley Baldwin ('the greatest of non-statesmen'). The result was deteriorated democracy, and weak and infirm government: 'decided only to be undecided, resolved to be irresolute, adamant for drift, solid for fluidity, all-powerful for impotence'.[31]

Weakness at home was bad enough by itself. But for Churchill, it was made worse by the fact that it inexorably led to weakness abroad. For Churchill as for Chamberlain, Britain's standing in the world was indissolubly linked to its will to rule and to retain its Empire. But their conceptions of Empire were very different. Chamberlain was most concerned with the great and growing British communities transplanted across the oceans. Churchill, by contrast, was most concerned with India. Without India, he believed, Britain's international prestige would be irretrievably damaged. And without the Indian Army, Britain would simply cease to be a great military power.[32] Hence his vehement opposition from 1930 to 1935 to the National Government's effort to grant a modest amount of constitutional reform in India. It was wrong because it indicated that the will to rule had been replaced by 'unimaginative incompetence and weak compromise and supine drift'. And it was wrong because this would mean the end of the Indian Empire, and thus the end of British greatness:

The continuance of our present confusion and disintegration will reduce us, within a generation, and perhaps sooner, to the degree of states like Holland and Portugal, which nursed valiant races and held great possessions, but were stripped of them in the crush and competition of the world.[33]

For Churchill, as for Chamberlain before him, and Thatcher after him, will-power, resolution, robustness and determination were all-important attributes. They were the very fibre and sinews of Britain's greatness. By contrast, the policies of appeasement so zealously and misguidedly pursued by the governments of the 1930s proclaimed to the world that Britain was a nation and an empire in decline, suffering from a potentially fatal 'disease of the will'. This was not how a great power should behave – or could behave. Appeasement in India was wrong because it was the negation of Britain's imperial mission. And the appeasement of Germany was also wrong because it represented the abdication of Britain's historic duty to ensure a continent free from tyrants and dictators. Giving way to Hitler was as bad as giving way to Gandhi: both were proof that 'the long, dismal, drawling tides of drift and surrender' had become government policy.[34] What was needed, Churchill insisted, in dealing with Nazi Germany, was a rediscovery of lost virtues, so as 'to raise again a great British nation, standing up before all the world'. There must be a 'supreme recovery of moral health and martial vigour', so the country could 'arise again, and take our stand for freedom as in olden time'.[35]

By the 1930s, Churchill had thus developed into a fully fledged alarmist, seeing enemies everywhere. Abroad, the foes were, successively, Lenin, then Gandhi, then Hitler. At home, there were the Labour Party, the trades unions and the National Government. No wonder that David Low drew a cartoon of a fabulous beast called 'The Winstonocerous', the caption beneath which read, 'Destroys Imaginary Enemies With Great Fury.' But for Churchill the enemies were very real, and during this period his rhetoric became increasingly apocalyptic, full of dark stairways, deep abysses and mortal perils.[36] Only by a reassertion of the national will, and by a return to the heroic values of an earlier age, preferably under his own leadership, could Britain's decline be averted. But, as contemporary critics and later historians have pointed out, this hardly amounted to a credible policy. On India, as Leopold Amery noted, Churchill was 'utterly and entirely negative, and devoid of constructive thought'. And on Germany, he was little better: 'fantastic', according to Lord Hankey, 'ignoring many realities'.[37] All he offered was rhetoric and resolution. This may have been admirable, but it was scarcely a solution to the underlying problem of reconciling too many commitments abroad with too few resources at home.

But in 1940, rhetoric and resolution were precisely what were needed. They served Churchill, and Britain, brilliantly, and never to more telling effect than in the peroration of his great speech of 23 June, where he warned of 'the abyss of a new dark age', while also holding up the prospect of the nation's 'finest hour'. But the very notion of 'their finest hour' carried with it the unacknowledged implication that, thereafter, things would only decline still further. And so, very soon, they did.[38] Rhetoric and resolution worked magnificently in Britain, but they conspicuously failed in Hong Kong, Malaya, Singapore and substantial parts of north-east India. To make matters worse, Churchill now found himself with two allies, Russia and the United States, both of whom disliked the British Empire, while cherishing, as he feared, imperial designs of their own. Once again, he responded defiantly. He did everything he could to thwart demands in London, New Delhi and Washington that he should undertake to give India self-government after the war. And in November 1942, he made this ringing declaration: 'We mean to hold our own. I have not become the King's first minister in order to preside over the liquidation of the British Empire.'[39]

In fact, the British Empire could only be recovered and retained on the sufferance of the Americans and the Russians. In 1945, it was the Iron Curtain and the Pax Americana which were expanding, while the British Empire in India was very soon to be in retreat. The bipolar world which Seeley had earlier foreseen had come into being: not for nothing did Churchill call the last volume of his war memoirs *Triumph and Tragedy*.[40] But as Leader of the Opposition, he soon returned to the apocalyptic rhetoric of the 1930s, laying the blame for what he insisted on seeing as Britain's continued but avoidable decline squarely at the feet of the Labour Government. The last six years, he thundered in 1951, have marked the greatest fall in the rank and stature of Britain in the world, which has occurred since the loss of the American colonies two hundred years ago. Our Oriental Empire has been liquidated, our resources have been squandered, the pound sterling is only worth three quarters of what it was when Mr. Attlee took over from me, [and] our influence among the nations is now less than it has ever been in any period since I remember.[41]

All this, to Churchill, was the inevitable result of ministerial 'apathy, indifference, and bewilderment', of a lack of 'moral strength and willpower' on the part of the government. Once more, what was needed was 'the regeneration of theme and spirit', and a 'new surge of impulse' to 'bring back all our true glories', so that Britain might 'rise again in its true strength'.[42]

As Churchill saw it, his task on returning to power in October 1951 was thus to take on again 'the hard and grim duty of leading Britain and her Empire through and out of her new and formidable crisis'.[43] But as in 1940, there were limits to what could be accomplished in practical terms. To be sure, he was himself the most admired statesman in the world. He sought to re-establish the 'special relationship' with America. And he ensured Britain possessed the hydrogen bomb. But he could not conceal his country's continued economic weakness, and its growing military dependency on the United States. Moreover, as he had himself predicted twenty years before, without India, Britain was no longer the power in the world it had previously been. Indeed, without India, much of the remainder of the British Empire was no longer necessary or worthwhile. Hence, in 1954, the withdrawal of British troops from the Suez Canal zone, an act denounced by die-hard Tories for the very same reason that Churchill had denounced the National Governments of the 1930s: it showed to the world that Britain's will to rule had gone.[44] But even Churchill had by now come to recognize that resolution alone was not enough. The 'liquidation of the British Empire', begun by Attlee in 1947, continued.

After his retirement in 1955, it gathered momentum. In the final months of his premiership, Churchill had come to believe that his chosen successor, Anthony Eden, was not up to the job, and his mishandling of the Suez crisis amply vindicated that view. On Eden's abrupt resignation, Churchill recommended Harold Macmillan, who promptly wound up what was left of the Empire. Like Chamberlain, Churchill's successors let him down, and like Chamberlain again, his last years were disappointed and unhappy. From 1930 onwards, he had devoted himself single-mindedly and whole-heartedly to what he described as 'the maintenance of the enduring greatness of Britain and her Empire'.[45] But by the time of his death in 1965, these great causes had long since become lost causes, something that his own magnificent state funeral tacitly acknowledged. For as everyone recognized on that cold, bleak January day, but no one dared mention, the ceremonials being staged with such dignified and moving splendour, were not only the last rites of the great man himself: they were also a requiem for Britain as a great power. In that sense, Churchill, like Chamberlain, had striven and fought in vain. Perhaps that was what he meant, when he observed, towards the close of his life, 'I have achieved so much, to have achieved nothing in the end.'[46]

III

To move from Churchill to Thatcher is thus to take a much bigger step down the slope of British 'decline', than it was to move from Chamberlain to Churchill, as the empire-state was superseded by the much-diminished island-state. Moreover, compared with Chamberlain's 'catastrophical theory of politics', and with Churchill's apocalyptic alarmism, Margaret Thatcher's rhetoric was less spacious and less highly coloured. But it was much more explicit, straightforward and insistent, with the words 'decline' and 'renewal' constantly appearing in her speeches as Conservative leader and British Prime Minister. Yet once again, there is a familiar pattern: for there was nothing in her life or career between 1925 and 1975 to suggest that she would later become so preoccupied with the parlous state of Britain, and so determined to revive it by the single-minded exertion of her own extraordinary will. From the Grantham corner shop, via Oxford University, marriage to a rich businessman, election to the Commons, and the Ministry of Education under Edward Heath, hers was a story of upward social mobility surpassing that of Joseph Chamberlain.[47] And for her generation, external circumstances were equally propitious: victory in war, the success-ful establishment of the Welfare State, thirteen years of Conservative dominance, and 'you've never had it so good'.

But it is at that point that the pattern ceases to repeat itself. Or perhaps it would be more accurate to say that by that stage of Britain's 'decline', it was no longer possible for the pattern to repeat itself. For the Thatcher transformation during the late 1970s, from welfare-state handmaiden to monetarist prophet and apocalyptic crusader, was not based on sudden disenchantment with the present, by comparison with which the immedi-ately preceding decades seemed bathed in the mellow light of a nostalgic, golden age. On the contrary, Thatcher came to believe that the problems of the late 1970s, culminating in the miners' strike, stagflation and the 'Winter of Discontent', were merely the culmination of a century-long period of national decline, mismanagement and retreat, of which the years since 1945 were the worst and most feeble period of all. It is still unclear precisely when, how and why she formulated these ideas. Certainly, there is no evidence that she was developing them during her time as Education minister.[48] But under the influence of Sir Keith Joseph, they soon took hold of her after she became Leader of the Opposition in 1975.

Thatcher's account of Britain's decline thus encompassed her own era, as well as those of Chamberlain and Churchill. By the time she came to political prominence, it had been going on much longer, and was correspondingly more advanced, than it had been in the 1900s or the 1930s. The rot had set in at precisely the time that Joseph Chamberlain had first noticed it: during the last quarter of the nineteenth century.[49] Sapped by the effete, insidious doctrines of the aristocracy, the civil service, the Church of England, the public schools and Oxbridge, the entrepreneurial spirit that had previously made Britain great was gravely weakened. The rise of trade-unionism and of the Labour Party at the same time only made matters worse. After the Second World War came the Welfare State, with too much socialism, too much planning, too much government spending and too much high taxation, which further eroded the spirit of enterprise. And in the 1960s came the permissive society, which added moral decay to economic degeneration. No wonder, by then, that Britain was widely regarded by the rest of the world, not as a great power, but as something between a national tragedy and a national joke.

According to Thatcher, this was the process whereby Britain had declined – morally, economically and internationally. As an historical account, it owes much to Martin Wiener and Corelli Barnett, and it is set out in full as the prologue to Thatcher's prime ministerial memoirs, where the phrase 'reverse national decline' is interminably repeated.[50] Nor is this mere retrospective invention. For the speeches Thatcher delivered between 1975 and 1979 had been full of the same stark simple message: decline, decay and degeneration on the one hand, and recovery, revival and renewal on the other. She quoted Churchill's words, which had indicted the National Governments of the 1930s, and turned them into an indictment of the Labour Government of the 1970s: 'the long, dismal, drawling tides of drift and surrender'. And in the 1979 election campaign she was even more apocalyptic:

Unless we change our ways and our direction, our glories as a nation will soon be a footnote in the history books, a distant memory of an offshore island, lost in the mists of time, like Camelot, remembered kindly for its noble past.

Or, as she put it more pithily in her last televised election broadcast: 'Somewhere ahead lies greatness for our country again. This I know in my heart.'[51]

How, then, did Thatcher set about halting and reversing what she saw as Britain's century-long decline and fall? In part, she was herself her own answer. Like the elder Pitt in 1757, she genuinely seems to have thought that she could save the country single-handedly, and that she alone could. More even than Chamberlain or Churchill, she believed that Britain's decline could be arrested and averted by the exertion and example of her extraordinary force of will. In her eyes, the major failure of the Heath government – indeed, the major failure of *all* British governments since 1945 – had been a lack of firmness and resolution, and it was a mistake she was determined not to repeat.[52] By her own example, she intended to 'renew the spirit and solidarity of the nation'. She worked prodigiously hard, relished confrontation, delighted in making enemies and dominated her Cabinet, the civil service and Parliament. As the Iron Lady, who was emphatically 'not for turning', she was determined to show that 'decline is not inevitable'. On the contrary, it was primarily an enfeebling and demoralizing state of mind. And it was a state of mind which could, should and must be changed. Such was Thatcher's 'inner conviction', on assuming power in 1979.[53]

For Thatcher, national decline was a *moral* question, and Thatcherism was thus a crusade, a cultural counter-revolution, to restore lost virtue.[54] In her eyes, the key to the revival of Britain was moral recovery and regeneration: the hedonism of the 1960s and the dependency culture of the Welfare State must both be renounced, and the more vigorous and admirable qualities which had once made the nation great, and which could make it great again, must be rediscovered, proclaimed and espoused. Hence her celebrated remarks about those 'Victorian values' which she had learned at her father's knee: thrift, sobriety, patriotism, hard work, self help, independence, personal responsibility.[55] As several historians have subsequently had the temerity to point out, this was a very selective picture of Victorian virtues, which also completely ignored Victorian vices. And it was far from clear how the values evolved in mid-nineteenth-century Britain could be grafted on to the very different economic and social structure of the later twentieth century.[56] Nevertheless, 'Victorian values' became the leitmotif of the Thatcher years: the idealization of the past to bring about a better future.

In what seemed an appropriately self-validating way, Thatcher's forceful leadership, and her campaign for moral regeneration, brought with them two spectacular and perfectly placed victories: one over the enemy without (General Galtieri), and the other over the enemy within (Arthur Scargill).

Both were presented as triumphs of will-power and determination, as no doubt to some extent they were. Both were important because they avenged earlier defeats which had been key episodes in the humiliating story of national decline. The Falklands atoned for the fiasco of Suez, which had itself been a vain attempt to blot out the humiliation of Munich; and victory over the miners was revenge for Heath's defeat at their hands in 1974.[57] And both were presented as emphatic evidence that decline had been halted, and that regeneration was under way. 'We are no longer a nation in retreat,' Thatcher proclaimed in the aftermath of the Falklands War. 'We rejoice that Britain has rekindled that spirit which has fired her for generations past, and which today has begun to burn as brightly as before.' Or, as the Conservative manifesto put it more succinctly for the 1987 general election: 'Great Britain is great again' – 'confident, strong, trusted.'[58]

That was, and still is, Thatcher's claim: that she 'restored Britain's reputation as a force to be reckoned with in the world'. But victories which matter because they atone for earlier defeats (the 'we have licked the Vietnam syndrome' syndrome) might also be seen as further evidence of the very decline which it is claimed they are denying. In any case, apart from these two symbolic successes, the rest of Thatcher's record was much more mixed. In foreign affairs, she was certainly a star on the international stage, who raised Britain's standing in the world.[59] But there is much less evidence to suggest that she lastingly reasserted British power or fundamentally changed British foreign policy. Try as she might (and she tried very hard indeed), she could not halt Britain's growing integration into Europe, nor could she prevent German reunification. She may have restored the 'special relationship' with the United States, but that was based on her close personal friendship with Ronald Reagan, it did not survive their departures from office, and there was never any doubt as to who was the majority partner. And for all her defiance over the Falklands, Thatcher was much more flexible and accommodating when dealing with such other remnants of Empire as Rhodesia, Northern Ireland and Hong Kong.[60]

Nor did she regenerate Britain domestically in the way that she hoped and claimed. True, there was talk during the early stages of the Lawson boom of a 'British economic miracle', on a par with those of Germany and Japan. But this soon ended when the boom collapsed, and taking the whole of her period of power, her record was no better than uneven. The chief gain seems to have been that productivity improved, although levels stayed considerably below those of Britain's international competitors. But investment and rates of growth remained slow and sluggish, the manufacturing base was eroded far beyond anything Joseph Chamberlain had feared, and much of what is left of British industry continues to be internationally uncompetitive.[61] Nor was intrusive and inhibiting government rolled back: the overall tax burden was not significantly reduced, centralized spending remained high, and the reach of the state was extended rather than withdrawn. As for popular attitudes, there is little evidence to suggest that the Thatcherite cultural revolution got very far. The welfare-state mentality has survived, the enterprise-spirit is distinctly lukewarm, the 'permissive' legislation of the 1960s was not repealed, and 'Victorian values' were preached but not practised.[62]

Had Thatcher gone 'on and on and on and on', as she herself once threatened, her regenerative revolution might have cut deeper. But in the end, her messianic, hectoring intolerance proved her undoing, and she was deposed in November 1990. As with Chamberlain and Churchill, her successor let her down. She supported John Major to thwart Michael Heseltine. But she already had her doubts, and Major's subsequent tenure of her office merely confirmed that he was 'wobbly', 'drifts with the tide', and was thus undoing her life's work.[63] Yet Thatcher's 'life's work', as she came to see it, only lasted from 1979 to 1990. As anyone who lived through those years can attest, it was an extraordinary performance. But only her most besotted and uncritical admirers would claim that her deeds matched her words. Here, instead, are the verdicts of two by no means unsympathetic journalists. Peter Jenkins concluded that Britain's decline had 'been temporarily arrested, although I doubt permanently reversed'. And Peter Riddell was more terse: 'she did not halt decline, no one could do that'. Perhaps, in her rather sad and deteriorated retirement, she has belatedly reached a similar conclusion. As she ruefully notes in her memoirs, 'in politics there are no final victories . . . arguments are never finally won.'[64]

IV

In a sense, of course, every major figure in British political life during the last one hundred years could be described as 'a statesman in an age of decline'. But very few of them were, or became, so obsessed with diagnosing that problem and proposing a solution as to merit that characterization. And even the three to whom that label may most appropriately be attached were in some significant ways extremely unalike. Joseph Chamberlain was a self-made industrialist, who never rose higher than the Colonial Secretaryship. Winston Churchill was the grandson of a duke, whose national leadership was more vigorous in war than in peace. And Margaret Thatcher was a shopkeeper's daughter, who had eleven uninterrupted years in which to impose her will on the country. Nor are these their only dissimilarities. In Chamberlain's time, Britain was a much greater force in the world than it was in Churchill's time. And in Churchill's time, it was a much greater force in the world than it was in Thatcher's. All of which is merely to say that they were different people, dealing with different phases of national decline, with different resources at their disposal, and with different policies in each case.

But for all these real variations in time and temperament, in circumstances and character, these three leaders conform to a recognizably atypical and charismatic type: messianic crusaders, convinced that they alone could reverse national decline, and bring about national regeneration. Like all such figures, from the Count-Duke of Olivares to Charles de Gaulle,[65] they were exceptionally difficult individuals – scornful of political conventions, adversarial in their style and rhetoric, frequently battling against their own erstwhile supporters, and more concerned to mould and mobilize public opinion than to follow it. At a particular stage in their lives – in each case, interestingly enough, soon after the onset of middle age – they repudiated their earlier political beliefs, became obsessed with the question of Britain's decline, and determined to change the course of the nation's history by their own exertions. But all three ended their political careers disappointed that they had accomplished less than they had set out to do. The most that can be said is that without Chamberlain, Churchill or Thatcher, Britain might have retreated more rapidly than it has. They may have slowed decline, but they neither halted nor reversed it.

Indeed, how could it possibly have been otherwise? For the whole point about a nation in a state of deeply rooted historical decline is that, by definition, such decline can be neither halted nor reversed. The diagnosis may be accurate, and the prescription the right one. But the patient not only refuses to recover: he (or she) stubbornly persists in getting worse. Chamberlain may have been correct in fearing the industrial might of the United States and the disintegration of the Empire; but there was nothing he could do about either. Churchill was prescient in fearing Indian independence and foreseeing German dominance. But notwithstanding his great efforts, India has been independent for over half a century, and Germany is once again the dominant power in Europe. And Thatcher may have been right about Britain's lack of an enterprise culture and its loss of sovereignty to the Brussels bureaucracy; but however hard she tried, there was little she could do to promote the one or to prevent the other. At the individual level, these were specific failures and disappointments. But collectively, they suggest that there was something inexorable and irreversible about Britain's twentieth-century decline. *Pace* Thatcher, it was not clear the 'decline is not inevitable'.

There is, however, a less gloomy and less self-lacerating way of putting this. For it cannot be too often stressed that the economic, naval and imperial dominance which Britain had enjoyed in the heyday of 'Pax Britannica' was in many ways a fluke – the accidental result of early industrialization, an empire run on the cheap, and the lack of credible continental rivals.[66] Once other, bigger nations caught up, once empires became harder to defend, and once military equipment became more expensive, it was inevitable that, sooner or later, Britain would revert – as it is, today, still in the process of reverting – to being what throughout most of its history it has always been: a small group of islands off the coast of Europe. Given the size and natural endowments of other countries and other empires, it was (and is) inconceivable that Britain could persistently play a very significant or autonomous part in international affairs, however much it may try to 'punch above its weight'. A country with such a small proportion of the world's resources and population cannot indefinitely deal on equal terms with developed nations bigger by anything between 50 and 400 per cent.[67] Thus described, British decline is not the moral or economic or military or imperial catastrophe of Chamberlain, Churchill and Thatcher: it is no more than a necessary (and perhaps even belated?) return to the normal state of affairs.

In believing that decline, thus reformulated and better understood, could be halted and reversed by the renewed exertion of the national will, these three leaders were all equally incorrect. But that was not the only error of judgement which each of them made. For their alarmist predictions of impending apocalypse were no less mistaken. Britain may indeed have fallen in the world rankings of prosperous and powerful countries. But it is still, despite everything that has happened during the last hundred years, one of the most prosperous and powerful countries in the world. And there seems no good reason to suppose that it will cease to be so in the foreseeable future. That, in turn, suggests an explanation for this second mistaken judgement: all three figures spoke the doom-laden language of *absolute* decline, when Britain was in fact – and is still, in fact – experiencing only *relative* decline. Moreover, compared with earlier nations and empires on the wane, Britain's retreat from greatness has been remarkably stable and trouble-free – no barbarians at the gates, no enemy invasions, no civil wars or revolutions, no end to civilization. Britain's decline has not only been relative, in a contemporary sense; it has also, in historical terms, been relatively gradual and relatively gentle.

Nor, despite many gloomy forebodings, has there been the sort of internal economic collapse which has usually accompanied nations and empires in decline. Quite the contrary. For it bears repeating that most Britons today enjoy a standard of living of which their late-Victorian forebears could scarcely have dreamed. A great power has surely been eclipsed, England has undeniably contracted, and Britannia has without doubt been overruled. But for the majority of the population, life has been getting, and is still getting, better and better and better. Small wonder, then, that the apocalyptic warnings of Chamberlain, Churchill and Thatcher fell on ears which were rarely less than half deaf, and were often considerably more so. And small wonder, too, that the majority of the nation's leaders from Lord Salisbury to Tony Blair left the issue of decline very much alone. By definition, being a self-appointed 'statesman in an age of decline' is always rather a thankless task. It is even more thankless when, as in the case of twentieth-century Britain, that age of decline was also an age of affluence.

3

Thrones: Churchill and Monarchy
in Britain and Beyond[1]

In early April 1955, on the eve of his retirement as Prime Minister, Sir Winston Churchill gave a farewell dinner at 10 Downing Street, at which the principal guests were Queen Elizabeth II and the Duke of Edinburgh. The occasion followed a precedent set by Stanley Baldwin in 1937, when he had invited King George VI and Queen Elizabeth, and it provided the immediate inspiration for Harold Wilson's resignation dinner in 1976, which was again attended by the Queen and Prince Philip. But the span and distinction of Churchill's career, and his long association with the crown, gave this valedictory gathering a unique significance and solemnity, of which all those present were well aware.[2] In proposing the loyal toast, the Prime Minister noted that he had enjoyed drinking another queen's health more than half a century ago, 'during the years when I was a cavalry subaltern in the reign of Your Majesty's great-great-grandmother'. At the end of the evening, as he escorted his sovereign to her car, the cameras caught the leave-taking scene: Churchill, full of years and honour, dressed in white tie and tails, wearing the Order of the Garter which she had given him, and the Order of Merit which her father had bestowed, beaming and bowing to the queen, whom he had earlier saluted as 'the young, gleaming champion' of the nation's 'wise and kindly way of life'.[3]

This sunset tableau, combining regal youth and statesmanly age, was reminiscent of Winterhalter's famous picture, painted almost exactly one hundred years before, which had depicted the venerable Duke of Wellington doing avuncular homage to the young Victoria, to Prince Albert, and to their son, Prince Arthur of Connaught, on the first of May 1851.[4] For Churchill, like the Iron Duke before him, was not only her majesty's greatest subject, a national icon and an international hero: he was also an ardent admirer of the institution of monarchy, and of the person and the character of the last British sovereign he himself would live to serve. Indeed, according to his wife, Clementine, he was the only surviving believer in the divine right of kings, and he took great pride and delight in being 'Monarchical No. 1', who valued 'tradition, form and ceremony'.[5] His public life, which spanned more than half a century, from the mid-1890s to the mid-1950s, was a veritable cavalcade of kings and queens, thrones and palaces, coronations and jubilees. By the end of his career, Churchill had been a Member of Parliament during the reigns of six successive sovereigns, he had held office as a cabinet minister under four of them, and he was by a substantial margin the senior Privy Councillor. These were distinctions which no contemporary politician could rival, they surpassed anything achieved by Walpole or Liverpool, Palmerston or Gladstone, and they bore ample witness to the length and closeness of Churchill's royal associations.

Nor should this come as any surprise. For Churchill was born – indeed, well-born – and grew up in what he later recalled as 'the days of Queen Victoria and a settled world order', when politics, society and government were still largely dominated by the traditional forces of monarchy, aristocracy and gentry, and by the highly coloured pageantry and spectacle that were associated with them. This was certainly the case in late nineteenth- and early twentieth-century Britain, and it was also true of every major nation and empire, with the exception of France, the United States and the republics of Latin America. As a result, kings and queens and lords and ladies were at the apex, not only of integrated national hierarchies, but of cosmopolitan, interconnected, international society. This was Churchill's world where, as C. F. G. Masterman noted in the 1900s, 'a benign upper class dispensed benefits to an industrious, bien pensant and grateful working class'. Almost half a century on, his views remained unaltered. In 1942, Herbert Morrison described him as 'the old, benevolent, Tory squire, who does all he can for the people – provided they are good, obedient people, and loyally recognise his position and theirs'.[6] Thus understood, Britain was a 'complex society', which 'descended through every class of citizen' from the monarchy at its apex to the workers, in their 'cottage homes', at the bottom, and it was because he saw it in this way that Churchill 'accepted class distinctions without thought'.[7]

Yet for all his deeply rooted belief in 'a natural, social, almost a metaphysical order – a sacred hierarchy which it was neither possible nor desirable to upset', Churchill's relations with the British royal family, and with monarchs generally and monarchy globally, were in practice more complex and contingent, contradictory and controversial, than that serene, sunset encounter with his sovereign suggests.[8] The toings and froings of Churchill's party-political allegiances, combined with his decade of unrelieved opposition during the 1930s, meant that there were times when he and the British crown were placed on contrary sides on the great issues of the day. Although he believed that monarchy was the best of all possible political (and social) systems, across Europe and throughout the Empire, there were other, practical considerations which often modified or overrode this general principle: if circumstances warranted, and they often did, Churchill would fight royal houses which ruled enemy nations, just as he would welcome republican – even communist – regimes, provided they were loyal and dependable allies. And notwithstanding his devotion to the institution of monarchy, he sometimes found individual sovereigns and their relatives, both at home and abroad, difficult to deal with, mistaken in their attitudes and personally unappealing – disparaging opinions of them which certain kings and princes were, reciprocally, inclined to entertain of him.

As a politician and statesman, Churchill's relations with British (and foreign) monarchs were also much influenced by his historical sense of how monarchy had evolved, by his constitutional sense of what monarchy ought to be and ought to do, and by his known, fierce loyalty to his own illustrious, but distinctly suspect, Marlborough forebears. During the first phase of his political career, until his fall in the aftermath of the Dardanelles disaster, he took European monarchies for granted as being an indissoluble part of the natural order of things, but he tended to see Edward VII and George V as obstructing his Liberal, reforming zeal. In the inter-war years, the collapse of the great continental ruling houses, combined with his own growing conservatism, meant Churchill became more appreciative of the stabilizing virtues of the British crown, and it was this very appreciation which clouded his judgement at the time of the abdication. But this divisive episode meant that in 1940, there were many fences to mend between the unexpected monarch and the unexpected prime minister, and it was only when this had been accomplished during the Second World War (when there were also many other sovereigns with whom he had to deal) that the final and mutually admiring phase of crown–Churchill relations was established. 'King and country, in that order,' noted Lord Moran, 'that's about all the religion Winston has.'[9] But it was not always in that order; and Churchill's beliefs sometimes seemed more heretical than orthodox.

I

Churchill's view of monarchy was grounded in the classic Victorian histories by Macaulay, Froude, Gardiner and Carlyle that he had initially encountered as a Harrow schoolboy and later read as a subaltern in Bangalore; and they were set out, virtually unchanged, in his *History of the English-Speaking*

Peoples, which was largely written during the late 1930s.[10] Notwithstanding the title, it was essentially a brightly lit cavalcade of the great public figures who had made up the nation's story, which was headed by kings and queens, most of them domestic and some of them foreign. They formed a varied and diverse collection, and Churchill judged them confidently, crisply and critically. There were outstanding leaders in war and forceful administrators in peace, such as Alfred the Great, William the Conqueror, Henry II, Richard I, Edward I, Henry V, Henry VII, Elizabeth I and William III.[11] But many monarchs were personally inept and politically disastrous, among them Stephen, John, Richard II, Richard III, Mary Tudor, James II, George III and George IV. As for overseas kings and queens: their relations with England fluctuated dramatically across the centuries. The Austrian Habsburgs were England's allies during the War of Spanish Succession, but opponents in the Seven Years War; the kings of Prussia were foes in the 1740s but friends in the 1750s; and the Emperor of Russia was a comrade-in-arms against Napoleon, but the enemy in the Crimea.[12]

The lesson to be drawn from this account was that English monarchs might be good or bad, while foreign sovereigns might be loyal or false and, in the course of his career, Churchill encountered kings and queens of all these stripes and types.[13] Yet amidst this constantly shifting kaleidoscope of royal dynasties, national alliances and sovereign individuals, two general themes did stand out, which formed the basis of his own constitutional beliefs. One was that, despite the delinquencies of many individual monarchs, the English crown was a sacred, mystical, almost metaphysical institution, which connected the past, the present and the future, and which proclaimed the unity and identity of the nation. As Lord Moran recalled, 'the history of England, its romance and changing fortunes, is for Winston embodied in the royal house'.[14] A second was that, while other European nations preferred (or suffered) kings and queens who were generally despotic and absolute, the English evolved a more admirable form of 'constitutional and limited monarchy'. Thanks to Parliament, which represented the nation as a whole, and the later advent of the two-party system, the sovereign's power was progressively eroded in a succession of episodes which were milestones in the advancing story of English liberties, extending from Magna Carta to the Glorious Revolution of 1688 and beyond. The result was a happy compromise, a 'permanent parliament and a docile monarchy', whereby the sovereign reigned above the battle of party, while the Lords and Commons legislated and the politicians governed.[15]

This, then, was the British crown as it had evolved and developed by the end of Victoria's reign, when young Winston was first learning about it. He had no doubt that she had been a great queen who, 'in spite of her occasional leanings', was 'a constitutional sovereign', who 'represented staunchness and continuity in British traditions', and who 'set a new standard for the conduct of monarchy which has ever since been honourably observed'.[16] In institutional (and Tory) terms, her crown embodied the nation's history, continuity and identity in its symbolic functions and ceremonial activities; and in practical (and Whig) terms, it was a convenient constitutional device, which left the people free to elect their representatives through whom they governed themselves. But during her reign, the monarchy also acquired two important new functions. Thanks to the happy home life of Victoria and Albert, it provided a moral example to the nation, of decent and dutiful domesticity, in a way that had not been true for much of the Stuart and Hanoverian dynasties. And Victoria was not only the head of the British nation but also became the 'great presiding personage' of the much wider British Empire. Largely on account of Disraeli's initiative and imagination, hers had become an imperial monarchy, the focus and cynosure of a diverse and far-flung British community, extended across the seas and around the world, which was united in fealty to the Queen Empress.[17]

This monarchy – by turns Tory and Whig, mystical and functional, symbolic and constitutional, individual and familial, national and imperial – was in the full flower of its late-Victorian abundance, confidence and ostentation as Churchill was growing up. It seemed an apt expression of the British genius for organic constitutional evolution and working political compromise, it was widely envied (and just occasionally emulated) around the globe and, in this particular settlement and configuration, it lasted the whole of his long life.[18] For Churchill, notwithstanding the occasional difficulties resulting from incompetent individuals or malevolent monarchs, it was beyond doubt the best of all possible worlds. 'Our ancient monarchy', he observed on the birth of Prince Charles in 1948, 'renders inestimable services to our country and to all the British Empire and Commonwealth of Nations.' And it did so because it was 'above the ebb and flow of party strife, the rise and fall of ministries and individuals, the changes of public opinion and fortune'. Domestically, it presided, 'ancient, calm and supreme within its functions, over all the treasures that have been saved from the past, and all the glories we write in the annals of our country'. And internationally, it provided 'the mysterious . . . the magic link which unites our loosely bound but strongly interwoven Commonwealth of nations, states and races'.[19]

But Churchill never forgot that while the mystical, unifying, moral and imperial functions of the monarch were important, the whole thrust of

English history had been to bring about a state of affairs where the king's government was carried on by ministers, who were primarily answerable to Parliament, rather than to the crown. He spelt out this minimalist doctrine of kingly power early in his political career. 'The royal prerogative', he insisted to his wife in 1909, 'is always exercised on the advice of ministers, and ministers and not the crown are responsible, and criticism of all debatable acts of policy should be directed to ministers, not to the crown.' He made the same point about Parliament's pre-eminence thirty years later, when he bluntly informed the exiled Duke of Windsor that 'when our kings are in conflict with our constitution, we change our kings', as had happened in 1688 – and as had happened again in 1936.[20] And in 1947, in *The Dream*, his imaginary conversation with his father, Churchill explained that the monarchy had survived because 'they took the advice of ministers who had majorities in the House of Commons'. This was the British throne as limited, constitutional, parliamentary monarchy. It put the crown in its place, and in political (though not social) terms, that was a subordinate place. Honouring the sovereign was right and good and necessary and splendid; but being governed by the sovereign had long since, and very properly, been given up.[21]

In any case, the British monarchy was not the only illustrious dynasty to which Churchill was devoted. For his loyalty to his own clan, the Marlboroughs, was no less fervent, and this veneration not only influenced his view of the crown (and his behaviour towards it), but also prejudiced the crown's view of him. As the highest ranking British aristocrats, ducal families enjoyed a particularly close relationship with the sovereign, by whom they were regarded as near social equals. Indeed, dukes were customarily referred to by kings as their 'right trusty and well-beloved cousins', and this was certainly a description which John Churchill, first Duke of Marlborough, was eager to win and proud to claim. For his rise to fame and fortune as a 'heaven-born general', and as a European statesman, were inextricably linked with the fate of the English throne. Along with the great Whig families, he had extended the invitation to Prince William of Orange in the Glorious Revolution, which made him a prime architect of that limited, Protestant monarchy which was the essence of the constitution. And during the reign of Queen Anne, he had been the linchpin of the Grand Alliance against Louis XIV, and achieved a succession of brilliant victories at Blenheim, Ramillies, Oudenarde and Malplaquet, which vanquished the French, secured the throne and the Church, and established England at the forefront of European powers.

In return, these monarchs were appropriately grateful, and John Churchill was made a baron by James II, an earl by William III and a duke by Queen Anne (he was in addition made a Prince of the Holy Roman Empire by the Emperor Leopold, a title which, Churchill proudly noted in his biography of Marlborough, 'has . . . descended to this day'[22]). In recognition of his great deeds, Queen Anne also bestowed on him the royal manor of Woodstock in Oxfordshire where, at the nation's expense, and with the assistance of Sir John Vanbrugh, Marlborough set out to construct Blenheim Palace as an enduring monument to himself, his greatness and his dynasty. By turns ornate, oppressive, Olympian and overwhelming, it is one of the most extraordinary houses in Europe, and one of the very few in Britain not inhabited by monarch or a bishop that was designated a palace.[23] Every year, on the anniversary of the battle of Blenheim, successive Dukes of Marlborough presented the king with a fleur-de-lys flag as rental for their royal estate, and across the generations, they were regularly Lord-Lieutenants of Oxfordshire, where they were among the greatest magnates in the county, and Knights of the Garter. Soon after Churchill was born, in 1876, the seventh Duke (his grandfather) was appointed Lord-Lieutenant of Ireland, at that time the most magnificent vice-regal position in the Empire, and he held sumptuous court in Dublin; and at the same time, his daughter, Lady Anne Spencer-Churchill, who was married to the Duke of Roxburgh, served Queen Victoria as Mistress of the Robes (as the great Duchess Sarah had served Queen Anne in an earlier generation).[24]

But this comfortable picture of courtly collaboration between monarchs and Marlboroughs was at best a partial version of the truth, for in many ways, and in many generations, the Churchills were neither reliable nor respectable from a royal point of view. 'Faithful but unfortunate' was their family motto, but in the case of the first duke, it was misleading on both counts.[25] Far from being a loyal servant of successive sovereigns, he was overweeningly ambitious and shamelessly opportunist, with his eye constantly to the main chance, and he had no qualms about abandoning one monarch and taking up with another. His initial rise had been thanks to the patronage and support of James II, but when things began to go badly for the king in the mid-1680s, the young John Churchill deserted him in favour of Prince William of Orange; two decades later, he was similarly unprincipled in plotting against William III, and in transferring his allegiance to Anne; near the end of his life, he changed thrones again, embracing the Hanoverian succession; and there were constant whispers that he was a closet Jacobite. Thereafter, and even when judged by the laxest aristocratic standards, successive Dukes of Marlborough tended to be morally wayward, financially irresponsible and politically unreliable, and these disagreeable family characteristics were abundantly displayed by Winston's father, Lord Randolph Churchill.[26]

As befitted someone with a well-deserved reputation for fast and rackety behaviour, he had originally belonged to the social set associated with the Prince of Wales. Indeed, Randolph first met his future wife, Jennie Jerome, at a reception and dance at Cowes, at which the Prince and Princess of Wales had been present in August 1873.[27] But in 1876, the prince and the politician fell out publicly and acrimoniously, when Randolph took his elder brother's side in a scandal involving Lady Aylesford, into which the heir to the throne had also been drawn. The complex, sordid details are of no concern here but, in the course of it, Lord Randolph threatened the Princess of Wales, challenged her husband to a duel, and claimed that some incriminating correspondence from the prince that had come into his possession meant he had 'the crown of England in my pocket'. The prince was outraged, and responded by ostracizing Lord and Lady Randolph, thereby effectively excluding them from high society from 1876 to 1884.[28] And this royal disapproval extended to the Queen-Empress herself. Like her son, she thought Lord Randolph was unstable, unprincipled and unsound; she resented his successful attempts, when Secretary of State for India, to thwart her scheme to appoint her favourite son, the Duke of Connaught, to the Bombay Command; she was furious that he wrote his letter of resignation as Chancellor of the Exchequer on Windsor Palace notepaper, while neglecting to inform her that he had done so; and she was relieved and delighted that he never again held political office.[29]

There was, then, ample ground across the centuries for royal disapproval; but as a great dynasty, who were closely (if intermittently) associated with their sovereigns, the Marlboroughs were undismayed. Although neither rich nor respectable by the highest ducal standards, they were undeniably *grand*: the bearers of one of the greatest names in the country, and the possessors of one of the finest houses. Like many dukes, they tended to look down on the British crown as being rather parvenu and, latterly, middle class: after all, they had seen off the houses of Stuart, Orange, Hanover and Saxe-Coburg-Gotha. In short, they were cavaliers – and they treated the monarchy cavalierly.[30] In return, successive sovereigns responded by regarding the Marlboroughs as distinctly suspect. These actions and attitudes would re-emerge, on both sides, in the course of Winston Churchill's life. For all his veneration of the throne as a national institution, he was never overawed by members of the royal family, and he often gave the impression, especially in the early stages of his career, that he did not think much of particular monarchs. He had, after all, been born in a *palace*, which was more than

George V or Edward VIII or George VI or Elizabeth II could claim. And so it was scarcely surprising that monarchs saw in him the defects to be expected in Lord Randolph's son and the great duke's descendant: he was a tactless, ambitious, egotistical opportunist, and a traitor to his class, who would never let royalty – or loyalty – get in the way of his own career.[31]

As young Winston was growing up, the relations between these two dynasties remained close but equivocal. Viscount Churchill of Wychwood, who was descended from a younger son of the fourth Duke of Marlborough, was lord-in-waiting to King Edward VII; but his private life was a shambles, and he separated from (and eventually divorced) his wife amidst great public scandal.[32] Churchill's mother, Jennie, had long since been forgiven for her husband's delinquencies, and returned to favour with the Prince of Wales; but her sister, Leonie, had formed a liaison with the Duke of Connaught, whom Lord Randolph had successfully kept out of the Bombay Command, which lasted from 1900 to 1938, and of which the Prince did not altogether approve. And 'Sunny', the ninth Duke of Marlborough, who was Churchill's cousin, and held the title from 1892 to 1934, was even less respectable. His marriage to Consuelo Vanderbilt brought money but misery to Blenheim. Their union was unhappy, and after their separation neither Edward VII nor George V would receive the duke at court, or meet him socially in private houses; he was asked to cease the annual practice of presenting the Blenheim flag; and it was only as a result of Churchill's personal intervention with the king in 1911 that the duke was allowed to attend the lunch at Windsor after the annual Garter ceremony.[33]

II

These complex dynastic interconnections meant that royalty was an integral part of young Winston's life from the very beginning, and during his early years he enjoyed the sort of friendship which in those days was commonplace between the scion of a great ducal house and the British royal family, characterized by a paradoxical combination of closeness and distance, approval and disapproval – and with eyes firmly to the main chance. The Prince of Wales enquired after his health when he was stricken with pneumonia in 1888, and Churchill first glimpsed the prince's cousin, the German emperor, on his visit to England in 1891, when he was memorably impressed by his extravagant uniform. His parents pulled strings with the Duke of Cambridge, the queen's cousin and Commander-in-Chief of the British Army, to get their son his commission, initially intended to be in the infantry, but subsequently in the cavalry. Such shameless lobbying was customary in high social circles at that time; but these were also the years of Victoria's imperial apotheosis, by which the young Churchill was deeply and lastingly affected. In Diamond Jubilee year, he was serving in India, and as he read accounts of how the queen had been made an empress, his romantic ardour was roused: 'I must', he told his mother, 'array myself with those who "love high sounding titles", since no title that is not high-sounding is worth having.'[34]

But as someone with a career to establish and a reputation to make, young Winston generally saw British royalty in terms of professional contacts and social connection. He served under the command of the Duke of Connaught in 1895 as a young officer at Aldershot, and thereafter (no doubt helped by his aunt Leonie) 'enjoyed his friendship'. Three years later, he sent the Prince of Wales a copy of his first book, *The Story of the Malakand Field Force*, and he professed himself 'Tory enough' to be delighted at the recipient's favourable response. Soon after, the prince wrote again, advising Churchill (rather shrewdly, as things turned out) that the 'parliamentary and literary life' would suit him better than 'the monotony of military life', and they continued to correspond when Churchill was in South Africa during the Boer War.[35] Thirty years later, in *My Early Life*, Churchill paid tribute to 'the extraordinary kindness and consideration for young people which the Prince of Wales always practised'. But on the queen's death ('a great and solemn event'), he had shown rather less obsequiousness in his attitude to the new king's accession. 'Will it entirely revolutionise his way of life? Will he sell his horses and scatter his Jews?' he asked his mother. 'Will he continue to be friendly to you? Will the Keppel be appointed first Lady of the Bedchamber?' These were the questions of someone well in touch with royal circles; but they were scarcely the reverent enquiries of a servile courtier. He was delighted at the prospect of knowing 'an Emperor and a King'; but admitted (quite rightly, as events later proved) that he needed to learn more about royal etiquette.[36]

When Churchill took up his 'parliamentary and literary life' in earnest, by becoming an MP for Oldham, he was soon invited to Balmoral. 'I have been very kindly treated here by the king,' Churchill reported to his mother, 'who has gone out of his way to be nice to me.' As Churchill began to make a reputation as Colonial Under-Secretary, Edward expressed delight that he was becoming 'a *reliable* minister and above all serious politician, *which can only be obtained by putting country before party.*' When he was sworn into the Privy Council, the king sent a further letter of encouragement: 'We have known your parents for many years (even before their marriage) and you and your brother since your childhood. Knowing the great abilities which you possess, I am watching your political career with great interest.' And when Churchill became engaged, Edward sent him a telegram of congratulation, and gave him a gold-headed malacca cane as a wedding present.[37] For his part, Churchill took pains in his biography of Lord Randolph to spare the royal family any embarrassment, glossing over the row between his father and the Prince of Wales, and urging that Randolph had opposed the appointment of the Duke of Connaught to the Bombay Command on constitutional rather than personal grounds. Far from being a royal critic, Churchill further insisted, the whole thrust of his father's career had been 'to rally the people round the throne, to unite the throne with the people, a loyal throne and a patriotic people'.[38]

But as so often in the history of the monarchy and the Marlboroughs, there was another, and less agreeable, side to the relationship. For Churchill's drive, brashness, ambition, opportunism, self-absorption and egotism soon grated on his sovereign, just as Lord Randolph had on Queen Victoria, and as he moved from being a junior Conservative backbencher to a junior Liberal minister, the king reluctantly concluded that he was 'almost more of a cad in office than he was in opposition'.[39] In 1905, he criticized 'those gorgeous and gilded functionaries with brass hats and ornamental duties who multiply so luxuriously on the plains of Aldershot and Salisbury', which Edward thought scarcely appropriate coming from 'a recent subaltern of Hussars!'. Once the Liberals were in power, Churchill lobbied hard for his uncle by marriage, Lord Wimborne, to be made Lord-Lieutenant of Dorset. The king (with good cause) disapproved of him (as he did his nephew) as a social climber and 'a political turncoat', and only agreed to the appointment with great reluctance. Soon after, in one of his earliest speeches as Colonial Under-Secretary, Churchill attacked Lord Milner in the House of Commons. The king was outraged by such 'scandalous' behaviour and 'violent and objectionable language', which he regarded as the negation of the sort of statesmanly conduct to which he had once hoped Churchill might aspire.[40]

These were relatively minor skirmishes. But they were cumulatively portentous, for as Churchill became more senior, and more radical, and began to embrace for a time the language of class conflict, the king's anxiety rapidly became alarm. In 1909, when President of the Board of Trade, Churchill made common cause with the Chancellor of the Exchequer, Lloyd George, to reduce the amount spent on the army in favour of old age pensions. The king responded by suggesting to the Prince of Wales, in a dazzling moment of sophisticated regal wit, that Churchill's initials, WC, 'are well named'. When Churchill made a speech in September 1909, attacking dukes as 'unfortunate individuals' and 'ornamental creatures' who were part of a 'miserable minority of titled persons who represent nobody', the king's private secretary, Lord Knollys, took the extraordinary step of writing to *The Times* to protest. But notwithstanding his much-prized Marlborough blood, Churchill was unrepentant. 'He and the king must really have gone mad,' he retorted. 'This looks to me,' he concluded, 'like a rather remarkable royal intervention, and shows the bitterness which is felt in those circles. I shall take no notice of it. It will defeat itself.' But Knollys was no less unforgiving. 'The very idea', he wrote, of Churchill's acting 'from conviction or principle . . . is enough to make anyone laugh.' Not surprisingly, Edward VII's anxiety about Churchill's conduct and character lasted to the end of his life.[41]

The same contrasts in attitude and behaviour were apparent during the early years of the reign of George V, whom Churchill had first met socially at Cowes in 1887. While he was Home Secretary, Churchill was scrupulous in giving his sovereign full reports of public disorders in the Rhondda in 1910 and in Liverpool in 1911; he successfully oversaw the trial for criminal libel of Edward Mylius, who claimed that George V had contracted a secret marriage in Malta in 1890, when serving with the Mediterranean fleet; and the king found the nightly reports of Commons proceedings which Churchill sent him at Asquith's request 'always instructive and interesting'.[42] In February 1911, Churchill substantially wrote the speech the king delivered at the unveiling of the Victoria Memorial, which ended with these rousing words: 'No reign in this kingdom ever gathered up more carefully the treasure of the past, or prepared more hopefully the path of the future.' Later that year, on exchanging the Home Office for the Admiralty, Churchill wrote with flattering grandiloquence: 'it has been a high honour to me to have stood so near to your majesty during the moving and memorable events of the first year of a happy and brilliantly inaugurated reign', and he looked forward to receiving the king's 'aid and support', based on 'a life-time of practical experience'. And there were further visits to Balmoral. 'The king', Churchill told his wife in September 1913, 'has been extremely cordial and intimate in his conversations, and I am glad to think that I reassured him a good deal about the general position.'[43]

But while George V recognized Churchill's zeal and energy, he was also influenced by his father's disapproval, and generally thought him 'irresponsible and unreliable', a view which his own experiences tended to confirm. In 1908, he had told Churchill that he did not consider Asquith to be a gentleman. Of course, and as he later admitted to Lord Esher, he should never have said such a thing, 'but Winston repeated it to Asquith, which was a monstrous thing to do, and made great mischief '.[44] At Edward VII's lying-in-state in Westminster Hall, Churchill had created a scene; and, during his first formal audience with the new monarch, he had tactlessly asserted that great change was necessary in the constitution, while expressing only perfunctory regret at the death of the late sovereign. There were also difficulties arising from the nightly reports of the Commons proceedings Churchill sent to the king, as when he observed that 'there are idlers and wastrels at both ends of the social scale'. George V opined that such views were 'very socialistic'; but Churchill stood by the offending phrase and objected to receiving 'a formal notification of the king's displeasure'. Peace was eventually restored; but the sovereign's private secretary saw this as further evidence that Churchill was 'a bull in a china shop', while he continued to think the royal reproof unjust and a sign of the king's lack of proper political impartiality.[45]

When Churchill moved to the Admiralty, matters did not improve. The new First Lord was a party politician and a zealous reformer; the king was a former naval person, head of the armed services, and a staunch believer in tradition and precedent. Churchill wanted to name a ship 'HMS Oliver Cromwell': not surprisingly, George V took violent exception to thus commemorating the regicide. Churchill then proposed 'HMS Pitt': but the king would not have that, either. In both cases, Churchill grudgingly gave way. 'I have always endeavoured to profit from any guidance his majesty has been gracious and pleased to give me,' he wrote rather stiffly and unconvincingly after this second royal rebuff.[46] Thereafter, their relations remained tense. In January 1914, the king disapproved of Churchill's threat to resign during the crisis over the Naval Estimates, and there were subsequent disagreements over promotions and honours. Churchill made no secret of his view that George V was a dim reactionary, and the king made it plain that Churchill was rude and inconsiderate. When he objected to the First Lord's proposal to withdraw battleships from the Mediterranean to safeguard British waters, in May 1912, Churchill exploded to his wife: 'The king talked more stupidly about the navy than I have ever heard him before. Really it is disheartening to hear this cheap and silly drivel with which he lets himself be filled up.'[47]

These two monarchs disliked Churchill because they thought he was insufficiently respectful of their person and their prerogative; Churchill was unintimidated, and objected to what he regarded as inappropriate royal interference in matters which were wholly within the realm of Parliament and government. But for all his blustering radicalism, he still took it for granted that Europe was – and should remain – a continent of nation states and empires linked together by the reigning monarchs at their heads and, as the grandson of a duke and a Cabinet minister, he moved easily and confidently in such glitteringly cosmopolitan circles. In 1906, Churchill visited Germany to watch military manoeuvres in Silesia, where he found the kaiser 'very friendly' and 'a most fascinating personality', and he subsequently sent him a copy of his life of Lord Randolph. In 1911, he met the recently deposed King Manuel of Portugal. 'He is extremely clever and accomplished,' Winston told Clementine. 'We made great friends. In harmony with my duties and British interests, I will do my best to help him.'[48] Early in 1914, he met King Alfonso XIII in Madrid, sent him editions of his books, and hoped his 'statesmanship and courage may long be preserved to the Spanish people'. And in July that year, when international affairs were everywhere tending 'towards catastrophe and collapse', Churchill vainly urged Asquith to propose a conference of European sovereigns with the aim of settling the impending crisis without war.[49]

But while, for all his radicalism, Churchill still believed in a traditional Europe of traditional monarchies, the British crown and court were firmly against him by the time war broke out later in 1914, and thereafter relations deteriorated still further. When Churchill urged that the British Navy would dig out the German Navy 'like rats in a hole', the king protested that such language was 'hardly dignified for a Cabinet minister'. Soon after, he rashly assumed command at Antwerp, which caused Lord Stamfordham to opine that he must be 'quite off his head!'. And when he urged the reappointment of Lord Fisher as First Sea Lord, George V objected on the (not unreasonable) grounds that he was seventy-three and lacked the confidence of the Navy; but Churchill insisted and the king had to give way.[50] All of which meant that his downfall over the Dardanelles disaster in 1915 was greeted at Buckingham Palace with scarcely concealed relief. 'It is', Queen Alexandra informed her son, 'all that stupid, young foolhardy Winston C's fault which has upset everybody.' And the king agreed. Churchill had become 'impossible', a 'real danger', and he was 'delighted' and 'relieved' that he had been got rid of. So was his son, the Prince of Wales and future Edward VIII: 'It is a great relief to know Winston is leaving the Admiralty,' he wrote to his father.[51] Thus ended the first phase of Churchill's involvement with the British crown, which scarcely presaged the mutual admiration that would characterize their relations in the last two decades of his life.

III

During the inter-war years, Churchill's attitudes towards monarchy, both in Britain and abroad, began to change, as the balance between criticism and approval, hostility and appreciation, shifted markedly in their favour. Like many pre-1914 Liberals, the First World War had left him saddened and uncertain, with his own reputation damaged and his career prospects diminished, and looking out on a social, political and international landscape so brutally transformed and disturbed that it bore little resemblance to what seemed, in retrospect, to have been the Edwardian *belle époque*, with its settled values, historic institutions, venerable titles and great estates. 'Injuries', he later wrote, 'were wrought to the structure of human society which a century will not efface, and which may conceivably prove fatal to the present civilisation.'[52] The ruling houses of Germany, Russia and Austria–Hungary had been fixed points around which much of Europe's history had evolved and revolved. Now they were gone, emperors and thrones alike, and the Spanish monarchy followed in 1931. Deprived of these symbols of order, tradition and continuity, 'woven over centuries of renown into the texture of Europe', the continent lapsed into anarchy, civil war, revolution and dictatorship (whether fascist or communist). Even Britain was not entirely free of this contagion: great aristocratic families were no longer as secure or prominent as they had been before 1914, and universal democracy threatened to get out of hand.[53]

In these troubled and terrible times, Churchill came to regret the demise of the great European monarchies, and his *The World Crisis* was not only a self-justification of his part in the Dardanelles campaign, but also an elegy for this vanished civilization. 'Nations and empires,' he wrote, 'crowned with princes and potentates, rose majestically on every side, lapped in the accumulated treasures of the long peace ... The old world in its sunset was fair to see.' He grieved that Russia which, he insisted, had been on the brink of victory early in 1917, had then fallen prey to the 'nameless beast' of bolshevism, which for the czar meant 'the down-fall of his house ... and a bloody cellar of Ekaterinburg', and for his people an 'abyss of ruin and horror'.[54] He depicted the aged Franz Josef as 'the weary, stricken, tragic, octogenarian heir of the ages and their curses', dying 'in harness', and he regretted the vanquishment of 'the once mighty Habsburg Empire' as it 'shivered into fragments'. And he wrote appreciatively of the military ability of the German crown prince, and sympathetically of the kaiser's ordeal, as his throne tottered and his empire disintegrated.[55] With the exception of Britain, all the great power monarchies – 'mighty organisms built up by generations of patience and valour, and representing the traditional groupings of noble branches of the European family' – had gone. Only on the edges of the continent, in the Low Countries, Scandinavia, Italy and the Balkans, did crowns and thrones now survive, uncertain, marginalized and diminished.[56]

These postwar changes, in continental circumstances and in Churchillian perceptions, help explain the substantial transformation in his relations with King George V. For he no longer regarded the British sovereign as the ignorant, blimpish reactionary of his radical Liberal days, but as the embodiment of decency, duty and tradition, in a world all too often characterized by strife, anarchy and revolution; and for his part, the king now warmed to Churchill both as an old friend and as a new conservative. The solution of the Irish problem seems to have had a great deal to do with this. Churchill greatly admired the 'unswerving sense of devotion' George V displayed in visiting Belfast in June 1921, when he urged Irishmen to 'forgive and forget'; and the king applauded Churchill's 'skill, patience and tact' in seeing the Irish Treaty through in the following year. Thereafter, the king was 'very sorry' about Churchill's defeat at Dundee in 1922 and, while he was Chancellor of the Exchequer between 1924 and 1929, their relations were much more cordial than they had been before the First World War.[57] When Churchill visited Balmoral in 1927, he 'enjoyed' himself 'very much' and had 'a very good talk about all sorts of things'. And when holidaying at Deauville, he observed the Shah of Persia at the gaming tables, dissolutely 'parting with his subjects' cash'. 'Really,' he observed to Clementine, 'we are well out of it with our own gracious monarch!'[58]

Churchill's new-found appreciation of old-world monarchy in the interwar years showed itself in more active and assertive ways. One indication was that he had wanted the kaiser treated leniently, unlike Lloyd George and many of his Cabinet, who had wished to see him brought to Britain and hanged. Another was the vehemency with which, between 1917 and 1922, he waged his increasingly obsessional campaign against the 'foul baboonery' of bolshevism. According to Lloyd George, his exceptional hostility was partly inspired by his rage at the destruction of the Russian crown, which meant his 'ducal blood revolted against the wholesale liquidation of Grand Dukes'. A more positive sign of Churchill's veneration for monarchy emerged in his handling of the Cairo Conference in March 1921, when he was Colonial Secretary. Urged on by T. E. Lawrence, he created new royal houses in the British-held League of Nations Mandates of Transjordan and Mesopotamia, where he delighted in establishing the two Hashemite kingdoms, ruled by Abdullah and Feisal respectively, to which (and to whom) he remained loyal all his life.[59] The models for these new Middle Eastern monarchies were the princely states of India, where Churchill had spent some of his happiest times as a serving officer. And so it was scarcely surprising that, along with such die-hard grandees as Lord Salisbury and the Duke of Westminster, he supported the ruling Indian princes in his battle against what became the Government of India Act of 1935. He regarded them as the Empire's loyalist allies, the embodiment of tradition, order and stability, and thus as the best corrective to the middle-class, urban-based nationalists of Calcutta, Bengal and Bombay, whom he distrusted and detested.

By this time, Churchill was out of office, and he was writing a great deal about thrones and crowns. In an article published in *Pearson's Magazine* in 1934, he posed the question, 'Will the world swing back to monarchies?', and answered it in the affirmative. Monarchy was the best antidote to anarchy and tyranny; it provided 'glamour, splendour, restraint and stability'; it was a 'silly idea' that republics were better governed than kingdoms; the twentieth-century 'holocaust of crowns' had been a huge folly; and the restoration of the historic royal houses in Germany and the successor states of Austria–Hungary should be hoped for and looked forward to.[60] In a similar vein, he wrote a sympathetic review of the kaiser's memoirs, and recalled with appreciation his meetings with him in 1906 and 1909. He was, Churchill opined, a decent man, on the side of order, aristocracy and tradition, who had been put in an impossible position in 1914, had behaved with great dignity in defeat and exile, and who deserved sympathy and understanding. If the Hohenzollerns had still been on the German throne, 'looking back upon the traditions of the past, and looking forward to a continuity in the future', he concluded, there would have been no Hitler. And he also wrote on King Alfonso XIII, another unhappy survivor from the old world, who had recently been exiled: to Churchill, he appeared brave, modest, decent, and high-spirited, 'the one strong, unmoving pivot around which the life of Spain revolved', whose 'sole object was the strength and fame of his realm'. Now he was gone, and the Spanish were 'tearing each other to pieces'. Was this progress? Churchill did not think so.[61]

By this time, he was deeply immersed in his biography of the great Duke of Marlborough, himself the product and ornament of an 'old world', and 'polite civilization', set in a 'formal frame', where 'rank and property' seemed 'secure and permanent', and unsullied, not only by the revolution of 1917, but by that of 1789, and where war was a chivalric contest fought out by kings and princes, aristocracy and gentry. As a Catholic, absolute monarch, Louis XIV was 'petty . . . mediocre . . . arrogant . . . the curse and pest of Europe' (no model sovereign he!); but in England, 'Marlborough's victorious sword established upon sure foundations the constitutional and parliamentary structure of our country almost as it has come down to us today.'[62] Indeed, between 1702 and 1708, England reached its pinnacle of glory, because Queen Anne 'determined to suppress her personal feelings in what she deemed a national interest', and allowed the duke, who invariably treated her with the extravagant deference due from servant to his mistress, virtually a free hand as 'master of events'.[63] But as always for Churchill, past history also taught contemporary lessons, as he pointed out in 1933 when he presented George V with the first volume of *Marlborough: His Life and Times*. 'This is the story', he wrote, 'of how a wise princess and queen gave her trust and friendship to an invincible commander, and thereby raised the power and fame of England to a height never before known, and never since lost.' 'And', he went on, 'it is submitted in loyal duty to a sovereign under whom our country has come through perils even more grievous with no less honour.'[64]

In the days of Marlborough, no less than in his own time, Churchill regarded the English monarchy as 'the crowned embodiment of the nation'. But there was also the 'broadening imperial theme', begun when Queen Victoria 'sought by every means in her power to bind her diverse people together in loyalty to the British crown', and Churchill was eager to safe-guard the King-Emperor as an imperial as well as a national sovereign.[65] Hence his dislike of the Statute of Westminster, passed in 1931, which declared that the dominions were autonomous nations, in no way subordin-ate to Britain, and thereby 'needlessly obliterating old, famous landmarks and signposts'. Hence his preference for the word 'Empire', which had strong and historic royal associations, rather than the use of the term 'Commonwealth', with its less happy Cromwellian connotations. And hence, too, his opposition during the early 1930s to moves towards further Indian self-government, which (as he saw it) threatened the position, not only of the ruling princes, but even that of the King-Emperor himself. In this unhappy inter-war world, increasingly characterized by shifting values and uncertain resolve, all that remained was 'tradition, good will and good sense', increasingly embodied in the institution of the monarchy, and in the person of the sovereign.[66]

Churchill developed these national, continental and imperial themes more fully in an obituary notice of King George V, which he subsequently revised and reprinted in *Great Contemporaries*.[67] In the course of the reign, massive changes had destabilized the world: empires and monarchies had fallen; dictatorship and anarchy had flourished; democracy had become incontinent and unfettered. Yet, 'at the heart of the British Empire', there was 'one institution, among the most ancient and venerable which, so far from falling into desuetude or decay', had 'breasted the torrent of events, and even derived new vigour from the stresses'. 'Unshaken by the earthquakes, unweakened by the dissolvent tides, though all be drifting', the 'royal and imperial monarchy stands firm.' This was 'an achievement so remarkable, a fact so . . . contrary to the whole tendency of the age', that it could not be 'separated from the personality of the good, wise and truly noble king whose work is ended.' He was 'uplifted above class-strife and party-faction'; he never feared British democracy; he reconciled labour and socialism to the constitution and the crown; he 'revivified the national spirit, popularized hereditary kingship'; and in so doing won the affection of his subjects and the admiration of mankind. 'In a world of ruin and chaos,' Churchill concluded, 'King George V brought about the resplendent rebirth of the great office which fell to his lot.'[68]

'HM always had a high regard for you,' his former private secretary wrote, appreciatively and tactfully, on reading the piece.[69] But then the crown passed to King Edward VIII, whom Churchill had known (and admired) for a long time. As Home Secretary, he had participated at the 'beautiful and moving ceremony' at Carnarvon Castle in 1911, when Edward was invested as Prince of Wales, and he had met him soon after at Balmoral, where they had gone through the First Lord's Admiralty boxes together. Edward's delight and relief at Churchill's fall in 1915 was soon abandoned, and he soon reverted to his earlier belief that Churchill was 'a wonderful man with great powers of work'.[70] During the 1920s, Churchill helped the prince with speech-writing and speech-making, he sent him copies of The World Crisis as the volumes appeared, they corresponded about public affairs and played polo together, and in 1932 the prince contributed to the cost of the Daimler that Churchill was bought by his friends on his return from America. Four years later, Edward was king, and Churchill wrote him a letter in the gracious and grandiloquent tone that he had by then perfected in his correspondence with royalty. He offered his 'faithful service and . . . heartfelt wishes that a reign which has been so nobly begun may be blessed with peace and true glory', and that 'in the long swing of events, your majesty's name will shine in history as the bravest and best beloved of the sovereigns who have worn the island crown'.[71]

These hopes were sincere and heartfelt, and rested on an exaggerated sense of the king's virtues, with a blind eye turned to his faults (especially his support of appeasement); but they were nullified by the abdication. In taking the king's side against the government, and thereby allying himself with his old friend, the legendarily mischievous Lord Beaverbrook, Churchill may have been seeking to embarrass Baldwin and upset the National Government. This was certainly the view of his critics at the time, but his motives were also more deeply grounded and disinterested than that.[72] He was a loyal friend, especially when the going got rough, and he sympathized with the king's wish for a happy home life to accompany the glitter and pomp of his lonely public position. Moreover, England had been through its constitutional revolution in 1688, when the royal succession had been abruptly interrupted and, in the uncertain 1930s, neither the country nor the monarchy needed any repetition of that disruption and disturbance. And he was sure that, given time, the king would – indeed, must – repent of his passion for Mrs Simpson, and thus retain (and adorn) his throne. On the basis of this analysis, Churchill's course was clear. With Baldwin's knowledge and consent, he rallied to the king, writing him letters, visiting him at Fort Belvedere, seeking to boost his morale, and urging him to be discreet in his relationship with Mrs Simpson. And he tried to play for time in Parliament, out of fear that undue pressure or excessive haste might lead Edward to make the wrong decision (abdication and marriage), and in the hope that given time and chance he might do the right thing and renounce her.[73]

In thus loyally championing the king, Churchill did his own reputation untold harm, with the public, with politicians and with the court. In a period of mounting tension and anxiety, his plea for extra time was derided by many as patently unrealistic; he failed to appreciate that Edward had already made up his mind to give up the throne for the woman he loved; and he seriously misjudged both the character of the sovereign and the mood of the country, which was turning decisively against the king. On 7 November, he rose in the Commons, for the third time in four days, to plead that 'no irrevocable step be taken'. The House turned angrily on him; the Speaker ruled him out of order; he shouted at Baldwin that 'you won't be satisfied until you've broken him'; and he stormed out of the chamber. Within three days, the king had abdicated, but Churchill, though shocked and disappointed, stood by him. Following Baldwin's announcement in the Commons, he praised Edward's 'qualities of courage, of simplicity, of sympathy and, above all, of sincerity rare and precious' which, he felt sure, 'might have made his reign glorious in the annals of this ancient monarchy'.[74] He helped to compose the ex-king's abdication broadcast, he was convinced his policy had been the right one, and he remained deeply unhappy at what had occurred. 'I believe', he wrote to Lloyd George at Christmas, when it was all over, 'the abdication to have been altogether premature and probably quite unnecessary. However, the vast majority is on the other side.'[75]

But while Churchill remained personally loyal to the Duke of Windsor (as Edward VIII became), he recognized that the British monarchy had to be carried on, and the throne had to be supported. In the aftermath of the abdication, he served on the Commons Select Committee charged with arranging the Civil List for King George VI and Queen Elizabeth. The government had expected him to cause further trouble over making financial provisions for the Duke of Windsor; but on learning of his substantial private fortune, Churchill agreed that the matter should be dealt with privately, so as to avoid the public embarrassment of parliamentary discussion. When the Committee's proposals were presented to the Commons, in March 1937, Churchill made what Henry Channon described as 'a stirring speech' in support of 'the honour and dignity of the crown'.[76] He believed the sovereign should be well provided for, in part because 'the glitter and splendour of ceremonial pageant' was intrinsically popular and exciting, and helped associate the mass of the people with the state. But he also insisted that 'the ancient constitutional monarchy of this country' was 'the most effective barrier against one man power or dictatorship, arising whether from the right or from the left'. Embodying tradition and custom, and sustained by Parliament, it brought decency and security to national life, and provided 'that element of unity, of the present with the past', which was 'the greatest hope of our freedom in the future'.[77]

IV

By this time, Churchill not only respected and revered the British throne as a powerful institution providing a beneficent antidote to contemporary chaos: after witnessing the coronation of King George VI and Queen Elizabeth at Westminster Abbey, he admitted to Clementine, 'You were right. I see now the "other one" wouldn't have done.' He published an effusive article on the new monarch in the *Strand Magazine* in May 1937, and in a speech in the following year opined that 'the king and his family play a part in our modern life more helpful and more fortifying to the state than in any former age'.[78] But this realistic recognition of royal realities did not mean he abandoned the duke. Indeed, Henry Channon believed that Churchill was 'pro-Windsor to the end'. Churchill and the duke exchanged letters regularly in the months after the abdication; Randolph Churchill was one of the few English friends who attended the wedding of the duke and duchess; and early in 1939, Churchill himself visited the Windsors in the south of France. When war broke out and Churchill was recalled to the government as First Lord of the Admiralty, the duke wrote to him, 'not as a minister of the crown, but more as a father'. And on one occasion, they met in the basement Secret Room of the Admiralty, where the disposition of the British Navy was recorded. Lord Crawford – the embodiment of responsible respectability – was not at all amused.[79]

So, in the aftermath of the abdication, Churchill was scarcely *persona grata* with the new king, the new queen or the new court. 'I know how devoted you have been, and still are, to my dear brother,' George VI had candidly written to him in the aftermath of his own coronation. Not surprisingly, George VI and Elizabeth had heartily loathed Wallis Simpson, and regarded any supporters of hers as enemies of theirs; and so, with equal vehemence, did Queen Mary. Indeed, they viewed the social circle centring around Emerald Cunard, Henry Channon and Winston Churchill as embodying all that was worst of the vulgar, morally suspect, American forces that seemed to be corrupting British society.[80] And these pro-Edward-and-Wallis delinquencies were further compounded by the fact that Churchill was implacably anti-Chamberlain and anti-appeasement. The new king and queen, by contrast, were devoted supporters of the Prime Minister. They shared with him a strong sense of decent moral values, and they invited him on to the balcony of Buckingham Palace after he returned bearing 'peace with honour' from Munich. When Chamberlain resigned on 10 May 1940, George VI told him he had been 'grossly unfairly treated' and 'greatly regretted' his going, while Queen Elizabeth wrote to him saying 'how deeply I regretted your ceasing to be Prime Minister. I can never tell you in words how much we owe you.'[81]

Chamberlain's departure was bad enough for the king and queen: the prospect that he might be followed by Churchill seemed even worse. His reverence for the institution of monarchy was not in question; but although he signed himself, as First Lord of the Admiralty, 'your majesty's faithful and devoted servant and subject', it was precisely that faith and that devotion to George VI which seemed to be so conspicuously lacking. Along with most of the British establishment, the king strongly preferred Halifax as Chamberlain's successor. He was sound, decent, religious, landed, a fox hunter and a family friend. Churchill, by contrast, was widely regarded as 'a cad', a 'half breed', a 'dictator', a 'rogue elephant', 'the greatest adventurer in modern political history' – judgements which would scarcely have come as a surprise to Edward VII, to Lord Stamfordham or to the young George V.[82] Jock Colville, the scion of a courtly family, and at that time private secretary to Neville Chamberlain, was singularly unimpressed by Churchill's 'record of untrustworthiness and instability'. And his mother, Lady Cynthia

Colville, who was a lady-in-waiting at Marlborough House, received a letter from Queen Mary saying she hoped her son would remain with Chamberlain and not go to the new Prime Minister. Had these people known that the Duke of Windsor had sent Churchill a letter of congratulation, thanking him for his 'great measure of practical and sympathetic support in the past', and clearly expecting more of the same in the future, they would have been even more alarmed.[83]

Such was the extent of courtly opposition when Churchill took office in May 1940, an appointment to which George VI, for all his scrupulous observance of the constitutional proprieties, was himself initially 'bitterly opposed'. The fact that Churchill immediately insisted – despite firmly expressed royal misgivings – on making the dreaded Lord Beaverbrook Minister of Aircraft Production, and the no-less unrespectable Brendan Bracken a Privy Councillor, only seemed to confirm the establishment's worst fears, namely that the 'gangsters' and the 'crooks' were now indeed in charge.[84] And, true to his old cavalier ways, the new Prime Minister was not always scrupulous in keeping the king informed, and he was often infuriatingly unpunctual for royal audiences or luncheons. 'He says he will come at six, puts it off until 6.30 by telephone, then comes at seven,' noted Colville. Chamberlain had been methodical, considerate and deferential, and the king and queen felt 'a little ruffled by the offhand way' in which Churchill treated them.[85] Moreover, he soon established himself as the personification of Britain's identity, unity and resolve, and as the nation's supreme warlord and grand strategist, which meant he inevitably upstaged the king. For he was eloquent, charismatic and heroic, which George VI was not. 'The King and Queen feel Winston puts them in the shade,' recorded Mrs Ronald Greville. 'He is always sending messages for the Nation which the King ought to send.'[86]

Nevertheless, their relations gradually improved. 'As the war proceeded,' Jock Colville recalled, 'the King and Queen became as devoted to Winston as he consistently was to them.' George VI soon came to recognize the vigour and brilliance and sheer indispensability of his wartime leadership: 'I must confess,' he wrote when giving permission in July 1941 for Churchill to leave the country to meet Roosevelt off Newfoundland, 'that I shall breathe a great sigh of relief when you are safely back home again.' And, although titanically busy, Churchill did do his best to keep his sovereign informed about the war, regularly lunched with him at Buckingham Palace, and sent the royal family presents on their birthdays and at Christmas.[87] In 1941, the king publicly expressed his confidence in his Prime Minister by making him Lord Warden of the Cinque Ports, and Churchill was 'much attracted by the historic splendour of the appointment', which had been held by the younger Pitt, Wellington and Palmerston. So close did their friendship become that when Churchill wrote his wartime memoirs, he noted with pride that 'as a convinced upholder of constitutional monarchy I valued as a signal honour the gracious intimacy with which I, as first minister, was treated, for which I suppose there has been no precedent since the days of Queen Anne and Marlborough during his years of power.' Once again, and to an extent that most of his readers could not have known, a sovereign had subordinated his personal feelings to work with a Churchill for the good of the country.[88]

For a second time in the nation's history, the royal and the ducal houses were joined together in a great patriotic collaboration, and Churchill was vividly aware of the historical parallels, as he played Marlborough to George VI's Queen Anne. One indication is that, throughout the war, his letters to his sovereign displayed what Ben Pimlott has rightly described as 'extravagant courtesy', and 'exaggerated shows of deference', and as such they were very much in the mode and manner of the great duke.[89] Here is one example. Early in 1941, George VI sent his best wishes for the new year, adding that he had 'so much admired all you have done during the last seven months as my prime minister'. Churchill replied that the sovereign's support had been 'a constant source of strength and encouragement'; that he had served the king's father and grandfather as a minister; that his own father and grandfather had served Queen Victoria; but that the king's 'treatment of me has been intimate and generous to a degree that I had never deemed possible'. The war, he concluded, putting things in a broader and more optimistic perspective, had 'drawn the throne and the people more closely together than was ever before recorded', and George VI and Queen Elizabeth were 'more beloved by all classes and conditions than any of the princes of the past'.[90]

Such letters, almost Disraelian in their flattering eloquence, were warmly received at Buckingham Palace; and while George VI was no wordsmith, he did his best to reciprocate the same elevated sentiments, even though he could not match the same high style. After the allied victory at Alamein in November 1942, he wrote to 'my dear Winston', sending his 'warmest congratulations', and in return, Churchill expressed himself 'deeply grateful' for 'the most kind and gracious letter with which I have been honoured . . . I shall', he continued, 'always preserve it during the remaining years of my life, and it will remain as a record of the support and encouragement given by the sovereign to his first minister in good and dark days alike . . . No minister in modern times,' he went on, 'and I daresay in long past days, has received more help and comfort from the king ... It is needless to me to assure your majesty of my devotion to yourself and family, and to our ancient and cherished monarchy – the true bulwark of freedom against tyrannies of any kind ... But', he concluded, 'I trust I may have the pleasure of feeling a sense of personal friendship which is very keen and lively in my heart, and has grown strong in these hard times of war.'[91] By now, when he signed himself 'your majesty's faithful and devoted servant', there seems every indication that he genuinely meant it, and also that the king knew he genuinely meant it.

But while Churchill's faith and devotion were as sincerely felt as they were eloquently expressed, he had not obtained supreme political power with any intention of sharing it with his sovereign. He kept the king fully supplied with the appropriate papers, and was impressed by his thorough mastery of them; but they were for information only.[92] From the outset, Churchill paid great attention to parliamentary opinion, he regularly (if reluctantly) deferred to his chiefs of staff, and in the later stages of the war he found it increasingly difficult to get his way with Roosevelt and Stalin. But as his intransigence about Beaverbrook and Bracken had signalled early on, he never seems to have changed his mind on a major matter of wartime policy or personnel at the behest of his sovereign. Here is another and later example. In October 1943, George VI wrote to his Prime Minister, expressing concerns about the invasion of the continent that was now being planned. Churchill's reply was blunt and brutal: 'There is no possibility of our going back on what is agreed.'[93] Only in smaller matters did the king occasionally insist, and the Prime Minister reluctantly give way. This was memorably demonstrated at the time of the D-Day landings, which Churchill was determined to watch at first hand from a nearby cruiser squadron. The king thought this was too great a risk, and in the end he prevailed. But even then, Churchill insisted that this in no sense overturned the general principle that as Prime Minister he alone could decide which theatres of war he should visit.[94]

V

In any case, George VI was not the only monarch with whom Churchill had to deal during these years. As he explained to Pierson Dixon in August 1944, 'I have had many kings on my hands,' one of whom was the ex-king and Duke of Windsor, who was clearly hoping for better times now he had a friend at 10 Downing Street.[95] But while Churchill remained personally sympathetic, this was another of those rare instances where he also had to take note, in what was a difficult and delicate family matter, and at a time when he himself was barely established in power, of the wishes of the king and queen. In July 1940, the duke and duchess were in Lisbon, having fled from France before the advancing German army. It was rumoured they were the object of Nazi plots and schemes, which made it imperative to get them out of the country. The duke wanted to return home, and to an important job. But the king, to say nothing of Queen Elizabeth and Queen Mary, were determined 'to keep him at all costs out of England'. Caught in the middle of this right royal row, Churchill offered the duke the Governorship of the Bahamas, and urged him to go there directly. Queen Elizabeth was 'bitterly opposed' to such an appointment, and the duke was 'cantankerous and maddening' in seeking to make conditions.[96] Nevertheless, it was a deft solution to a difficult problem. 'He'll find it a great relief,' observed Lord Beaverbrook of the duke. 'Not half as much as his brother will,' replied Churchill. 'I have done my best,' the Prime Minister told Windsor, who recognized that he had. But in keeping him out of the country, Churchill also went far in mending his own damaged fences with the king and queen.[97]

The very different challenges presented by the career considerations of the king's cousin, Lord Louis Mountbatten, were a great deal easier for Churchill to deal with. For here his task was not reluctantly to relegate a tainted royal to the margins of events, but enthusiastically to propel a glittering royal towards the centre of affairs. As well as being the great-grandson of Queen Victoria, Mountbatten was young, brave, gallant, confident and dashing (and delighted in playing polo): in short he was an ambitious, well-connected officer, very much after Churchill's own heart. Moreover, he was the son of Prince Louis of Battenberg, who had been obliged to resign as First Sea Lord in October 1914 when Churchill had been First Lord of the Admiralty, on the wholly groundless accusations that because of his German 'birth and parentage' he was unpatriotic in his sympathies.[98] So Churchill had many reasons for wishing Lord Louis well, and he did just that, appointing him successively Chief of Combined Operations in 1941, and Supreme Allied Commander in South East Asia two years later, positions of exceptional seniority to be given to an impetuous (and foolhardy?) sailor, who was still only in his early forties. And in July 1945, with the end of the war in the Far East approaching, Churchill urged Mountbatten to come to see him. 'We will talk about your future', he told him, 'as I have great plans in store.'[99]

The Duke of Windsor and Lord Mountbatten were domestic royal matters; but they were also part of the wider world of cosmopolitan royalty, in Europe, the Middle East and beyond, with which Churchill had to deal during the war. Those monarchs who were enemies of Britain, or who hampered the war effort, received short shrift. There was King Leopold III of Belgium, who capitulated to the advancing Germans in May 1940, and was 'castigated soundly' for refusing to leave his country and become a focus of resistance – very different behaviour from his predecessor in 1914, who had preserved 'an unconquerable majesty amid the ruin of his kingdom'.[100] There was the King of Sweden, who in August 1940 proposed a conference 'to examine the possibilities of making peace'. But Churchill told Halifax 'the intrusion of the ignominious King of Sweden as a peace-maker, after his desertion of Finland and Norway, and while he is absolutely in the German grip . . . is singularly distasteful'. There was the King of Italy, whom he had previously admired for supporting Mussolini; now Churchill denounced him for supporting Hitler as a 'miserable puppet'. 'So much for the House of Savoy!' remarked Jock Colville.[101] There was Prince Paul, regent of Yugoslavia since 1934, who signed a pact with the Axis powers in March 1941, whom Churchill nicknamed 'Palsy', and in the Commons called 'a weak and unfortunate prince'. And there was the pro-Axis King Farouk of Egypt, dismissed by the Prime Minister as 'an oriental despot who on every occasion has proved himself a poor friend of England', who was coerced by the British, in February 1942, into installing a more pro-allied government.[102]

But there were other monarchs for whom Churchill retained a high regard, out of a mixture of historical connections and loyal support. Just before he became Prime Minister, he put out feelers as to whether the kaiser might 'desire to seek asylum here', where 'he would be received with consideration and dignity'. He declined. Among his favourite sovereigns were those who refused to surrender to the Nazis, but fled to London to carry on the fight: Wilhelmina of the Netherlands (Churchills had always got on with the House of Orange); and Haakon VII of Norway (who was married to a sister of George V, and who, on the eve of his departure, averred that he 'believed that the Allies would win in the end').[103] He supported Haile Selassie (also for a time exiled in London) against the Italians, and in May 1941 the British replaced the emperor on the throne from which Mussolini had evicted him five years before. And he was a staunch admirer of Abdullah in Jordan (the allies' most reliable supporter in the Middle East), of the Regent Abdullilah in Iraq (whom the British restored in the spring of 1941 after a brief pro-Nazi coup), and of Ibn Sau'd in Saudi Arabia (whom he met in Egypt in February 1945). 'My admiration for him was deep', Churchill recalled, 'because of his unfailing loyalty to us. He was always at his best in the darkest hours.'[104]

These sovereigns, whether enemies or friends, were very much within

Britain's early spheres of wartime involvement: Western Europe and the Middle East. But as the war became more extended, protracted and complex, and as Britain acquired new allies (and enemies), Churchill's dealings with kings became correspondingly more elaborate and difficult, especially in Italy (where fascism first collapsed) and the Balkans (where the communist threat first presented itself). This was partly because these were nations where royal houses were not historically well rooted, were not widely esteemed, did not behave with dignity and decency, and were further compromised by their fascist collaborators and dictatorial inclinations. However much he might have wished it otherwise, these were not 'constitutional monarchies' as evolved, practised and admired in Britain.[105] But it was also because, as a member of this latter-day grand alliance, Churchill found himself with co-combatants who deeply disliked kings and queens, and who led nations which had been created and defined in conscious and audacious opposition to old world royalty. At Yalta, Stalin made it plain that 'he had always been against kings, and that he was on the side of the people and not that of any king'. And Roosevelt, too, was the leader of a nation which in 1776 had rejected crowns and titles, which prided itself on its egalitarian hostility to hierarchy, and which did not share Churchill's 'weakness for kings'.[106]

But for his part, Churchill's view of things was very different, as befitted his position as a product of the old, royal European world which both Stalin and Roosevelt, albeit from very different political perspectives, equally disliked and rejected. To be sure, individual monarchs might misbehave, disappoint, be disloyal and go over to the enemy; but, all other things being equal, Churchill genuinely believed (as Harold Macmillan later recalled) that 'any king is better than no king'. And having witnessed the chaos into which post-1918 Europe had fallen, because (as he saw it) the great kings and emperors had been overturned, Churchill was determined that the same should not happen again. In the inter-war years, he was sure that monarchy might have been a successful bulwark against fascism; now, as the war dragged on, he came to regard it as a no-less-necessary bulwark against inexorably advancing communism. The result was that, by the end of 1944, it was widely believed that (in Jock Colville's words) 'we support the monarchies of Europe as a matter of principle, whatever the will of the people'.[107] But as so often with Churchill, rhetoric was one thing, reality another. The sovereigns whom he wished to support were rarely people of substance, plausibility or significance, and there were real (and increasing) limits to Britain's capacity to intervene, let alone to impose on nations and peoples a political system they no longer wanted.

All this is well illustrated in the case of Italy, where these problems and contingencies first came to the fore. In previous periods, Churchill had been a supporter of Victor Emmanuel III for embracing the Duce, and then an enemy of Victor Emmanuel III for embracing the Fuhrer. But by the summer of 1943, Mussolini was finished, and under these circumstances Churchill changed his mind again, 'adamantly' supporting the Italian king, and Marshal Badoglio, on the grounds that they had abolished fascism, that they wanted to make peace, and that, as the nearest thing to an historically legitimated government, they could 'deliver the goods'. 'When I want to lift a pot of coffee,' Churchill explained to Harold Macmillan, in a metaphor that vividly illustrates both his utilitarian and historical sense of monarchy, 'I prefer to keep the handle.'[108] But the reality was that Victor Emmanuel was impossibly compromised by his support of Mussolini, and in April 1944, he handed over his powers to his son, Crown Prince Umberto, who was created lieutenant-governor of the realm. The King of Italy, Churchill later noted, had 'slipped through my fingers'. But he hoped Umberto might 'play his part in building up a constitutional monarchy in a free, strong, united Italy', and it was agreed there would be a plebiscite once the war was ended and over.[109]

The situation in Greece was both similar and yet different. During the First World War, King Constantine I, who was married to the kaiser's sister, had vetoed Greek co-operation with the British in the Dardanelles campaign, which had been a source of particular annoyance and disappointment to Churchill, and he had subsequently abdicated after a military revolt in 1922.[110] By contrast, his son, King George II, inclined to the allies, and he retired to London, where he joined other monarchs in exile when the Germans overran his country in 1941. Although Greece was bitterly divided between those who supported the king, and those who supported the communists, Churchill was initially determined to do everything he could to ensure that the king should return to his country, and in October 1944 he gave George Papandreou, the Greek Prime Minister, what Harold Macmillan described as a 'homily . . . in praise of monarchy in general, and of King George of Greece in particular'. But there was strong resistance in certain quarters to the return of the monarch, King George became increasingly unhelpful, difficult and uncooperative, and it was only by journeying to Athens late in 1944, and reluctantly agreeing to the establishment of a Regency under Archbishop Damskinos, that Churchill was able to keep open the possibility that the king might return, pending the result of a postwar plebiscite.[111]

Meanwhile, in Yugoslavia, the Regent Prince Paul paid a high price for signing the Nazi pact in March 1941. He was immediately overthrown in a *coup d'état*, taken into custody by the British, and eventually exiled to South Africa. The young Crown Prince Peter was thereupon proclaimed king, and became a national hero by renouncing the Nazi pact. But the Germans invaded his country, and he, too, was forced to leave his kingdom and bide his time in London. Once again, Churchill supported the sovereign-in-exile, as he made plain in a speech at the Quebec Conference in August 1943: 'the kings of Greece and Yugoslavia' had 'never faltered for one moment in their duty', and he hoped to see them 'restored to their thrones by the free choice of their liberated peoples'. But this task was made more difficult as Tito's pro-communist partisans became the prime focus and expression of indigenous resistance.[112] There was no love lost between the king and Tito, and Churchill's attempts to bring them together met with little success. In August 1944, he urged Tito not to let the king down, gave him a 'homily on the blessings of constitutional monarchy', 'and expressed his conviction that Yugoslavia's international position would be stronger under a king than as a republic'. Thereafter, his prime policy was to persuade the king to come to terms with Tito: but this was not easy. 'I have fought hard for George and Peter,' Churchill mused to Pierson Dixon in August 1944; but in the Yugoslavian case with even less prospect of success than Greece.[113]

In each of these three countries, Churchill's preferred aim was to establish democratic government under a constitutional monarchy. He believed that this was the best of all possible political worlds and, as he explained to Anthony Eden in October 1944, 'If none of the kings are allowed to go back into any of their countries, and strike a blow on the allied side, the establishment of Soviet-controlled republics will be the universal pattern.' But in practice, there were limits to what he could achieve. This was partly because, as he admitted to Stalin in Moscow at the same time, he could not 'force' monarchs on them: the people of these countries should 'have a free and fair chance of choosing' whether they wanted a republic or a monarchy.[114] It was partly because the sovereigns themselves were, unlike Wilhelmina and Haakon, exceptionally difficult individuals to deal with. As Colville noted early in 1945, clearly echoing his master's voice, 'it would be hard to find two worse advertisements for hereditary monarchy than George of Greece and Peter of Yugoslavia'. It was partly because monarchy as an institution was less resonant and appealing: 'it was', Eden explained to Churchill, 'impossible to regard kings in most of these Balkan lands as other than coming and going, like a Labour Government at home'. And it was partly because discredited absentee monarchs had far less binding claims on their former subjects' loyalty than pro-communist partisan leaders, fighting for freedom on the spot.[115]

The result was that by early 1945, Churchill had distanced himself from the kings of Italy, Greece and Yugoslavia, recognizing that constitutional monarchy was an unlikely prospect in any of their countries, despairing of getting the kings to agree to compromise proposals, and accepting there was no more he could do to help them keep or regain their thrones. But although he had no choice but to recognize these political realities, he did not like them. To add to his woes, the royal scene elsewhere in the Balkans was, by this time, even darker. In Albania, the local communist partisans refused to allow King Zog, who had fled when Mussolini had invaded in April 1939, to return. Churchill deeply regretted 'dropping' him. 'Another king gone down the drain!' he ruefully minuted to Eden in October 1944.[116] It was no better in Romania, which was fast becoming a Soviet satellite. In August 1944, King Michael turned out the fascist dictator, General Antonescu, and declared war on the Germans. But it was impossible for the British to give him any support, and in March 1945 the Soviets insisted he sack his government, and replace it with one more sympathetic to Moscow. This did not bode well for the king's future, and Churchill was 'deeply disturbed by this news which', across the whole of the region, 'formed a pattern of things to come'.[117]

As the war in Europe drew to a close, royal prospects in the Balkans thus seemed distinctly unencouraging. But the situation was very different in Britain. On 8 May 1945, Churchill appeared on the balcony of Buckingham Palace with King George VI and Queen Elizabeth, and soon after, he moved a loyal address to the king in the Commons. 'We have', he observed, 'the oldest, the most famous, the most honoured, the most secure and the most serviceable monarchy in the world.' It was, he insisted, 'an ancient and glorious institution', the 'golden circle' which embraced the loyalties of all the states and peoples of the empire and commonwealth, and 'the symbol which gathers together and expresses those deep emotions and stirrings of the human heart which make men travel far to fight and die together'. The king himself was a model monarch, 'because of his courage, his simple way of living, his tireless devotion to duty', and Churchill recalled with pride and gratitude the 'personal kindness and encouragement' which he had shown him.[118] For his part, George VI was as dismayed to lose 'my dear Winston' in the 1945 general election as he had been reluctant to appoint him five years before. 'I was shocked at the result, and I thought it most ungrateful to you personally after all your hard work for the people,' he wrote, with a fine indifference to the conventions of constitutional impartiality. 'I shall miss your counsel to me more than I can say.' He duly offered Churchill the Order of the Garter (which he refused) and later the Order of Merit (which he accepted).[119]

VI

Unlike the great Duke of Marlborough, Churchill had been dismissed by the electorate rather than by the sovereign, and he remained a firm favourite with the royal family, by many of whom he was now regarded more 'as a friend' than as an ex-prime minister. The king continued to consult him about speeches and letters, Churchill sent copies of his history of the Second World War as successive volumes appeared, and he spoke effusively in Parliament on the occasion of their majesties' silver wedding.[120] He was delighted when Princess Elizabeth became engaged to Lieutenant Philip Mountbatten; in seconding the Commons address of congratulation, he noted that the monarchy and the royal family 'play a vital part in the tradition, dignity and romance of our island life'; and when he arrived (late) for their wedding in Westminster Abbey, 'everyone stood up, all the kings and queens'.[121] As this remark of Henry Channon's suggests, Churchill was by now no less a favourite of European royalty, especially those he had supported in the war, and he visited the Queen of the Netherlands and the King of Norway, participating in 'pageants of honour and kindness' in a manner reminiscent of Marlborough's visits to the great continental courts in the aftermath of Blenheim. He also remained a foul-weather friend to the Duke of Windsor: he unavailingly supported his search for an honorary post at the British Embassy in Washington, and Winston and Clementine celebrated their fortieth wedding anniversary with the duke and the duchess in the south of France in 1948.[122]

By this time, Churchill was deep in his war memoirs where, as in so much of his writing, he was much concerned with royalty. Once more, he put forward the view that 'if a grandson of the Kaiser had been left on the [German] throne after 1918, Hitler would never have seized power'; he reiterated his lament at the break-up of the Austro-Hungarian Empire; and he again regretted 'the prejudice of the Americans against monarchy', which he felt had caused so much mischief at Versailles and thereafter.[123] But there was also more recent royal business which had to be dealt with, both domestic and foreign, and he dealt with it very artfully indeed. He printed the letter he had received from George VI at the time of his coronation, claiming, quite disingenuously, that it showed he had enjoyed the king's support from the very outset of his reign. He made no mention of the protracted difficulties he had had with the Duke of Windsor. And he reproduced many of the fulsome exchanges between himself and his sovereign. He also went to great lengths to show how much trouble he had taken to shore up the monarchies in Italy, Yugoslavia and Greece, and insisted that he had been vindicated by subsequent events. And he wrote with great charity about the Emperor of Japan whom he claimed 'admired the secure majesty of the English monarchy'.[124]

As always with Churchill, past history and present politics were inextricably intertwined: for the postwar world was not a happy one for monarchs and this caused Churchill regret and disappointment. He was dismayed at Indian independence, which involved both the loss of the king's imperial title, and also the subsequent coercion of great princely states like Hyderabad. (Indeed, for all his earlier admiration and support, Churchill never forgave Mountbatten for 'giving away' the Raj, for presiding over the massacres associated with partition, and for preferring Hindu India to Muslim Pakistan, and their relations were never as close or as cordial again.[125]) It was no better in Europe, where Churchill's worst forebodings were realized, as thrones disappeared in Italy, Yugoslavia, Albania, Romania and Bulgaria, in all cases except the first because of irresistible communist pressure. These were, as Churchill wrote to ex-King Michael of Romania, 'the bitter winds that blow'. Only in Greece, after a postwar plebiscite, was the king allowed to return to his country. But that was Churchill's sole (and, as it turned out, impermanent) royal success in the Balkans. 'In bygone ages,' he recalled in a speech in Geneva in 1946, 'Europe was linked by many ties together . . . there were the aristocratic ties which were cosmopolitan, the great association of reigning houses which in the days of Queen Victoria gave something in common between countries.' 'But', he noted, with evident regret, 'all have disappeared.'[126]

On Churchill's final return to power in October 1951, the king was as delighted to see him back as he had been dismayed in 1940. 'In Winston's approach to the throne,' Lord Moran reported, 'his sense of history invested the monarch with a certain mystique, so that he always spoke of the royal house with touching reverence.'[127] The death of George VI in January 1952 moved him deeply: 'the demise of a sovereign', his doctor observed, 'seemed to him like a revulsion of nature', and his broadcast and parliamentary eulogies were vibrant with emotion: 'during these last months, the king walked with death, as if death were a companion, an acquaintance, whom he recognized and did not fear'. And he saluted him for being 'so faithful in his study and discharge of state affairs, so strong in his devotion to the enduring honour of our country, so self-restrained in his judgement of men and affairs, so uplifted above the clash of party politics'. It may have been 'the hardest reign of modern times'; but throughout, the king remained 'a spirit undaunted'. In short, his conduct on the throne was 'a model and a guide to constitutional sovereigns throughout the world today, and also in future generations'. But what Churchill meant by that was clear and revealing: George VI 'mastered the immense daily flow of state papers', and this made 'a deep mark' on his mind; but even in this generous tribute, he never suggested that the king made any serious impact on government policy.[128]

The Prime Minister's feelings towards the king were genuinely warm; but they were less tender towards his mother, Queen Mary, whose hostile courtly attitudes of the 1910s and 1930s seem to have lingered long after the Second World War.[129] She had been an implacable foe of Churchill's appointment in 1940, and although Jock Colville later claimed that 'even' Queen Mary had developed 'an immense admiration' for the new Prime Minister, there is no evidence that she was ever fully reconciled to him. When she died in 1953, on the very eve of her granddaughter's coronation, Churchill's eulogies, both in Parliament and on the wireless, were distinctly uneloquent and lukewarm, compared to his resounding tributes to George VI, lacking emotion and the personal touch: 'she looked a queen, she acted like a queen . . . a figure of almost legendary distinction'.[130] 'Winston was adequate,' Henry Channon noted of his speech in the Commons, 'but definitely not at his best. Curiously enough, Attlee was the more moving, and Winston, realising this, looked restless and nettled.' 'Perhaps', Channon concluded, 'he did not like the old lady, or did they cross swords over the Abdication?' The first question was well posed, and the answer to the second was definitely 'yes'. Beyond that, we can only speculate: in James Pope-Hennessy's official biography of Queen Mary, there are only two references to Churchill, which hardly suggests close or cordial contact, even in the closing phase of her long life.[131]

But with the new monarch, the situation was very different, for here all was indeed sweetness and light. Churchill had first met Princess Elizabeth at Balmoral in 1928, when she was two. She was, he told Clementine, 'a character', with 'an air of authority and reflectiveness astonishing in an infant'. Now she was queen, and the ageing Prime Minister saw himself playing Melbourne to her Victoria, and offering her the sort of 'respectful yet sentimental devotion' that John Churchill had once given to Queen Anne. He was, after all, the experienced world statesman, with an authority matchless and unrivalled; she, by contrast, was the young sovereign, new to her great responsibilities. The Prime Minister thought her 'lovely, inspiring', he wore a frock coat and top hat for their (increasingly lengthy) weekly audiences, they talked about polo, horses and his early life as a subaltern in India, and he returned 'overflowing with her praises'.[132] The queen, for her part, was 'very fond' of her first Prime Minister; she enjoyed his company at the races and at Balmoral; she gave him the Order of the Garter, which he had previously declined from her father; and she commissioned a portrait bust by Oscar Nemon to be placed in Windsor Castle. Mutual admiration could scarcely go further, and was one of the reasons why Churchill determined to stay on to see the new queen crowned, and he was very much the high priest of the secular-cum-sacred splendours of her coronation.[133]

Among the greatest pleasures of Churchill's second premiership were the opportunities to give public expression to his romantic, chivalric feelings for the institution of monarchy, and for the person of the new monarch. When saluting Elizabeth's accession, he hoped her reign would witness 'a golden age of art and letters', and a 'brightening salvation of the human scene'. On the evening of her coronation, he described the sovereign as 'crowned in our history, and enthroned for ever in our hearts'. She was, he went on, 'a lady whom we respect because she is our queen, and whom we love because she is herself'. And when she and her husband returned from their six-month, post-coronation Commonwealth tour in May 1954, Churchill was even more magniloquently expansive. The 'gleaming episode' of this 'royal pilgrimage' had, he averred, cast a 'clear, calm, gay and benignant' light 'upon the whole human scene', and he assigned 'no limits to the reinforcement which this royal journey may have brought to the health, the wisdom, the sanity and hopefulness of mankind'.[134] Small wonder that on Churchill's eightieth birthday, the whole royal family bought him a present of four silver wine coasters. 'You have been, and are, such an inspiration to our people,' the Queen Mother wrote in congratulation, 'and we are all *very* proud of you' – a complete and conspicuous bouleversement from the damning opinions she had entertained of him fifteen years before.[135]

But there was also serious and sensitive royal business with which Churchill as Prime Minister had to deal. Much of this concerned two familiar figures: the Duke of Windsor, who remained a problem, and Lord Mountbatten, who had recently become one. The duke still wanted an official job; but there was nothing Churchill could do, try as he might (and he clearly did). He also wanted to attend Queen Elizabeth's coronation, but Churchill strongly and successfully advised against. For his part, Churchill tried to prevent, then delay, the publication of German Foreign Office documents from 1940, which showed the Duke of Windsor in none too favourable a light in Lisbon in July 1940. (They eventually appeared in 1957.)[136] As for Lord Mountbatten: he was convinced that the marriage of his nephew to Princess Elizabeth meant the house of Mountbatten had become Britain's ruling house when the princess became the queen. But Churchill (strongly urged on by Queen Mary and Alan Lascelles) took the greatest exception to this idea, and the name of Windsor remained. He probably needed no urging, partly because of Mountbatten's actions in India, and partly because of his oft-repeated Labour sympathies, which Churchill thought inappropriate in a serving officer. As a result, he was less sympathetic to Mountbatten's determined wish to be First Sea Lord than he might once have been, and it was only towards the very end of his premiership that sentiment won out, and in October 1954 Churchill appointed him to the office from which his father had resigned in undeserved disgrace forty years before.[137]

At the same time, a new royal reign, and a new royal generation, brought with them additional problems for Churchill. There was the question of televising the coronation, to which the Cabinet and the queen were initially opposed, and which the Prime Minister thought would be too great a strain for the young monarch. Eventually, they were all forced to change their minds in response to public opinion. There was the problem of Princess Margaret, who wished to marry the divorced Peter Townsend: Churchill, ever the romantic, was initially favourable, believing 'the course of true love must always be allowed to run smooth'; but he was persuaded by his wife that this would be an error of judgement comparable to that of the abdication, and he threw his weight (and the Cabinet's) against the scheme.[138] There was also the future of the Queen Mother to consider: on the death of her husband, she was initially inclined to retire into private life, but Churchill persuaded her otherwise, and even held out the prospect that she might become Governor-General of Australia. And there was the need to assuage the Duke of Edinburgh, who had felt slighted when told that his wife had not taken his surname. At the very end of his prime ministership, in March 1955, Churchill suggested to the Cabinet that Philip might be created a Prince of the United Kingdom, a proposal eventually carried through by Harold Macmillan two years later.[139]

Meanwhile, it was not only in Europe that thrones had been tottering: in the Middle East, the same trend was now apparent. Churchill had placed King Abdullah of Jordan on his throne in 1921, and in the postwar period he regarded him as 'the only reliable and stable ruler of that region', who must not be treated in the same indifferently cavalier way as the Nizam of Hyderabad. When Abdullah was assassinated in 1951, Churchill 'deeply regretted the murder of this wise and faithful Arab ruler, who never deserted the cause of Britain'.[140] In a Middle East increasingly convulsed by militant Arab nationalism, even the overthrow of King Farouk of Egypt was cause for concern and regret: 'They have lost their king', Churchill minuted on a telegram in July 1953, in remarks ruefully reminiscent of those on King Zog a decade earlier. Indeed, the assassination of the young King Feisal of Iraq in July 1958, whom Churchill had addressed as a schoolboy at Harrow ten years before, tempted him to consider a rare post-retirement foray into active politics. The king, his uncle and Nuri Pasha, Churchill observed, 'were most loyal servants of their country and true friends of their allies. They were swept away in the convulsion of the Arab people that is still going on.' None of this Churchill welcomed: but as he recognized, 'the days of Queen Victoria and a settled world order' were now 'far gone'.[141]

By then, Churchill was well into his retirement, which had begun in April 1955. He had declined the dukedom which his sovereign offered him in his final audience, and he conspicuously refused to give 'advice', believing that the choice of his successor was a matter for the monarch alone. (In fact, of course, it was no such thing: Eden had for years been Churchill's acknowledged heir-apparent, and Churchill had advised George VI of that in June 1942.) And the queen not only attended his farewell dinner: she wrote to him in her own hand, thanking him 'with deep gratitude' for all his services as her first (and favourite) Prime Minister, a position in her affections that he has retained to this day. 'I had a lovely letter from her,' Churchill told Lord Moran, 'eight pages in her own writing. It took me a whole morning to reply.'[142] Thereafter, sovereign and subject continued to correspond, he sent her copies of the *History of the English-Speaking Peoples*, he dined occasionally at Buckingham Palace, and the queen consulted him about the succession to Eden in 1957 (he recommended Macmillan). Towards the very end of his life, there was one last episode which literally completed the story, when Princess Alexandra, who was the niece of George VI and cousin of Elizabeth II, married Angus Ogilvy in 1963. For he was the son of the Earl of Airlie, from whose forebears Clementine was descended in the female line. Thus the Churchills and the crown were finally and familiarly connected.[143]

The queen's appreciative affection for her first and favourite Prime Minister were fully displayed on his death in January 1965, when she behaved impeccably and with great generosity and imagination. For it was at her instruction, and with Parliament's acquiescence, that Churchill was given a state funeral – arrangements which represented a conspicuous reversal of the previous occasion, when Parliament had had to petition the (extremely reluctant) Queen Victoria to accord a similar honour to Gladstone.[144] Setting aside all precedent and precedence, Elizabeth II attended in person (something even Victoria had not done for Wellington, and would never have dreamed of doing for the Grand Old Man) to mourn the passing of her greatest subject, as did almost the entire royal family (with the exception of the still-unforgiven Duke and Duchess of Windsor), along with the kings of Belgium, Norway, Greece and Denmark, Queen Juliana of the Netherlands and the Grand Duke of Luxembourg.[145] Indeed, one of the most memorable images from that day was of the sovereigns and princes of Europe, gathered together in a royal tableau on the steps of St Paul's, saluting Churchill's coffin as it was carried away. Born in a Vanbrugh palace, and given his obsequies in a Wren cathedral, Churchill (like Marlborough before him) had lived and died a grander and greater life than any sovereign in a nation where monarchs were expected to reign rather than rule.

VII

As with many aspects of Churchill's public life and political career, his relations with monarchs, both British and foreign, was a uniquely rich and varied story, which unfolded at several different levels. There was a high rhetorical plane of history, drama, romance and sentiment, only equalled among British prime ministers by Disraeli and (more briefly) Lord Rosebery. From this grandiloquent and dynastic perspective, Churchill regarded successive British sovereigns as kindred social beings, national symbols and imperial icons, whose affairs he was proud to conduct, and whose encouragement, recognition and admiration he deeply cherished. In the same way, he saw monarchies in Europe and the Middle East as the embodiment of tradition and order, and the best bulwark to anarchy, fascism and communism that had yet been devised. At another level, and this was especially demonstrated in his instinctive feelings towards the marginalized Duke of Windsor, the widowed Queen Elizabeth, the humiliated Prince Philip and the matrimonially troubled Princess Margaret, Churchill had a genuine sense of the loneliness, sadness and tragedy which was never far from the public pomp and glitter of the throne. And at yet a third level, of workaday politics and practical affairs, he often saw individual monarchs as flawed personalities, political opponents and tiresome nuisances, with inflexible attitudes, reactionary opinions and obscurantist instincts, who deserved neither deference nor sympathy.

In practice, this meant that virtually everything was negotiable – and renegotiable. For, as Churchill had earlier put it in his life of Marlborough, 'when kings forswear their oaths of duty and conspire against their peoples, when rival kings or their heirs crowd the scene, statesmen have to pick and choose between sovereigns of fluctuating values, as kings are wont to pick and choose between politicians according to their temporary serviceableness.'[146] As the record shows, 'picking and choosing between sovereigns' was how Churchill spent much of his political life. Among foreign royalty, his views of the kings of Greece, Italy, Belgium and Yugoslavia changed more than once: sometimes he was effusively and admiringly loyal; on other occasions he was vituperatively scornful. Likewise, among British monarchs, his opinions of Edward VII, George V, Edward VIII and George VI all underwent serious and significant modification. Only Queen Victoria and Queen Elizabeth II seem to have been the beneficiaries of his unstinted admiration. And, of course, what was negotiable from Churchill's side was also negotiable from the monarchy's side: Edward VII and George V certainly changed their minds about Churchill, and so, even more significantly, did King George VI and Queen Elizabeth, as initial alarm was replaced by 'temporary serviceableness' and eventually by life-long admiration. For just as he came to modify his opinion of them in the light of events, so they in turn came to alter their opinion of him. Constitutional monarchy, like political activity, was (and is) very much the art of the possible.

But not everything was negotiable. Above all, the principle and practice of 'constitutional monarchy' was, for Churchill, inviolate. The crown was to be revered and respected as an institution, and individual sovereigns might be courted and flattered with Disraelian artifice. But 'the supremacy of Parliament over the crown' was, for Churchill, the cardinal axiom of British political life, and of his political practice. As he put it in his *History of the English-Speaking Peoples*, the crown was 'the instrument of Parliament', the king was 'the servant of his people', and the Commons was 'the dominant institution of the realm'.[147] And so, it was 'the duty of the sovereign to act in accordance with the advice of his ministers', and Churchill never wavered in this belief. To be sure, he was prepared to give way, throughout his career, on minor points: the naming of ships in the Royal Navy, the employment of the Duke of Windsor, his own attendance at the D-Day landings. But in all great matters – the personnel of politics, domestic statecraft, the grand strategies of war and peace – he was determined to get his way and, as Philip Ziegler rightly notes, 'it is hard to think of a single instance in which Churchill changed his views or his course of action on any important question in accordance with his perception of the wishes of the monarch of the time'.[148]

From one perspective, there was an extraordinary symmetry and completeness to Churchill's relations with the British monarchy. He began his public life at the end of the reign of one great queen, and he ended his public life at the beginning of what he felt sure would be the reign of another. 'I,' he observed on Elizabeth II's accession, 'whose youth was passed in the august, unchallenged and tranquil glories of the Victorian era, may well feel a thrill in invoking, once more, the prayer and the anthem, "God save the queen".'[149] So, indeed, it had been; and so, indeed, he did. But from another perspective, the serenity of these final years, as with so much of Churchill's stormy and controversial career, was late happening and hard won. Of course, and as befitted the grandson of a duke, he had never been a social revolutionary: indeed, even before 1914, one perceptive contemporary had opined that the 'whole tenor of his mind' was 'anti-radical'.[150] But in his early liberal, crusading years, he seemed on the side of change and reform to an extent which made successive sovereigns uneasy, and he also carried with him an accumulation of dynastic delinquencies and personal short-comings which meant monarchs were disinclined to trust him – a hostile view which his misguided loyalty to Edward VIII seemed amply to vindicate. Only as he got closer to the British throne in the reigns of King George VI and Queen Elizabeth II, did he come to see more fully their virtues; and, reciprocally, they came to see the virtues in him.

But there were also deeper trends and feelings at work. For as the first half of the 'terrible twentieth century' followed what he regarded as its uniquely dreadful course of 'woe and ruin', Churchill did become more socially and politically conservative, which meant he increasingly regarded the institution of monarchy – not just in Britain but virtually anywhere – as the best available antidote to the excesses of democracy, revolution, dictatorship, fascism and communism, by which the world seemed increasingly blighted. Indeed, the brutal overturning of so many royal and princely houses, 'the sweeping away of long-established dynasties' during the course of his lifetime, caused him increasing sadness and growing dismay.[151] That the British crown remained, despite all this, stable and secure became, by contrast, a source of singular pride and gratification to him. It defied the course of history, and in his years of power and triumph, Churchill took great delight in helping and encouraging it to become even 'stronger than in the days of Queen Victoria'. 'No institution', he told Lord Moran on the accession of Elizabeth, 'pays such dividends as the monarchy.' Small wonder that at his funeral, the queen's wreath bore the appreciative inscription, 'In grateful remembrance: Elizabeth R.' For she, like her parents, had much to thank him for.[152]

4

Language: Churchill as the
Voice of Destiny

When Sir Winston Churchill celebrated his eightieth birthday as Prime Minister, in November 1954, there had been nothing like it in British public life since the days of Palmerston and Gladstone. Indeed, in one significant respect, his anniversary surpassed theirs: for he received an unprecedented, all-party tribute from members of both Houses of Parliament in Westminster Hall.[1] His speech in reply has rightly been described as a 'gentle masterpiece': 'the puckish humour, the calculated asides, the perfectly modulated control of voice, and that incomparable moral sturdiness made him look, and sound, years younger than his true age.' Referring to the alleged impact of his wartime words, he offered the following self-deprecating observation:

I was very glad that Mr Attlee described my speeches in the war as expressing the will not only of Parliament but of the whole nation. Their will was resolute and remorseless and, as it proved, unconquerable. It fell to me to express it, and if I found the right words, you must remember that I have always earned my living by my pen and by my tongue. It was a nation and a race dwelling all round the globe that had the lion heart. I had the luck to be called upon to give the roar.[2]

But this was scarcely the whole truth of things, for luck is when preparation and opportunity meet, and Churchill had spent the whole of his long life preparing his words and his phrases for the time when he hoped they might make history – which, in 1940, they certainly did.

As his friends never doubted, and as even his enemies conceded, Churchill was the most eloquent and expressive statesman of his time, truly the master, but sometimes also the slave, of the English language. Here is Asquith, himself no mean wordsmith, recording in his diary of October 1915 an encounter with Churchill:

For about a quarter of an hour he poured forth a ceaseless cataract of invective and appeal, and I much regretted that there was no shorthand writer within hearing, as some of his unpremeditated phrases were quite priceless.[3]

And here, from much later in his career, is an appreciation from Oliver Lyttelton, another friend who also wielded a felicitous pen:

His effects were procured with all the artfulness which a lifetime of public speaking had given him. He began usually, and of course on purpose, with a few rather stumbling sentences; his audience was surprised that the phrases did not seem to run easily off his tongue. The tempo was slow and hesitant. Then gradually the Grand Swell and the Vox Humana were pulled out, and the full glory of his words began to roll forth.

In short and, as Churchill himself put it on one occasion, 'I have in my life concentrated more on self-expression than self-denial.'[4]

Indeed, his extraordinary career may fittingly be regarded as one sustained, brightly lit and scarcely interrupted monologue. Day after day, and often night after night, he turned out words and phrases in tumultuous torrent and inexhaustible abundance – inspiring, exhorting, moving, persuading, cajoling, thundering, bullying, abusing and enraging. In private engagement or public appearance, Cabinet meeting or Commons debate, car or boat, train or plane, dining-room or drawing-room, even bedroom or bathroom, his flow of oratory never ceased. Dozens of books, scores of articles, numerous state papers and countless memoranda bear literally the most eloquent witness to his unfailing verbal resource, his prodigious rhetorical ingenuity and his lifelong love of language. From the time of his election to the Commons in 1900, until his last weeks as Prime Minister in 1955, Churchill was someone of whom it could properly be said that he almost never seemed lost for words. As Lord Moran once noted, 'few men have stuck so religiously to one craft – the handling of words. In peace, it made his political fortune; in war it has won all men's hearts.'[5]

Because he was essentially a rhetorician, who dictated and declaimed virtually every sentence he composed, most of Churchill's words were spoken rather than written. But some were more spoken than others. For it was as an orator that he became most fully and completely alive, and it was through his oratory that his words and his phrases made their greatest and most enduring impact. With Churchill, as it was said of Gladstone, 'speech was the fibre of his being': indeed, more so, for in the number (though not the length) of his orations, Churchill was emphatically ahead: 2,360 to Gladstone's 2,208.[6] During his own lifetime, more of his speeches were published in book form than those of any other political contemporary; the definitive edition runs to eight vast volumes, containing well over four million words; and his most memorable phrases – not just 'blood, toil, tears and sweat', 'their finest hour', 'the few' and 'the end of the beginning', but also 'business as usual', 'iron curtain', 'summit meeting' and 'peaceful co-existence' – have become part of the everyday vocabulary of millions of men and women. As Churchill himself once remarked, 'words are the only things which last for ever', and this confident prediction has also become an incontrovertible epitaph.[7]

I

From almost his earliest years, Churchill was enthralled by the art and craft of oratory, and determined to succeed at it himself. He wanted to be an heroic historical figure, commanding great events, and stirring men's souls, and he saw speech-making as the way to achieve these ends. While serving as a subaltern in India, he wrote an essay on 'The Scaffolding of Rhetoric', which set down his early thoughts on the subject. There were, he believed, 'certain features common to all the finest speeches in the English language': the continual employment of the best possible words to express the full meaning of the speaker; a particular balance and rhythm to the phrasing, producing a cadence which resembled blank verse rather than prose; the careful accumulation of argument through 'a rapid succession of waves of sound and vivid pictures'; the use of colourful and arresting analogies to render established truths more comprehensible, or new ideas more appealing; and powerful perorations which would arouse and electrify the listeners. By 'observation and perseverance', Churchill concluded, the secrets of rhetoric, the power to move audiences, the 'key to the hearts of men', might be found; and the speaker who could command such oratorical resources would always be a force to be reckoned with:

Of all the talents bestowed upon men, none is so precious as the gift of oratory. He who enjoys it wields a power more durable than that of a great king. He is an independent force in the world. Abandoned by his party, betrayed by his friends, stripped of his offices, whoever can command this power is still formidable.[8]

At the same time, Churchill was working on his only novel, *Savrola*, and the eponymous hero, who is clearly the author's idealized version of himself, displays many of these qualities.[9] For Savrola believes in freedom and hates tyranny; he hopes to be the saviour of his country, Laurania; and his main weapon in this quest is his unrivalled power of oratory. Early in the novel, Churchill gives this description of Savrola putting his words and phrases together:

His speech – he had made many and knew that nothing good can be obtained without effort. These impromptu feats of oratory existed only in the minds of the listeners; the flowers of rhetoric were hothouse plants.

What was there to say? Successive cigarettes had been mechanically consumed. Amid the smoke he saw a peroration, which would cut deep into the hearts of a crowd; a high thought, a fine simile, expressed in that correct diction which is comprehensible to the most illiterate, and appeals to the most simple; something to lift their minds from the material cares of life and to awake sentiment. His ideas began to take the form of words, to group themselves into sentences; he murmured to himself; the rhythm of his own language swayed him; instinctively he alliterated. Ideas succeeded one another, as a stream flows swiftly by and the light changes on its waters. He seized a piece of paper and began hurriedly to pencil notes. That was a point; could not tautology accentuate it? He scribbled down a rough sentence, scratched it out, polished it, and wrote it in again. The sound would please their ears, the sense improve and stimulate their minds. What a game it was! His brain contained the cards he had to play, the world the stakes he played for.[10]

With minor modifications and embellishments, such as the presence of a long-suffering secretary prepared to take dictation at almost any hour of the day or night, this was exactly how Churchill would set about composing his own speeches throughout the whole of his career.

Later in the novel, Savrola delivers his great oration to a large and enthusiastic crowd. Beforehand, he quivers with scarcely suppressed excitement, and his composure was merely assumed. Initially, he seemed nervous and halting, 'and here and there in his sentences he paused as if searching for a word'. But gradually he mastered his audience, and the phrases and sentences began to flow, evoking 'a hum of approval', and conveying 'an impression of dauntless resolution'. He ridiculed the tyrannical president of Laurania, and 'every point he made was received with cheers and laughter'. He 'spoke of the hopes of happiness to which even the most miserable of human beings had a right', and 'silence reigned throughout the hall'. Time and again, 'sound practical common sense' was expressed with 'many a happy instance, many a witty analogy, many a lofty and luminous thought'. For an hour, Savrola had conveyed 'his passions, his emotions, his very soul' to the thousands in his audience. And so to the peroration:

Each short sentence was followed by wild cheering. The excitement of the audience became indescribable. Everyone was carried away by it . . . His sentences grew longer, more rolling and sonorous. At length he reached the last of those cumulative periods which pile argument on argument as Pelion on Ossa. All pointed to an inevitable conclusion. The people saw it coming, and when the last words fell they were greeted with thunders of assent.[11]

Churchill was in his early twenties when he wrote these words, and he had scarcely made a public speech, let alone faced a large audience or moved a multitude. But already, he knew the speech-maker he wanted to be, and this account sets out, with vivid imaginative force, and in arrestingly prescient detail, the sort of speech-maker he did eventually become, and that Oliver Lyttelton later portrayed and saluted. Indeed, as a description of the great perorations with which he would end his wartime speeches, more than forty years later, these early words are hard to surpass. And in depicting Savrola's behaviour at the close of his address, Churchill was no less accurate in foreseeing the sense of anxious and expectant exhaustion he himself would later feel:

Then he sat down, drank some water, and pressed his hands to his head. The strain had been terrific. He was convulsed by his own emotions; every pulse in his body was throbbing, every nerve quivering; he streamed with perspiration and almost gasped for breath . . .

Savrola turned to [his colleague:] 'Well Louis . . . how did it sound? I liked the last words. It is the best speech I have ever made.'

Inspired by his uplifting words, the Lauranians storm the presidential palace and depose the tyrant, and Savrola returns in triumph to the capital, 'the ancient city he had loved so well'.[12]

In more senses than one, *Savrola* was a rhetorical romance. But in order to become his own Savrola, young Winston had a great deal of work to do, for he was in no sense a born orator, and 'in truth', as Lord Moran noted, 'he did not seem to be designed by nature for his part'. He was physically unprepossessing and uncharismatic, not much above five feet tall, with a hunched frame, a stooping walk, a weak upper lip, a delicate skin and a waistline which became self-indulgently expanded in middle age. He felt deeply his lack of an Oxbridge education – partly because it left him with an abiding sense of intellectual inferiority in the company of such cerebral sophisticates as Balfour, Asquith and F. E. Smith, and partly because it meant he 'never had the practice which comes to young men at university of speaking in small debating societies impromptu on all sorts of subjects'.[13] Although his conversation was widely regarded as brilliant, and while his repartee could be devastating, Churchill never mastered the art of extemporaneous public-speaking except for making a few brief remarks at social gatherings or at the beginning of his speeches. Most distressing of all, his voice was unattractive and unresonant, and he suffered from a speech impediment, part lisp and part stammer, which in his early years often made it painful to listen to him. As one observer noted, he was 'a medium-sized, undistinguished young man, with an unfortunate lisp in his voice . . . and he lacks face'. Or, as Lord Birkenhead bluntly put it to Churchill later on, 'it isn't as if you had a *pretty* voice'.[14]

The main reason why Churchill's oratory eventually took the ornate and memorable form it did was that he had to overcome these many debilitating disadvantages. Like Savrola, he only mastered his chosen craft by 'hard, hard work', by 'extraordinary self-discipline', and by serving a 'long and painful apprenticeship'. He studied, and often memorized, the greatest orations of Cromwell, Chatham, Burke, Pitt, Macaulay, Bright, Disraeli and Gladstone. He knew his father's speeches off by heart, and deliberately emulated Lord Randolph's dress and mannerisms. He laboured heroically to overcome his lisp and his stammer, by visiting voice specialists, by constant practice and perseverance, and (like Aneurin Bevan, another stammerer-turned-orator) by choosing unusual words and phrases so as to avoid the treacherous rhythms of everyday speech.[15] He spent hours in front of the looking-glass, rehearsing his gestures and practising his facial expressions. And he steeled himself to succeed, using all his will-power to still his nerves and calm his racing heart before rising to speak. Yet despite this monumental resolution and dedication, the prospect of composing a speech always hung over him like a cloud; he was constantly afraid, in his early years, that he would blurt out some unpremeditated remark in the Commons; and to the very end of his career he remained apprehensive before making any major speech, and was on edge until he was satisfied that his words had not misfired.[16]

Above all, he was obliged, again like Savrola, to lavish hours on the detailed construction of the speeches themselves. Whether delivered in the Commons, on the platform or at the microphone, Churchill's orations were, as Arthur Balfour once observed, far from being the 'unpremeditated effusions of a hasty moment'. For he took enormous care 'to weigh well and balance every word which he utters', creating speeches which were formal literary compositions, dictated in full beforehand, lovingly revised and polished, and delivered from a complete text which often included stage directions.[17] As such, they were indeed 'hothouse plants': meticulously constructed set-pieces, carefully planned from beginning to end, with ample documentation to support the case being made, and with the arguments flowing in ordered sequence, until the peroration was finally reached. Inevitably, this process occupied a great deal of Churchill's time. His first major speech in the Commons took six weeks to put together; a forty-five minute oration usually took him between six and eighteen hours to perfect; even during the darkest and busiest days of the Second World War, he was never prepared to shirk or skimp the task of composition; and his last great address in the Commons took twenty hours to draft and structure and polish. Although he sometimes made speeches which were ill-judged or unsuccessful, he rarely made a careless or a slovenly one.[18]

To this extent, Churchill mastered the techniques of speech-writing and speech-making in ways that best compensated for his physical, temperamental and intellectual disadvantages. But, like Savrola yet again, he also fashioned a personal style which was essentially his own. He began by combining the stately, rolling sentences of Gibbon with the sharp antitheses and pungent wit of Macaulay, the two authors he had read so carefully during his days as a soldier in India. Among living orators, he was most indebted to Bourke Cockran, an Irish-American politician out of Tammany Hall, whose best speeches were even more eloquent than those of William Jennings Bryan. The resounding perorations which soon became such a marked feature of Churchill's utterances were modelled on those of the younger Pitt and Gladstone, while for invective and vituperation, there was always the strikingly successful example of his father, Lord Randolph. To this exceptionally heady mixture, Churchill added his own personal ingredients: detail, humour and deliberate commonplace. The result, as Harold Nicolson noted during the Second World War, was a remarkably arresting 'combination of great flights of oratory with sudden swoops into the intimate and the conversational'. 'Of all his devices,' Nicolson went on, 'it is one that never fails.'[19]

In addition, Churchill was himself a true artist with words. For a self-educated man, no less than for a career politician, his vocabulary was uncommonly large and varied. From the time when he was an otherwise unpromising schoolboy at Harrow, he took an almost sensuous delight in military metaphors, arresting alliterations, polished phrases, apt antitheses and explosive epigrams. His speeches, like his paintings, were full of vivid imagery, sunshine and shadows, and rich, glowing colour. He relished evocative, assertive and often bookish adjectives: 'silent, mournful, abandoned, broken' – his description of Czechoslovakia in the aftermath of the

Munich settlement. He loved short, strong, robust nouns: 'blood, toil, tears and sweat' – all he could offer on becoming Prime Minister in 1940. He became the master of the unexpected but apt choice of word, as in his description of the Mississippi as 'inexorable, irresistible, benignant', where the last, unusual adjective breaks the predictable alliterative pattern to great effect.[20] Above all, he was unrivalled among his political contemporaries as a fertile maker of memorable phrases. His remark at the time of the General Strike, 'I decline utterly to be impartial as between the fire brigade and the fire', is one well-known example. And his later description of Russia as being 'a riddle, wrapped in a mystery, inside an enigma' is another.[21]

The combined result of such remorseless determination, diligent application and consummate artistry was that Churchill very rapidly acquired the most rhetorical style of any statesman in British history. From department to department, from one crisis to another, from government to opposition and back again, he took his glittering phrases with him, modifying and reworking well-tried word patterns to meet new circumstances. Consider his famous panegyric on the Battle of Britain fighter pilots in 1940: 'Never in the field of human conflict was so much owed, by so many, to so few' – a sentence of classic simplicity and seemingly effortless perfection, rendered the more memorable by its echoes of Shakespeare's Henry V ('We few, we happy few, we band of brothers').[22] But it had been through many different permutations before reaching its final, unforgettable form. 'Never before', Churchill had observed at Oldham in 1899, 'were there so many people in England, and never before have they had so much to eat.' And nine years later, as Colonial Under-Secretary, he made this comment on a projected irrigation scheme in Africa: 'Nowhere else in the world could so enormous a mass of water be held up by so little masonry.' One of the reasons why his rhetoric flowed so easily and so splendidly in 1940, when Churchill was a titanically busy man, was that so many of the phrases were already well honed and established, and were standing to attention, just waiting to be used again.[23]

But they were also there because they exactly expressed his true personality. For Churchill's speeches were not just accomplished technical exercises in rhetorical composition, verbal ingenuity and public histrionics. He also spoke in the language he did because it vividly and directly reflected the kind of person he himself actually was – or thought himself to be. His own sense of himself breathed through every grandiloquent sentence – a character at once simple, ardent, innocent and incapable of deception or intrigue, yet also a character larger than life, romantic, chivalrous, heroic, great-hearted and highly coloured. As Asquith's daughter Violet noted, shortly after meeting him for the first time in the 1900s, 'There was nothing false, inflated or artificial in his eloquence. It was his natural idiom. His world was built and fashioned on heroic lines. He spoke its language.' In the darkest days of 1940, Vita Sackville-West was comforted by essentially the same thought: 'One of the reasons why one is stirred by his Elizabethan phrases', she told her husband, 'is that one feels the whole massive backing of power and resolve behind them, like a great fortress: they are never words for words' sake.'[24]

For all these reasons, Churchill's oratory soon became a remarkably well-tuned and well-practised political instrument. Indeed, considering that he never built up a regional power base in the country or a personal following at Westminster, that he changed his party allegiance twice, that his judgement was often faulty, that his administrative talents were uneven, and that his understanding of ordinary people was minimal, it is arguable that oratory was, in fact, Churchill's *only* real instrument. 'Without that feeling for words', Lord Moran agreed, 'he might have made little enough of life.'[25] For it was that feeling, and that facility, which enabled him to make his reputation as a young MP, to survive the vicissitudes of the First World War, to recover his position in the 1920s, to wage his solitary campaign against appeasement, to rally the forces of freedom during the Second World War, and to play the part of world statesman in the years which followed. At best, by sheer eloquence, he imposed his own vision, and his own personality, on people and on events, expressing noble sentiments in incomparable speeches which possessed a unique quality described by Isaiah Berlin as 'formal magnificence'.[26] For Churchill was not just speaking for the moment, however important that was: he was also speaking for posterity; and, as he intended, posterity is still listening.

II

Nevertheless, despite the remarkable and transcendent qualities of Churchill's best speeches, the fact remains that for much of his career they were ultimately ineffective, in that they did not enable him to achieve his supreme ambition of becoming Prime Minister. Indeed, it may be argued that, for all its undeniable brilliance, and for all the remarkable reputation which it enabled him to make, the very nature of his oratory made it harder, not easier, for him to get to the very top in public life. In part, no doubt, this was because his glittering phrases, his polished performances and his unconcealed delight in his own hard-won oratorical prowess provoked a great deal of envy in the majority of lesser, greyer and duller men. But it was also true that for most of his career his speeches frequently failed to persuade, and offended and antagonized as much as they captivated and impressed. As Herbert Samuel remarked in the Commons in 1935, 'When the Rt. Hon. Gentleman speaks . . . the House always crowds in to hear him. It listens and admires. It laughs when he would have it laugh, and it trembles when he would have it tremble . . . but it remains unconvinced, and in the end it votes against him.'[27] What, then, were the defects of Churchill's oratory – and of the less attractive side of his character which that oratory seemed to reveal – which meant that this appreciative but damning verdict held so true for so much of his public life?

Part of the problem was that the very luxuriance of Churchill's rhetoric, the disconcerting ease with which it was so readily mobilized in support of so many varied and even contradictory causes, only served to reinforce the view, which became widespread very early in his career, and which lasted until 1940 and beyond, that he was a man of unstable temperament and defective judgement, completely lacking in any real sense of proportion. For it was not just that he constantly yearned for excitement and action, and that he exaggerated the importance of everything he touched, true though all this was. It was also that his rhetoric often seemed to obscure his reason, and that his phrases mastered him, rather than he them.[28] Any policy, any scheme, any adventure which could be presented with verbal ingenuity and rhetorical attractiveness immediately appealed to him, regardless of its substantive merits – or drawbacks. As Charles Masterman once complained, 'he can convince himself of almost every truth if it is once allowed to start on its wild career through his rhetorical machinery'. Later on, General Smuts agreed that his 'ornate phraseology . . . soared above the sober and often intransigent facts of reality'. All too often, Churchill seemed to be guilty of the charge which Disraeli had previously levelled at Gladstone, of being 'a sophisticated rhetorician, inebriated with the exuberance of his own verbosity' – and this was a charge which stuck throughout his career.[29]

So, in 1917, Lord Esher noted that Churchill 'handles great subjects in rhythmical language', but became 'quickly enslaved by his own phrases', which meant 'he deceives himself into the belief that he takes broad views', when his mind was 'fixed upon one comparatively small aspect of the question'.[30] These comments were made in the year of the Dardanelles disaster, which seemed a quintessential Churchillian enterprise: easily presented rhetorically, but insufficiently thought through operationally. During the Second World War, even an admirer like Harold Nicolson regretted that the Prime Minister could never 'avoid the cadences of a phrase', and he was right: 'the soft under-belly of the Axis' was a memorable mot, but it proved far harder for the allies to advance up the Italian Apennines than these easy and optimistic words had implied.[31] And in July 1953, while convalescing from his stroke, Churchill surprised his doctor when 'suddenly he spouted with great feeling a speech by a country-man against towns'. ' "Who said that?" Lord Moran enquired. "I did," Churchill replied. "I just made it up." ' Even then, when he was far from well, and when most mortals would scarcely have been able to speak at all, the words still came too easily, too fluently, too eloquently, too torrentially. He knew it, but could not help it and never showed any inclination to regret it. 'During a long life,' he observed towards the end of it, 'I have had to eat my own words many times, and I have found it a very nourishing diet.' But his critics did not share this self-regarding view.[32]

A further difficulty was that his carefully prepared and highly polished orations were literary, dramatic, theatrical, set-piece speeches, which were ill-suited to what Churchill himself admitted was the intimate, domestic, informal, conversational atmosphere of parliamentary debate. As Clement Attlee once remarked, his speeches were 'magnificent rhetorical perform-ances', but they were 'too stately, too pompous, too elaborate, to be ideal House of Commons stuff '.[33] Like Burke's effusions in an earlier era, they were an impressive exposition of his own views, they read superbly in Hansard, and they have captivated posterity; but they rarely reflected the mood of the House, they often contributed little to the debate itself, and they were sometimes completely out of place. On several occasions, this resulted in conspicuous parliamentary humiliation, when Churchill failed to anticipate the mood of the Commons correctly, but was so tied to his text that he could only plough on inexorably towards disaster. Early in his career, Balfour (who was a brilliant extempore speaker) poured scorn on Churchill's 'powerful but not very mobile artillery', and much later, Aneurin Bevan (who was equally quick on his feet), using the same metaphor, complained that 'he had to wheel himself up to battle, like an enormous gun'.[34]

Even Churchill came briefly to recognize these limitations, during the lengthy debates on the Government of India Bill, as the sheer number of speeches he felt compelled to give forced him for a time to change his manner of parliamentary speaking.[35] When the bill was in Committee, he told Clementine that he was 'in the House all day long, two or three days a week, speaking three or four times a day. I have', he went on, 'been making short speeches of five, ten and fifteen minutes, sometimes half an hour, always without notes.' After more than thirty years in Parliament, this was something entirely new for him. 'At sixty,' he concluded soon after, 'I am altering my method of speaking . . . and now talk to the House of Commons with garrulous unpremeditated flow.' 'What a mystery', he winningly admitted, 'the art of public speaking is! It all consists in my (mature) judgement of assembling three or four absolutely sound arguments and putting these in the most conversational manner possible. There is', he concluded, 'apparently nothing in the literary effect I have sought for forty years.'[36] But such wisdom and such recognition came late in the day, and for all his delight in this new-found conversational approach to speech-making, and for all his recognition of its merits and appeal, he soon reverted to his customary, formal, premeditated ways.

This elaborate preparation carried with it other political disadvantages. For it was precisely because Churchill's words were so carefully crafted and highly polished that they often gave the very greatest offence, thereby reinforcing another widespread criticism that he was exceptionally belligerent and vituperative, and almost completely insensitive to the feelings of others. He may have been great-hearted and magnanimous, but if he had nothing constructive to say, he often fell back on invective which was (in Balfour's words) 'both prepared and violent', and this was something which his victims rarely forgot or forgave.[37] Early in his career, in a pompous and patronizing speech, Churchill dismissed Lord Milner, the darling of the British establishment, and a considerable (albeit controversial) figure, as a man who 'has ceased to be a factor in public events', and (according to Edward Marsh) 'appeared to be taunting a discredited statesman with the evil days on which he had fallen.' Six years later, he launched this attack in the Commons on Lord Charles Beresford, using words which could never be applied to himself:

He is one of these orators of whom it was well said: 'Before they get up, they do not know what they are going to say; when they are speaking, they do not know what they are saying; and when they sit down, they do not know what they have said.'[38]

Like his father's vituperation, this was clever, memorable and funny; but unlike Lord Randolph, it smelled too much of the lamp.

But Churchill never learned to amend his ways and, to the end of his public life, there remained much validity in Balfour's early criticism. In the early 1930s, he brutally described Ramsay MacDonald as 'the boneless wonder', the only politician he knew who could fall down without hurting himself. Soon after, he caricatured Gandhi as 'a seditious Middle Temple lawyer', a 'half-naked fakir' – scornful, boorish, wounding phrases that were never forgiven (or forgotten) in India.[39] In 1945, there was his notorious 'Gestapo' jibe at his Labour opponents in his first party political broadcast of the general election – a terrible thing to say about men who during the previous five years had yielded nothing to him in patriotic zeal. And four years later, in the aftermath of the devaluation of the pound, he mounted a swingeing attack on Sir Stafford Cripps, the Labour Chancellor of the Exchequer, a figure of unimpeachable integrity, and also his former colleague in the wartime Coalition. For Churchill, this was merely the small change of party politics, but for Cripps, it was a wholly unmerited besmirching of his character, he declined to receive an honorary degree from Churchill's hands at Bristol University, and it took to the very end of his life to forgive. There was, then, ample justification for Attlee's view that 'Mr Churchill is a great master of words', but it was 'a terrible thing when the master of words becomes a slave of words', because there was 'nothing behind these words, they are just words of abuse.'[40]

Much of Churchill's oratory, especially after the lights of liberalism went out in 1914, was also implausibly pessimistic and apocalyptically gloomy. In lurid and vivid phrases, he depicted a succession of terrible threats to the very survival of the British nation and Empire: the bolsheviks, the trade unions, the Indian nationalists, the nazis, the postwar Labour governments and the atomic bomb. Each one was for him the most dire and deadly peril. And he described them in very similar language. 'On we go,' he thundered in 1931, when the danger was India, but it might equally well have been Germany, 'moving slowly in a leisurely manner, jerkily onwards towards an unworkable conclusion, crawling methodically towards the abyss' (this last an especially favourite Churchillian noun).[41] But it was not just, as Leo Amery remarked, that many of these speeches were 'utterly and entirely negative, and devoid of all constructive thought'. It was also that many of these menaces were at best exaggerated and at worst quite imaginary. By using phrases so similar to describe threats so varied and sometimes so implausible, Churchill effectively devalued his own rhetoric of alarmism by crying wolf too often. No wonder Parliament did not heed his warnings over German rearmament. He had said it all before. It had become boring. Why should he be right this time? 'He likes to rattle the sabre', one MP observed in the aftermath of Churchill's Munich speech, 'and does it jolly well, but you always have to take it with a grain of salt.'[42]

While much of Churchill's oratory was too melodramatic and doom-laden, it was also too high-flown and, however sincerely meant, it often sounded false, flatulent, bombastic, histrionic, overblown. In the humdrum world of the inter-war years, and in the Socialist era of 1945–51, when new, deflating styles were established by Lytton Strachey and George Orwell, his rhetoric was too bright, too rich, too vivid, too exuberant, and what had once been the 'grand manner' now seemed 'so much tinsel and hollow pasteboard'. One woman, after hearing Churchill thunder at a public meeting, thought him 'a preposterous little fellow', who was 'detestable as anything except a humorous comic entertainer', with 'his folded arms, tufted forelock and his Lyceum theatre voice'.[43] And as the wireless began to supersede the political meeting, he became increasingly out of touch and out of date: as a broadcaster, he lacked the low-key, conversational style which was appropriate to the medium and also to the times, and he remained more interested in the sound of his own words than in their effect on his audience. Not surprisingly, politicians like Baldwin and Attlee, who made a virtue of being down-to-earth and matter-of-fact, who were much more sensitively attuned to the mood of the nation, and who despised rhetoric and distrusted rhetoricians, often got the better of him – both in the country and in the Commons.[44]

The fundamental flaw in Churchill's oratory was that its defects were thus inseparable from its virtues, and were very much on the same Olympian scale. His speeches were meticulously prepared, but this meant they were ponderously inflexible. They often clothed noble sentiments in majestic language, but they could also ring hollow and sometimes gave wounding and lasting offence. They were endlessly inventive in their word-play, but this merely reinforced the widespread opinion that Churchill was a man of unsound judgement and indiscriminate enthusiasms. 'To speak with the tongues of men and of angels . . .', Asquith once observed of him, 'is no good if a man does not inspire trust.'[45] For all their brilliance, polish and fireworks, they could bludgeon an audience into indifference or insensibility as easily as they could persuade it into admiration or acquiescence. But their greatest weakness was that they were the speeches of a self-absorbed egotist who was uninterested in the opinions of anyone else. 'He usurps a position in this House', complained George Lansbury, 'as if he had a right to walk in, make his speech, walk out, and leave the whole place as if God Almighty had spoken . . . He never listens to any other man's speech but his own.' And if he was not prepared to listen to others, is it any wonder that, on many occasions, others were not prepared to listen to him?[46]

III

As Churchill's career unfolded, the balance between the strengths and weaknesses of his oratory shifted very markedly, even though the speeches themselves scarcely altered in their vocabulary, structure and technique. During his early years, from his election to Parliament in 1900 until his resignation in the aftermath of the Dardanelles disaster in 1915, Churchill was learning his craft as an orator and trying to master the House of Commons. Inevitably, given his physical, educational and vocal disadvantages, he made mistakes and suffered setbacks. On one occasion, when speaking on the Trades Disputes Bill in April 1904, he broke down in the Commons in mid-sentence, having completely lost the thread of his words, and thereafter, as he later admitted to Lord Moran, 'he dreaded getting up to speak more than ever'.[47] His earliest speeches were often crude in expression, and his attacks on what was, after all, his own Conservative front bench were excessively (and implausibly) violent. 'To keep in office', Churchill observed of them, 'for a few more weeks and months there is no principle which the government are not prepared to betray, and no quantity of dust and filth they are not prepared to eat.' It was infelicitous and unconvincing efforts such as this which drew Balfour's memorable riposte: 'If there is preparation, there should be more finish; and if there is so much violence, there should certainly be more veracity of feeling.'[48]

Nor did Churchill find the transition from opposition to government, and from Conservative to Liberal, particularly easy, for this required a very different style of speaking which it took him time to master. His first major speech as a junior minister, which included his long-remembered and long-resented assault on Milner, was fatally ill-tuned to the mood of the Commons. It was dismissed by Lord Winterton as 'a complete failure', and Joseph Chamberlain also took delight in seeing the Tory turncoat flounder as Liberal minister: 'Winston Churchill', he observed in April 1906, 'has done very badly as a speaker since he has been in office.'[49] As Asquith's government headed for a showdown with the upper house, Churchill's early attacks on the House of Lords were crude in thought and vulgar in expression, as when he described it as being 'filled with old doddering peers, cute financial magnates, clever wirepullers, big brewers with bulbous noses'. Time and again, young Winston seemed like a schoolboy speaker or the Union debater he had never been, trying on adult rhetorical clothes, but finding them too big. Indeed, some of his early phrases were so prolix, so antithetical and so polysyllabic as to be almost comical in their uncontrolled verbal luxuriance, and it was sometimes impossible to understand what, if anything, he actually meant by them. To say, as he did in the Commons in 1908, that the London docks, 'which have already been called obsolescent, may have to be allowed to obsolesce into obsoleteness', was little more than sheer rhetorical nonsense.[50]

Nevertheless, Churchill's dogged persistence, tireless application and undoubted flair for fine phrases soon brought him real and important rewards. As a Tory backbencher, he was constantly in the limelight, and some of his early attacks struck home, as when he observed of Balfour that 'the dignity of a Prime Minister, like a lady's virtue, is not susceptible of partial diminution'.[51] And as Colonial Under-Secretary, he soon recovered from his unpromising beginning, delivering speeches on the granting of self-government to the Transvaal which were remarkable not only for their mastery of detail, but also for their breadth and generosity of view. Here is the peroration from his speech of 31 July 1906, which in its lofty language and elevated sentiments provides an early anticipation of the oratorical heights he would later reach:

We are prepared to make this settlement in the name of the Liberal Party. That is sufficient authority for us; but there is a higher authority we should earnestly desire to obtain. I make no appeal, but I address myself particularly to the right Hon. Gentlemen who sit opposite, who are long versed in public affairs, and who will not be able all their lives to escape from a heavy South African responsibility. They are the accepted guides of a party which, though in a minority in this house, nevertheless embodies nearly half the nation. I will ask them seriously whether they will not pause before they commit themselves to violent or rash denunciations of this great arrangement. I will ask them, further, whether they cannot join with us to invest the grant of a free constitution to the Transvaal with something of a national sanction. With all our majority, we can only make it the gift of a party; they can make it the gift of England.[52]

As this last sentence suggests, Churchill was learning quickly, and as he was promoted rapidly up the Liberal ministerial ladder, his oratorical talents blossomed. While Colonial Under-Secretary, he had coined the phrase 'terminological inexactitude' as a euphemism for lie, which was clever, funny, memorable, and greatly superior to 'economical with the truth'. At the Board of Trade, and as Home Secretary, he steered through many important measures in speeches which bore all the hallmarks of a mature style: careful construction, abundant detail, vigorous argument, striking phrases and resounding perorations. And as First Lord of the Admiralty he introduced the naval estimates in 1914, in a speech lasting over two hours, which was generally regarded as a masterpiece of lucid and cogent exposition.[53] 'The applause of the House', Lloyd George noted, had become 'the very breath of his nostrils'. At the same time, Churchill acquired a formidable reputation as a platform speaker, especially during the controversy surrounding the 'People's Budget' and the House of Lords constitutional crisis. His attacks on the peers soon became more fluent and polished, and when he dismissed their lordships' chamber for being 'one-sided, hereditary, unpurged, unrepresentative, irresponsible, absentee'. And in one particularly effective speech, he gave a memorable riposte to Lord Curzon's questionable claim that 'all civilization has been the work of aristocracies'. 'The upkeep of aristocracies', Churchill retorted, 'has been the hard work of all civilizations.'[54]

The second phase of his career lasted from his return to power in 1917 until the outbreak of war in 1939. As a leading member of the Lloyd George Coalition, Churchill made many fine speeches, among them those introducing the army estimates in 1920 and in support of the Irish Free State Bill two years later. They were long, detailed, eloquent and, to all but his fiercest critics, loftily persuasive. And as Chancellor of the Exchequer, from 1924 to 1929, he found ample scope for memorable phrase-making. 'I would', he observed on one occasion, 'rather see Finance less proud and Industry more content.' The purpose of returning to the gold standard, he later opined, was so that 'the pound can look the dollar in the face'.[55] In particular, his budgets were widely acclaimed for their superb presentation and great sense of occasion, and they were praised for being almost Gladstonian in their length and mastery of detail. His speech in 1927 was described by Lloyd George as providing 'over two and a half hours of extraordinarily brilliant entertainment'. 'No one', Harold Macmillan later recalled, 'could withhold admiration for the wit, humour, ingenuity and rhetorical skill which he displayed.' This was, indeed, a widely held view. As Lord D'Abernon put it in 1930, 'as a speaker and debater' Churchill was 'in the front rank; as a coiner of phrases unequalled among his contemporaries'.[56]

But as at all stages of his political career, there was another, less positive side to Churchill's oratorical accomplishments during the 1920s. It was partly that matters such as import duties on hops, road-fund grants and rating reform were too complex and too arcane to be ideal subjects for his grandiloquent rhetoric. It was partly that in the era of a mass electorate and the Bright Young Things there was a growing feeling that his mannered, Victorian style was becoming out of date, increasingly resembling (as

J. H. Plumb has memorably put it) 'St Patrick's Cathedral on Fifth Avenue'.[57] And it was partly that in the destabilizing aftermath of the First World War, when the familiar landmarks of his youth had been disrupted and overturned, Churchill began to cultivate a lurid, pessimistic, gloomy style, at best exaggerated, at worst paranoid, as in this attack on the bolsheviks, of January 1920:

The theories of Lenin and Trotsky . . . have driven man from the civilisation of the twentieth century into a condition of barbarism worse than the Stone Age, and left him the most awful and pitiable spectacle in human experience, devoured by vermin, racked by pestilence, and deprived of hope.[58]

In the context of such accumulated mistakes as Tonypandy, Antwerp, the Dardanelles, Chanak and the General Strike, such exaggerated rhetoric scarcely inspired confidence. As Neville Chamberlain put it in 1925: Churchill's 'speeches are extraordinarily brilliant, and men flock to hear him . . . The best show in London, they say.' But he went on, 'so far as I can judge, they think of it as a show, and are not prepared at present to trust his character, still less his judgement'.[59]

It was against this discouraging background that Churchill fought his two great oppositional campaigns of the 1930s, which showed him at his worst and then at his best as a speech-maker. From 1929 to 1935 he waged what Sam Hoare later called 'Winston's Seven Years War' against the Government of India Bill. It was a determined display of persistent and resourceful eloquence, but rarely can so much effort have been expended on a cause so completely misjudged. The purpose of the measure was to give India a modest constitutional advance, but to Churchill it was 'a hideous act of self-mutilation', embodied in a measure he dismissed as 'a gigantic quilt of jumbled crotchet-work, a monstrous monument of shame built by pygmies'.[60] Much of his language was even more apocalyptic than that he had used against the bolshevik menace. Here is one example from January 1931:

The struggle will go on; it will only be aggravated; it will proceed under conditions in which British rule will be shorn of all its argument and half its apparatus. It will proceed steadily towards the goal which those who are driving this policy forward, both here in this country and in India, no longer hesitate to avow, namely the goal of complete severance between Great Britain and India of every tie except tradition, to which India is adverse, and sentiment, which in India is hostile. Sir, I say that is a frightful prospect to have opened up so wantonly, so recklessly, so incontinently and in so short a time.

Churchill thought the Commons were 'delighted' by such extravagant effusions; but Stanley Baldwin expressed the general view when he observed that these die-hard opinions were essentially those of George III couched in the language of Edmund Burke.[61]

It was largely because of the hostility Churchill aroused by this ferocious but futile campaign (the recklessness and the incontinence were mainly his) that his closely argued and powerfully documented speeches against the nazi threat attracted much less notice than they deserved during the second half of the decade. As a sustained, one-man crusade, and as displays of parliamentary courage, they may be described in the words he himself had written in 1897 – 'abandoned by his party, betrayed by his friends, stripped of his offices, whoever can command this power is still formidable.'[62] Here is the peroration to his speech in protest against the Munich settlement:

I do not begrudge our loyal, brave people, who were ready to do their duty no matter what the cost, who never flinched under the strain of last week – I do not grudge them the natural, spontaneous outburst of joy and relief when they learned that the hard ordeal would no longer be required of them at the moment. But they should know the truth. They should know that there has been gross neglect and deficiency in our defences; they should know that we have sustained a defeat without a war, the consequences of which will travel far with us along our road; they should know that we have passed an awful milestone in our history, when the whole equilibrium of Europe has been deranged; and that terrible words have for the time being been pronounced against the Western democracies. And do not suppose that this is the end. This is only the beginning of the reckoning. This is only the first sip, the first foretaste of the bitter cup which will be proffered to us year by year, unless by a supreme recovery of moral health and martial vigour, we arise again and take our stand for freedom as in olden time.

But full though the documentation was, and magnificent the rhetoric, speeches such as this were often delivered to a half-empty chamber. 'For five years', Churchill candidly lamented in 1938, 'I have talked to this House on these matters – not with very great success.'[63]

How right he was. In 1933, Herbert Samuel noted in the Commons that Churchill made 'many brilliant speeches on all subjects, but that is no reason why we should necessarily accept his political judgement. On the contrary,' he went on, 'the brilliance of his speeches only makes the errors in his judgement the more conspicuous . . . I feel inclined', he concluded, 'to say of him what Bagehot wrote of another very distinguished Parliamentarian [Disraeli]: "His chaff is excellent, but his wheat is poor stuff." '[64] Stanley

Baldwin, himself an exceptionally accomplished rhetorician, but in a low-key, art-which-conceals-its-art style, was of the same view. 'One of these days', he observed to Tom Jones in 1936, in words very reminiscent of those Asquith had used a generation earlier,

I'll make a few casual remarks about Winston. Not a speech – no oratory – just a few words in passing. I've got it all ready. I am going to say that when Winston was born, lots of fairies swooped down on his cradle bearing gifts – imagination, eloquence, industry, ability. And then came a fairy who said, 'No one person has a right to so many gifts', picked him up and gave him such a shake and twist that with all these gifts, he was denied Judgement and Wisdom. And that is why, while we delight to listen to him in his House, we do not take his advice.

Or, as R. A. Butler put it, 'Winston was entranced by his own imagery; he loved to hear himself as he knew others did, but whereas he was profoundly moved by his own words, others were not.'[65]

IV

Between 1939 and 1945, however, the Commons, the nation and the world were much more attentive. Throughout the 'Phoney War', Churchill made a succession of vigorous, fighting speeches as the recently recalled First Lord of the Admiralty, which gave a reassuring (sometimes misleading) impression of resolute confidence and robust competence. But it was only when he became Prime Minister, in the perilous circumstances which he had been waiting and hoping all his life to command, that his oratory fully and finally and magnificently caught fire. For this was no mere interior personal fantasy: it was authentically the hour of fate, the crack of doom, the deep abyss that he had so often (and often so vainly) foretold. And the issues seemed appropriately Churchillian in their momentous and noble simplicity: victory or defeat, survival or annihilation, freedom or tyranny, civilization or barbarism. To such an unprecedented national crisis – actually terrible yet potentially heroic – Churchill's magniloquent rhetoric, so often so out of place and so out of date, was for once perfectly attuned. The drama of the time had suddenly become fully equal to the drama of his tone. In 1940 Churchill finally became the hero he had always dreamed of becoming, and his words at last made the historic impact he had always wanted them to make. 'It was', Lord Moran recalled, 'his favourite part, and when he was offered the role . . . he proved to be word-perfect.'[66] For now, and for a time, he was truly and triumphantly his own Savrola.

During the early stages of his premiership, Churchill's oratory served three different purposes with equal success. In the first place, he reported regularly to the Commons about the progress of the war – the formation of the Coalition Government, the fall of France, the Battle of Britain, and so on. Many of his most famous speeches were essentially parliamentary news bulletins, with an additional, uplifting paragraph added on at the end, when the feelings he had hitherto kept in check gave wings to his words, as in the peroration to his speech delivered on 4 June 1940 in the aftermath of the Dunkirk evacuation:

Even though large tracts of Europe and many old and famous states have fallen or may fall into the grip of the Gestapo and all the odious apparatus of Nazi rule, we shall not flag or fail. We shall go on to the end, we shall fight in France, we shall fight on the seas and oceans, we shall fight with growing confidence and growing strength in the air, we shall defend our island whatever the cost may be; we shall fight on the beaches, we shall fight in the fields and in the streets, we shall fight in the hills, we shall never surrender; and even if, which I do not for a moment believe, this island or a large part of it were subjugated and starving, then our Empire beyond the seas, armed and guarded by the British fleet, would carry on the struggle until, in God's good time, the New World, with all its power and might, steps forth to the rescue and liberation of the old.[67]

The second purpose of these speeches was to rally and reassure the British people as a whole. We shall never know whether Churchill inspired them – something he himself always denied – or whether he merely expressed the emotions they all shared but lacked the means to express. Either way, his oratory, so often a monologue with himself, became, for the first (and only?) time, a dialogue with the nation at large. 'Since 1940', Lord Moran observed, 'we do not think of the PM as handicapped by living apart from the people. His countrymen have come to feel that he is saying what they would like to say for themselves, if they knew how.'[68] But Churchill did know how, and never to more telling effect than in this speech, initially delivered in the Commons on 18 June 1940, and subsequently broadcast:

What General Weygand called the Battle of France is over. I expect that the Battle of Britain is about to begin. Upon this battle depends the survival of Christian civilisation. Upon it depends our own British life, and the long continuity of our institutions and Empire. The whole fury and might of the enemy must very soon be turned on us. Hitler knows that he will have to break us in this island or lose the war. If we can stand up to him, all Europe may be free, and the life of the world may move forward into broad, sunlit uplands. But if we fail, then the whole world, including the United States, will sink into the abyss of a new Dark Age, made more sinister, and perhaps more protracted, by the lights of perverted science. Let us therefore brace ourselves to our duties, and so bear ourselves that, if the British Empire and its Commonwealth last for a thousand years, men will still say, 'This was their finest hour'.[69]

The third purpose of these speeches was to convince world – and especially American – opinion, both of the plight of Britain's position and of the strength of Britain's resolve and, as the two previous examples make plain, Churchill lost no opportunity to mention, and draw in, the United States whenever he could. Here, again, the words were perfectly judged, as with the peroration of his 20 August speech on the Battle of Britain pilots, in which he described the possibility of the destroyers for bases agreement, and welcomed the prospect of increasing Anglo-American co-operation in a memorable simile:

These are important steps. Undoubtedly this process means that these two great organisations of the English-speaking democracies, the British Empire and the United States, will have to be somewhat mixed up together in some of their affairs for mutual and general advantage. For my own part, looking out upon the future, I do not view the process with any misgivings. I could not stop it if I wished. No one can stop it. Like the Mississippi, it just keeps rolling along. Let it roll on full flood, inexorable, irresistible, benignant, to broader lands, and better days.[70]

At a time when Britain was on the defensive, when invasion seemed possible at almost any moment, and when victory was virtually unthinkable, these speeches were themselves the best (and sometimes the only) weaponry available. They may have expressed a confidence the Prime Minister did not always feel; many of the phrases were being recycled for the umpteenth time; and critics like Lord Halifax thought them vulgar and histrionic.[71] But between May and December 1940, Churchill talked his way to immortality, and as these magnificently defiant words were soon accompanied by equally defiant deeds, they acquired an iconic status and historic significance they have retained to this day. They were generally well received by the public, and his friends and admirers rejoiced that Churchill's great gifts had finally been matched by great events. Harold Nicolson thought 'we shall fight on the beaches' was 'the most magnificent speech that I have ever heard'. Violet Bonham Carter claimed that Churchill's panegyric on 'the few' beat 'your old enemies, "the classics", into a cocked hat'. And Sir Alan Lascelles, the king's private secretary, opined that the Prime Minister alone 'of living orators, could make one realise what it must have been like to hear Burke or Chatham'. But the best appraisal came from the American journalist, Edward R. Murrow, who observed that in 1940 Churchill 'mobilized the English language, and sent it into battle'.[72]

Inevitably, it proved impossible for him to maintain this high pitch of emotional excitement and oratorical intensity for the entire duration of what he himself admitted was 'a long, hard war'. As the conflict dragged on there were signs of discontent at home, and a run of defeats in the Far East led to criticism of Churchill's leadership for being, in Aneurin Bevan's phrase, 'a succession of oratorical successes accompanied by a series of military disasters'.[73] The stark and simple issue of surrender or survival was soon replaced by the more intractable and less heroic problems of allied co-operation and postwar reconstruction; it was no longer so easy for Churchill to simplify and dramatize complex military and political problems; it was difficult to strike a balance between the secrecy essential for conducting operations in wartime, and the need to keep the Commons fully informed; and he was increasingly obliged to defend and to justify allied policies of which he himself disapproved, but which he lacked the power to influence or to change. Under these circumstances, it is scarcely surprising that even Churchill was moved to remark in November 1941 that 'no sensible person in wartime makes speeches because he wants to: he makes them because he has to'.[74]

As these words also implied, most of the work of running what had become this vast, global war was done by committee and correspondence and conference.[75] But as long as Churchill was in charge in Britain, there were still many memorable oratorical moments. There were world broadcasts: 'Give us the tools, and we will finish the job.' There was an address to a joint session of the United States Congress: 'What kind of a people do they [the enemy nations] think we are? Is it possible that they do not realise that we shall never cease to persevere against them, until they have been taught a lesson which they and the world will never forget?' There was a no-confidence motion repulsed with ease: 'I offer no apologies, I offer no excuses, I make no promises.'[76] There was a eulogy of Lloyd George: 'as a man of action, resource and creative energy, he stood when at his zenith without a rival'. There was a tribute to Roosevelt: 'the greatest champion of freedom who has ever brought help and comfort from the new world to the old'. And when Germany surrendered, there was this appropriately majestic victory broadcast:

I told you hard things at the beginning of these last five years; you did not shrink, and I should be unworthy of your confidence and generosity if I did not still cry: forward, unswerving, unflinching, indomitable, till the whole task is done, and the whole world is safe and clean.[77]

V

Yet as soon as this victory was achieved, what remained of the binding spell of Churchill's wartime oratory was abruptly broken. Even to an admirer like Vita Sackville-West, his party political broadcasts during the general election of 1945 seemed 'confused, woolly, unconstructive, and so wordy that it is impossible to pick out any concrete impression from them'. Speaking as a partisan leader rather than a national hero, and obliged to concentrate on domestic policy rather than global statecraft, he once again fell back on vituperation and vagueness: 'on with the forward march! Leave these Socialist dreamers to their Utopias or their nightmares. Let us be content to do the heavy job that is right on top of us.'[78] Thereafter, as Leader of the Opposition, he could rarely resist the temptation to be savagely partisan towards the government. 'I'll tear their bleeding entrails out of them,' he informed Lord Moran in June 1946. The result was a succession of slashing attacks, predicting in familiar apocalyptic mode the direst consequences that would result from the nationalization of industry, the independence of India and the devaluation of the pound. As with his speeches in the House of Commons delivered during the 1920s and 1930s, they invariably provided superb, and often rollicking, entertainment. But they were not always convincing, and in different ways, both the laconic Attlee and the more flamboyant Aneurin Bevan regularly managed to get the better of him.[79]

Nevertheless, Churchill's best speeches remained great parliamentary occasions, and he could still rise to unrivalled heights of feeling and expression, as in his final survey of the war, made from the opposition front bench in August 1945:

I have great hopes of this Parliament, and I shall do my utmost to make its work fruitful. It may heal the wounds of war, and turn to good account the new conceptions and powers which we have gathered amid the storm. I do not underrate the difficult and intricate complications of the task which lies before us; I know too much about it to cherish vain illusions; but the morrow of such a victory as we have gained is a splendid moment, both in our small lives and in our great history. It is a time not only of rejoicing, but even more so of resolve. When we look back on all the perils through which we have passed, and at the mighty foes we have laid low, and all the dark and deadly designs we have frustrated, why should we fear for our future? We have come safely through the worst.[80]

But significantly, Churchill's greatest oratorical successes during these post-war years were achieved outside Parliament and outside Britain. At Fulton ('an Iron Curtain has descended across the Continent') and at Zurich ('we must build a kind of United States of Europe') his words were those of a private citizen who had recently been dismissed by the electorate from all further conduct of his country's affairs, and they were the familiar Churchillian amalgam of gloom and uplift. But the stature of the speaker, the novelty of the occasions and the timing and content of his speeches meant that they made an immense impact, not only in the Western world, but in Russia too.[81]

In October 1951 the Conservatives narrowly won the general election, and Churchill brought his words and his phrases back to power for the last time. Inevitably, the mood was very different from what it had been fourteen years earlier, and of necessity his rhetoric was less inspirational and more emollient: 'what was magic in 1940', Jock Colville later observed, 'would have been melodrama in 1955'. Moreover, Churchill himself was by now a very weary Titan indeed, the composition of his speeches became more of a burden to him, and he sometimes used drafts which had been prepared for him by other hands. The words no longer flowed as easily or majestically as they once had, and he admitted to Lord Moran that impending speeches now hovered over him 'like ... vultures'.[82] In the early summer of 1953, Churchill suffered a stroke, which temporarily incapacitated him, and between May and October he delivered no public speech, the longest period of official silence in the whole of his political career. Thereafter, his strength ebbed rapidly and visibly, he was deaf and increasingly unsteady on his feet, his words were often blurred and slurred, and he sometimes failed to master his own script, or to show much interest in what he was saying. 'Nowadays', Lord Moran noted in 1954, with the sort of morbid relish that so often characterizes his diary, 'one does not ask whether a speech went well, but only "Is he all right?" It has come to that. Just to get through is an achievement in itself.'[83]

Thus did Churchill's speaking career come almost full circle, as the fears and anxieties of his youth, which he had striven so hard to allay and so successfully to master, returned to haunt him in his oratorical old age. Part of him wanted to die in office and in harness, collapsing Chatham-like on the floor of the Commons in the midst of a speech; but another part of him, to say nothing of his family and friends, dreaded the embarrassment and humiliation of such a final and very public breakdown. And there were, indeed, some very close calls during these last years. In April 1954, Churchill made one parliamentary speech so partisan, so ill-judged and yet so unalterable that he was virtually howled down in the Commons. 'All expression had gone from his voice', observed Lord Moran, 'which quavered into the high-pitched speech of a very old man.'[84] In October that year, he addressed the Conservative Party at its conference at Blackpool, but it was a distinctly lacklustre performance: the text was poorly delivered, his manner was halting and hesitant, and he fumbled and stumbled over his words. And a month later, in a speech to his Woodford constituents, Churchill blurted out some remarks about the contents of a wartime telegram he had sent to General Montgomery which caused widespread embarrassment.[85]

As Roy Jenkins has rightly remarked, much of Churchill's last premiership was spent trying to persuade people – himself, his family, his friends, the House of Commons, the British people and other world leaders – that he was still up to the job. That was why he continued to make speeches and, with appropriate medical stimulants, he could still sometimes rise to great occasions with unrivalled eloquence. His address to the American Congress in January 1952 was a vigorous (if vain) reassertion of Britain's independent role in the world. His broadcast eulogy of George VI later that year touched the hearts of his listeners as never before: 'after a happy day of sunshine and sport, and after "good night" to those who loved him best, he fell asleep as every man or woman who strives to fear God and nothing else in the world may hope to do'.[86] His first speech after his stroke, to the Conservatives at Margate in October 1953, was a triumphant surmounting of a formidable obstacle: 'Never before', Churchill told Lord Moran, using a familiar word pattern, 'has so much depended on a single bloody speech.' His contribution to the debate on the address in the Commons in the following month was widely praised: 'an olympian spectacle', according to Henry Channon; 'in eighteen years in this honourable House, I have never heard anything like it'. And his last great parliamentary speech, on the threat of nuclear war and the impact of the hydrogen bomb, was meant to be 'one of his great utterances, something the House would long remember'.[87]

'If you never make another speech,' his son-in-law Christopher Soames commented at the end of it, 'that was a very fine swan song.' So it was; and so it proved to be. Within a month, Churchill had resigned, and he scarcely spoke in public thereafter. 'I don't want to make any more speeches,' he told Lord Moran. 'Why should I?' There was nothing left for him to say or to prove, and even if there was, he himself was now no longer capable of doing either. In November that year, Henry Fairlie, writing in the *Spectator*, urged Churchill to return to the Commons, to deliver the sort of grand, panoramic, inspirational address that had been commonplace in his prime. But such feats were by now beyond him: 'He would make no more speeches that mattered. If he had to get on his legs all he could now hope for was that he would not make a fool of himself.' Yet almost to the end, Churchill remained haunted by oratory, and by the orator he himself had once been. In April 1957, he told Lord Moran he had 'had a dream that he made a very good speech, and when he woke, he felt he could'. 'But', Moran went on, 'after a little he realized that he could not speak for forty minutes; he could not make a speech at all.' For more than half a century, words and phrases had truly been the fibre of Churchill's being; and when he ceased to be able to make speeches, his own life was as good as over.[88]

VI

'A hundred and fifty years ago,' Churchill observed towards the close of his career, 'dramatic art was conspicuous in great orators. It was my ambition, all my life, to be master of the spoken word.' That he achieved that ambition is undeniable; and that he worked hard to achieve it is no less certain. But as with so many aspects of Churchill's career and character, his oratory must be seen as a whole, in the full perspective of his long and controversial life, and not merely from the majestic standpoint afforded by the Periclean peaks of 1940. At his worst, it bears repeating. Churchill was a bombastic and histrionic vulgarian, out of touch, out of tune and out of temper: in short, the very figure so searingly (and so upsettingly) depicted in Graham Sutherland's long-since-destroyed eightieth-birthday portrait. The politest thing that may be said about it is that for much of his career, Churchill's oratory was far more important and interesting to himself than it was to the British political classes or to the British people in general, and that he was often rude and vituperative, bullying and overbearing, apocalyptic and irresponsible. 'Even now,' Lord Moran noted, 'at the end of his life, when the nation, regardless of party, insists on looking to him as the sagacious world statesman . . . his tastes lie in the rough and tumble of the House of Commons. He loves a fight.' So he did. Notwithstanding his later years of fame and apotheosis, there was still about him a touch of Eatanswill, and for all its stately and studied magnificence, his oratory was rarely entirely free of it.[89]

Nevertheless, the fact remains that when Churchill retired as Prime Minister in April 1955, there went out of British public life a breadth of vision, a poetry of expression and a splendour of utterance which it seems highly unlikely will ever be seen or heard or witnessed again.[90] In part this is because post-Churchillian, post-imperial Britain is a lesser place, where the high-flown rhetoric appropriate to great causes and great issues no longer seems relevant or right. In part it is because in the world of television and the confrontational interview, there is neither the scope nor the opportunity for the grand manner and the majestic style. In part it is because politicians have ceased to train themselves to be orators in the deliberate, laborious and demanding way that Churchill did, not least because ministers speak far less in the Commons than they used to.[91] And in part it is because they lack both the time and the talent to lavish hours on the creation of memorable set-piece speeches, or even on the coining of unforgettable phrases. Compare the many memorable quotations which Churchill bequeathed to posterity with those most readily associated with his successors – Harold Macmillan ('You've never had it so good'); Harold Wilson ('A week is a long time in politics'); Edward Heath ('We shall cut prices at a stroke'); Margaret Thatcher ('No, no, no'); and John Major ('Put up or shut up') – and we have clearly moved into a different, and lesser, world.

Where, then, should we take our leave of Churchill the orator, in one guise a hectoring bully and self-absorbed egotist, incontinently prolix and wearingly verbose, in another a wordsmith of genius, the supreme phrase-maker of his time who, like Savrola, lifted people's 'minds from the material cares of life' and beckoned them towards 'broad, sunlit uplands'?[92] It could be during the early stages of his career, as he painfully and painstakingly learned to practise his craft and master his art. It could be during the inter-war years, as he waged his long, vain, lonely battles against the Government of India Bill and the policy of appeasement. Or it could be during the Second World War, as he defied tyranny in its fleeting hour of triumph, with magnificent words and splendid phrases that have rightly become immortal. But it is surely most appropriate to leave him with these closing words from his last great speech in the House of Commons, delivered in April 1955, which he meant as his farewell to politics, to Parliament and to public life, and which, nearly half a century after they were spoken, still move by their eloquence, their wisdom, their compassion and their hope:

The day may dawn when fair play, love for one's fellow-men, respect for justice and freedom, will enable tormented generations to march forth, serene and triumphant from the hideous epoch in which we have to dwell. Meanwhile, never flinch, never weary, never despair.[93]

PART TWO

POLITICS IN DIVERSE MODES

5

Locality: The 'Chamberlain Tradition' and Birmingham[1]

Between the accession of Queen Victoria and the outbreak of the Second World War, the Chamberlains of Birmingham were a quintessentially middle-class family – in their ancestry, their clannishness, their education, their sources of income, their religious beliefs, their styles of life, their choice of marriage partners, their cultural aspirations and their attitude to honours. But they were less than typically bourgeois in their political importance and their worldly success. Joseph Chamberlain, who was born a year before Victoria became queen, was the greatest Mayor of Birmingham, an inveterate opponent of Irish Home Rule, and a famously forceful Colonial Secretary, who raised British imperial consciousness to unprecedented heights. His elder son, Austen, was an MP for more than forty years, was twice Chancellor of the Exchequer, served as Foreign Secretary from 1924 to 1929, and won the Nobel Peace Prize for negotiating the Locarno Treaty in 1925. And Joseph's younger son, Neville, was the most successful of them all: Lord Mayor of Birmingham from 1915 to 1917 (following his father), twice Chancellor of the Exchequer (following his half-brother), and Prime Minister from 1937 to 1940 (outdoing them both).[2]

This meant that in their time, and it was a long time, the Chamberlains were the most prominent middle-class dynasty in British politics and, during the last two hundred years, they have been rivalled only by the Cannings before them, and the Hoggs since. Not surprisingly, their sense of family pride and collective identity was exceptionally well developed, and in private and public, Austen and Neville remained abidingly loyal to 'the clique' and especially to their father's memory.[3] But the Chamberlains were also unusual in that they were so closely identified, across the generations, with one particular British city. For it was Birmingham which provided the source of their considerable wealth, an unrivalled arena for municipal endeavour, and the base from which they sustained themselves in parliamentary politics. Much has been written about these three men, as local worthies and as national figures. The purpose of this chapter is to take a fresh look at the

Chamberlains in their civic setting: to re-evaluate their political position in Birmingham across the decades, to outline the cultural and ceremonial resources they mobilized in stamping their mark on the city, and to explore the interconnections between their local standing and their national endeavours. It seeks, in short, to describe the rise, zenith and decline of something which disappeared from Birmingham's collective civic consciousness in 1945, but which in its heyday was an integral and defining element in the city's political and cultural life: the 'Chamberlain tradition'.

I

When Joseph Chamberlain became Mayor of Birmingham in 1873, having been elected to the council only four years before, he inaugurated a municipal revolution, which was of lasting significance in his adopted town, and which set so successful an example to the nation and Empire that Birmingham became recognized as a 'municipal mecca' and the 'best-governed city in the world'.[4] The outlines of this story are well known. Along with his nonconformist relatives and friends, many of whom were important local businessmen, Chamberlain elevated the status and standing of the office of mayor, and transformed the city council from a byword in myopic incompetence into 'the pivot on which the whole life of the community has turned'. During his three-year mayoralty, the gas and water supply were taken into municipal ownership, and the Corporation Street improvement scheme was inaugurated. Thereafter, this vigorous civic crusade was continued by Chamberlain's relatives and associates, as Birmingham acquired a Welsh water supply, a bishopric and a university. In 1889 it was raised to the rank of a city, in 1896 its mayor was transformed into the Lord Mayor, and in 1911 it was enlarged into Greater Birmingham, 'the second city in the Empire'.[5]

But this was only the municipal side of the story. For in 1876, having already established himself as the dominant force in the National Education League, Chamberlain resigned the mayoralty and was returned unopposed as one of the town's three Liberal MPs at a by-election. As in the Council House, so in the Commons, he was regarded as an advanced radical – hostile to the aristocracy and the monarchy, master of the Birmingham caucus, and the architect of the new National Liberal Federation.[6] He remained an MP for the next thirty-eight years, transferring to West Birmingham, one of the seven single-member constituencies created by the third Reform Act. For much of that time Chamberlain was the city's most celebrated public figure, and this was either despite, or because of, the many changes in his politics: separating from Gladstone over Home Rule, creating a new electoral organization to supersede the Liberal caucus, becoming a Unionist and embracing imperialism, and resigning from Balfour's government to campaign for Tariff Reform. Throughout these unexpected turns and developments, Chamberlain's Birmingham 'duchy' held firm. Such sustained dominance by one man of one city was distinctly unusual.[7]

All this is well enough known. When Birmingham men and women talked, as they did by the 1900s, of the 'Chamberlain tradition', they were referring to a potent and unique amalgam of personal charisma, civic vigour, electoral success and national political importance, apparently dating back a quarter of a century. But for much of that time, Chamberlain's so-called 'fortress' was less secure than that word implies. On the municipal front, there was opposition in his own day from the Ratepayers' Association and the Conservatives, and later from the Liberals and the new Labour Party. Nor was it any easier in the constituencies. At the 1880 general election, there was a strong Conservative revival in the city, and Chamberlain was returned with fewer votes than the other two successful Liberal candidates. In 1885, the Conservative vote went up again, and Chamberlain left the veteran MP John Bright to rebut the challenge mounted by Lord Randolph Churchill in Birmingham Central.[8] During both of these elections, he was much criticized: for the expense of the Council House, the Art Gallery and Corporation Street, for his lack of interest in the housing of the poor, and for the dictatorial methods of the caucus. Indeed, the dominant Birmingham Liberal in these years was not Chamberlain, who in age and votes was the junior partner, but John Bright, who had been MP for the city since 1857.[9]

During the later part of the 1880s, Chamberlain's local position remained weak, as he did not so much lead slavish Birmingham opinion in a rightwards direction as follow it in an uncertain search to find a new accommodation with it. His first responses to Gladstone's Home Rule proposals were far less decisive than John Bright's.[10] Once it was clear in 1887 that there would be no reunion with the Gladstonian leadership, Chamberlain was obliged to create a new organization in Birmingham from scratch. There was much animosity from the Liberals (his former friends) he was leaving behind, and distrust from the Conservatives (his former enemies) who were now expected to make way for their old adversary. Only the disarray of the Birmingham Liberals enabled him to secure victory for himself and his allies in the elections of 1886, not until the election of 1892 was his local position fully consolidated, and not until 1895 did he become a serious player at Westminster again. And it was only during the early 1900s that the idea of a 'Chamberlain duchy' in the West Midlands as a whole, and a 'Chamberlain tradition' in Birmingham itself, became generally recognizable.[11]

That Chamberlain, his relatives and associates worked hard for Birmingham's (not always reliable) votes cannot be doubted. Much less appreciated are the other ways in which they sought to stamp their mark on the town and win popular support. The image of Birmingham which they projected during the last quarter of the nineteenth century was that of an Italian city state – proud, free and independent. They saw their town as a latter-day Renaissance Venice, and themselves as latter-day oligarchs, a hereditary patriciate, governing and beautifying their town in the interests of all its inhabitants, with the same skill and virtue, piety and patriotism, wisdom and disinterestedness that Venice had shown in its prime.[12] This self-image did not completely square with the partisan nature of Chamberlainite council and party politics; but nor was it wholly fanciful. For the 'civic renaissance' was not just about gas and water: it was also about promoting the arts, elevating the taste of ordinary citizens, and nurturing in them a collective sense of civic identity. As *The Times* obituarist noted on Chamberlain's death, 'he held up the ideal of a self-sufficient community with stately and beneficent public institutions, and a dignified public life'.[13]

The most visible expression of this civic gospel were the public buildings constructed during that period: 'the projection of values into space and stone'.[14] This was partly because of the need to house the expanding municipal bureaucracy, and partly as a way of asserting the importance of the town and the council. But it was also a deliberate attempt at enlightened municipal patronage. 'Art', observed John Thackeray Bunce, a friend of Chamberlain's and editor of the *Birmingham Daily Post*, 'must . . . permeate and suffuse the daily life, if it is to become a real and enduring influence.' There must be 'public buildings, ample and stately and rich enough in their ornament to dignify the corporate life', which would promote 'a municipal life nobler, fuller, richer than any the world has ever seen'. Hence the construction of the Council House, between 1874 and 1879, and the City Museum and Art Gallery from 1881 to 1885. And the images projected by these buildings perfectly accorded with Bunce's vision. Above the portico of the Council House was a relief of 'Britannia Rewarding the Birmingham Manufacturers', the inscription stone of the Art Gallery bore the words 'By the Gains of Industry We Promote Art', and the Art Gallery boasted a campanile, modelled on San Marco in Venice.[15]

This was a portent of things to come. For while the Council House and Art Gallery were mainly neo-classical, the Chamberlainites soon developed their own distinctive architectural style, which was Venetian or Ruskinian

Gothic. It was characterized by red brick and terracotta, by high, pointed windows, gables, towers, chimneys and spires, and by elaborate ornamentation in ironwork, glass, marble, granite and tiles.[16] During the last quarter of the nineteenth century, most of the public buildings in Birmingham were constructed in this style, including Mason College, the extensions to the Birmingham and Midland Institute and the Central Reference Library, and the Birmingham School of Art. The shops and offices which fronted on to Corporation Street were also built in Venetian Gothic, as were more than thirty board schools, which became as characteristic of Birmingham's inner suburbs as Wren's churches were of the City of London. Even the hardware princes of Edgbaston turned from suburban stucco to Gothic villas, inspired by The Grove, where Archibald Kenrick lived, and by Highbury, the grandest palazzo of them all, constructed for Joseph Chamberlain in 1880.[17]

Most of these buildings were designed by John Henry Chamberlain who, though no relation, was a Liberal friend of Joseph Chamberlain's, and closely involved with the Birmingham Society of Artists, the Birmingham School of Art and the Birmingham and Midland Institute. It was said that he 'cared for the municipal life of our town with a steadfast and passionate feeling', and he was the de facto official architect to the civic gospel. As such, he successfully projected the image of Birmingham as a latter-day Venice in the most public and enduring way. He was Ruskin's most ardent practising disciple, and he firmly believed in the social responsibilities of architects, and in the appropriateness of Venetian Gothic for the great buildings of Victorian towns.[18] They established a direct continuity with an earlier golden age of urban life; they were majestic expressions of civic patriotism and municipal high-mindedness; and they enriched and informed the lives of all who saw them. As J. T. Bunce declared in an obituary notice, 'to the whole community he spoke ... by the buildings with which his creative skill had adorned the town,' thereby 'teaching daily lessons of beauty and refinement to the crowds who daily pass them.'[19]

J. H. Chamberlain's buildings were the cathedrals of the new civic gospel, and he also assisted in the celebration of its saints and evangelists. In the centre of the city, surrounded by the Town Hall, the Art Gallery, the Reference Library and Mason College, was established Chamberlain Square, 'adorned with monuments commemorating, either by design or association, the achievements of Liberalism in politics, in science, in eloquence or in local work'. Here were placed statues of such worthies as George Dawson, the most influential preacher of the civic gospel, and Josiah Mason, who founded the local science college from which the university eventually developed.[20] But pride of place went to the Chamberlain Memorial, a 65-foot

Gothic spire, richly ornamented with mosaics and a portrait medallion of Joseph Chamberlain himself. It was designed by his namesake, and unveiled in 1880, the year in which Chamberlain resigned from the town council, and proclaimed the Liberal values of municipal enterprise. Nearby, in Council House Square, another commemorative project was also begun, with statues of Joseph Priestley, the radical scientist, and John Skirrow Wright, a long-serving Liberal councillor.[21]

J. H. Chamberlain's early death in 1883 meant that for the two great public buildings of a later period, the city was forced to turn to London. But Aston Webb, the architect selected for both commissions, designed very much in Chamberlain's established idiom. The Victoria Law Courts, constructed on Corporation Street between 1887 and 1891, were another richly ornamented terracotta extravaganza, complete with stained-glass windows depicting episodes in Birmingham's history and celebrating its industries. The courts were much admired, and inspired such neighbouring buildings as the General Hospital and the Methodist Central Hall.[22] Twenty years later, Joseph Chamberlain summoned Webb again to design the new university of which he was Chancellor, promoter and chief fund-raiser. In addition to the buildings devoted to education, teaching and research, Chamberlain wanted something distinctive – partly as another monument to himself, partly to make the university a landmark in the city, and partly to proclaim that it was a place of general culture belonging to a great European tradition. Not surprisingly, he settled on an Italian campanile – primarily based on Siena, but also with touches derived from the tower of San Giorgio Maggiore at the entrance to the Grand Canal of Venice.[23]

Like the rulers of Renaissance Venice, the Chamberlainites of Victorian Birmingham sought to glorify civic life, and to advance their civic crusade, by staging grand ceremonials against the backdrop of the buildings and spaces they had created.[24] From the time of Chamberlain's mayoralty, the scale and tempo of municipal festivities considerably increased. Between 1874 and 1882, the foundation stones of the Council House and Mason College were laid, and the buildings declared open; there was a dinner given to Chamberlain on his resignation as Mayor and there was the inauguration of Chamberlain Square; and there was the laying of the inscription stone of the Art Gallery and the reopening of the Central Reference Library. Each of these occasions was notable for large crowds and speeches on the importance of local civic endeavour. In 1883, there were week-long celebrations of the silver jubilee of John Bright's first election as MP for the town. There was a procession through five miles of streets, a mass meeting in Bingley Hall, a banquet at the Town Hall, and a civic address and reception. Towards the end of the decade, Chamberlain was made the first honorary freeman of the borough in March 1888, and a year later, there was a public reception to welcome him with his new wife.[25]

As Chamberlain and Birmingham moved from Liberalism to Unionism, the royal family was also brought to the centre of the civic stage. The Jubilees of 1887 and 1897 were celebrated with loyal extravagance – thanksgiving services, public holidays, addresses, processions, illuminations and fire-works – and the monarchy became directly involved in ceremonials of civic aggrandizement. From 1858 to 1885, there were no official royal civic visits, but from the mid-1880s, there was a sudden upsurge. The queen appeared in Golden Jubilee year, to lay the foundation stone of the Law Courts which would bear her name; the Prince of Wales visited in 1885 and 1891 to open the Art Gallery and the Victoria Law Courts; and the Duke and Duchess of York laid the foundation stone of the General Hospital.[26] And this new but increasingly close connection between royal visits and civic aggrandizement was recognized in more permanent ways, as Council House Square, hitherto a monument to Liberalism and nonconformity, was completely transformed. In 1901, a statue of the Queen-Empress was unveiled, and the place was renamed Victoria Square. In 1913, Priestley and Wright were moved to Chamberlain Square, and a statue of Edward VII was unveiled by Princess Louise. Within a generation, radical and civic Birmingham had been super-seded by royal and imperial Birmingham.[27]

Interleaved with these royal occasions were later ceremonials connected with Chamberlain himself – now no longer a politician on the defensive, but an international statesman. On his farewell to Birmingham in November 1902, prior to his visit to South Africa, there was a lengthy civic dinner, a horse-drawn procession along a route illuminated by 4,000 torch-bearers, from the city centre to Canon Hill Park, and a great fireworks display, ending in a fire portrait of Chamberlain and his wife. It was this elaborate extravaganza which established Chamberlain's position as 'analogous to that of Mr Bright a generation ago', and for decades after, it was remembered as 'the greatest display of affection ever shown to a politician' in his own city.[28] But even this was surpassed by the celebrations of July 1906, to mark Chamberlain's seventieth birthday and his thirtieth anniversary as Birmingham's MP, which were modelled on the John Bright jubilee of more than twenty years before. There was a civic lunch in the Council House, at which Chamberlain delivered his last panegyric on public service in muni-cipal life. There was an eighty-car procession through seventeen miles of decorated streets. There was a speech in Bingley Hall where Chamberlain reviewed his political life. And there was another torchlit procession, followed by fireworks. This was the most elaborate and inclusive ceremonial ever to have taken place in the city, and it was estimated that half the population of Birmingham had turned out for it.[29]

There were also great public occasions marking Birmingham's evolution as a city. On 24 July 1904, the Corporation and guests were taken by train to Rhayader in North Wales, to witness the official opening of the Elan Valley Water Supply Scheme by King Edward VII, who knighted the mayor, Alderman Hallewell Rogers. Less than a year later, Charles Gore was enthroned as the city of Birmingham's first bishop, before a large congregation in St Philip's Cathedral. Although this was a religious occasion, Gore's sermon was a Chamberlainite 'eulogy of the civic spirit'. 'Very much', he observed, 'of what is best, noblest, most beautiful, most intellectual in the world's history . . . is bound up with the intense life of cities, with men's love for their city.'[30] Finally, on 7 July 1909, there was the opening of the new university buildings, by King Edward VII and Queen Alexandra. There were seven miles of street decorations and six triumphal arches; there was a civic luncheon, at which the king declared that Birmingham was 'the home of the best traditions in municipal life'; the absent and ailing Chancellor sent a message; and there were fireworks, illuminations and medals.[31]

In Joseph Chamberlain's Birmingham, these buildings, and the ceremonies to which they provided the backdrop, were more important than has generally been recognized. They involved Birmingham people in all sorts of ways, creating a vivid sense of excitement, identity, tradition and inclusion that partly depended on broader national developments, but which also had local ingredients that were peculiarly its own. They simultaneously projected an image of the managing oligarchy, at once confident and benevolent, powerful and socially responsible, politically partisan yet community-minded, which was not without its critics and its opponents, but which *does* seem to have enjoyed an increasingly broad base of support. As the *Birmingham Daily Post* put it on Chamberlain's return from South Africa, it was his 'forceful but *non partisan* personality which is so well known in Birmingham'.[32] It was not so well known elsewhere. In the aftermath of the Home Rule split, Chamberlain was the most hated man in British politics, and Gladstone thought him 'the greatest blackguard I have ever come across'. Two decades later, Tories hostile to Tariff Reform took the same view: according to John Strachey, 'the Chamberlain tradition is that you must give no quarter in politics and that the spoils are to the victors'.[33] But in Birmingham, it generally meant something very different.

However it was regarded, the 'Chamberlain tradition' was much attenuated after 1906. In the aftermath of his seventieth-birthday celebrations,

Joseph suffered a stroke and thereafter played no public part in municipal or national life. Since 1892, he had been joined in the Commons by his elder son. But Austen sat for East Worcestershire, which was not Birmingham, he was fully taken up with events in London, and in the city itself, Unionist zeal and organization flagged. 'I fear', Neville Chamberlain wrote to Bonar Law in 1913, 'that one day there will be a very unpleasant awakening to realities.' In local government, by contrast, the 'Chamberlain tradition' continued into the next generation. Joseph's nephew Norman became a councillor, and in 1911 he wrote an article acclaiming Birmingham as a 'city state' still characterized by strong 'civic feeling', religious commitment to the public good, and 'easy co-operation of classes in matters of common interest'.[34] In that year, Norman was joined by his cousin Neville, who was active in business and philanthropy in the city. 'I am', he noted on his election, 'only following out the traditions in which I have been brought up, and which it is my earnest desire to maintain.' He became Lord Mayor in 1915, bringing 'a new atmosphere of initiative and energy' into local affairs, especially as regards town planning, the city orchestra and the municipal bank. And when he was re-elected Lord Mayor in 1916, William Cadbury observed that 'the municipal career of Joseph Chamberlain would always remain an inspiration to the people of Birmingham. His son had worthily carried on that tradition.'[35]

But this is to anticipate, for in July 1914, Joseph Chamberlain died in London. His family refused a burial in Westminster Abbey, and his body was brought back to Birmingham where he was buried in Key Hill Cemetery, alongside his relatives and other makers of modern Birmingham: Kenricks and Martineaus, Dawson and Dale. Thousands of his fellow-citizens lined the streets to see his final journey, and the local press mourned him as 'Birmingham's greatest son' no less than as a world statesman. Even *The Times* admitted that during his mayoralty, the city 'rose to a level of dignity and autonomous power surpassed by no other civic community in the world'.[36] But all that now seemed in the past. Chamberlain's widow remarried in 1916, left the city and settled in London. Austen inherited Highbury, but with insufficient money to keep it up. He sold the orchids and the contents, disposed of the adjoining lands and eventually gave the house to the corporation. From 1915 to 1918, it was used as a military hospital, and thereafter, it was a home for disabled ex-servicemen and aged women. Another planned commemoration was a large-scale biography to be completed by J. L. Garvin 'in two years'. But nothing came of it for a decade. 'Damn Garvin!' Austen raged in 1931, 'Why can't he get on?'[37]

II

Nevertheless, Joseph Chamberlain's memory and the 'Chamberlain tradition' lived on in his city for another generation, kept alive by his two sons. On his father's death, Austen moved to his constituency of West Birmingham, and in 1914 and 1918 was returned unopposed. His 1922 election posters contained two portraits, of himself and of his father, with the slogan: 'You voted for Joe. Vote for Austen.' So they did. 'I have', Austen told his sister Ida, 'not only inherited but made personal to myself much of the old Chamberlain feeling.' In 1926, he was made a freeman, and spoke with pride of his native city: 'I was born in Birmingham, I was bred in Birmingham, Birmingham is in my blood and in my bones; and wherever I go and whatever I am, I shall remain a Birmingham man.'[38] Meanwhile, his half-brother Neville had been elected MP for the Ladywood division in 1918, as 'the second son of Birmingham's greatest citizen'. Although he spent much of the 1920s in office, he was still actively involved in civic affairs. As Minister of Health, he nudged the corporation towards an innovative project for a new hospital centre, next to the university, combining treatment and teaching. In 1925, he attended the unveiling of a bust of his father to celebrate the municipal jubilee of the gas department. He spoke, 'both as a citizen and a son', of the importance of civic endeavour, and concluded that 'the relations between the city and the various members of my family are unique'.[39]

Both Austen and Neville continued to represent Birmingham until their deaths, carrying on the 'Chamberlain tradition' at the national, parliamentary level. But they did not enjoy the local rapport that their father had had. 'There was not really much of Birmingham about [Austen],' Harold Macmillan recalled; 'sometimes he almost seemed a *grand seigneur*'. He had never been in business or in local government in the city, he spent his time in Sussex or London, and preferred the Commons or international diplomacy. He was also stiff and aloof, a notoriously inattentive constituency MP, and at the 1929 election only scraped in by forty-three votes.[40] Despite his stronger local roots and greater attentiveness, Neville was little better. His 'manner freezes people', Austen wrote in 1925, in words equally applicable to himself. 'His workers think he does not appreciate what they do for him. Everybody respects him and he makes no friends.' For all his conscientiousness, Neville was ill at ease in Ladywood, the most working-class constituency in the city. His majority fell at the elections of 1922 and 1923, and in 1924, Oswald Mosley came within seventy-seven votes of capturing the seat. In 1929, which was just in time, Neville removed himself to safe, solid and suburban Edgbaston.[41]

It was developments such as these which caused Lord Beaverbrook to opine that 'in Birmingham itself, the Chamberlain dominion is worn out'. This was an exaggeration, but there was some truth in it. For it was not just that Austen and Neville failed to catch the imagination of Birmingham's citizens in the way their father had done: it was also that the clan itself was much depleted in these years. Joseph's brothers were all dead; two members of the next generation, John Chamberlain and Norman Chamberlain, were killed on active service during the war; and another cousin, Arthur junior, retired from business in Birmingham to become a Devon country gentleman. Of Joseph's three surviving daughters, Hilda and Ida (who were Neville's sisters) moved away to Hampshire when Highbury was closed as the family home, and Beatrice (Austen's sister) died in the influenza epidemic of 1918–19. This was a serious diminution of Birmingham-based talent and energy, and Norman's death was a particularly severe blow. Had he lived, he would almost certainly have been an inter-war Lord Mayor, and he would probably have joined Austen and Neville in national politics. But his death meant there was no Chamberlain left to carry on the family tradition in local government during the inter-war years.[42]

At the same time, the city itself was becoming a different place. The enlargement of Birmingham's boundaries significantly altered its character: it was diminishingly a 'great village' with a strong sense of community and increasingly a great metropolis, with more segregated housing, and a much expanded administration. Its constituency politics changed, too: in the aftermath of the fourth Reform Act, the number of Birmingham MPs was increased from seven to twelve, and more seats to fight meant a larger organization to fund and facilitate the fighting. Birmingham's economy was also evolving, as the small workshops were gradually replaced by larger factories and new industries such as electrical engineering, aluminium and motor cars, often owned by companies which were nationally rather than locally based. One result was that conditions of work improved, and the city missed the worst unemployment of the inter-war depression.[43] Another was the growth in the strength and success of the Labour Party. During and after the First World War, its organization was much strengthened, and in the elections of 1924 and 1929 Labour scored its first victories, breaching the hitherto impregnable bastion of Chamberlainite Unionism. In 1924, Labour captured its first seat, and in 1929, it won six of the twelve constituencies, with its best results in the country.[44]

Taken together, these changes in the Chamberlain clan and developments in the city of Birmingham significantly altered the tone and the tempo of municipal life, which became less theatrical and more prosaic. The brief flowering of the creative arts in the service of the civic gospel during the late nineteenth century spawned no inter-war successor, the Venetian idiom of a latter-day city state vanished from public speech and public buildings, and the civic spectaculars built around the Chamberlain family virtually disappeared.[45] Most local effort after 1918 was centred on the monuments and rituals associated with Remembrance Day, and also on royal visits, which were themselves often associated with the city's attempts to commemorate the First World War. The financing and construction of Birmingham's war memorial were very protracted, with debates over what it ought to be, where it ought to be, how much it should cost and how it should be paid for. Eventually, the foundation stone of the Hall of Memory was laid by the Prince of Wales in 1923, and it was opened by Prince Arthur of Connaught two years later. But while such occasions brought the citizenry together, there was nothing specially Chamberlainite about them, and indeed nothing about them that was unique to Birmingham.[46]

Such municipal effort as there was during the 1920s centred on planning a new civic centre, complete with City Hall, Mansion House, Municipal Offices, a Natural History Museum and a Public Library, with the Hall of Memory as the focal point. As Birmingham grew, there was a need for more office accommodation for local government, and also for a public space larger than Chamberlain Square and Victoria Square. The purchase of land, along Broad Street and to the north-west of the old city centre, was begun in 1922.[47] A competition was announced in October 1926, and the winning entry was by Maximilian Romanoff of Paris, whose extravagant plan took little heed of existing buildings and thoroughfares. Unlike John Henry Chamberlain in an earlier generation, Romanoff had 'no personal knowledge of Birmingham, and no sort of personal regard for its traditions, its general character or its resources', and his scheme was 'a clean break with the past' – a piece of grandiose monumentality which had more in common with Hitler's Berlin, Mussolini's Rome or Roosevelt's Washington than with the Birmingham of Joseph or of John Henry Chamberlain. In the end, the scheme was declared to be too expensive and was never implemented.[48]

For all the continuation by Austen and Neville of the 'Chamberlain tradition', it is clear the 1920s represented a falling away from the intensity and involvement of the pre-war era. But there was something of a revival during the 1930s. The Labour challenge was much weakened – partly because of the failure of the 1929 administration, and also because of the Party split following the formation of the National Government. In the general elections of 1931 and 1935, the Birmingham Unionists swept the board, recapturing the seats they had lost in 1929, and both Austen and Neville were safely returned – Austen with an increased majority in Birmingham West, and Neville more comfortably in Edgbaston than he had ever been in Ladywood.[49] When campaigning in 1935, Austen met people who had borne torches in the processions in 1903 and cherished his father's memory. As a visiting journalist explained: 'Joe Chamberlain's spirit is not dead. Indeed, it is still a potent political force . . . Labour canvassers are still told, "My father voted for Joe Chamberlain and what was good enough for him is good enough for me." It is as if Joe were still alive.'[50]

At the same time, the individual reputations of the Chamberlains also revived, beginning with Joseph's. Between 1932 and 1934, J. L. Garvin belatedly produced the first three volumes of his much-delayed official life, covering its most successful period up to 1900. He told the story of the Birmingham mayoralty and the civic renaissance, the struggle with Gladstone over Home Rule, and the early years at the Colonial Office, culminating in the Boer War.[51] Then, in 1936, came an unprecedented opportunity for civic homage: the centenary of Joseph Chamberlain's birth. In London, there was a rally at the Albert Hall, which dwelt on the continuing relevance of his imperial vision. But in Birmingham, the celebrations were more domestic. There was a special meeting of the City Council in the Town Hall; the vice-chancellor of the university delivered an oration; the council passed a resolution recording its appreciation of Chamberlain's 'distinguished and valuable services' to the city; Neville replied that his father had set local government 'on a new pedestal of dignity and honour'; wreaths were laid on the Chamberlain Memorial and on his grave; and there was a civic reception for those who had 'grown up under his shadow'.[52]

During the same decade, Austen's standing also improved somewhat. After 1929, he was out of office, and spent more time in his constituency. From sheer financial necessity, he also turned to writing. His first effort, *Down the Years*, consisted of 'random recollections of men and events', and it was rightly remarked that his father was 'present in every line of the book'. The second, *Politics from Inside*, was even more filial in content, consisting of the letters Austen had written to his stepmother to keep his father informed during his period of incapacity from 1906 to 1914. Both books (published 1935 and 1936) tied him more closely to Joseph – and thus to Birmingham – than ever before.[53] Within a year, Austen was dead. 'National figure as he was,' opined the *Post*, 'he never ceased to be a man of Birmingham.' This was pious exaggeration, as evidenced by the fact that Austen's remains were buried in London rather than beside his father in his home town. But the Lord Mayor acclaimed him for 'the way in which, through the whole of his life, he identified himself with his native city', and at the memorial service in the cathedral, he was eulogized as 'a Birmingham man, carrying on the great Birmingham tradition'.[54]

Meanwhile Austen's younger brother was 'still with us and carrying on the great Birmingham and Chamberlain tradition'. On the formation of the National Government, he had become Chancellor of the Exchequer, and in 1932 introduced a scheme of protection which he described as the fulfilment of the Tariff Reform programme which his father had conceived but failed to carry, and which he laid before the Commons 'in the presence of one and by the lips of the other of the two immediate successors to his name and blood'. 'How proud father would have been of Neville', Austen had written, 'and how it would have moved him that Neville should complete his work.'[55] As a result, Neville was given the freedom of Birmingham, following his father and his brother, and in May 1937, scarcely ten weeks after Austen's death, he duly became Prime Minister. Soon after, he was given a civic banquet, and in his speech, he recalled the great reception given to his father on *his* seventieth birthday, spoke of his work on Birmingham city council, and reiterated his pride in the fact that 'I was born and bred in Birmingham'. 'It reminded me of the old days', he noted, 'when the people used to run after Father's carriage.'[56]

By agreeable coincidence, this meant Neville Chamberlain was Prime Minister when Birmingham marked the centenary of incorporation in 1938. Although no one could have known it, these celebrations were the last local hurrah of the 'Chamberlain tradition', politically, architecturally and ceremonially. In 1935, a second competition for a Civic Centre had been won by Cecil Howitt of Nottingham, with a design of orthodox, neo-Georgian monumentality, 'reminiscent of the Cunard offices in New York'. The foundation stone was laid in the centenary year, and the Lord Mayor described it as the most important occasion 'since Joseph Chamberlain laid the stone of the present Council House'.[57] The year 1938 also witnessed the completion of the new Birmingham Hospital Centre in Edgbaston, located in Neville Chamberlain's constituency, and completed in considerable part thanks to his efforts. The foundation stone had been laid by the Prince of Wales in 1934, and the buildings were opened by the royal visitors in incorporation year. They were described as 'a synthesis of the accumulated civic consciousness of a hundred years, handed over with both hands by the Birmingham of today to the Birmingham of tomorrow'. But as with the Civic Centre, there was nothing in their style or ornamentation which embodied or articulated this view.[58]

The visit of the king and queen to open the new Hospital Centre was the climax of the centenary celebrations themselves. These were staged on a scale which surpassed the royal Jubilees of 1887 and 1897, and even those of John Bright and Joseph Chamberlain. Once again, there were street decorations, floodlighting and fireworks. But there were also broadcasts, souvenir programmes and a newly commissioned history of the town, in all of which pride of place went to Joseph Chamberlain.[59] The main event was a pageant of Birmingham, organized by Gwen Lally, who had stage-managed previous spectaculars at Tewkesbury, Coventry and Warwick. Planned and rehearsed over a period of three months, and involving six thousand performers drawn from all parts of the city, it told the story of Birmingham from the dinosaur to modern times. On 14 July, Neville Chamberlain accompanied the royal visitors to a special performance, and watched the panorama of the city's history unfold, in a succession of tableaux, the last one devoted to the greatest figures from Birmingham's past, in which special homage was paid to his own father. That evening, at the centenary civic banquet, Neville proposed the health of the City of Birmingham.[60]

Thereafter, the Prime Minister's reputation, and that of the 'Chamberlain tradition', were inexorably tied to national and international events unfolding in countries far away from Birmingham. When Neville returned from Munich later in 1938, bearing 'peace with honour', the local press celebrated its 'own son's triumph in the role of peacemaker', and there were rumours that, like Austen, Neville would be awarded the Nobel Peace Prize. The Lord Mayor sent a telegram, 'Birmingham is especially proud today', and opened a Thanksgiving Fund in appreciation of the Prime Minister's efforts.[61] Commemorative souvenirs were issued, including a plate depicting the three Chamberlains as 'Britain's most famous political family', and which bore this inscription: 'In appreciation of Mr Neville Chamberlain securing peace for Europe during the crisis of September 1938.' And the whole dynasty was memorialized by Sir Charles Petrie in a book entitled *The Chamberlain Tradition*, which showed 'what Great Britain and the British Empire owe to the Chamberlain family', and drew 'attention to those qualities which the father and two sons possessed in common': 'courage and optimism, foresight and vigour'.[62]

But during the next eighteen months, Neville Chamberlain lost his reputation and his job, and there was growing opposition to his foreign policy, even among some local Unionists. Eventually, it was his fellow Birmingham MP, Leopold Amery, who was a great admirer of Joseph Chamberlain, and whose son Julian eventually completed Garvin's biography, who quoted the terrible words of Oliver Cromwell in the parliamentary debate which brought Neville down in May 1940. But elsewhere, Birmingham support continued strong to the end. In January 1939, he addressed the Jewellers' Association, and described the 'demonstration of loyalty and affection' as 'only a continuation of the favours you have always accorded to members of my family'.[63] In March, on the eve of his seventieth birthday, he made what turned out to be his last speech in the Town Hall, and throughout the defeats and disappointments of his final months the *Birmingham Post* remained loyal. On his death in November 1940, the Lord Mayor paid tribute to one of the city's 'most distinguished sons', and at the memorial service, Bishop Barnes eulogized him as 'Birmingham's most renowned citizen'. But like his brother, and unlike his father, Neville did not return to his home city: instead, he was buried in Westminster Abbey.[64]

III

One of the most remarkable aspects of the 'Chamberlain tradition' is the abruptness and completeness with which it disappeared. For the death of Neville Chamberlain was 'the end of an era, the end of eight decades in which the Chamberlains and their friends had guided Birmingham through an age of unprecedented growth, prosperity, and good government'.[65] Why was this? As the foregoing account makes plain, part of the answer was undoubtedly the fact that their grip on the city and the region was never as strong or as invincible as the ardent (or critical) rhetoric of the 'Chamberlain tradition' suggested, and that for most of the time, they had to work hard to retain their power. During the late 1860s and early 1870s, the late 1890s and early 1900s, and again in the 1930s, their position was certainly secure. But in between, they were much more vulnerable: Joseph during the crisis over Home Rule, both Austen and Neville in the aftermath of the First World War, and Neville alone once the Second World War had broken out. From this perspective, the most extraordinary aspect of the 'Chamberlain tradition' is not that it collapsed so suddenly, but rather that it had survived for as long and as successfully as it had.[66]

For the very idea of a 'Chamberlain tradition' presumed a greater degree of social harmony than generally existed in Birmingham, and also that the city carried a greater weight in the counsels of the nation than it actually did. With this uncertain base and background, it was scarcely surprising that the whole clan suffered by association from the lasting damage done to Neville's reputation by the events of 1939 and 1940, and this may help explain why, at the personal level, the Chamberlain line simply gave out.

Neither Austen's son, Lawrence, nor Neville's son, Frank, showed any inclination to carry on the family involvement in local or national politics. As a result, the general election of 1945 was the first since 1874 when there was no Chamberlain to solicit the votes of Birmingham's electorate. But that election was a turning point in other ways too: during the war, there was growing enthusiasm for Labour, and its organization had strengthened while the Unionists had stagnated. There was a 23 per cent swing to Labour, higher than in any other city in Britain, and Labour won ten of the thirteen seats. Although the Tories were later to win back some constituencies, 1945 meant the end of the old-style, locally based Unionism of the Chamberlain era.[67]

Here was the 'unpleasant awakening to realities' which Neville Chamberlain had feared over thirty years before.[68] And what was true of constituency politics was also true in local government. The surviving members of the extended Chamberlain clan played their part in Birmingham's social and philanthropic life for another generation, but in the Council House, their dominion passed away, as municipal politics became increasingly partisan confrontations between Labour and the Tories, which mimicked and reflected national trends rather than local allegiances. At the same time, the creation of a 'new' Birmingham was a deliberate rejection of the Victorian and Venetian pretensions of John Henry Chamberlain and his ilk. Much of his city centre, including parts of Chamberlain Square itself, was torn down and replaced by hideous concrete blocks, devoid of local articulation, 'owing nothing to historical precedent', and lacking any significant civic meaning. Birmingham's buildings, like its politics, were becoming indistinct from those of any large metropolitan area, and so were its much-attenuated civic ceremonials. The centenary of Joseph Chamberlain's mayoralty was largely ignored, and the hundred and fiftieth anniversary of his birth was barely noticed.[69] The 'Chamberlain tradition' has passed into history.

6

Piety: Josiah Wedgwood and the History of Parliament[1]

For Colonel Josiah Wedgwood, 1930 was his Staffordshire *annus mirabilis* in more ways than one. Since 1906, he had been Member of Parliament for Newcastle under Lyme, first as a Liberal, but more recently for Labour. As his biographer was later to observe, he was exceptionally attentive to constituency affairs, and 'never ceased to be at heart a Staffordshire man, a true son of the pot-bank, steeped in local tradition, sympathetic to local loyalties, the first to speak and the best informed on the conditions and interests of the workers in the Potteries, and a determined advocate of the rights and dignity of the ancient borough of Newcastle under Lyme.'[2] So indeed he was. The rapid inter-war growth of the federated city of Stoke-on-Trent led to a scheme for its further extension which involved the annexation of Newcastle. But its inhabitants were vehemently opposed to the loss of their identity and independence, and the result was a long battle, in the press, in Parliament, and for public opinion. In Newcastle and in London, the pre-eminent campaigner for the town's continued autonomy was Josiah Wedgwood, and when the annexation proposal was defeated in the Lords in the spring of 1930, he was given the two highest honours the town could bestow, in appreciation of his steadfast loyalty, fighting spirit and sterling services. He was made an honorary freeman, and from 1930 to 1932 he served as mayor.[3]

But this was not the only way in which Wedgwood achieved a kind of local apotheosis at this time. For 1930 was also the two hundredth anniversary of the birth of the first and most famous Josiah Wedgwood, who was the Colonel's great-great-grandfather, which meant that North Staffordshire was *en fête* for much of the year, with pageants, lectures, exhibitions, receptions and dinners.[4] As part of these celebrations, the latest Josiah composed, in the manner of Plutarch, an imaginary dialogue between himself and his most illustrious forebear. They discussed the American War of Independence, developments in the pottery industry, nineteenth-century family news and the local and national political scene. In the course of their conversations, the younger Josiah explained that, although he had represented Newcastle for twenty-four years, it was not at the behest of the Leveson Gowers (in whose control the constituency had been in old Josiah's day), but because 'forty thousand electors sent me to Westminster'. Their exchange concluded with these words:

'What are your politics?'
'Yours, sir! Hatred of cruelty, injustice and snobbery, and an undying love of freedom.'
Then I heard a voice say: 'Carry on,' and the Prince of Potters vanished.[5]

Together, these two episodes tell us much about the character and career of the younger Josiah Wedgwood, and they hint at a great deal more. They suggest that he was animated by strong feelings of family pride and local attachment, which were informed by a powerful, sentimental and highly personal sense of the past. They suggest that he felt a deep reverence for democracy, for free speech, for the electoral process and for Parliament. They suggest that he was fascinated by politicians and by politics, that he held views which were fiercely independent and (sometimes) infuriatingly idiosyncratic, and that he was better and happier in opposition than in government. And they suggest that he was a passionate believer in individual liberty, who was vehemently hostile to injustice, oppression or official interference, whether by the national government or by a local authority. That Colonel Wedgwood was all of these things is well attested in the pages of his autobiography, published in 1940, three years before his death, and in the affectionate memoir produced by his niece, C. V. Wedgwood in 1951. But how do his character and career look in the longer perspective afforded by the passing of another half-century? And how do they help us understand the genesis and early years of a well-intentioned but initially troubled enterprise, which has nevertheless survived to become his most enduring monument, the history of Parliament?

I

'One can judge fairly of no man', Josiah Wedgwood once observed, 'without seeing his contemporaries and circumstances,' and this dictum may indeed be applied to him. But it has to be applied with caution and care. He was born in 1872, which means he belonged to the late-Victorian generation of high imperialism which culminated in the Boer War. Appropriately enough, he hankered after a military career, but he could not pass the necessary medical tests. Instead, he trained at Greenwich to be a naval architect and engineer, and worked in the Admiralty's Portsmouth dockyards and at Armstrong's Elswick shipyards. In 1899, he volunteered for service in the Boer War, and he stayed on in South Africa until 1904 as a member of Lord Milner's Kindergarten, where he was Resident Magistrate for the District of Ermelo in the Transvaal. In the First World War, he volunteered again, and he took part in the Gallipoli expedition (in which he was wounded, and awarded the DSO), and he later served under General Smuts in East Africa.[6] Hence the military title by which he was known, though his family and friends always called him 'Jos' or 'Josh'. Such a career suggests he was devoted to war and the military, and to empire and authority, and that his patriotism was of a blimpishly unquestioning brand. But while this was true of many members of the upper and upper middle classes of Wedgwood's generation, such a characterization of him would be completely wrong.

For he was at least as much the product of his dynasty as a child of his time. He had been born at Barlaston, and although he was not himself a potter, his father, his elder brother and his younger son were successively in charge of the family business, and he felt a deep sense of loyalty to its history, its products and its workmen. Etruria, he opined, was not so much a firm as an institution, where the management style was paternalistic, and industrial disputes were virtually unknown.[7] All Wedgwoods, he believed, were reserved, unostentatious puritans, but they spoke their minds plainly and fearlessly, formed their own opinions about others, and 'refused to accept antiquated shibboleths simply because other people accept them'. The greatest Josiah had been a friend of Priestley and Franklin and Clarkson, had welcomed freedom for the American colonies, and had been a determined opponent of slavery. One of his descendants supported the Great Reform Act because he 'thought it was right', and had invited Kossuth and Garibaldi to Barlaston. They were 'sure of their position and themselves', were 'markedly independent and free in thought', and emphatically on the side of tolerance, liberty and progress. Wedgwood was justifiably proud of his forebears, believed his relatives mattered more than any friends, and his great aim was to make his name more famous than it already was. 'Family pride,' he was later to remark, 'properly applied, provides one with backbone.'[8]

But the Wedgwoods were not only a distinguished dynasty: they also formed part of that broader, interlocking intellectual aristocracy which was so marked (and so influential) a feature of British life from the 1830s onwards. In earlier generations, several Wedgwoods had married into the

Darwin family, which also connected them to the Sidgwicks, the Keyneses and the Gosses; and Josiah's mother was the daughter of James Meadows Rendel, one of the most famous Victorian engineers.[9] His own parents took the life of the mind very seriously, and although Josiah did not attend university, he was exceptionally well educated. He read a great deal of history, from the *Iliad* to Macaulay and Motley; he learned about places and dates, maps and trains, soldiers and armies; and he won the Gold Medal for History at Clifton School. He was also an accomplished linguist, and was one of the last MPs who regularly used Latin quotations in the House of Commons. And through his younger brother Ralph, a Cambridge under-graduate, he came into close contact with the Trevelyans: with Sir George Otto, whose blend of scholarship and statesmanship he much admired; with his eldest son, Charles, a fellow Liberal MP, who also crossed the floor to Labour; and with Charles's younger brother George, whose 'literary and liberal' style of history greatly appealed to him.[10]

Wedgwood's scholarly interests showed themselves early, and he became a lifelong devotee of genealogical research and local history, set in a broadly Whiggish, progressive, dissenting and patriotic framework. 'Provide a man with a pedigree', he once remarked, 'and he will never remain your enemy.' 'Knowledge of this sort of ancestry', he observed on another occasion, 'gives a personal interest to history.' He had also been encouraged in these interests by a chance remark of Gladstone (he was then eighty-one) about the impor-tance of family and tradition.[11] But the most direct and immediate influence on him was the Hon. George Wrottesley, a scion of one of the county's grandest families (his brother was Lord-Lieutenant), who was described by J. H. Round as the Nestor of genealogists. After his retirement from the army in 1881, Wrottesley devoted himself to Staffordshire scholarship, and it was to further this activity that he became the driving force behind the establishment of the William Salt Archaeological Society. He was the Society's Secretary until his death in 1909, and a regular contributor to its annual publications, of which he was the de facto editor. Much of his work was concerned with publishing Staffordshire material, which he extracted from the plea rolls and the feet of fines in the Public Record Office, and he also produced local family histories of the Giffards, the Okeovers, the Bagots and his own.[12]

Josiah Wedgwood joined the William Salt Society soon after his return from South Africa. He was on close terms with Wrottesley, whose influence can be detected in his early publications: histories of the Audley and Har-court families, and a record of heraldry in Staffordshire. He was Wrottesley's chosen successor as Secretary of the Society, he contributed the entry on him to the *Dictionary of National Biography*, and his first substantial book was dedicated to him.[13] It was a genealogy of the Wedgwood dynasty, which traced the family back to medieval times, and sought to revive 'in particular persons the life of a class and of a locality'. He later revised and extended these researches into a comprehensive history of the Wedgwoods across the centuries and around the world. In the course of these books, he took issue with those biographers who had dared to criticize the great Josiah, and he stressed 'the persistence among his descendants of the qualities he possessed'. Between these two works of family piety, Wedgwood produced a general history of the Potteries, describing the evolution of the industry from home to factory production, and exploring the rise of machinery, steam power and mass production. Naturally, the great Josiah was once again the hero of the story – an innovator and entrepreneur of genius – but the book also paid attention to the many other families and firms in the industry, like Ridgway, Minton, Doulton, Copeland and Spode.[14]

This history was affectionately dedicated 'to my constituents who do the work'. On his return from Africa, Wedgwood had taken up residence at Barlaston Hall, and since he did not need to earn his living he had thrown himself into local affairs. By this time, most of his family had abandoned the earlier dissenting radicalism that had been the Wedgwoods' hallmark, and had moved across to the Conservatives. But Josiah remained true to the creed of his forebears, and in 1906, he was elected Liberal MP for Newcastle under Lyme. His parliamentary friends such as C. P. Trevelyan, Charles Buxton, H. A. L. Fisher and Walter Runciman tended to be on the radical wing of the party (he was also close to Winston Churchill, at whose instigation he was elected a member of the Other Club) and along with Trevelyan and Buxton, Wedgwood left the Liberals for Labour in 1919.[15] Under this new party label, he continued to represent Newcastle for another twenty-three years (and he was also a Staffordshire county councillor from 1910 to 1919). Considering that the majority of the Wedgwood family was against him, that he endured much adverse publicity immediately after the First World War because of his controversial divorce, and that he changed his party affiliation, the fact that he retained his seat for so long was a remarkable tribute both to his unrivalled local appeal, and to the fidelity of the voters. Indeed, after his great labours of 1930, he was returned unopposed in the 1931 election, and again in 1935.[16]

It was this combination of family pride, local connection and parliamentary activity which encouraged Wedgwood to undertake his most sustained and influential piece of research: his *Staffordshire Parliamentary History from the Earliest Times to the Present Day*, which he began shortly after his election to the Commons, and which was published in four instalments covering the years 1213–1603, 1603–1715, 1715–1832, and 1780 to 1841, by the William Salt Society between 1917 and 1933.[17] The survey was intended as a monument to local identity: it was 'the political history of Staffordshire and a gazetteer of its leading citizens'. Among them, were many families such as the Harcourts, the Sneyds and the Leveson Gowers, who were still active in county affairs; and some of his biographical entries concerned his own Wedgwood forebears, though he noted with pride that his 'own great grandfather was too radical for an eighteenth-century parliament'. Drawing on a wide variety of published and unpublished sources, and helped by local antiquarians, he described the changing structure of parliamentary representation, provided histories of constituencies and elections, and produced biographies of MPs. For Wedgwood, this was a prodigious labour of love: he once claimed that he had spent as many hours in the Public Record Office as in the House of Commons.[18]

These antiquarian and genealogical findings were set in a broader interpretational framework, for each section of the Staffordshire parliamentary history was prefaced by a general introduction, outlining national developments, which Wedgwood believed helped explain changes in the pattern and personnel of parliamentary representation. As befitted someone who had grown up with the late nineteenth- and early twentieth-century textbook surveys of English history, he saw these as a pageant of almost pre-ordained sequences: the twelfth century was the era of the 'feudal monarchy', when the magnates determined who should go to Westminster as knights of the shire. Then came 'the rise of parliament', when recognizable county families first made their appearance. This in turn led to the Tudor era of 'autocracy', and in Parliament, from 1553, 'the first clear indication of party'.[19] This provoked the Stuart period of 'revolution', during which 'the Whig and Tory parties began', and 'a seat in the House' became 'the most prized of possessions'. This was followed by 'the oligarchy', which governed from 1715 to 1832, during which time the Leveson Gowers and the Ansons established themselves as the foremost parliamentary powers in the county.[20]

Wedgwood's devotion to his family, his locality and his county was only equalled by his devotion to Parliament, where he was an exceptionally – some said infuriatingly – active MP. In 1919, his busiest year, he asked 402 questions and made speeches running to 230 columns of Hansard. Because he was comfortable, confident and enjoyed a secure majority, he was renowned (or notorious) for the independence of his opinions. He did not find the pre-war Liberals radical enough, and he was disappointed that they did not embrace the single-tax doctrines of Henry George, with which he became preoccupied – some said obsessed.[21] He then fell out with the Lloyd George Coalition because he thought its taxation policies too regressive, and he repudiated the 'coupon' in 1918. And although he changed to Labour, and was vice-chairman of the party from 1921 to 1924, he did not like Ramsay MacDonald, and his brief period of office, as Chancellor of the Duchy of Lancaster in 1924, was not a success. He railed against what he saw as increasingly rigid party discipline, he was a bad team player – and he was proud of it. He relished being a one-man opposition and on the side of the underdog: like his forebears, he was 'markedly independent and free in thought'. But while this won him friends in all parts of the House, it meant he never realized his full potential, and any hopes he might have had of playing a creative and constructive part in government were dashed after 1924.[22]

But for Wedgwood, personal freedom was more important than government office, and freedom meant having a parliament where independent voices could be heard and where contrary opinions could be expressed. Hence his championing of the liberties of imperial subjects – Home Rule in Ireland, native land rights in Africa, a national settlement for Jews in Palestine, independence for India – and his belief that the Empire should be a free association of democratic peoples.[23] Hence, too his growing anxieties about the erosion of freedom across Europe in the inter-war period. President Wilson and the League of Nations had been a false dawn, and he was as much repelled by communism as by fascism. He hated the destruction of liberties in Soviet Russia. He disliked the postwar tyrannies established in Hungary and Bulgaria, opposed Mussolini almost from the beginning, and was a fierce critic of Franco's Spain. He was also one of the earliest MPs to notice the menace presented to peace and freedom by Hitler and, throughout the 1930s, he worked hard to help refugees from nazism and was a tireless campaigner against appeasement. As he saw it, the seventeenth century had witnessed a European reaction against religious liberty in the form of the Catholic Counter-Reformation. Now the twentieth century was witnessing another European reaction against political liberty in the form of communist and fascist totalitarianism. It was a reaction Wedgwood was determined to resist.[24]

These national and international concerns, stressing freedom and liberty at home, abroad and in the Empire, were partly the consequence of his own secure independence and fierce family pride. But they also arose out of, and helped inform, his study of Staffordshire MPs. For Wedgwood, the outstanding characteristic of Parliament was that it connected locality and nation, 'the records of county with national history'. As he saw it, the history of Parliament – as revealed through the biographies of the men who were sent there, a knowledge of their constituencies, and a study of the way in which the Commons evolved and functioned – was synonymous with all that was best in the history of the nation. 'The history of England,' he observed at the outset of his Staffordshire survey, 'or the part of it of which we are most proud, is the history of how we came to govern ourselves, and taught others to do the same.'[25] The British Parliament was unique – in the unbroken continuity of its history; in the way in which it had always been a national forum; in the way in which the legislature, the executive and the judiciary were all represented there; and in its gradually unfolding story of liberty, freedom and democracy. From this history, Wedgwood drew conclusions which inspired his own oppositional preferences: Parliament's purpose was primarily to check the executive, secondarily to raise money and only thirdly to legislate.[26]

As a long-serving MP, Wedgwood loved Westminster – what it had been, what it was and what it stood for – as much as he loved Etruria and Barlaston. Parliament was the place where he could be simultaneously patriot and dissenter, conformist and rebel, critic and clubman, local representative and national personality. It was where his generosity, his integrity and his wit were much admired, and where his lack of judgement, his wild knight-errantry and his incorrigible bloody-mindedness were gently tolerated. All this was spelt out in the opening pages of his Staffordshire history, in words he was to repeat, with modifications and embellishments, in later publications:

To me, personally, Parliament is everything; the members are the staunchest friends man ever had; the life combines the mental gymnastics of college with the fresh wind of the outer world; only the recesses are intervals of stagnation. There is no other Parliament like the English. For the ordinary man, elected to any senate, from Persia to Peru, there may be a certain satisfaction in being elected . . . But the man who steps into the English Parliament takes his place in a pageant that has ever been filing by since the birth of English history . . . York or Lancaster, Protestant or Catholic, Court or Country, Roundhead or Cavalier, Whig or Tory, Liberal or Conservative, Labour or Unionist, they all fit into that long pageant that no other country in the world can show. And they one and all pass on the same inextinguishable torch – burning brightly or flickering – to the next man in the race, while freedom and experience ever grow. These men who have gone by, who have had the glimmer of the torch on them for a little time, are those whose memories I want to rescue, and in so doing reincarnate a small section of the Parliaments which made us.[27]

This was, no doubt, a rose-tinted and excessively Whig view of Parliament and of parliamentary history. But although the late 1920s and early 1930s were the unheroic age of MacDonald and Baldwin, of 'Safety First' and National Governments, in which Parliament was thought by some to be declining in effectiveness and esteem, there *was* something to be said for Wedgwood's alternative and more positive view. He was not alone in being moved by the patriotism shown by many of his parliamentary colleagues between 1914 and 1918, especially those who were killed in action, and he cherished the ambition of writing 'a true history of what MPs did in the war'.[28] As the centenary approached of the passing of the Great Reform Act, this seemed an appropriate opportunity to celebrate Britain's unique, hundred-year-long journey from aristocratic oligarchy to stable and success-ful democracy, a journey which had just been completed by the granting of the 'flapper' vote in 1928. As the traditional governing families withdrew from active involvement in the Commons and the Cabinet, it was important to remind MPs of different social backgrounds of the magnificent heritage to which they were the heirs, occupationally and electorally, even if no longer genealogically and dynastically. And as democracy, liberty and free-dom were being subverted and snuffed out across so much of continental Europe, it was no less important to proclaim the British constitution as 'a stronghold of Parliamentary democracy in a world of authoritarianism'.[29]

It was in these circumstances, by turns dispiriting and encouraging, anxi-ous and inspiring, that Wedgwood conceived his most ambitious historical project, part scholarly enquiry, part institutional handbook, part contem-porary celebration. He may also have been encouraged in this endeavour by the reluctant recognition that there was now no further prospect of government office, and that if he *was* to adorn and enhance his family name, it would have to be by other means. It was with these mixed motives that he set down, in the closing pages of his Staffordshire parliamentary history, a preliminary sketch of the much larger scheme that was developing in his mind:

My aim has been, partly to link the county with the country history, but far more to pioneer out a new and living view of all the parliaments that have made and registered England through seven centuries. Staffordshire was a sample of what could be done ... Having taken a vertical section through the ages, I am now engaged on a horizontal section through the whole country, taking the dark, blank age, 1439 to 1509. When the two sections are finished, we may sometime get an adequate history of the men and methods which framed democracy and left us free.[30]

In these characteristically uplifting words, Wedgwood announced the inception of the most challenging and controversial piece of scholarship he would ever undertake: the history of Parliament.

II

Wedgwood's idea for such a scheme naturally grew out of his local, familial and genealogical researches, and was informed and animated by his powerful passion for democracy and freedom.[31] But while these were a very personal amalgam of interests, they were also to some extent those of his class and generation. During the last quarter of the nineteenth century, when he was growing up, the practice of amassing information about British individuals, group experiences and institutions, and of publishing it in as many volumes as possible, had been almost epidemic. Monumental works of reference were initiated and produced on the peerage, archbishops of Canterbury, judges and generals, Catholics and Huguenots, and Oxford alumni, to say nothing of the *Dictionary of National Biography*. Between 1876 and 1891, at Parliament's behest, there was published, extended, revised and corrected the 'Return of Members', which sought to set out the names of Westminster MPs from medieval times to 1885, of members of the Irish House of Commons to 1800, and of elected members of the Scottish parliament to 1707.[32] And during the same period, local constituency histories were produced on Cumberland and Westmorland, Lancashire and Cornwall, the English Northern Counties, and Scotland and Wales. Such works not only provided the model and inspiration for Wedgwood's Staffordshire researches: they also indicated what could be done – and what needed to be done – on a broader, national scale.[33]

Moreover, although the years from 1924 to 1939 were indeed those of 'Safety First' and National Governments, they were also a time when Whiggish beliefs in liberty and freedom, Parliament and progress, were reasserted and celebrated anew. In addition to the centenary of the Great Reform Act in 1932, there was the 250th anniversary of the Glorious Revolution in 1938; and between them, in 1935, was the Silver Jubilee of George V, when the king spoke of the slow evolution of Parliament as the embodiment of liberty and freedom. This was also the period when G. M. Trevelyan produced his *History of England* (1926), his *England Under Queen Anne* (1930–34) and his study of *The English Revolution, 1688–89* (1938); and when Winston Churchill completed his pietistic and grandiloquent biography of his great ancestor, the first Duke of Marlborough (1934–8).[34]

Appropriately enough, Wedgwood had been friends with both Trevelyan and Churchill since the 1900s, when they had all been new Liberals together. By the 1930s, Trevelyan was a Baldwinite Tory and Churchill seemed a marginalized reactionary. But although their party political views had evolved along different lines, they all remained Whigs in their essential belief in 'the panorama of English history', and they were all busy proclaiming such values in the decade before Hitler invaded Poland.[35]

Wedgwood's contribution to this efflorescence of inter-war Whig history was to launch his national project to compile 'lists of all Members of Parliament, for all counties, for all Parliaments', and to provide full biographical details of the 75,000 people this would include. In this form, as he later admitted, the scheme was 'a gigantic genealogy, quite as much as the apotheosis of parliament'. In May 1928, he sent a letter to The Times, outlining the scheme, and he spent the rest of the year mobilizing support among the press, MPs and peers.[36] The Prime Minister, Stanley Baldwin, was sympathetic, and in March 1929 a committee was appointed 'to report on the materials available for a record of the personnel and politics of past Members of the House of Commons from 1264 to 1832, and on the cost and desirability of publication'.[37] Wedgwood himself was made chairman, and he effectively chose his colleagues, comprising equal numbers of MPs and professional historians. Among the former were John Buchan (the novelist and biographer), the Hon. J. J. Astor (whose family owned The Times), Sir William Bull (Maltravers Herald Extraordinary and Conservative MP for Hammersmith) and Sir Robert Hamilton (Liberal MP for Orkney and Shetland). Among the latter were T. F. Tout, A. F. Pollard, J. E. Neale, C. W. Previté-Orton and Lewis Namier, and they were later joined by the American, Wallace Notestein.[38]

Wedgwood's committee spent two and a half years consulting scholars and collecting evidence, and in July 1932, the very month of the centenary of the passing of the Great Reform Act, it issued what was intended to be its first interim report.[39] It described previous attempts at compiling lists and biographies of MPs, and writing constituency histories. It outlined the materials which existed for this larger task, which the 'Official Return' had not used, including unprinted rolls in the PRO, parliamentary diaries, contemporary lists of members, and municipal records. It discussed contested elections, set out a list of all parliaments which had been summoned from 1258 to 1832, and enumerated various local archive sources. And it sketched an outline of the finished product. The 600-odd years of Parliament's past would be divided into 'significant historical periods'.[40] Each section would be treated in three ways: a list of members, arranged under constituencies; a biographical dictionary of MPs; and an introduction. It was hoped that the scheme could be completed in between five and ten years, at an estimated cost of £30,000, and that it might later be rounded off with lists and biographies of Scottish MPs before 1707 and Irish MPs down to 1800.

Most of these conclusions were set out in the lifeless prose of an official document. But the report also included a justification for the enterprise in eloquent words that were unmistakably Wedgwood's:

The importance of Parliament itself is a measure of the importance of its history . . . We were the first people to govern ourselves through responsible representatives. We may be the last. The institution is so peculiarly English, has been so envied by other nations, and has been so widely copied and discarded and fought over, that the world has come to accept parliamentary government as a symbol of freedom.

But, he continued, 'of the men who gave the institution life, who shaped it, and in so doing shaped our history and even our minds, no record has ever been attempted'. It was these men he wished his history to rescue from oblivion, and there had never been a more pressing time to undertake this enterprise than now. For, he went on,

There is some danger of Parliament losing its dignity and prestige, even in our own country. A wider franchise has tended to exclude from public life, both in the House of Commons and on municipal councils, many public-spirited people whose unwillingness any longer to take part in government is a loss to the State. To give members a sense of their community in a famous inheritance might do much to restore the dignity of their service.

In a decade, he concluded, when the centenary of the Reform Bill and the fourth centenary of the Reformation Parliament were being celebrated, 'the prestige of Parliament itself is a thing to be cared for', and this need was all the more compelling since all around them parliaments were 'being broken in other countries'.[41]

On the whole, the report was well received, especially in *The Times* and *The Times Literary Supplement* (it had been a shrewd move to put Astor on the committee).[42] But thereafter, the going for Wedgwood got much harder. In ways that could not have been predicted at the outset, the early 1930s turned out to be a very unpropitious time to get such an enterprise launched. One problem was financial, for this venture was clearly going to be expensive: a dozen or more historians superintending each period, a small army of professional scholars doing the detailed research, and extended, multi-volume publication. Wedgwood had initially hoped that the historians he had put on his committee would undertake the supervisory work for nothing, but only Notestein was prepared to do so. To make matters worse, the stock market crash of 1929 and the slump which followed meant that government expenditure was savagely cut, that the incomes of philanthropic bodies were much diminished, and that rich individuals were distinctly less wealthy than they had been in the twenties. These were not ideal circumstances in which to try to generate £30,000 (the equivalent of £600,000 in today's terms). The British government would not contribute a penny, attempts to raise money from the American Rockefeller Foundation were unsuccessful, and putting such a sum together from individual donations was bound to be an uphill task.[43]

The second problem which soon confronted Wedgwood was academic. For while the Whig view of the past which underpinned this enterprise remained popular in the public mind, it was markedly in retreat among the new generation of professional historians. In 1931, a young, iconoclastic Fellow of Peterhouse, Cambridge, named Herbert Butterfield, published a book entitled *The Whig Interpretation of History*, which attacked the whole scholarly tradition celebrating progress, protestantism and freedom as a 'gigantic optical illusion', and seemed directly aimed at such patrician popularizers as Churchill and Trevelyan.[44] At the same time this Whiggish history was also being undermined in detail. A clutch of young medievalists, building on the work of Maitland, Richardson and Sayles, demolished William Stubbs's earlier picture of medieval parliaments, which had stressed how they foreshadowed or illuminated subsequent constitutional developments.[45] And with equal cogency and conviction, Lewis Namier assailed the Whig myth that George III was a tyrant and a monster, the enemy of party and Parliament and progress. To be sure, Namier shared Wedgwood's view that it was a 'marvellous microcosmos of English social and political life', an 'extraordinary club' – which was why Wedgwood had put him on his committee in the first place. But Namier was a Tory who was deeply sceptical of the importance of ideas in history and who hated Whigs. From his perspective, the biographies of MPs were atomized stories, about money and intrigue and place: they did not add up to a grand patriotic pageant of progress and freedom.[46]

In such an unpromising financial and academic climate, Wedgwood's committee had turned out, as he himself later admitted, to be 'a terrible business'. Despite his own initial high hopes, the MPs had rarely attended (Buchan was ill for much of the time and Bull died in January 1931), the historians had not cared for the non-professional element, the medievalists and modernists disagreed among themselves, Previté-Orton resigned in June 1929, and Tout died in January 1931.[47] Moreover, Wedgwood was an insufficiently sensitive, expert, subtle and emollient figure to smooth away these differences of aim and outlook, and he later came to regret that Pollard had not been in the chair. Although the interim report had been 'agreed' in October 1931, this had only been accomplished by 'whipping in' the MPs to vote against the professionals. Even Wedgwood recognized this was 'a very bad start for a co-operative enterprise', and it did not bode well for the future of the project. In any case, it was far from clear by this stage whether the project had a future. Wedgwood had intended that his committee would be permanently constituted so as to superintend the work until completion, and that it would publish the volumes of the parliamentary history in a manner similar to the *Annual Reports* of the Royal Commission on Historical Manuscripts. But in the grim financial climate of 1932, the Treasury seized upon the appearance of the 'interim' report to declare it 'final', and dissolved the committee.[48]

Undismayed by these financial constraints, and undeterred by this scholarly scepticism, Wedgwood resolved to continue, raising the money himself and disregarding the academic snipers. In March 1933, he called a meeting of MPs and peers, to which no historians were invited. Its purpose was to consider how best to find the necessary funds, and how to redefine the project in the light of these rather dispiriting developments. A committee of the two houses, with Lord Salisbury in the chair, was appointed by the meeting to take on the task of raising enough money to begin the work, and on 8 June an appeal was launched in *The Times*, under the patronage of the Speaker, and all three living premiers, Ramsay MacDonald, Stanley Baldwin and Lloyd George.[49] The Pilgrim Trust gave £2,000, the Carnegie Endowment made a gift of $10,000, there were some individual benefactions, and Wedgwood wrote personally to MPs and ex-MPs, soliciting contributions. Winston Churchill sent two guineas, *The Times* newspaper gave £100, and the Astor family donated £200. The Chancellor of the Exchequer, Neville Chamberlain, agreed that when £15,000 had been raised, the Stationery Office would publish the results at public expense. By May 1935, that sum had been found.[50]

In order to make it easier to appeal for money, Wedgwood and his new committee had significantly extended the scope of their parliamentary history. The chronological span was carried forward to 1918 (in the hope of interesting current MPs), and the House of Lords would be included as well as the Commons (with a view to obtaining money from the peers).

Wedgwood elaborated this new outline in an article in the *Fortnightly Review* in July 1935. The history would be divided into particular periods, and each scholar in charge would have a budget of £2,000, with which to produce three volumes. The first would contain the biographies of the MPs, the second would provide lists (and analyses) for each parliament of all those summoned to the Lords or elected to the Commons, and the third would consist of studies of franchises, elections, legislation, committee work, and relations between Parliament, party, the public and the crown – 'conclusions as to the movement towards democracy' which would be 'useful to all mankind'. Wedgwood ended with another panegyric on Parliament:

We owe much, perhaps most, to our religion – character. We owe much to those who on sea and land have died for England – our safety, our Empire, and our good pride. To many men of diverse minds we owe a language of unsurpassed utility and a literature unequalled for its beauty. But to those who made Parliament we owe our freedom and our justice, and in that Parliament is our hope. It is time that its history be written and set out in print by a grateful country as a memorial to the dead and a reminder to the living.[51]

Not surprisingly, the professional historians were increasingly unsympathetic to these developments. As scholarly experts, they had resented being outmanoeuvred and outvoted on the original 1929 committee, and several of them were highly critical of the lists of parliaments which had been printed as an appendix to the 'interim' report.[52] By (as they saw it) deliberately excluding the historians from his 1933 committee, Wedgwood had only made things worse, and they were fiercely dismissive of the more elaborate proposal which he had put forward in 1935. There was much criticism that Wedgwood was an amateur who was mistakenly trying to undertake work which should have been theirs, and that he had wilfully gone against the earlier 'interim' report by broadening the scope of the enterprise so much. As professional scholars, steeped in the many and multifarious sources, and aware of the complexities associated with their interpretation, the historians thought it inconceivable that Wedgwood's project could encompass *all* MPs and *all* peers and *all* parliaments in a mere ten years. And they were sure that in seeking to draw general conclusions, he would produce statements that were at best superficially Whiggish, and at worst simple-mindedly unscholarly. As Namier rightly put it, Wedgwood was venturing into 'many subjects which expert historical advisors would have warned the committee against'.[53]

But Wedgwood was unrepentant. He thought the historians were too negative, too critical, too aware of problems, and insufficiently interested in possibilities and opportunities. If it had been left to them, he concluded, they 'would have made the task seem so impossibly difficult that nothing further would have been attempted'. And at a time when liberty was increasingly in jeopardy across Europe, Wedgwood thought their lack of appreciation of England's freedoms, and of Parliament's part in establishing and preserving them, was little short of treason. Not surprisingly, he viewed 'with profound distrust the attack on the Whig interpretation of English history by the younger scholars of the twentieth century'. He was also convinced that as self-regarding professionals, the historians resented his amateur intrusion on to their own jealously guarded turf. 'No Trades Union', he was later to write, 'ever raged so furiously against a blackleg as the historians against me.'[54] There was much truth in this, and it is easy to see why Wedgwood became so irritated and so impatient. But there was also something to be said for the other side. For Wedgwood treated the professional historians, not as experts on the subject (which they were), but as parliamentary opponents who had to be swotted out of the way (which they were not). And this, in turn, merely confirmed their view that he was an ignorant, blustering amateur, who was going to rush and bungle a project that needed more time and thought and expertise than he could ever appreciate, let alone possess or provide.

The result was that the professionals played little part in Wedgwood's history of parliament as it finally took shape in the second half of the decade. An advisory subcommittee was formed in the summer of 1935, but it lacked experts on the Commons and the Lords: of those who had served on the earlier 1929–32 committee, only Wallace Notestein was a member. A scheme was drawn up, allocating particular periods of Parliament to particular historians to supervise: F. M. Powicke and E. F. Jacob for the years before 1509; Pollard for 1509 to 1603; Notestein for 1603 to 1689; G. M. Trevelyan for 1689 to 1714; Namier for 1714 to 1832; and H. A. L. Fisher for 1832 to 1918.[55] But it came to nothing, and subsequent attempts to persuade scholars such as Namier and Neale to rejoin the project were also unsuccessful. The professionals were fiercely critical of Wedgwood's own work, and demanded a degree of general editorial control which he was not prepared to yield to them. Belated efforts at mediation by F. M. Powicke, the Regius Professor of Modern History at Oxford, failed to make any headway. Apart from Notestein, the only historians who now stood by Wedgwood were Pollard and Trevelyan. But even they recognized that once his own research was done and published, the whole project must then be placed on a more sound and scholarly footing.[56]

Under these far from propitious circumstances, Wedgwood's grand historical enterprise in collective research and public education made little headway. 'It is my property', he stubbornly insisted, 'and cannot be tampered with.' But with the majority of the professorial 'trades union' against him, progress was both difficult and slow. It was not easy for him to recruit (let alone train) young researchers, who naturally feared for their careers by being associated with something that their academic superiors regarded as an irredeemably tainted project.[57] And it was even harder for Wedgwood to find senior figures to superintend the production of the volumes, since no professor was prepared to be involved. He tried several times to persuade Churchill to oversee the period 1885 to 1918, partly because his name would guarantee sales, and also because he was the ideal person to write about those magnificent MPs who had served and died in the First World War. But Churchill was too busy. An attempt to launch a parallel history of the Irish Parliament down to the Act of Union began promisingly, but then collapsed.[58] In the end, the only sustained research was undertaken on the English parliaments of the fifteenth century – and that, predictably, was by Wedgwood himself.

III

The result was two volumes, covering the period 1439–1509, which were published by the Stationery Office in 1936 and 1938. (Appropriately enough, they were bound in covers of Wedgwood blue.) They were compiled in accordance with the more comprehensive scheme outlined in 1935. The first provided biographies, in alphabetical order, of 2,500 known Members of the Commons. To keep the work within bounds, the average biography was limited to 150 words, and was confined to essential personal and professional information, plus 'a chronological account of his public life'. But even so, that meant the total text was in excess of 400,000 words. The main sources were the Roll series in the PRO, plus municipal and private collections. Wedgwood undertook the lion's share of the work himself, but he was assisted by A. E. Stamp and M. C. B. Dawes of the PRO, A. T. Butler who was Windsor Herald, and a host of local historians and collaborators.[59] The second volume reassembled this data for each successive parliament, enumerating principal office holders and subsequent changes in appointments, furnishing a diary of events and legislation, and providing lists of those summoned to the upper house and returned to the lower house. This was followed by entries on each constituency, naming and analysing the

MPs returned, with further notes added on the electorate. Again, the result was a mammoth tome, running to well over 800 pages.

Both volumes were primarily genealogical and antiquarian, but they also contained extensive introductions, in which Wedgwood again extolled the virtues of Parliament and its history, and set his findings in a broader, Whiggish framework. Even in this medieval period, he was sure Parliament had captured England's imagination: 'the excitement, the news, the trip to town, the gossip and the exaggerations'. The MPs and peers were the 'people who created democracy and hope', and it was already possible to discern a growth in party identity, the elaborate franchises of the eighteenth century 'in embryo', and 'that contact between the Executive and the representatives which is the distinctive and saving feature of English Parliamentary government'.[60] Thus regarded, Parliament was 'a true mirror of England', 'as necessary a part of England as the sea or the Royal Family or *The Times* newspaper'. The Commons had not yet established its supremacy, 'but that, too, would come'. 'Five hundred years before our day, and three hundred and fifty years before any such light dawned in Europe, almost unselfconsciously the foundations of freedom were laid by Englishmen.' Such was his ringing conclusion to the second volume. And the first had ended on no less elevated a note, with a reworking of the peroration from his Staffordshire parliamentary history, and a dedication to those 'who died for the greater glory of this Honourable House'.[61]

This was a heady (and inimitable) mixture of scholarship and sentiment, genealogy and rhetoric. But as Wedgwood candidly admitted, perhaps in an effort to forestall criticism, there was much about his volumes that was imperfect or incomplete. He and his co-workers had only been able to find information on 2,500 of a possible 3,800 men elected to the Commons, and he accepted that much of that was from sources so doubtful that it was often unreliable, and that many of the identifications might be incorrect. The spelling of surnames was fraught with difficulty, and many of the dates of birth, marriage and death, as well as individuals' occupations, were often little more than guesses.[62] He also conceded that many relevant sources had not been consulted: among them the Plea Rolls at the PRO, unprinted wills from York, Bristol and elsewhere, most borough records and the lawyers' unpublished Year Books. He allowed that the use of the letters 'MP' was 'blatantly anachronistic', he admitted he knew very little about 'the electorate', that the use of the term 'party' was probably an oversimplification, and that 'ministers' did not resign collectively signifying a 'change of government'. But he was characteristically unrepentant. 'Because they themselves never attempted the task and fear reproach,' he concluded, throwing down the gauntlet once again, 'the professional historians hold up hands in horror, and exclaim that it is either "too soon" or "not new" or in the wrong hands.'[63]

Given the nature of the project, the fame of its author and the prodigious labours that had gone into the undertaking, the publication of these volumes inevitably attracted considerable public attention. One thousand copies of the first instalment were printed, and the enterprise was acclaimed by *The Times* as 'a national monument', 'a great task of research and compilation'.[64] But the scholarly reception was extremely hostile, reminiscent to that 'outburst of criticism' which had greeted the 'Return of Members' more than half a century before. The professionals whom Wedgwood had spurned and scorned were no doubt determined to prove that the amateur was not up to the job, and he gave them plenty of opportunity. They were disappointed that he had neglected to consult many relevant documents. They noted his too-ready assumption that MPs elected for one parliament would continue to sit for others. They criticized his presumption that men with the same name were obviously related. They thought his choice of terminal dates perverse, and that he did not understand the scholarly complexities of 'the most obscure and difficult century of our history', and they dismissed the extravagant statements in his introduction about freedom and democracy as 'absurdities'. The whole enterprise, one reviewer concluded, was not only premature: it took too little account 'of the labours of those trained scholars who, from Stubbs downwards, have devoted their abilities to a study of medieval parliaments in accordance with the laws of historical evidence'.[65]

Wedgwood's response was both unsuccessfully belligerent and inadequately accommodating. He unwisely took issue with his anonymous reviewer in the correspondence columns of the *TLS*, who was none other than A. F. Pollard.[66] But Pollard's article had been the more damning because it had been couched in well-disposed and admiring terms, and he refused to reply. He did not need to, and probably did not want to. Having praised Wedgwood, pointed out some of his mistakes and observed that 'the editor has too marked an individuality and lives too vividly in the twentieth century to divest himself of his and its characteristics and to feel at home in the fifteenth', he had clearly said enough. Wedgwood's second response was to print fourteen pages of addenda and corrigenda to the first volume in his second volume. He insisted that most of these corrections had been provided by his co-workers on the project, and that they were remarkably few compared with the errors that had been detected in the 'Return of Members'. But for all his determined defiance, this did rather corroborate his critics' case.[67] The result was that when the second volume appeared in 1938, it was virtually ignored in the academic journals, and received a brief and hostile review in the *TLS*. Once again, Wedgwood defended himself and his project in the correspondence columns, but this time the reviewer responded, and the exchange soon lapsed into quarrels and quibbles over details, from which no one emerged the victor.[68]

Even worse for Wedgwood, *The Times* now abandoned its earlier support, and in a leading article regaled its readers with an account of the 'lamentable rift' between the Colonel and the professors which had dogged the project since 1929.[69] It accused Wedgwood of 'hastiness of judgement', noted that his first volume was tainted by 'a great number of errors', and urged that the scheme be put on a more secure financial and academic footing. This led to a letter from Professor Powicke, explaining that he had tried to mediate between Wedgwood and the professors, but that the Colonel had been impossibly intransigent, and was also 'strangely reluctant' to submit his own work to expert scrutiny. Under these circumstances, Powicke concluded, it was scarcely surprising that the professors refused 'to have anything to do with what might have been a great work of co-operative scholarship'. This was followed by a letter from A. F. Pollard, who now publicly joined the ranks of the critics. It had been a great mistake, he insisted, to extend the scope of the original scheme down to 1918, and to add on the House of Lords and more general matters. Even the earlier project, restricted to the Commons before 1832, was a vast enterprise, and it was 'humanly impossible for any single man' to 'co-ordinate and edit [it] with real scholarship'. If the project was to continue, he concluded, it should certainly be under Wedgwood's leadership, but he should abandon the peers, postpone the Victorian age, and hand over the supervision and preparation of subsequent volumes to expert editors.[70]

More than half a century on, it is easy to see why both sides in the quarrel felt so deeply, and why they came to take up positions and attitudes which were so intransigent. Wedgwood believed that it was a noble, patriotic, public-spirited enterprise to 'reincarnate the Parliaments which made us', and a significant contribution to 'real knowledge' and 'English culture'. Moreover, he had conceived the scheme, raised the money, and done more work on it than all the professors put together. He dismissed them as cowardly and carping pedants, who wanted a source book while he wanted a real history: not merely 'the Commons, nor Parliament, nor democracy, but the whole government of a people'. 'I do enjoy hitting back at the historians, at traitors, at catholics, at liars, at anybody,' he wrote to his daughter Camilla at this time – hardly the most measured of statements.[71] For their part, the historians thought Wedgwood was in too much of a hurry, did not understand the historical or evidential complexities of the period, had taken on a task which was too large to be manageable, had wilfully disregarded expert professional advice, and had impugned the motives of those who proffered it. With the opinion of the press and the professors so stacked against him, even he recognized that the scheme could not continue to go on under his leadership, and in its present form. Having achieved 'neither peace nor an apology', he wrote to *The Times*, 'sheathing the sword'. He had done what he could: if others were not satisfied with his labours, then they must try to do better.[72]

The publication of these two volumes, and their critical reception among the professorate and in the press, effectively brought the project, as Wedgwood had conceived, financed and managed it, to an end. His third volume, drawing general conclusions from the material presented in the first two, never materialized, and although work continued on other periods, there were no more publications during his lifetime. Although £17,000 was eventually raised, it was calculated that another £27,000 would be needed to complete the task. Meanwhile, the parliamentary committee, now chaired by Lord Onslow, resolved that something must be done to re-establish the intellectual credibility of the enterprise, and to set it on a more permanent basis than that afforded by their unofficial body.[73] The Prime Minister refused a request for a Royal Commission, and turned the matter over to the Master of the Rolls. He, in turn, urged the formation of a trust, to take over responsibility for the project, with an editor-in-chief who would be responsible for superintending the completion of the history. That trust (of which Wedgwood was a member) was duly established in December 1940, with Lord Macmillan as its chairman. Soon after, Macmillan issued a report, which included an account of the venture thus far that sought to do justice to all parties involved. It was, according to Wedgwood, 'a most kind and soothing – and even truthful report'. 'My begging letters [to MPs]', he explained to Macmillan, 'always insisted on the importance of keeping up the standards of recruits for Parliament by giving them a touch of immortality.'[74]

At the same time, the trustees sought to take stock of the enterprise for which they had assumed responsibility, especially in the light of the criticisms levelled at Wedgwood for broadening its scope by including the House of Lords (which risked duplicating information already available in *The Complete Peerage*), and by calling for general conclusions (which were bound to be interim and controversial, and thus inappropriate in an official publication). Accordingly, they turned for advice to Professor F. M. Stenton, then President of the Royal Historical Society, who made several suggestions. He urged that during the war, research should continue, albeit by a reduced staff. He proposed that after the war, a new committee of historians should be appointed, responsible to the trustees, who would provide academic supervision, and that a general editor should also be recruited who would oversee the day-to-day running of the enterprise. He agreed that the treatment of the House of Lords, and the provision of general conclusions, should be given up, and he urged that future effort should be concentrated on MPs and their constituencies, as envisaged by the original committee and report of 1929–32. There, for the time being, the matter rested, and for the remainder of the war, and during the early years of Attlee's government, no further progress was made.[75]

In any case, from 1939 onwards, Wedgwood's attention, like that of most Britons, had turned to more immediate and pressing matters, and he had less time or energy to spare for the history of Parliament: freedom now needed to be defended by more direct and vigorous means. As Neville Chamberlain's appeasement policy crashed into ruins, Wedgwood became more than ever convinced that the Prime Minister would have to go, and that he must be replaced by his old friend and fellow Whig, Winston Churchill. 'You or God', he wrote at the time of Munich, 'will have to help if this country is now to be saved.' To his unconcealed delight, both did. 'Thank whatever God there be,' Wedgwood exulted to Churchill on his appointment as First Lord of the Admiralty in September 1939. 'Now we shall win.'[76] But he still hankered after a change of leader, and he was a conspicuous participant in the Commons debates in early May 1940 which resulted in Chamberlain's resignation, leading the singing of 'Rule Britannia' by dissident MPs. Thereafter, he remained a staunch supporter, writing after the new Prime Minister's 'we shall fight on the beaches' speech following the Dunkirk evacuation, that it was 'worth 1,000 guns and the speech of 1,000 years'. 'You might do something for Jos,' Churchill wrote to Anthony Eden soon after. 'He is a grand hearted man.'[77]

The rest of Wedgwood's career was a predictably vigorous diminuendo. Later in 1940, in collaboration with Allan Nevins, he published *Forever Freedom*, an anthology of Anglo-American literature of liberty. In his introduction, he hit out at his scholarly enemies, the authors of 'the new history', which 'blackens England's past in an endeavour to belittle liberalism and exalt authority'. Soon after, he published his autobiography, appropriately entitled *Memoirs of a Fighting Life*, which he dedicated 'to all members of parliament', and which included a foreword by the Prime Minister, praising his 'old and gallant friend' for 'his single-minded pursuit of truth and justice'. It also included a final protest at the 'perpetual bitter opposition and obloquy' which he believed he had suffered at the hands of the professional historians.[78] Wedgwood declared the wartime parliament 'better than any in which I have sat', and concluded with a ringing defence of his country, 'at last taking its proper place, sacrificing all, standing against evil'. In January 1942, and surely at Churchill's suggestion, the Colonel left the Commons for the upper house, and took the title Lord Wedgwood of Barlaston. It was an apt acknowledgement of his family pride and local roots, and it complemented the title Wedgwood of Etruria which had been taken by his younger brother Ralph, who had been given a baronetcy at the same time.[79]

In these last years, Lord Wedgwood continued his work on the history of Parliament and on a yet more elaborate family tree, and he published a final book, *Testament to Democracy* (1942), in which he reasserted his belief in the greatness and uniqueness of the British Parliament and in the abiding importance of liberty and freedom.[80] He reaffirmed his view that Parliament's prime purpose was to control the executive and to *prevent* it making laws, and he regretted the increase in party control, Cabinet power, government legislation and state intervention. It was reviewed by his friend-then-enemy Lewis Namier, who insisted that Wedgwood was 'sometimes inconsistent in argument, confused in thought, inaccurate in his "facts" – not a painstaking historian'. But he also recognized that 'a light burnt in him, a fire, more valuable than logic and precision, and far more sacred than mere intellectual achievements', and he saluted him as 'a passionate lover of his country, jealous of its honour and moral integrity, a knight-errant of Englishry'. As a critical yet generous epitaph, it was only slightly premature, for Wedgwood died in London in July 1943, and was buried in Barlaston. He had already chosen the author of his biography (his niece C. V. Wedgwood) and the title (*The Last of the Radicals*), and he hoped the book would be 'a clarion call against the constructors of a safe and unjust society'. It was also, without the least paradox or contradiction, a memorial to Wedgwood's 'passionate love of English history and unwavering pride and faith in his country's traditions'.[81]

IV

The biography was published in 1951 and, quite by chance, another memorial to Wedgwood was already in the making. For thanks to the efforts of Lord Macmillan, the government agreed, in February that year, to assume responsibility for funding the history of Parliament, by making available

£17,000 annually for the next twenty years. The management of this enterprise was handed over to a revived Board of Trustees, who were responsible
for administering the funding, and to an editorial board chaired by Stenton
which, with a view to avoiding the disagreements and divisions of the 1930s,
was deemed supreme in academic matters.[82] There were many ironies about
this rejuvenated enterprise. One was that, even in the absence of Wedgwood,
the professors continued to quarrel and prevaricate among themselves:
writing history by committee is always, by definition, slow and painful
work.[83] Another was that, for the next ten years, the moving academic spirit
was none other than Sir Lewis Namier, who on his retirement from his chair
at Manchester University took on responsibility for producing the volumes
concerned with the years 1754–90. Although he had been a fierce critic of
the Wedgwood approach to parliamentary history, he devoted the last years
of his life to furthering what he regarded as a much more rigorous and
scholarly version of the same enterprise. The three volumes were published
in 1964, soon after Namier's death, since when many more have appeared,
so that the period from 1386 to 1832, encompassing almost the whole of
Wedgwood's original time-span, is now virtually complete.[84]

But Namier's later reinvolvement was not the only irony. For him, the
biographies of MPs were everything, and he was only grudgingly persuaded
to include histories of constituencies. The broader questions – debates,
procedure, legislation, private and public bills, the growth of party, the
formulation of policy, the electoral and popular world beyond Westminster
– were all but disregarded. Unlike Wedgwood, Namier was an anatomizer,
not a visionary, a Tory not a Whig.[85] He wanted facts, detail, information,
but as in all his work, wider generalizations were beyond his ken and his
capacity. His volumes were not so much a history as a work of reference,
of value to eighteenth-century specialists, but of minimal appeal to current
MPs, and of even less interest to the general public. As a result, Namier's
books were widely criticized (as were their successors) for their narrow-
ness and their myopia, and for their determined refusal to deal with most
aspects of Parliament's functions and parliamentary life. This was scarcely
a history of the Commons in any collective or operational sense, let alone a
history of Parliament as a functioning national institution.[86] In the era of
Welfare State Whiggery, Wedgwood's more imaginative approach to the
subject, which had been so fiercely criticized by the professionals in the
1930s, had been embraced again by their successors. Here was another
irony, and one which Wedgwood would surely have relished as a kind of
posthumous vindication.

This, in turn, leads to a further irony which from Wedgwood's standpoint is even happier still. Sixty years after his original proposals, and with the biographies of MPs and the history of their constituencies almost complete, the history of Parliament is beginning, albeit belatedly, to turn its attention to those broader issues which, after 1933, Wedgwood came to think were so important and integral a part of the enterprise: the House of Lords, parliamentary matters and general conclusions. If future work does indeed move forward in these directions, it may well be that the final history will bear a closer resemblance to Wedgwood's conception than anyone would have thought possible in 1938 or 1951. Of course, such a history will be far more accurate and authoritative than Wedgwood could ever have made it, and the conclusions will be less triumphantly patriotic and complacently whiggish than he would have wished. Today, the power and renown of the British House of Commons are significantly less than they were in his day, and no history of Parliament, however comprehensively conceived, is likely to reverse that trend. Here is yet a final irony – but this time it is not one which Wedgwood would have appreciated.

It was said by both his supporters and his opponents that Colonel Josiah Wedgwood was a staunch ally in any cause, because of his vigour and his fearlessness, but that he was also a doubtful ally because of his poor judgement and impetuosity. There is much about his involvement with the history of Parliament which bears out both these verdicts. The project he wanted was a genealogist's and a politician's history, rather than a scholar's or an historian's. Inevitably, he clashed bitterly with those professionals who thought his views too simplistic, too present-minded, too propagandist, and his methods too rushed, too crude, too slipshod. But the fact remains that without his imaginative determination and vigorous lobbying, there would never have been a history of Parliament in the first place, and the longer the project continues, the closer it may eventually approximate to his more comprehensive vision. Although Wedgwood spent much of his public life as a critic and in opposition, he was also, like many of his forebears, an initiating, creative, enabling force, and the history of Parliament thrives today as a monument to that initiative, that creativity and that forcefulness. Appropriately enough, the London building in which it is located is called Wedgwood House. It is a long way from Staffordshire. But it is another, and more enduring, form of apotheosis.

7

Emollience: Stanley Baldwin and Francis Brett Young

When Stanley Baldwin was appointed British Prime Minister in succession to Andrew Bonar Law in May 1923, he was dismissed by the Marquess Curzon of Kedleston, who believed that *he* should have been preferred, as someone 'of the utmost insignificance'. This turned out to be a fatal misjudgement, for Baldwin soon established himself as the dominant figure in British politics, a position he was to retain and consolidate until his retirement in 'a blaze of affection' in May 1937, by which time Curzon had been dead and gone for more than a decade.[1] One sign of Baldwin's commanding position was that he was Prime Minister on three separate occasions, not only in 1923, but again from 1924 to 1929, and finally from 1935 to 1937 – an achievement which rivals only Gladstone and Salisbury among his predecessors, and which none of his twentieth-century successors ever equalled. Another was the extraordinary list of those public figures whom he bested, marginalized and defeated: Lords Beaverbrook and Rothermere among the press barons; Austen Chamberlain, Winston Churchill and Lord Birkenhead among front-ranking politicians; Lloyd George and Ramsay MacDonald as prime ministers; and Edward VIII as king and emperor.

These are impressive political statistics and no-less-impressive individual scalps: but they do not give the full measure of Baldwin's importance. For in addition to being thrice Prime Minister, he was also the dominant figure in the National Government of 1931–5, which meant that during his years as Tory party leader he was only out of office when the minority Labour administrations of 1924 and 1929–31 were unhappily and uncertainly in power. Indeed, during the inter-war years, the Conservatives were by far the most successful political party, adapting with ease and rapidity to the mass electorate which the fourth Reform Act of 1918 had brought into being.[2] And the lion's share of the credit for this lay with Baldwin, who believed that the Tories had nothing to fear from universal adult suffrage, who extended the vote to young women in 1929, and who established a close rapport with large sections of the British public. Uniquely among the party leaders of the 1920s and 1930s, he was admired as a trustworthy, decent and honourable man, wedded to the wholesome, consensual, patriotic values of country life, public duty, social reconciliation and the Christian religion.[3]

In reality, this was only part of the picture for, as well-informed contemporaries recognized, Baldwin was a very complex character. He was born in 1867 into the rich, provincial, upper middle classes; his father was MP for the local constituency of Bewdley; he was educated at Harrow School and Trinity College, Cambridge, where he acquired a lifelong love of history, literature and the classics; and until early middle age he was busy as a company director, and Worcestershire ironmaster. But he was also highly strung, suffered occasional spells of nervous collapse and exhaustion, and inherited from his Scottish mother a melancholy Celtic strain. Indeed, Harold Macmillan (who was no admirer) claimed that Baldwin's emolliently English image was entirely created and manipulated by the media:

In the days about which I am writing, the public character of any leading politician seldom bore any close relationship to his true nature. It was largely represented or distorted by party bias, by rumour, and above all by the press . . . Of all those with whom I was associated or watched from a distance, this distortion particularly applied to Stanley Baldwin . . . He was not at all the kind of man which he was popularly believed to be, or that the Conservative Central Office wished in their propaganda to portray.

Harold Laski was of the same opinion, and G. M. Young put forward an identical interpretation in his unsympathetic official biography.[4] But other observers, including Harold Nicolson, Montagu Norman and W. P. Crozier, as well as Baldwin's close friend J. C. C. Davidson, took the less hostile view that the reassuringly bucolic persona was undoubtedly a part – albeit only a part – of the whole man.[5]

For Baldwin's belief in the regenerative power of 'spiritual values' derived from the English countryside was genuine enough, and as such it also caught, shared and intensified a widespread inter-war mood. It was this concern for the beauty of the landscape, and for the moral uplift and spiritual nourishment which it provided, that lay behind such varied organizations as the National Trust, the Council for the Preservation of Rural England, the Youth Hostels Association and the *Victoria History of the Counties of England*.[6] And these sylvan and spiritual sentiments were shared by many men of power and influence, including Sir Edward Grey, Lord Halifax and the young R. A. Butler among politicians, Edward Elgar, Arnold Bax and

Ralph Vaughan Williams among composers, G. M. Trevelyan, John Buchan and the young Arthur Bryant among writers and historians, and Hugh Walpole, P. G. Wodehouse and Compton Mackenzie among novelists. In such a climate, and in such company, Baldwin's recommendation of Mary Webb's novel *Precious Bane*, set in the Severn Valley, not only helped turn the book into a best seller, but also consolidated his popular reputation as a cultured gentleman and Christian countryman.[7]

But Baldwin's closest relationship with a writer of fiction, at both the personal and the political level, was probably with his Worcestershire friend, neighbour and near-contemporary, Francis Brett Young. His early novels, written immediately before and after the First World War, were largely experimental in theme and form, and they were unsuccessful commercially. But in 1927, the year after the General Strike, he published *Portrait of Clare*, which became an immediate best seller and was awarded the James Tait Black Memorial Prize. Thereafter, Brett Young was a consistently popular author, producing a steady stream of novels: *My Brother Jonathan* (1928), *Jim Redlake* (1930), *Mr & Mrs Pennington* (1931), *The House Under the Water* (1932), *This Little World* (1934), *White Ladies* (1935), *Far Forest* (1936), *Portrait of a Village* (1937), *They Seek a Country* (1937), *Dr Bradley Remembers* (1938), and *Mr Lucton's Freedom* (1940). Described as 'long, comfortable, charmingly-written and classically composed', Brett Young's books projected and celebrated the same wholesome, consensual, rural values, locally rooted in the Worcestershire countryside, that Baldwin epitomized and advocated in his years of fame and power. For both men, politics was about culture more than it was about politics; and culture was about tranquillity rather than excitement.

I

During the 1920s and 1930s, the key to Baldwin's long-lasting and high-toned reputation was, as Laski grudgingly admitted, his 'power to evoke a sense of trust which transcends the divisions of parties', both inside and outside the House of Commons; and the explanation for this was that he 'appeared to be not a politician, but a plain man in politics'.[8] After 1922, being a 'plain man' in politics carried with it a particular – and highly beneficial – connotation: for it meant rejecting the Lloyd George Coalition, which had disintegrated amidst widespread public disapproval and claims of corruption earlier that year. More precisely, it meant rejecting Lloyd George himself, 'the first Prime Minister since Walpole to leave office flagrantly richer than he entered it, and the first since the Duke of Grafton to live openly with his mistress'. It meant rejecting Lord Birkenhead, who was widely regarded as too clever by half, who was thought to have links with shady characters like Maundy Gregory, and who was drunk for much of the time. And it meant rejecting Winston Churchill, who had been responsible for the Dardanelles disaster and the Chanak fiasco, and whose matchlessly fluent oratory inspired at least as much distrust as admiration by this time.[9]

The best way to avoid being likened to these super-large egos, these first-class brains, these incorrigible buccaneers and these suspect characters was to stress the virtues of plainness and ordinariness, and during the inter-war years, no one was better placed to do this than Baldwin.[10] For in his case, this was not only appearance: it was also substantially rooted in reality. During his first forty years as a Worcestershire industrialist, he had lived a life of virtuous obscurity, known only in the provincial, Severn-side society which had recently been immortalized in Elgar's 'Enigma Variations'. And from 1908, when he succeeded his father as MP for the local constituency of Bewdley, he had spent most of his time in the Commons inconspicuously perching on the back benches. Hence Curzon's damning observation; but hence, too, Baldwin's constant (and plausible) later claims to ordinariness which were to prove such a powerful political weapon. 'I am', he once told his Worcester neighbours, 'just one of yourselves, who has been called to special work for the country at this time.' He was, he insisted, a 'plain Prime Minister . . . the ordinary man who is attempting the task of government'. And the implication was clear: unlike the members of the Lloyd George Coalition, Baldwin might have a second-class brain; but, unlike them again, he did not have a second-class character.[11]

Indeed, throughout his years of power and pre-eminence, Baldwin went to great trouble to stress his unexceptional averageness and reassuring plainness, by turning self-deprecation into a minor art form, long before George W. Bush. At different times, and to different audiences, he insisted he was an 'ordinary man' among classicists, an 'outsider' among artists, an 'onlooker' among archaeologists, an 'amateur' student of history, a 'layman' among clerics and an 'ignoramus' among geologists.[12] More generally, Baldwin presented himself as a 'typical Englishman', who made no claim to any special skills, and who lacked the temperament to seek, and the talent to win, those 'glittering prizes' which had so captivated (and so corrupted) the adventurers of the Lloyd George Coalition. Baldwin, by contrast, described public life as 'a great trial', and high office as 'the loneliest job in the world', an 'almost intolerable burden', which only a strong and selfless desire to be of service to the nation enabled him to bear. As he said to a journalist shortly after he first became Prime Minister, in a phrase which artfully blended a reassuring lack of assurance with a commitment to public service and clear evidence of religious feeling, 'I need your prayers rather than your congratulations.'[13]

And in many cases, Baldwin actually got them, for he was the most devout Tory leader since the great Lord Salisbury, and no other prime minister between 1916 and 1945 could compete with him in his sincere (and well-advertised) Christian convictions. Even in ostensibly secular settings, Baldwin's vocabulary was suffused with religious imagery, as when he spoke of political 'gospels', of party workers as 'missionaries', and of the national need for 'salvation' and 'redemption'. And two of his most famous and effective parliamentary orations ended with explicitly religious injunctions: '"Faith", "Hope", "Love" and "Work"', and 'Give Peace in our time, O Lord'.[14] They were effective because, uniquely among the leaders of his generation, Baldwin *was* a Christian gentleman. Hence his disapproval of Lloyd George, the 'Goat', the 'dynamic force', the 'real corrupter of public life'. Hence his dislike of smart parties and high society, which marked him off not only from Lloyd George but also from Ramsay MacDonald. Hence his wish to bind 'together . . . all classes of our people in an effort to make life in this country better', which distinguished him from the bellicose and belligerent Churchill. And hence the ease with which he befriended Labour MPs, which contrasted strongly with the cold, haughty approach of Neville Chamberlain, who either despised or patronized them.[15]

The favourable impression Baldwin made in Westminster, where his wholesome ordinariness gave him unrivalled moral authority, was also conveyed to the wider audience outside, in large part by the frequency and felicity of his public speeches. As one reporter put it in 1926, 'much of Mr Baldwin's influence . . . springs from the occasional addresses he delivers'.[16] Indeed, and especially in his early years at the top, there were so many of them that the word 'occasional' was scarcely appropriate. Universities, learned societies, church meetings, county associations; in London, Birmingham, Leeds, Glasgow or Cornwall: no audience was too small, no town too remote. Indeed, much of Baldwin's time as Prime Minister and Conservative leader was taken up in preparing and giving these speeches, and he regarded it as time well spent: talking to his fellow Englishmen and women was something he believed in, and did exceptionally well. Here, if anywhere, is to be found the key to what G. M. Young described as Baldwin's 'insatiable conquest of the English heart'. And that conquest was intensified by the five published selections of his speeches, bound in large, comfortable, blue volumes, the first of which, *On England*, sold over 30,000 copies, and went through six reprints in twelve months.[17]

The title is revealing, for the published addresses were not those of a partisan politician deliberately seeking confrontation or revelling in conflict. As the preface to one later collection put it, 'throughout this volume, he speaks as the statesman and Englishman, not as the party leader concerned with immediate issues'.[18] Indeed, of the 137 speeches published, only twelve were delivered in the Commons, and seven of these were of a non-partisan nature, such as eulogies of Asquith or Curzon, or proposing the construction of monuments to past worthies. They were always sensitive to the audience, the locality and the occasion; they were soothing, eirenic, even sentimental in tone; and they showed a greater acquaintance with history and literature than Baldwin's claims to plainness and ignorance suggested. They also contained general messages of broader significance: the importance of religion and duty, the need for social reconciliation and class coexistence, the claims of country and community. Thomas Jones, Baldwin's right-hand man and who, after all, should have known, summed up perfectly the impression these anthologies were intended to make, and did make, when he wrote in his diary apropos of *This Torch of Freedom*:

It will help to establish confidence in his, or what people think is his, typical Englishness. The speeches are professedly non-party about Scott, Burne Jones, John Wesley and so forth, but really about Stanley Baldwin. By the time you are through the book it is his character which emerges.[19]

Not only did it emerge in the subject-matter of the speeches: it also came out in the style. Whether inside or outside Parliament, Baldwin always eschewed (and criticized) rhetoric as the 'harlot of the arts'. Instead, he offered low-key, humdrum utterances, with homely metaphors, extensive extempore passages, and simple, sentimental perorations in the plain man's language of his audience rather than in the self-consciously superior style of a well-practised and highly polished orator. When giving his Rectorial Address at Glasgow University in 1930, for instance, he warned his audience not to 'expect from him the skill in composition which you would rightly expect from a Barrie or a Kipling or a Shaw'.[20] But once again, this was self-deprecation as a political weapon: for he was deliberately doing himself less than justice. Kipling (who was his cousin) once described Baldwin as 'the real pen in our family' and with the help of Thomas Jones, he took great care to think out his speeches in advance, in terms of general structure, overall tone and pitch, and particular words and phrasing. This was skilful artistry: but it was the skill of the artist who conceals his art. Baldwin impressed just because he did not appear to try to impress, offering instead what seemed a 'plain, unadorned account'.[21]

This technique reached its fullest development in his speech to the Commons in December 1936 describing the events immediately prior to the abdication of Edward VIII, 'the quintessence of his artistry: apparently an informal account of events, unpremeditated, told with the aid of a few notes jotted on scraps of paper'. By common consent, it was a masterly parliamentary performance: 'I must tell', Baldwin began, 'what I have to tell truthfully, sincerely, and plainly, with no attempt to dress up or adorn.' In fact, of course, he had gone to the greatest trouble with the speech, which was a carefully crafted defence of his own conduct and that of the king, and was designed to protect and preserve the crown as the central feature of the constitution: once again, it was the art which concealed its artistry.[22] Here, as so often, Baldwin was advantageously contrasted to other inter-war parliamentary performers. He avoided the severely classical, architectonic style of Asquith, the magical, scintillating metaphors of Lloyd George, the searing, scorching vituperation of Birkenhead, and the highly polished, extensively prepared rhetoric of Churchill. In Parliament as in the country, they performed whereas he communicated. They impressed as orators; he inspired trust as a statesman. As one paper put it: 'When we compare his quiet, helpful speeches with the whirling words of Mr Lloyd George, it is easy to understand why the country trusts the one and not the other.'[23]

Hence Baldwin's unrivalled success on the radio, that new medium of mass communication, the value of which he was the first political leader to recognize. With his calm, homely, reassuring voice, he invented the 'fireside chat' a decade before Franklin D. Roosevelt, realizing that the key to success lay in addressing people in a conversational, intimate way, rather than as if they were at a public meeting. Here is a picture of him at the microphone in 1931:

The light and flexible tones and the extreme simplicity of language smacked more of conversation than of a set address ... The mode is a tactful one, for broadcast oratory is largely fireside oratory, and Mr Baldwin might easily have had his feet on our fender ... Too often the more flamboyant orator baffles the listener by a range of cadence that sways from declamation to inaudibility. If Mr Baldwin had nothing of fresh consequence to say, he at least said it simply, pleasantly and equably.[24]

Not surprisingly, Baldwin's election broadcasts, in 1924, 1929, 1931 and 1935 were easily the most popular and accomplished. He took great care in preparing them, even to the extent of enquiring of Sir John Reith, the Director General of the BBC, about the surroundings in which people listened to radios, so he might pitch his remarks appropriately. Neither Lloyd George nor MacDonald ever really mastered the technique of broadcasting, being too much set in the ways of hustings oratory, and even Churchill only became an effective radio speaker during the Second World War when, for a short time, his sonorous rhetoric seemed appropriate.[25]

This contrast in speech was accentuated by differences of dress. Even after 1922, the former members of the Coalition continued their essentially pre-war appearances: Austen Chamberlain with his wing collar, pin-striped trousers, spats and monocle; Lord Birkenhead with his well-cut, expensive suits, cigar and top hat; Lloyd George with his long hair, moustache, walking-stick and cloak; and Churchill, with his frock-coat, cigar and multifarious headgear. All these outfits dated from that time when clothes were a device by which class and professional distinctions were reinforced. But Baldwin's outfits were essentially postwar, seeking to blur rather than reinforce class divisions, and expressing ordinary plainness rather than privileged individuality. Soon after becoming Prime Minister, he attended the Eton and Harrow match in a baggy suit and shabby soft felt hat. This earned him a rebuke from the editor of the *Tailor and Cutter*, who described his clothes as 'suburban'. But as one of Baldwin's earliest biographers recognized, it was also a political masterstroke:

Nothing suited Baldwin better than to be described as 'suburban'! From this time on, the public were deluged with descriptions of his simplicity, urbanity, suburbanity, and rusticity, and were offered a picture of a man so like themselves – and even inferior to themselves – in simplicity, common sense and the absence of all outstanding talents (such as had made Mr Lloyd George, Mr Winston Churchill and Lord Birkenhead so irritating) that they could not but be gratified.[26]

This sense of trustworthy ordinariness was further enhanced by Baldwin's use of his pipe. From his first days as Prime Minister, he was almost invariably photographed with it, and extra sparkle was added to a provincial news story when he was seen without it. As another early biographer noted, the pipe 'became one of his props, like Charlie Chaplin's little cane. Impossible for Baldwin to be photographed without his pipe! Impossible for Baldwin to meet interviewers without modestly asking their permission to light up!'[27] And as with his choice of clothes, his use of the pipe was exactly in tune with the times. Like Baldwin himself, and unlike Lloyd George and the Coalitionists, his pipe was, in A. J. P. Taylor's words 'respectable without being ostentatious'. Indeed, in April 1923, *The Times* drama critic had made the same point:

The pipe is the great thing. It is the human touch. Everybody in the kingdom can understand that pipe, and will feel drawn towards its owner. It is a symbol of homeliness, of a philanthropic and ruminative temperament, of the wise preference of comfort to luxury, and of the *juste milieu* to extremes. In a word, it is the pipe of popularity.[28]

So it was; and so it remained throughout his career.

Underlying these 'ordinary' attributes of decency of character, directness of speech, and plainness of dress lay the no-less-appealing persona of the English country squire. His critics thought such an image preposterous, noting that Astley, his Worcestershire home, had an estate of but one hundred acres, and that it was financed by the dividends from the Baldwin ironworks. And even Baldwin's son has admitted that his father

never took a direct hand in the work of the soil nor showed any practical interest in the organization of his small estate . . . His wife, or head gardener attended to the organization and the details of the place. In holiday time, the master was in the library reading or working, or else on a walk; never supervising the grafting of a fruit tree, the stacking of a rick, or the diet of a middle-white porker.[29]

But Baldwin's rustic image was far from being the cynical invention of Conservative propagandists. Thomas Jones, who was close enough to know, noted his 'deep attachment to the English countryside', and J. C. C. Davidson later recalled that 'he really did like leaning over a gate and scratching a pig'. 'I am so glad', Baldwin told the young R. A. Butler after visiting him at Stanstead Hall in Essex, 'to have seen you at home in the country. You must go on coming down every weekend. Life in the country makes you see things whole.'[30]

There seems no doubt that that was genuinely Baldwin's view. 'To me,' he observed in one of his most famous early speeches,

England is the country, and the country is England . . . The sounds of England, the tinkle of the hammer on the anvil in the country smithy, the corn crake on a dewy morning, the sound of the scythe against the whetstone, and the sight of the plough team coming over the hill . . . The wild anemones of the woods in April, the last load at night of hay being drawn down a lane as the twilight comes in.[31]

And it was from this rich vein of genuine rural attachment that he dug out material for some of his most effective speeches, such as his eulogy of Austen Chamberlain:

When our long days of work are over here there is nothing in our oldest customs which so stirs the imagination of the younger Member as the cry which goes down the lobbies, 'Who goes home?' Sometimes when I hear it I think of the language of my own countryside, and my feeling that for those who have borne the almost insupportable burden of public life there may well be a day when they will be glad to go home. So Austen Chamberlain has gone home.[32]

It was words and phrases such as these which established Baldwin as the unrivalled 'interpreter of England' of his generation, in whose sentimental orations the nation's spirit was brought alive.

But for all its undoubted sincerity, Baldwin's attitude towards the country *was* essentially romantic, mystical and quasi-religious. He was not concerned with the actuality of rural life in the 1920s and 1930s, with the squalor, disease, poverty and crime that lay behind the picturesque façade. On the contrary, he was enamoured of those aspects of country life which came to him 'through my various senses – through the ear, through the eye, and through certain imperishable scents'.[33] From this perspective, country cottages were not insanitary hovels (as many of them were), but the embodiment of rural tradition and spiritual hope:

Nothing is more characteristic of England's countryside than the village homes which, for century upon century, have sheltered her sturdy sons of toil. Who has not felt a thrill of admiration on catching sight of some old-world village round a bend of the road? The roofs, whether thatched or tiled; the walls, weather-boarded or half-timbered, or of good Cotswold stone – have been built with a material ready to the hand of the craftsman and, painted with the delicate pigments only to be found on the palette of Father Time, have grown amid their surroundings just as naturally as the oaks and elms under whose shade they stand.[34]

For Baldwin, such cosy rural dwellings were the essence and epitome of the real England, which everyone ought to share and venerate. Of course, he was forced to concede that during the last hundred years, 'we have become largely an urban folk', but he remained convinced that it was the countryside which embodied those 'eternal values from which we must never allow ourselves to be separated'. Indeed, it was his most ardently held conviction that, despite the Industrial Revolution, the growth of factory production, and the massive expansion of towns, there lay, 'deep down in the hearts even of those who have toiled in our cities for two or three generations, an ineradicable love of country things and country beauty, as it may exist in them traditionally and subconsciously', which only needed to be 'fanned into life'. And the proof of this could be seen, he felt, in the way in which town-dwellers cultivated their gardens, and the working classes of Birmingham escaped at every available opportunity to fish in the River Severn. For he was convinced that they, like him, knew in their bones that the country, not the town, was their spiritual home, where a more ordered, traditional society prevailed; and that was why he spent so much time talking to urban audiences about rural values.[35]

Baldwin's love of the countryside, and his belief in the essential spiritual nourishment that it might provide for the nation as a whole, were derived from his upbringing in, and fierce attachment to, what he called that 'delectable corner of England' in the region of the Severn Valley. As he once put it, 'One knows in one's bones that one is a Worcestershire man – there is nothing like it.'[36] He knew the highways and byways of the county intimately, and as a youth had explored the more distant lands west of the Severn. But there was more to the country than peace, beauty and repose. In his pre-prime ministerial days, he had learned the arts of leadership and conciliation through his service on the local parish council, the Wilden School Managers and Worcestershire County Council, and in the years of his wider public fame he never forgot his local roots: if anything, they became more important to him. As Prime Minister, he remained devoted to Worcestershire cricket, and when time permitted he was a regular visitor to the county ground, superbly located close by the Severn and the cathedral. He was much admired throughout the county, and on receiving the freedom of Worcester, his words were as genuine as they were well chosen:

I suppose there have been many ceremonies at which I have been present which were more magnificent than this, and made much more noise in the world, but I have never been to one that has touched me more, or one in which all the elements that can grip the heart of man have been more present.[37]

Indeed, Baldwin was in his element at the annual meetings of the Worcestershire Association, which was founded in 1926 'to revive personal associations and promote good fellowship among Worcestershire folk wherever resident, and to foster love of county and pride in its traditions', and of which he was first president.[38] Each year, at the annual London dinner, he made speeches 'felicitous in phrase and feeling, expressing, as few can, the significance of local patriotism and deep love of the Worcestershire countryside'. Day after day, he noted in his speech at the inaugural banquet, when he was confined to London, he thought

of what I can see from my own garden in the most beautiful view in all England. I see the hills known to all of you, beginning in the north-east, the Clents; and beyond, in Warwickshire, Edgehill, where the English squire passed with horse and hounds between the two armies; Bredon, the beginning of the Cotswolds, like a cameo against the sky, and the wonderful straight blue line of the Malverns, little shapes of Ankerdine and Berrow Hill and, perhaps most beautiful and graceful, his two neighbours, Woodbury and Abberley; and Clee Hills, opening up another beautiful and romantic world and presenting a circle of beauty which I defy any part of England to match.[39]

Thereafter, Baldwin's touch at these Association dinners never deserted him. He could recount a local anecdote expertly, or recognize old friends from his county council days with touching intimacy and real conviction. As the *Daily Telegraph* remarked:

The Prime Minister's sense of county patriotism is strong, and on no subject does he speak more delightfully. To sound the praises of Worcestershire is to him an occupation no less agreeable than to a Saint to sound the praises of Zion. When he is vexed with politics, serenity returns at the mention of the name Worcestershire.[40]

As a mark of appreciation and respect, it was the Worcestershire Association which presented him, on his retirement as Prime Minister, with the wrought-iron gates which were hung at the main entrance to Astley, and which were later to cause so much trouble, when Lord Beaverbrook piratically requisitioned them as Minister of Aircraft Production in 1940. 'As to what I have done for the Association,' Baldwin said in a characteristically gracious reply, 'it has been a labour of love.' There can be no doubt he meant it.[41]

This fully developed Baldwin persona – 'the unimaginative, stolid, Anglo-Saxon figure depicted by the popular press', complete with pipe, baggy clothing, and a benevolent look – was a remarkably resonant and enduring fixture on Britain's inter-war political scene. Like George V, but in a less grand way, Baldwin gave a reassuring sense of dutifulness and service, wholesomeness and permanence, in an era when everything seemed to be changing for the worse, with bolshevism and fascism in Europe, and industrial depression and unprecedented unemployment at home. As Lord Blake puts it:

To the public [Baldwin] seemed to embody the English spirit, and his speeches to sound the authentic note of that English character which they so much admired and so seldom resembled. Pipe-smoking, phlegmatic, honest, kind, common-sensical, fond of pigs, he represented to Englishmen an idealised and enlarged version of themselves.[42]

So, indeed, he did. On Baldwin's retirement, Sir Bernard Partridge, *Punch*'s chief cartoonist, depicted him in farmers' raiment as 'The Worcestershire Lad'. 'Well done, Stanley,' John Bull observes, 'a good long day and a rare straight furrow.' And in a final act of local homage, Baldwin took both of his titles from the region: Earl Baldwin of Bewdley, the constituency he had represented in the Commons for nearly thirty years; and Viscount Corvedale, the Shropshire village where his forebears had originated.[43]

II

One of Baldwin's fellow speakers (and admirers) at the eighth annual London dinner of the Worcestershire Association in 1934 was Francis Brett Young, then at the height of his long-since-forgotten fame. 'I owe Mr Brett Young a great deal of gratitude for his books,' observed Baldwin. 'I have read nearly all of them, and with great pleasure.'[44] By then, he was far from being alone in that activity. *Portrait of Clare* became 'almost a household name' and was reprinted eighteen times between 1927 and 1948; *Dr Bradley Remembers* would eventually sell more than 300,000 copies; and the sales of *Mr & Mrs Pennington* reached 24,000 in the first five weeks after publication. And with commercial success went critical acclaim. John Masefield hailed Brett Young as the 'most gifted, most interesting mind among the younger men writing English', and Hugh Walpole, when comparing him with his contemporaries, 'could not see anyone who gives so much promise of being first of the bunch as he does'. In the early 1930s, praise reached its zenith, when Brett Young was described as a 'literary giant', the 'successor to Galsworthy', 'a commanding figure in contemporary letters', and 'the most distinguished writer of prose now practising the novel in England'. Among popular novelists, he was undoubtedly one of the pre-eminent figures of the age of Baldwin.[45]

Francis Brett Young had been born in 1884 in the small Worcestershire town of Halesowen, which was equidistant from the coal mines and blast furnaces of the Black Country, the great provincial metropolis of Birmingham, and the hills and plains of the Severn Valley. Although he attended

Birmingham University and (like his father) qualified as a doctor, it was to the countryside rather than the city, and to writing rather than medicine, that his youthful thoughts, feelings and ambitions were drawn.[46] As a small boy, he longed to know what lay to the west of the nearby Clent and Walton Hills, which he was later to describe as 'the navel of my life', 'the twin hubs of the universe'. Then, one day, he reached the summit of Walton Hill, and as he contemplated for the first time the whole of the Severn Valley laid out at his feet, his imagination took wing. For he saw below him

all the kingdoms of the earth. It seemed like that. Even today, I doubt if I could ever wholly overcome the awe of that prospect, for it is one of the widest and fairest in all England: the dreamy, green expanse of the Severn Plain; the level line of the Cotswolds – pale blue as the chalk hill butterfly; Bredon (beloved hill!), a half-strung bow; Malvern, peaked and fantastic like scenery on a stage; Abberley, with its tower; two waves of Clee; and, beyond it all, a tangle of unnamed hills.[47]

This was Baldwin's country (and Baldwin's language), and in the long Edwardian summers Brett Young explored it all: from Worcestershire to the Severn and Wye Valleys, and to the Welsh Marches and beyond.

For Brett Young, as for Baldwin, this was the landscape of his life, his aesthetic and his morality. For Baldwin it would provide the inspiration to his politics, and for Brett Young it would furnish the inspiration for his fiction. 'Ever since my childhood,' he later recalled, in Baldwinian cadences redolent of 'spiritual values', 'my soul has wandered over these beloved hills, and brooded over them, tenderly.'[48] And absence only made his heart grow fonder. For having qualified as a doctor, and having married in 1908, Brett Young set up in general practice in Brixham, Devon. Then came the war, in which he saw service in South and East Africa; then, with his health undermined, and his finances decidedly uncertain, he went into exile in Italy; and then, from 1928 to 1933, he took up residence in the Lake District. But all the time he was writing – about the region he had come to know and love in his youth. For in the coronation summer of 1911, accompanied by his wife Jessica, he had been on a walking holiday to the lands west of the River Severn, and during that vacation he formulated his great literary enterprise – of 'illuminating, by a number of sections through its social strata, the life of the western Midlands during those impressionable years when I was best qualified to observe it'.[49]

This was, in the manner of Arnold Bennett and the 'Five Towns', a fictionalized but recognizable version of that part of England which he had seen as a boy from the summit of Clent and Walton Hills, which were thinly disguised as 'Pen Beacon' and 'Uffdown' in his novels. 'Nothing that has happened in my English books', he later wrote, 'took place outside the limits of that superb vista.' To the north was the Black Country: 'Dulston' (Dudley), 'Halesby' (Halesowen), 'Wedensford' (a 'composite Black Country town', owing much to Wednesbury), 'Wolverbury' ('not quite Wolverhampton') and 'Sedgebury'. To the north-east was 'North Bromwich', the 'city of iron' (Birmingham), with its suburbs, 'Alvaston' (Edgbaston), 'Winsworth' (Winson Green) and 'Sparkdale' (Sparkhill). And to the south and west, there lay the countryside: the Severn Valley and the Welsh Marches. There are small Worcestershire villages ('Monks Norton', 'Chaddesbourne d'Abitot' and 'Grafton Lovett') obviously adapted from their real-life equivalents (Redmarley d'Abitot, Abbots Morton, Chaddesley Corbett, Grafton Flyford and Elmley Lovett). The 'Garon Valley' is the Elan Valley complete with a 'North Bromwich' water scheme; and further west 'Forst Fawr' is a more frightening version of the Rhayader Massif.[50] This was what became known for a time as the 'Brett Young Country', and in the (aptly named) 'Severn Edition' of his novels, a map of it was provided as the endpapers.

His early fiction, written in accordance with this grand design – *Undergrowth* (1913), *The Dark Tower* (1915), *The Iron Age* (1916), *The Young Physician* (1919), *The Black Diamond* (1921), *Cold Harbour* (1924) – concentrated on the working and middle classes in North Bromwich and the Black Country, the sort of people he had met in his father's surgery and during his own medical studies. They dealt with the years from the 1880s until the outbreak of the First World War, and they concentrated on the darker side of urban and industrial life. 'The scheme is ambitious,' Brett Young wrote in 1919, 'but it has been long and carefully planned.'[51] 'North Bromwich' was described in *The Young Physician* as 'not a place from which men have wilfully cast out beauty, as one from which beauty has vanished in spite of man's pitiful attempts to preserve it', and he missed no opportunity to mock the philistine, materialist views of the city fathers. The Black Country ironmasters fared no better in *The Iron Age*, where Brett Young introduced 'old' Walter Willis: 'he did not worship gold; he worshipped iron', and regarded the First World War as 'the crowning mercy of his life, the thing above all for which he had lived'. As for the workers: whether labouring down the coal mines or in chain-makers' shops, or living in squalid slum dwellings, they were degraded, diseased, unhappy and uncouth.[52]

But the lowly born heroes of Brett Young's early novels, who are confined and constrained by this harsh, grimy urban environment, are also endowed with their creator's desire to escape to those green lands to the west to which they find themselves powerfully drawn.[53] Edwin Ingleby, the son of a Halesby chemist, studying medicine at 'North Bromwich' University, never abandons his childhood belief that the countryside to be seen from the summit of 'Uffdown' is the 'land of his heart's desire'. And Abner Fellows, having liberated himself from the captivity of being a coal-miner, contemplates that very same view:

Even now, the sun was drinking up the mists that concealed it, revealing sombre woodlands heavy in leaf, yellow cornfields, the smoke of hidden towns or villages and, here and there, a shining bend of river. From that high post, indeed, he gazed upon the pastoral heart of England, the most placid and homely of all her shires; but the national schools had taught him nothing of these things and, as the mists ascended, showing the cliffs of Cotswold long and level, Bredon, an island dome, May Hill and Malvern, Abberley, Clee, and all the nearer hills of Wales, he only knew that it was green and big, and that it promised freedom.[54]

As Brett Young's *Times* obituarist later noted, 'much of his quality' as a regional novelist resided in 'the effect of a distant romantic landscape which he carried into his minute and intimate observations of Midland life and manners'.[55]

Once again, this was the language and attitude of Baldwin before Baldwin's time had come. But by the mid-1920s, Baldwin's time had indeed arrived, and in *Portrait of Clare*, Brett Young produced his first self-conscious foray into Baldwinian fiction. For, like Baldwin's politics, it was deliberately an exercise in nostalgic retrospection. In revulsion against the disorientation of the First World War, and the brittle superficiality of the 1920s, it sought to put the clock back to an earlier, more wholesome era. For as Brett Young later explained, *Portrait of Clare* embodied

an instinctive reaction on my part against the kind of heroine who had become fashionable in the fiction of those strained and excited years which immediately followed the great war. To many of us who had known in our not very recent youth a coolness and quietude of life with which those writers who had grown up during the war were impatient, the kind of existence they portrayed appeared even more revolting than pitiful. The idea of inventing a woman who did not 'live on her nerves' to an accompaniment of negroid music made as strong an appeal to the contrariness of my nature as did the prospect of writing a romance of Victorian dimensions at a time when novels generally were tending to become shorter and shorter.[56]

Here was an authorial agenda which exactly paralleled Baldwin's political programme. For just as Baldwin represented an explicit rejection of the frenetic, tawdry, discredited world of the Lloyd George Coalition, and sought to return high politics to its pre-war standards of probity, so Brett Young set out to put the clock back to the days before Freud and Bloomsbury had changed – perverted, even? – the course and content of the English novel.

This approach proved to be a winner, and Brett Young held to it through-out the rest of his productive life, his subsequent novels averaging more than 500 pages in length, each of them bound in handsome, blue octavo volumes which closely resembled the published anthologies of Baldwin's speeches. And the critics welcomed this return to the old ways. 'We have to go back sixty years', observed one reviewer of *Portrait of Clare*, 'for any parallel in size and subject to this entirely English tale.' It was a longer and more leisurely treatment than in his earlier novels, and it was set in Worcestershire and the countryside rather than in Birmingham and the Black Country. Thereafter, the rustic scene came to predominate, and of his later books, only two – *My Brother Jonathan* and *Dr Bradley Remembers* – were set in the Black Country. For the rest, Brett Young preferred the villages of Worcestershire and the Marches of Wales, and he increasingly came to set his stories in the 1920s and 1930s, rather than in the pre-war days of his childhood. But it was more than an enlargement of expositional scale, an updating of the temporal setting, and a shift in geographical location, that were being signalled here. The publication of *Portrait of Clare* proclaimed Brett Young's wholehearted acceptance and eager embrace of the person and the politics of Stanley Baldwin.

Soon after it appeared, and perhaps in the hope of some beneficial pub-licity, Brett Young had sent the Prime Minister a copy of *Portrait of Clare*. He scored an immediate bull's-eye. 'More power to your elbow,' Baldwin replied from 10 Downing Street, 'and I hope you will write much more of our own folk . . . I shall make myself acquainted with your books without delay.' It seems as though he did precisely that, for only three months later, when speaking in Quebec, he quoted from the autobiographical *Marching on Tanga*, one of Brett Young's earlier works. Thereafter, Baldwin received a copy of every new Brett Young novel, and he read and enjoyed them. 'I am bearing [*My Brother*] *Jonathan* off to Chequers for the week', he wrote on receiving it in 1928, 'and looking forward keenly to starting on it.'[57] With *Jim Redlake*, Brett Young sent Baldwin his 'best wishes – political and otherwise', and in 1932 it was even suggested that Baldwin might become president of a Francis Brett Young Society.[58]

The scheme came to nothing, but the flow of books did not abate, and nor did Baldwin's appetite for them. In October 1932, Thomas Jones noted in his diary that Baldwin had been reading *The House Under the Water*. 'I know', wrote Brett Young two years later, enclosing a copy of *This Little World*, 'that its scene, a Worcestershire village, and its subject, that village's ordinary life, are as dear to your hearts as they are to mine.' 'We are really grateful when you send us your books,' wrote Baldwin on receiving *Far Forest*:

> If I may say so, without impertinence, there are now two things about your books that give me complete satisfaction. Your craftsmanship – how I respect a good workman! And your capacity to give the smell and the spirit of the choicest county in the world. You get it both ways, physical and spiritual.[59]

By then, the Baldwins and the Brett Youngs were regularly visiting each other in their respective Worcestershire homes, and tramped the countryside together. Indeed, on Baldwin's retirement, he and Brett Young spent a day exploring Corvedale, the latter learning at first hand 'the whole story of the Abdication'. Shortly after, their friendship reached its most publicized point, when Brett Young dedicated *They Seek a Country* 'To the Earl Baldwin of Bewdley, K.G., with the homage and gratitude of a friend and neighbour'.[60]

As these words imply, Brett Young's great commercial success had eventually allowed him to return to his favourite county in triumph – not to Halesowen but to Craycombe House near Pershore, and not as a practising doctor or impoverished author but as a country gentleman with literary leanings. 'I have become a Worcestershire landowner,' he wrote ecstatically to Baldwin in 1932, and there he remained until 1945, playing to perfection the part of the local squire in the county which was the 'prime passion' of his life.[61] He lavished money on restoring the house to its eighteenth-century splendour; he grew fruit and vegetables on the small estate; he was on visiting terms with local grandees like the Cobhams and the Beauchamps; his wartime service entitled him to be called 'Major'; and he was regularly seen walking the country lanes, clad in tweeds and smoking a pipe. Like Baldwin, he was an ardent admirer of Worcestershire cricket, he served on the executive committee of the Friends of Worcester Cathedral, and he was vice-chairman of the local branch of the Council for the Preservation of Rural England, vice-president of the Worcestershire Association, and president of the Midland Ramblers Association.[62]

This was Brett Young fully established and identified as Baldwin man; and from *Portrait of Clare* until the outbreak of the Second World War, his novels were very much established and identified as Baldwin fiction. Time and again, Brett Young claimed that he wrote with no didactic purpose, and that he was uninterested in politics. This was merely another way of saying that he had no politics, but voted Conservative for the good of the country, and that his books were pervaded by the sort of wholesome, non-political values that every right-thinking English man and decent English woman might – and should – applaud. Between the covers, they were long, leisurely and ruminative stories, mirroring and mimicking Baldwin's reputation for calmness, reliability and placidity. In their rejection of city-bred, cosmopolitan intellectuals, the parallel with Baldwin's philosophy is again evident: none of Brett Young's heroes and heroines may be thus described. And characters like Diana Powys and Jack Ombersley, who embodied the brash, irresponsible, promiscuous outlook of the 1920s and 1930s, were roundly condemned and held up to ridicule.[63]

As in his earlier books, those characters who were still unfortunate enough to be confined by the city find a means of escape to the lush lands further west. So: Jonathan Dakers, in need of a holiday after the strain of general practice during the First World War, went on a walking tour beyond the Severn Valley, the very same area where Baldwin went to recuperate during the summer of 1936. So: David Wilden, after qualifying as a teacher in 'North Bromwich' returns to work in Shropshire; and John Bradley – another reluctant town dweller – chooses to practise as a doctor in the Black Country town of 'Sedgbury' because from the nearby ridge the same wondrous view that so moved Abner Fellows may be seen. And in *Mr Lucton's Freedom*, the escapist motif reached its most extreme development when Owen Lucton, a respectable North Bromwich solicitor, vanishes for two blissful months from the cares of family and business to the shires beckoning far beyond. Again, he begins his journey by recalling his childhood memories of the view from atop 'Uffdown': 'It was odd, he reflected, how all through his life, that prospect had drawn his imagination westward.'[64]

When it came to describing the countryside to which these characters aspired and escaped, Brett Young was no more interested in the limitations and shortcomings of rural life than Baldwin. To be sure, in *This Little World* and *Portrait of a Village*, he referred to the squalor of some rural cottages as being a 'social disgrace', but the references to their lack of water, to their leaking roofs, and to their thin walls, were made very much in passing.[65] In the same way, the inhabitants were depicted very superficially, as types rather than individuals: the schoolteacher, the doctor, the vicar, and so on. In essence, Brett Young described village life as town dwellers wanted to see it, a world of pretty gardens, cricket matches, country dances and choral societies. Here, for instance, is the sight which greets Mr Lucton as he enters a Worcestershire village:

The dim, straggling street was full of signs of warm and friendly life: smoke rising straight from a dozen cottage chimneys; the voices of children which echoed in the deepening dusk; swallows (or were they bats?) darting under the eaves of thatch and circling the church tower; a colony of agitated rooks that seemed loth to alight on their nests in the elms that guarded the green; a late cuckoo, distantly calling with the cracked note of June.

Similar passages may be found in many of his books and, in their style, their substance and their sentiment, they could be inserted into any number of Baldwin's speeches without incongruity.[66]

In fact, it was not so much the everyday life of Worcestershire villages which attracted Brett Young as the lives of the country gentry who lived near them and dominated them, and it was on the Abberleys of 'Monks Norton', the Ombersleys of 'Chaddesbourne d'Abitot', and the Pomfrets that he lavished some of his most sentimentally purple prose:

No title or abundant wealth has ever come their way; no brilliant blossom has ever adorned their family tree; its sole virtue consists in its astonishing permanence . . . Wars may redden the land, revolutions may change its face and dynasties may divide it, but the Abberleys still go on: they are so near to the soil, their roots reach so far down, that mere accidents such as these are powerless to remove them.[67]

Even after the First World War, they are – thankfully – still there. But only just. For when Miles Ombersley succeeds to the Chaddesbourne estate in 1922, he finds nothing but a 'thousand-odd acres of land, for the most part neglected, and a staggering load of death duties for which, characteristically, his father had made no provision'. Determined to carry on, Miles reckons without his son's refusal to co-operate, and his rejection of what he sees as the outdated and uneconomic enterprise of 'traditional' landownership. And he is soon faced with additional financial demands which leave him no choice but to sell off some of the estates: 'the losing battle was over: he had been forced to capitulate'.[68]

But, as if by a miracle, the Chaddesbourne estate is saved at the eleventh hour: a road accident brings Miles's son to his senses (which means, essentially, seeing things in the same way as his father), and an even more convenient windfall bolsters up the family finances. As one authority noted, 'the book is exceptionally full of difficulties solved'.[69] Instead of being a realistic account of the gentry's decline, *This Little World* is an escapist monument to their reassuring permanence. Here, for instance, is Brett

Young's account of Miles Ombersley's state of mind when, for the first time, he views the body of his late father:

The qualities which he had admired in his father were not personal: their two natures were far too like each other for that. No, the admiration he felt – and his present emotion showed that this was genuine – was for what his father represented as the vehicle and instrument of a tradition, the incarnation of that sense of duty, that faith – in their Chaddesbourne, in England – which had devolved on every bearer of the name for the last four hundred years. That old man, lying there, with his cold features waxed in candlelight, had kept the light burning for the better part of a century. He, Miles Ombersley, was prepared to carry the torch a stage further.

And the book ends on a similar note of decent and dignified dutifulness, with the dedication of the village war memorial, the stiff-upper-lipped behaviour of the Ombersleys (who had lost two sons in the war), and the whole village singing 'Jerusalem'.[70]

The scene, the setting and the sentiments were quintessentially Baldwinian: a local community brought together in a display of order and consensus; the virtues of public service and patriotic sacrifice asserted and proclaimed; the losses recognized, but the feelings kept firmly under control; and all this with the sanction and support of the Church of England. These were Baldwin's inter-war images and beliefs, and they were Brett Young's, too. They might have been working in different mediums, but their concerns and their messages were essentially the same: the linking, as Baldwin had earlier put it, of the 'physical' and the 'spiritual'. This was politics as culture, as comfort and as consolation – so much so, indeed, that it scarcely seemed to be politics at all. As Brett Young explained, when sending Baldwin his inscribed copy of *They Seek a Country*, he saw the by-now former Prime Minister as

representing my own thoughts and feelings in these troublous times – and above all during the messy business of the abdication, and I am thankful that in the House of Lords you will still be able to speak for people like myself, who have no great concern with politics, but a deep, an almost religious feeling, for the English manner of thought. I explain myself badly, for the thing is hard to define; but I think that you, better than any man living, will understand what I mean.[71]

III

During the eighteen eventful years which separated the Lloyd George Coalition of 1922 from the Churchill Coalition of 1940, Britain was largely ruled by what has rightly been described as 'the respectable tendency', and that rule was as much exercised through culture and the countryside as it was through government and Parliament.[72] As such, it was a widely supported enterprise, and among those who gave it shape and substance, Stanley Baldwin was the pivotal political figure, and Francis Brett Young a significant literary force. Like many Britons during the 1920s and 1930s, they were bewildered, disoriented and dismayed – by the catastrophe of the First World War, by the corruption of the Lloyd George Coalition, by the descent of Europe into bolshevism and fascism, by the depression in British industry and the social unrest in British society, and by the collapse of religious beliefs and settled values almost everywhere. In such circumstances, the most that could be realistically achieved was to persuade Britons to come to terms with their grief and their sense of loss, to abandon class warfare and sectional interests, to turn away from material greed and political corruption, to eschew the extremism of continental ideologies, to endure uncomplaining the hardships of poverty and the humiliations of unemployment, and to try to live together in amity, friendship and brotherhood, by putting the community and the country before their own selfish interests, and by returning to the consoling tenets of Christian religion.

It was to that great enterprise of social amelioration and spiritual regeneration that Stanley Baldwin devoted his years of power and his considerable gifts of insight and expression, and it was a similar mission and message which, from 1927, Francis Brett Young undertook and proclaimed in his novels. Of course, both had their contemporary critics. The political buccaneers like Lords Birkenhead and Beaverbrook despised Baldwin for being self-righteous and second-rate; Lloyd George and Sir Oswald Mosley thought he should have done something about urban unemployment rather than merely invoking rural images; and Churchill thought he should have done more about Hitler than merely praising English decencies. Many intellectuals and industrial workers found his rustic bromides nauseating and condescending, and his squirearchical pose insincere and unconvincing; and for all his appeals to consensus, conciliation and community, Baldwin was emphatically on the side of 'the nation' and 'the public' rather than 'the people' or 'the working class'.[73] In the same way, Brett Young's novels were dismissed by the intelligentsia for being old-fashioned, lazy and bland, for parading rural platitudes as moral profundities, and for offering nostalgic, sentimental banalities, when something more bracing, more engaged, more realistic and more adventurous was needed. Niceness, in short, was not enough.

More generally, the case put by the clever men and the critics was that Baldwin (and Brett Young) were provincial, mediocre and narrow-minded; that they wasted their time, and everyone else's, dishing out escapist fantasies, Christian clichés and soothing pap; that they were all style (we would now say spin) and no substance, putting 'Safety First' but nothing else behind it; and that they were intellectually idle and politically timid – afraid of first-class minds with bright ideas, who might have solved the otherwise intractable problems of the inter-war years, but whom they ruthlessly kept out of office and out of power. To which the 'respectable tendency' retorted that for all their intellectual limitations, their characters were more decent, honourable and reliable; that their insight into the country's affairs was in fact the clearer and the truer; that their sympathies with the people were wider, deeper and more genuine; that the electorate regularly and repeatedly voted for them and against the self-styled clever men; that the problems by which inter-war Britain was beset could not be solved by brittle politicians with bright ideas but no sense of human reality; and that under these circumstances, the best that could be hoped for was to try to bring everyone together and to pull the nation through.

For most of the 1920s and 1930s, this was the view that generally prevailed, as decency and duty – suitably exemplified and expressed by Baldwin, and echoed and endorsed by Brett Young – triumphed. Lloyd George never held power again after his coalition fell in 1922; Lord Birkenhead died of drink, debts and disappointment in 1931; Oswald Mosley abandoned the politics of Parliament for the scuffles of the streets; and by the 1930s, Winston Churchill seemed marginalized as a die-hard and embittered class warrior.[74] So, when Baldwin retired in May 1937, having eased King Edward VIII out, and having presided over the coronation of King George VI and Queen Elizabeth, his public and parliamentary standing were at their peak, and he departed hoping for 'a few peaceful years of life in the county in which one was brought up, to look out once more upon those hills, and ultimately to lay one's bones in that red soil from which one was made'. As for Brett Young, his novels had never sold better, the fictional future seemed set fair, and he achieved his ultimate triumph as a Worcestershire gentleman, when *Country Life* published his own article on Craycombe House.[75]

But by then, the tide of politics and public opinion was emphatically turning against both of them. The Second World War, Chamberlain's fall, Churchill's encounter with destiny, and Labour's massive electoral victory in 1945, signalled the end of popular approval for the values Baldwin and Brett Young had each, in their different professions, embodied and celebrated. Those who had venerated Baldwin in his heyday now came to hate him, and with Neville Chamberlain's death in November 1940, he became the prime target for those in search of 'Guilty Men', and the abusive letters, the caustic articles and the vindictive episode of the Astley railings are all familiar features of his declining years.[76] The best Baldwin could hope for was that most people, preoccupied by the trials and tribulations of war, survival and victory, would forget him. 'The last person many people want to hear is a survivor from the days of 1931–1937,' he told Thomas Jones in September 1941. 'We are out of date.' Lonely, widowed and infirm, Baldwin lingered on, his eightieth birthday passing virtually unnoticed outside his family, and the household at Astley never recovering its pre-war scale. As G. M. Young put it, with rather morbid relish, 'Baldwin was living in a landscape no longer to be seen from any window.'[77]

He died just before Christmas 1947, and as befitted this loyal son of his county, he was buried in Worcester Cathedral. Soon after, Francis Brett Young offered this commentary on his friend's career and character, which tells us a great deal about both men:

I knew him for many years, mainly in an unofficial capacity, as a Worcestershire neighbour, who happened to be interested in my series of Mercian novels and, as he showed me, knew and appreciated every word of them, having even taken the trouble to verify my topography by following in the footsteps of my imaginary characters on their wanderings.

He was an odd mixture of personal simplicity and political shrewdness; and his greatest asset in both was his power of identifying himself with that part of the nature of masses and individuals which can only be described as their essential 'Englishness'.

He had a passionate love for the particular patch of the Western Midlands in which we were both born and which was illuminated for both of us by the memories of childhood: that is to say, the enchanted countryside which lies between the River Severn and the Welsh Border. He knew every highway and byway in it intimately, and I spent many happy hours with him in exploring what we already knew.

This interest was at the centre of his life, and I think his absorption in it explains his comparative disinterest [sic] in foreign affairs, which he was inclined to neglect because he had little sympathy with them or understanding of them. It was this limitation, this concentration on what he did understand, this insularity, which gave him his strength and influence as an English Prime Minister.

He was at his best in the handling of local problems, such as the General Strike and the Abdication of Edward VIII, in both of which he played a part for which he was personally qualified, with complete success. Though he was not in any sense a scholar, he had a great love for Literature, particularly the Literature of Tradition, and for History just so far as it had a bearing on the life of our Island.

He was not, in other respects, a 'strong' man. In some respects it would be fair to say that he was lazy. He was at heart a Quietist, who suddenly, and to his own surprise, found himself thrust into a key position in a most unquiet world which was little to his taste and which he had not the capacity to control.

Although he was ambitious and enjoyed the great position which he attained, I think he would have been a happier man if he had never become Prime Minister, an office which deprived him of many of the things he loved, and imposed too great a strain on an easy-going nature.

He had great personal charm, and (in his private life) a disarming frankness. He never pretended to be anything more than he was; and that, I suppose, is one of the characteristics of greatness.

As to his part in the critical events which preceded the Second World War: we must leave these to History; but there is no doubt that he did his duty according to his lights, and was satisfied, to the end, that he had done it, and serenely confident that Time would do him Justice. That remains to be seen.

At the moment we can do no more than mourn the loss of a good man and a loyal friend, a human type which has grown rarer and rarer in these catastrophic years, but which is still characteristic of the English character at its best.[78]

As the allusion to 'these catastrophic years' suggests, Brett Young had fared little better during the Second World War and in the years immediately after. His weak heart compelled the sale of Craycombe in 1945 and exile in the kindlier climate of South Africa, and he never recovered from parting with his house ('the material thing I loved best in all the world and in all my life') or leaving Worcestershire ('wherever I am, a picture of my native country-side is stamped indelibly on my mind'). His epic poem, *The Island*, written in a mood of high and fervent patriotism during the Second World War, and which he regarded as 'the epitome and crown of all I had to say', failed to establish him as a significant presence in the new cultural climate of the Churchillian consensus, and he lived long enough to see his fiction lose its pre-war popularity. 'It is already out of date', he wrote of *The Island* in 1948, 'and I am out of date with it', a pathetic echo of Baldwin's words to Thomas Jones of seven years before.[79] His letters became more sad and embittered, with ravings against the 'totalitarian' Labour government in England, and his love for the 'vanished splendours' of rural, aristocratic life, which he now believed to be irrevocably gone, became an obsession. In *Wistanslow*, his final work of fiction (published posthumously), he sought to write their requiem, but ill-health meant he abandoned work on it. So, with no major new novel published since the war, his death in 1954 'passed almost unnoticed by the literary press'.[80]

Since then, their respective reputations have remained largely in the doldrums. In politics, Baldwin's consensual, Christian, countrified emolli-ence was a world away from Churchill's heroic defiance, Attlee's radical nationalization, Macmillan's affluent materialism and Thatcher's confron-tational patriotism. Meanwhile, Churchill took terrible revenge in his war memoirs, where he described Baldwin as confessing to 'putting party before country', Lord Beaverbrook's implacable vendetta was carried on after his death by A. J. P. Taylor in his histories and biographies, and Baldwin's enthusiasm for rural values was an early target for those seeking an expla-nation for Britain's inter-war industrial decline.[81] To be sure, there was a postwar revival of interest in what is now called the 'national heritage', but this was more concerned with the country house than with the country side, and today the safeguarding of the 'environment' is seen as a secular mission in defence of the planet rather than as a moral crusade in support of 'spiritual values'. Assuredly, Baldwin has in recent decades found a clutch of appreciative biographers. But for all their recognition of his charms and cleverness, his skills and decency, his importance and significance, he remains among the least remembered or recognized of Britain's twentieth-century prime ministers. And the fact that Harold Wilson appropriated Baldwin's pipe, and that John Major borrowed a debased version of his rural rhetoric, did neither them, nor him, much good.[82]

Just as Baldwin's inter-war image still seems tarnished beyond rehabili-tation, so the mirror which Francis Brett Young held up to it has been broken, apparently beyond repair. Of course, even in the 1920s and 1930s, he was never as dominant a force in English literature as Baldwin was in English politics, and he never succeeded in transcending the geographical limitations of his novels to offer insights of general significance in the way that Baldwin for a time managed to do. To be sure, there have been many postwar authors who have made rural nostalgia their stock in trade, from R. F. Delderfield to Winston Graham (to say nothing of *The Archers*: an 'everyday story of country folk'), but Brett Young has failed to benefit from this renewed cult of the country. In the years immediately after his death, his widow constantly but vainly predicted a revival of interest in his work, her own biography of him failed to stimulate such a trend, his books have received little scholarly attention, and today he is all but forgotten.[83] Yet in his heyday, Brett Young *was* a significant novelist, not only because of what he wrote, and because he was widely read, but also because of his friendship with the dominant political figure of his time. It is not often that politicians and novelists establish such a close rapport, conveying the same messages and images to voters and readers alike. But on the rare occasions when they do, historians are well advised to take note. Politics is always about politics; but it can sometimes be about culture as well.

8

Diplomacy: G. M. Trevelyan
and R. B. Merriman[1]

The early months of 1939 were difficult and challenging times for the Foreign Office in London and the State Department in Washington, as well as for the occupants of 10 Downing Street and the White House. Appeasement and neutrality remained the respective policies of the British and American governments towards Nazi Germany, and they were still being robustly defended in public by Neville Chamberlain and Franklin D. Roosevelt. But in the aftermath of the Munich agreement of September 1938, at which large parts of the Czech Sudetenland had been ceded to Germany, doubts were beginning to creep into official circles on both sides of the Atlantic as to whether, and for how long, these policies could be plausibly pursued and successfully sustained. In these circumstances, thinking the unthinkable about the future was becoming increasingly unavoidable. The prospect might have to be faced that the Fuhrer could not be indefinitely placated, in which case there was no point in continuing to try to appease him. The possibility that war between Britain and Germany could not be prevented was thus becoming ever more real, but it was not clear what the outcome of such a conflict would be. And if it happened, this war might eventually involve the United States as well as the United Kingdom, but who could say whether this would be on the basis of strict or benevolent neutrality or of open and allied belligerence?[2]

As is well known, these momentous changes in policy and purpose did eventually come about: Britain renounced appeasement, America progressively gave up neutrality, and the Anglo-American Grand Alliance duly defeated Hitler (albeit with considerable assistance from the Russians). But however pre-ordained this triumphant outcome may seem in retrospect, there was nothing inevitable about it in prospect. The English-speaking peoples might share a common language, but they had rarely made or shared a common foreign policy. Their brief collaboration during the First World War was the exception rather than the rule, and during the late 1930s, Anglo-American relations were once more characterized by 'suspicion and hesitation on both sides'.[3] This meant that in early 1939, the British did not know if, or how, or when, or to what extent, the Americans would abandon neutrality, in which case they were not sure they should or could give up appeasement. It also meant that the Americans did not know if, or how, or when, or to what extent, the British would give up appeasement, in which case they were not sure they should or could abandon neutrality. Inevitably, then, it took time for the two nations, assisted by both Hitler and Hirohito, to inch and feel their way towards the successfully belligerent collaboration which finally began in December 1941.

It bears repeating that none of this could have been realistically expected or predicted in January or February of 1939, and it was in that gloomy period, when established policies seemed increasingly in doubt, when Anglo-American relations remained in their usual state of flux, and when no one in either country could know who the American President would be after the election due in November 1940, that two great historians tried to nudge and coax their respective governments towards making common cause against the threat to freedom posed by Nazi Germany. The instigator of this diplomatic initiative was Professor Roger Bigelow Merriman of Cambridge, Massachusetts, and his unsuspecting (but not unwilling) collaborator was Professor George Macaulay Trevelyan of Cambridge, England. In the complex history of pre-war Anglo-American relations, their endeavours have rightly received little more than the briefest notice.[4] But when set in the common context of their family and professional lives, and their shared views of the world, their intervention deserves more sustained attention than it has received from historians of official policy and international relations.

I

It was an agreeable and suggestive coincidence that Merriman and Trevelyan were both born in the same year – 1876 – for their backgrounds, careers, interests and opinions were strikingly similar, and by 1939 they were old and close friends. Roger Merriman traced his paternal ancestry back to Nathaniel Merriman, who had been born in England in 1613, had arrived in Boston in 1632, and settled in New Haven in 1640. The tercentennial of Nathaniel's birth was celebrated with a Merriman reunion, held at Wallingford in Connecticut, the town he had helped to found in 1670. Thereafter, the family remained concentrated in that state, but Daniel Merriman established himself in Boston, where he was remembered as 'a noted Congregationalist preacher and a man of wide influence'.[5] In 1874, Daniel married Helen Bigelow, whose forebears were descended from John Bigelow, who had settled at Watertown in Massachusetts in 1637, and fathered twelve children. Among later generations of Bigelows were inventors, economists, lawyers, educators, surgeons and physicians, and many of them became associated with the foremost institutions of Greater Boston: Harvard University, the Massachusetts Institute of Technology, the Massachusetts General Hospital and the Boston Museum of Fine Arts. One of them was Erastus Brigham Bigelow, who was best known as the inventor of the carpet loom, which brought fame and fortune to his branch of the family; and Helen Bigelow, who became a writer, an artist and the editor of her husband's sermons, was his only surviving child.[6]

By the late-nineteenth-century standards of east coast America, these were illustrious pedigrees and, as the firstborn son of Daniel and Helen, Roger Bigelow Merriman naturally grew up with a strong sense of ancestral pride, dynastic identity and religious commitment. Like many Boston Brahmins of his generation, he was educated at Harvard, where he graduated in 1896, and obtained his Ph.D. six years later. He immediately became an instructor in the History Department, was a full professor by the age of forty-two, and in 1929 was named Gurney Professor of History and Political Science. In 1904, he had married Dorothea Foote, whose family was as venerable and distinguished as the Merrimans and the Bigelows. Her relatives were scattered throughout Massachusetts, Connecticut and New York, her father was the Revd. Henry Wilder Foote, minister of King's Chapel in Boston, and her uncle was the New England composer Arthur William Foote.[7] But there were even grander connections, for Dorothea Foote's uncle by marriage was Charles William Eliot, President of Harvard University from 1869 to 1909, the greatest educator of his generation, and according to Theodore Roosevelt, the 'First Citizen of the Republic'. With such grand connections, it was scarcely surprising that, between 1931 and 1942, Merriman was the founding Master of Eliot House, where he presided with such 'splash and flourish' that it rapidly became the pre-eminent Harvard house.[8]

Trevelyan's family background was very similar, and his scholarly career ran in almost exact parallel. He was descended from the cadet branch of a 'very old family' of Cornish gentry, who in the nineteenth century had established themselves at Wallington in Northumberland, where they acquired by marriage a great house and estate.[9] His grandfather, Sir Charles Trevelyan, was a civil service reformer and Indian colonial governor; his great uncle was Lord Macaulay, by turns a poet, a politician, and the most widely read historian of his day; his father, Sir George Otto Trevelyan, held office in every Gladstone government, and was the biographer of Charles James Fox and the historian of the American Revolution; and his elder brother Charles was a minister in the Liberal governments before the First World War and again in the Labour administrations of 1924 and 1929. Moreover, in marrying (as he did in 1904) Janet Penrose Ward, Trevelyan linked his own family with a dynasty which, while less venerable, was no less distinguished than his own. For Janet was the granddaughter of Thomas Arnold, the niece of Matthew Arnold, and one of her aunts married into the Huxley clan. As a result, one favourite pastime of George and Janet was to play what Bertrand Russell called 'the game of great uncles', when they tried to decide, half-jokingly, half-seriously, whose relatives had been the more eminent.[10]

Like Roger Merriman, Trevelyan thus belonged not only to his nation's aristocracy of birth, but also to its aristocracy of talent, and in his own life, he more than measured up to these exacting standards. He was educated, like his father, at Harrow school and Trinity College, Cambridge, where he was elected to the Apostles and numbered among his friends and contemporaries John Maynard Keynes, Lytton Strachey and Ralph Vaughan Williams (to all of whom he was also related), and Bertrand Russell. He took a First in History in 1896, and was elected a Fellow of Trinity two years later. But in 1903, he left Cambridge for London, to throw himself into metropolitan life and promote the cause of 'literary and Liberal history'.[11] In 1927, he returned in triumph to academe, when the Prime Minister Stanley Baldwin (who had also been educated at Harrow and Trinity) appointed him Regius Professor of Modern History at Cambridge. Three years later, he was made a member of the Order of Merit, as his father had been before him, and in 1940, another Harrovian Prime Minister and near-contemporary, Winston Churchill, appointed him Master of Trinity College. Like Macaulay's, Trevelyan's was (in Gladstone's words) 'an extraordinarily full life of sustained exertion', a 'high table-land without depressions', with 'success so uniform as to be almost monotonous'.[12]

As befitted someone from his background and generation, Roger Merriman was an abidingly ardent anglophile. Between 1897 and 1899, he studied at Balliol College, Oxford, under F. York Powell and Arthur Lionel Smith, and his research eventually appeared as a two-volume study of Thomas Cromwell. This formative period left him with a lifelong devotion to the English system of élite education, and also to Tudor history. He was one of the principal promotors of the tutorial system at Harvard, regarded Oxbridge colleges as the ideal model for Harvard houses, and proudly hung his Balliol oars in his Eliot House study. He was renowned for his appreciation of Shakespeare and Jacobean prose, and was thought 'Eliza-bethan' in his zest and love of life.[13] Although his scholarly interests shifted to continental Europe, he continued to keep up with new work in the field, and to teach Tudor and Stuart history, stressing 'the development of the English constitution and institutions during the important formative period, 1485–1714'. Throughout the inter-war years, Merriman was a regular summer visitor to Europe, where he 'maintained his friendships with men prominent in British scholarship and public affairs'. He received honorary doctorates from the universities of Oxford (1922), Glasgow (1929) and Cambridge (1935), and in this latter distinction the Regius Professor of Modern History must surely have had a hand.[14]

For his part, Trevelyan's interest in America was virtually synonymous with his family name. His father's history of the revolution was much admired in the United States (it had, according to his son, been partly written to improve Anglo-American relations), and he was the close friend of Theodore Roosevelt, Henry James, John Hay, Elihu Root and Henry Cabot Lodge. In the next generation, Trevelyan corresponded extensively with American scholars, including William Roscoe Thayer, Wallace Notestein, William Aitken, Allan Nevins and Willard Connely. He paid his first lengthy visit to the United States in 1915, when he gave a series of addresses putting the British case for involvement in the First World War.[15] Ten years later, he delivered lectures at Harvard that were eventually developed into his one-volume *History of England*, a book he dedicated to another anglophile, Lawrence Lowell, who was Eliot's successor as president of the university. In 1935, his son Humphry spent a year as a graduate student at Yale, at the end of which he married Mary Trumbull Bennett, whose forebears came from the same patrician stock as the Merrimans, the Bigelows and the Footes, and who was described by her prospective father-in-law as 'a very nice New England girl of the right breed'. Throughout the inter-war years, Trevelyan was a regular supporter of the Anglo-American conference of historians, held each year at the Institute of Historical Research in London, and as wartime Master of Trinity, he entertained many visiting American servicemen in Cambridge.[16]

Trevelyan and Merriman were not only fellow patricians in the Anglo-American republic of letters: they also wrote a similar sort of history – large-scale, multi-volume works, based on detailed, archival research, rang-ing widely in space and time, which were intended to reach a broad public audience. Merriman's models were Bancroft, Motley, Prescott and Park-man; Trevelyan's were his great uncle and his father. After his life of Thomas Cromwell, Merriman turned to a four-volume history of the Spanish Empire in the old world and the new, from medieval times to the death of Philip II, which he completed between 1918 and 1934, and he went on to produce a survey of revolutions in seventeenth-century Europe, and a biography of Suleiman the Magnificent. Trevelyan published two trilogies, on Garibaldi and *England Under Queen Anne*, surveys of seventeenth- and nineteenth-century England, in addition to his one-volume general history, and a clutch of biographies. Both men believed history provided the best 'liberal education' for those who sought to understand how the world they inhabited had come to be the way it was. As they conceived of it, taught it, and wrote it, history was not about impersonal economic or social processes, but was a dramatic narrative of nations and individuals: 'a pageant, animated, grand, compelling'.[17]

But their similarities were not confined to the sort of history they preached and practised. Throughout their writings, both men projected and proclaimed comparable values, preferring freedom, Protestantism and progress to despotism, Catholicism and obscurantism. All Trevelyan's work is shot through with a burning love of liberty, often associated with the countryside and the high hills of Northumberland, with a fierce hostility to the Catholic despotisms of France and Spain, and with a marked preference for stories with 'happy endings'. The Garibaldi trilogy charted the triumph of secular progress and personal liberty over the clerical reaction of the papacy and the despotic governments of Sicily and Austria.[18] In *England Under the Stuarts*, and in *England Under Queen Anne*, Trevelyan celebrated parliamentary and religious freedom as the strongest bulwarks against continental absolutism. He wrote one book to commemorate the Glorious Revolution of 1688, and another to memorialize the life of Earl Grey who had passed the Great Reform Act of 1832. And these themes received their fullest elaboration in the *History of England*, where Trevelyan fondly traced the development of the nation's 'peculiar characteristics, laws and institutions', as they had evolved and endured across the centuries.[19]

Merriman's histories of England and Spain were written from a very similar viewpoint. His Thomas Cromwell was the unlawful creator of Tudor despotism, a figure who inspired 'madness and terror', but who fortunately failed to undermine English liberties or significantly thwart their development. By contrast, the English revolution of the mid-seventeenth century was the most important of those which occurred in Europe, because of the new ideas of religious toleration and personal freedom which it embodied and unleashed.[20] As a devout Congregationalist, Merriman was also vehemently anti-papist, and he scornfully denounced Catholic-American scholars who tried to argue that the Inquisition had been a 'good thing' and that the Reformation had been no less bad.[21] And as befitted an admirer and follower of Prescott, he argued that Spain and its empire had failed because of their backward-looking religion and inhibiting, indolent absolutism, whereas Britain and its empire had succeeded because of their forward-looking religion and vigorous, liberating democracy. Merriman's Spain and Trevelyan's England were thus corroborative contrasts, the opposite sides of the same liberal, Whiggish, Protestant coin.[22]

We do not know when these two historians first met: perhaps it was on Merriman's early, extended visit to England as a graduate student, or perhaps during Trevelyan's long visit to the United States during the First World War. But whenever it was, they soon discovered they were kindred spirits, they greatly enjoyed each other's company, and they also took a shared delight in country walking. By the 1920s, they were in regular correspondence, and each new work by Merriman was enthusiastically received by Trevelyan.[23] That admiration was clearly reciprocated, and a photograph of Trevelyan hung in the library of Eliot House. When the Merrimans made their regular summer visits to Britain, they stayed with the Trevelyans, sometimes at Garden Corner in Cambridge, but also at Hallington in Northumberland. There the two professors walked across the moors where the air was 'like champagne'; they visited Sir Charles Trevelyan at Wallington; and they engaged in endless conversations 'ranging over every conceivable subject', which were punctuated by quotations from Latin, Greek and the poets. Merriman loved 'messing about' among Trevelyan's collection of Lord Macaulay's books and 'imbibing the historical atmosphere'; and Trevelyan presented him with two copies of his father's *History of the American Revolution*, one for Harvard University, the other for the Massachusetts Historical Society.[24]

II

Merriman and Trevelyan were not only close friends and practitioners of a similar sort of history: they were both as much public men as university professors in their day could be. They came from distinguished families, which gave them dynastic pride and ancestral authority; they wrote books which reached a broad, educated and appreciative audience; and this combination of connection and attainment impelled them to the heart of their respective national establishments. As befitted someone of his class and clan, Trevelyan regarded figures such as Pitt the Younger, Charles James Fox and Lord John Russell, not as distant historical characters but as personal acquaintances, social equals and close contemporaries. Through his father, he had met most of the leading lights of Gladstonian Liberalism, and he himself had friends or relatives in every twentieth-century British Cabinet until 1955. Among Prime Ministers, he was related by marriage to A. J. Balfour, he was read by Asquith, MacDonald and Lloyd George, and he was especially close to Baldwin and Churchill, albeit in rather different ways. Among first-ranking politicians, his friends included Sir John Simon, Sir Edward Grey (whose biography he wrote), Walter Runciman and Hugh Dalton. And he moved with effortless ease across the networks and bastions of the British Establishment: *The Times*, the BBC, the Apostles, the Athenaeum, the British Academy and the Order of Merit.[25]

There has never been an exact equivalent of the American east coast to the British Establishment. But during the 1930s, Merriman's connections to the corridors of power in Washington were even closer than Trevelyan's in London.[26] As a junior instructor at Harvard, one of his students had been the young Franklin Delano Roosevelt. FDR was not an outstanding scholar, did not read very much, habitually confused concepts like feudalism and tyranny, and only obtained a C in History 1, the famous outline course Merriman taught on European history from the Fall of Rome to the Present. But this was a less dishonourable grade then than it would be now, and Merriman recognized that Roosevelt was 'bright, slick and politically oriented'.[27] They became firm friends, they met and corresponded during the 1920s, and as President, FDR stayed in touch with his mentor. 'Your ancient teachings', he wrote from the White House in November 1933, 'have stood your old pupil in good stead in the development of more modern history.' But as befitted a Boston Brahmin, Harvard Professor and Republican supporter, Merriman was unintimidated by the fact that his former pupil was now the nation's president. When FDR attempted to pack the Supreme Court, Merriman spoke out vigorously against him. To both men's credit, they remained friends, nonetheless.[28]

It was thus not only as historians who cherished European freedom and English liberties, but also as men close to government and (largely) sympathetic to the governors, that Trevelyan and Merriman were both becoming increasingly worried about European affairs and Anglo-American relations by the late 1930s. To be sure, Trevelyan believed that Germany had been badly treated after the First World War; he was a supporter of Baldwin, Chamberlain, appeasement and Munich; and he distrusted Churchill's character and political judgement, even though he admired his books. But as a Whig who cherished freedom and feared continental despots, he had supported the decision to go to war in 1914, he hated what Mussolini had done to Italy, and he had no doubt that Hitler was a barbarian and a tyrant.[29] And his biography of Sir Edward Grey, published in 1937, was taken by many as an exemplary account of how an earlier Foreign Secretary had prepared for the possibility of war while simultaneously continuing to work for peace in the years before 1914. By the winter of 1938–9, Trevelyan was resigned to the fact that the Munich settlement had not guaranteed 'Peace in Our Time', and that Britain would probably have to fight Germany again, in a war which he was sure would destroy European civilization as he knew it and loved it.[30]

As an anglophile Whig, with a strong European sense, and a shared belief in liberty and freedom, Merriman had reached similar conclusions about world affairs, albeit by slightly different routes. He had been a champion of Anglo-American co-operation and a critic of United States isolationism long before America entered the First World War, and he had served in the US military as an army captain in 1918.[31] Predictably, given his areas of academic expertise and his hostility to Catholicism, he was greatly concerned about Spain's descent into civil war, and he was a vehement critic of Franco's new and more brutal brand of Catholic despotism. He also, by extension, deplored the dictatorial regimes of Hitler and Mussolini, and contemplated with horror the prospect of a continent overrun by these Fascists, of a beleaguered and besieged Britain, and of an indifferent and unconcerned United States.[32] By 1938, he feared that American neutrality was inexorably veering towards isolationism, regretted that there was not more active support in Washington for Britain, and worried that Europe was prey to dictators whom no one in American seemed prepared to condemn, let alone try to stop.

It was in this mood that Merriman initiated a correspondence with Trevelyan which he hoped would enable him to bring these points home to American policy-makers at the highest level. He did so by stealth and with considerable subtlety. In November 1938, he wrote to a young Harvard graduate student, who was then a Henry Fellow at Peterhouse, Cambridge, enclosing a letter of introduction to Trevelyan. In the course of it, Merriman also asked Trevelyan to set down his views on the current world situation. Appropriately enough, the young courier of this missive was the son of another Harvard history professor, who would himself go on to write biographies and multi-volume histories in the 'literary and Liberal' mode, and also play some part in the broader public life of his country. His name was Arthur Schlesinger, jr. But at that point, Merriman's initiative stalled almost before it had begun, for it was not until January 1939, having been reminded by his father, that Schlesinger acknowledged receipt of the letter, and finally delivered it to Trevelyan. The Regius Professor duly invited the student to lunch, they talked about the world situation, and towards the end of the month Trevelyan sent Merriman his reply.[33]

It was a remarkable communication. Trevelyan began by admitting that his general views were 'very gloomy', and he then set down a robust defence of the British policy of appeasement, insisting that Neville Chamberlain had been right not to fight over Czechoslovakia the previous October, because such a war could not possibly have been won. The only potential ally had been Russia, but it was 'down and out and can be written off – she won't or rather can't even save China from Japan'. The only possible course, some argued, was for Britain and France to launch an *offensive*, land-based, European war, in order 'to smash through Germany to Czechoslovakia'. But Trevelyan was sure this could not have been accomplished: 'our military and well-informed people all said and say' this was a 'hopeless task'. The conclusion was clear. 'If your fellow citizens think we ought to have fought this war, I think they misunderstood the possibilities.' In any case, the United States had remained neutral throughout the crisis, which had not helped. Munich, he insisted, 'saved the Czechs so far as it was possible to save them'. And, in a real if unheroic sense, it saved the British too.

Nevertheless, Trevelyan went on, this sensible decision not to fight over Czechoslovakia did not also mean 'that if (as seems likely soon) Germany and Italy attack France and England, that we shall be conquered in a *defensive* war'. 'We may or may not be,' he continued, 'but we are preparing to die in the last ditch at worst.' Yet there was also another possible, and preferable, way forward. Given that 'Hitler and Mussolini are both "rabid men"', the only thing, he felt, 'that will stop a war coming pretty soon', would be 'the US letting them know that you will take part if they make aggression'. But since he understood there to be 'little chance of that, I think the prospects are very bleak indeed'. In the last war, Trevelyan recalled, 'England and France and Italy and Russia and Japan and (halfway through) the US only just beat Germany and Austria.' How, he enquired, 'do you expect England and France alone to "crush the dictators" with Germany, Austria, Italy and Japan against us?' 'If ', he insisted, 'you don't want Europe and Africa to be prostrate at the feet of Germany and her allies, with Japan in possession of Asia, you had better be reconsidering your isolation policy before you are indeed "isolated"'.

This was a shrewd, wide-ranging and deeply felt letter which, unbeknown to Trevelyan, should have served Merriman's diplomatic purposes perfectly. The justifications for appeasement and for Munich were cogently put: it was an unavoidable necessity but no guarantee of lasting peace. There was a reluctant but realistic acceptance that this policy could not go on for much longer, and that war with the Axis powers was thus increasingly likely. There was an apt and undeceived characterization of the fascist dictators. There was a vigorous assertion that if and when war came, Britain would fight them. There was an accurate recognition that Britain and France versus Germany, Italy, Austria and Japan would be a hopelessly unequal contest. And there was a clear call for an end to American isolationism and for a more determinedly anti-German foreign policy. Trevelyan's conclusion was patriotically buoyant, but personally depressed. He was sure that if and when war came, the British 'will put up a jolly good fight', and he underlined these words. But he was also sure that whoever emerged the winner, 'nothing will be left of civilisation' as he knew it, and that 'everything I care for will disappear'. 'If Europe remains,' he concluded, 'how soon are you coming to visit us?' 'Dearest love', he added, 'to you, your family and your country.'[34]

Merriman could scarcely have written a better letter himself, and he hastened to pass it on to the President. 'I have', he informed FDR in characteristically grand and Olympian style, 'been following with interest and, on the whole, with approval the course of your foreign policy.'[35] 'I send you a quotation', he went on, 'from one of my oldest English friends.' (In fact, he sent virtually the entire letter, minus the personal pleasantries and family remarks.) Trevelyan, he explained, was Regius Professor at Cambridge, and 'author of many books, most of which you have doubtless read'. (Roosevelt certainly owned, and might even have read, *Grey of Fallodon*, Trevelyan's most recent biography.[36]) 'One has to "make allowances"', Merriman went on, 'in considering the verdicts of all Trevelyans' – an allusion to the political waywardness of George's elder brother Charles, and to the latter's propensity for walking the moors in a state of complete undress. But, he continued, 'George is saner than most of them, closely in touch with the people who count in Downing Street, and not (like your old teacher) a "mere don".'

Merriman clearly hoped Trevelyan's words would impress FDR with Britain's determination to fight, and also with the need for more conspicuous demonstrations of American friendship and support. But while Roosevelt found the communication 'extremely interesting', he did not see things this way. He interpreted Trevelyan's letter as showing that the British wanted assistance and assurances from the United States *before* they were prepared to stiffen their resolve. But FDR would only consider giving that assistance and those assurances *after* the British had first demonstrated they were worthy of them, by themselves displaying more firmness and spirit. 'I wish', the President replied, 'the British would stop this "we who are about to die, salute thee" attitude.' Lord Lothian had been visiting recently, FDR went on, had admitted that Hitler could no longer be treated as a 'semi-reasonable human being', and urged that the Americans must now take over from the British as 'the guardians of Anglo-Saxon civilisation'. 'I got mad clear through', FDR continued, 'and told him that just so long as he or Britishers like him took that attitude of complete despair, the British would not be worth saving anyway.' 'What the British need today', he concluded, 'is a good stiff grog, inducing not only the desire to save civilisation, but the continued belief that they can do it. In such an event, they will have a lot more support from their American cousins – don't you think so?'[37]

Merriman was not entirely convinced by the president's criticism of the British, and rightly so, since Trevelyan's letter had not expressed feelings of 'complete despair', but had more than once affirmed Britain's will and determination to fight. (It is unlikely Merriman would have forwarded it to the White House if it had not.) 'I think', he replied to FDR,

you are a bit hard on 'the average Britisher'. Some of his itinerant exports over here are intolerable . . . but the bulk of the stay at homes are of better quality. The fact is I think a lot of those who come over here for the first time don't quite know how to behave with us, and hit the wrong note at the outset.

But he undertook to relay a copy of the president's letter to Trevelyan, telling him that he would mark it 'private' and cautioning that as an indication of American official attitudes to Britain, it must be deployed 'with discretion' in 'the right quarters'.[38] In passing on to Trevelyan 'the enclosed rise from FDR', Merriman assured him that he had told the president 'that he ought not to judge "the regular Britisher" by his itinerant exports over here', and he reaffirmed that the letter could and must be used, but with great care.[39]

Trevelyan was suitably taken aback to learn that his personal note written to a Harvard friend had been forwarded to the White House in an effort to influence United States foreign policy.[40] 'Well I'm damned!' he wrote to Merriman on 25 February. 'You went and sent that scrawl to himself. I feel as if I could sink through the floor.' But on balance, Trevelyan was more pleased than embarrassed, 'as it has drawn that lovely letter from him about Lord Lothian etc. . . . I am', he went on, recognizing the importance of the contents, 'using the copy you sent me with great discretion, but I'm using it . . . The style and the spirit', he added, referring to the Roosevelt–Trevelyan correspondence of an earlier generation, 'remind me of the letters another president of his name used to write to my father . . . So glad', he concluded, 'that you are to be here this year. Let us know when you come, or before you come, and arrange to visit us here', either in Cambridge until mid-July, or thereafter at Hallington in Northumberland.

Trevelyan duly communicated Roosevelt's response to official circles in London. On the same day that he replied to Merriman, he also wrote to the Foreign Secretary, Lord Halifax, explaining that he had sent his American friend a letter, 'which was roughly a defence of our proceedings at Munich and since – why we could not successfully fight a strategically offensive war to get through Germany to save the Czechs, but could and would put up a jolly good fight if forced to a defensive war to save Western Europe – though such war if it came would be the end of all I cared for in civilisation.' The letter, Trevelyan added, had been sent on to FDR 'without my knowledge', and had elicited the reply which he also now enclosed. 'It is hard to say,' Trevelyan went on, a touch artlessly, 'but I cannot help thinking that the President would not be averse to my showing you this. Whether I ought to show it to anyone else is another matter: perhaps Baldwin before he goes to Canada?'[41] It is impossible to know whether Trevelyan discussed it with the former Prime Minister. But he certainly read out Roosevelt's letter to Michal Vyvyan, another scion of a family of ancient Cornish gentry, who had recently been elected a Fellow of Trinity, having resigned from the Foreign Office in 1938 in protest at the continued policy of appeasement. Vyvyan thought FDR's remarks of 'extraordinary interest and importance', and he passed them on to former colleagues at the Foreign Office like William Strang.[42]

III

At this point, the Merriman–Trevelyan intervention in Anglo-American relations came to an end. What, if anything, did their endeavours achieve? In the short run, on the British side, their impact was more disruptive than helpful, albeit unintendedly so. For there were some at the Foreign Office who interpreted Roosevelt's remarks as an explicit criticism of Lord Lothian, who had recently been selected to go to Washington as the new British Ambassador. During much of the 1930s, Lothian had been a well-known appeaser (although, as Roosevelt's words make plain, he had recently come to recant that[43]), he had been a member of the 'Clivenden set', and he was not a career diplomat. He had been chosen as the successor to Sir Ronald Lindsay despite Foreign Office opposition, but his appointment had not yet been made public, and Roosevelt's critical letter seemed to provide ammunition to those officials like Sir Alexander Cadogan (the Permanent Secretary), and Oliver Harvey (who was Halifax's private secretary), who now made one final effort to prevent it.[44] But at the time when he met him, FDR did not even know that Lothian had been selected, and he raised no objection when Lindsay, acting on official instructions from London, asked him about the matter directly. Lothian's appointment duly went through, and he took up residence in Washington in August 1939.[45]

On the American side, Roosevelt's somewhat unenthusiastic response to Trevelyan's letter, rather downplaying its eloquent expressions of British resolve, and ignoring the appeals for greater United States involvement in European affairs, meant Merriman's intervention achieved virtually nothing. From the President's perspective, isolationist opinion was still very strong in America, the war between Britain and Germany had not yet happened and still might not happen, and even in the event of such a conflict, it was impossible to know what sort of a fight Britain would actually put up, or what sort of assistance, if any, should or could be given. In such uncertain circumstances, Roosevelt was surely correct in responding to Merriman (and to Trevelyan) as he did: urging greater resolve on the part of the United Kingdom, personally inclining to their side rather than to Germany's, but not publicly committing the United States in any way.[46] Only after Hitler had subdued much of Europe, and Britain under Churchill had shown both the resolution and the ability to fight on, would it become possible for Roosevelt to push hard against the limits of neutrality by giving more active American support. And only after Pearl Harbor would it become possible for the United States to declare war on Germany as well as on Japan. In the broader context of presidential policy-making, Merriman's well-intended but politically insensitive initiative had come much too soon.

But on the British side, once the furore over Lothian's appointment had died down, Trevelyan's intervention was more propitiously timed. In the aftermath of Munich, opinion was hardening at the Foreign Office that appeasement was not working, and that the way must be prepared for a change to a less accommodating and more resolute policy – precisely the sort of policy for which Roosevelt was asking. This fundamental shift in thinking was taking place both at the junior level, among the permanent officials such as Vyvyan's former colleague William Strang, and also at the very highest level, in the mind of Lord Halifax himself. The Foreign Secretary was famous for never changing his views rapidly, and always tested the ground carefully before signalling a shift in policy. But by January and February 1939, he was increasingly coming to sense that appeasement was bankrupt, and began to distance himself from the Prime Minister, who continued to believe in it. Accordingly, in the early months of 1939, Halifax made a succession of speeches, more firm and defiant than any he had delivered before, which must certainly have been 'more to the President's taste'.[47] It is impossible to know how far Trevelyan's letter had influenced him or encouraged him, but it would surely have added extra authority to the growing weight of evidence that a change in (and stiffening of) British policy was needed.

Merriman duly visited Europe during that last pre-war summer of 1939, when he and Trevelyan must have discussed the even gloomier state of the world, and the limited success of their initiative in doing anything to alleviate it. Germany's occupation of Prague in the spring of 1939, in open defiance of the Munich settlement, had vindicated those who were now calling for an end to appeasement, and Britain's unconditional guarantee to Poland followed shortly thereafter. When war eventually came, Trevelyan regarded it with scarcely concealed horror, but he recognized that Hitler had to be fought and had to be beaten. Despite his earlier doubts, he soon came to appreciate that Churchill was the only man who could do this, and in the summer of 1940 he wrote eloquently and publicly in support of the war effort. It was for him a bitter-sweet irony that the new Prime Minister appointed him Master of Trinity, one of the supreme positions in the British civilized world, at the very moment when that world and that civilization seemed most in jeopardy, and when he was writing their epitaph in his *English Social History*.[48] And while he rejoiced that Britain had successfully defied Hitler, he knew that without full-scale American assistance, the chances of victory were slim.

On the other side of the Atlantic, Merriman remained a fierce critic of American neutrality, and continued to urge more vigorous support for beleaguered Britain. In May 1940, he denounced an anti-war petition intended to remind Roosevelt that Harvard undergraduates would 'never follow in the footsteps of the students of 1917', insisting instead that America 'can and should pour money and supplies into the Allied cause as fast as possible'. The students, he went on, 'totally fail to see the moral issue' and 'fail to discern that a Hitler victory would vitally affect the United States'. In his valedictory lecture, delivered exactly a year later, Merriman again spoke of the importance of liberty and security, and urged that 'there is no such thing as isolationism today'. 'No matter on what side of the Atlantic,' he opined, 'it is the duty of mankind to resist Hitler. The Atlantic Ocean today is no wider than the English Channel in Napoleon's time.' By October that year, American opinion had perceptibly shifted in the direction he had long wanted it to move. He rejoiced that the United States was 'virtually in an undeclared war now', and was delighted that Harvard was 'ninety nine per cent in favour of doing everything it could to help defeat the Germans'.[49] By this time, Pearl Harbor was scarcely a month away, and so was the Anglo-American alliance to which he had so long looked forward.

The rest of this story is easily told. Both Merriman and Trevelyan survived to see the final triumph of the Anglo-American alliance, the defeat of Nazi Germany, and the destruction of imperial Japan. But they never met again. Soon after VJ day, Roger Merriman died at his summer home at St Andrews-by-the-Sea in New Brunswick, and Trevelyan later sent this tribute to his friend's widow, Dorothea:

It is still difficult to believe that Roger Merriman is dead. He was always so very much alive, so highly charged with physical and mental energy, with interest in and affection for others; and when his great frame came swaying into a room, the rest of us at once became more happy and more aware of life. My recollections of long, swift walks with him across country in England and America are among my happiest thoughts today. So great a scholar and historian, so warm a friend, so good a citizen, a spirit of such quick response to all fine effort and achievement, is seldom to be found. He was a personality unique and irreplaceable. His friends in Cambridge, England, will never forget him, and never cease to love him.[50]

But these words were not only a salute from one distinguished contemporary and fellow-historian to another: they were also the summation of a long association, based on similar backgrounds, a shared sense of the past, a like-minded view of the world and common ideas of public-spirited behaviour. These words, as Merriman himself had observed in another context, were 'a truly beautiful tribute to the depth and power of scholarly solidarity and friendship'.[51]

PART THREE

VANISHING SUPREMACIES?

9

Tradition: Gilbert and Sullivan
as a 'National Institution'[1]

Gilbert and Sullivan were self-made products of the Victorian era who, for all their wit, humour and lightheartedness, might have stepped straight from the pious pages of Samuel Smiles's book, *Self-Help*. They were both born in unpromising circumstances, but their ascent to the high peaks of fame and fortune was even more successful than that of such renowned Gilbertian social climbers as the judge in *Trial by Jury* and Sir Joseph Porter in *HMS Pinafore*. This was very largely the result of the series of comic operas which they created together. Their partnership began tentatively, with *Thespis* (1871), *Trial by Jury* (1875) and *The Sorcerer* (1877), but it was only with the production of *HMS Pinafore* (1878) that they effectively established themselves. During the next decade, they produced a rapid succession of new works: *The Pirates of Penzance* (1879), *Patience* (1881), *Iolanthe* (1882), *Princess Ida* (1884), *The Mikado* (1885), *Ruddigore* (1887), *The Yeomen of the Guard* (1888) and *The Gondoliers* (1889). But then Gilbert and Sullivan fell out (ostensibly over the costs of new furnishings for the Savoy Theatre), and their last two operas – *Utopia Limited* (1893) and *The Grand Duke* (1896) – were not a success.

Taken as a whole, however, their remarkable partnership is unique in the history of popular entertainment, far surpassing either Rodgers and Hammerstein or Lerner and Loewe in its duration and productivity. For over one hundred years, their operas have been enhancing the gaiety of nations, with their 'innocent merriment', their 'ballads, songs and snatches' and their 'magic and spells'. Mr Gladstone went to see *Iolanthe*, and happily acknowledged 'the great pleasure which the entertainment has given me'. Queen Victoria commanded a performance of *The Gondoliers* at Windsor, and found it 'quite charming' throughout.[2] More recent admirers have ranged from Winston Churchill via Franklin D. Roosevelt to Harold Wilson. In the summer of 1980, *The Pirates of Penzance* was so successfully restaged in Central Park, New York, that it was transferred to Broadway and London's West End. And six years later, Jonathan Miller's audacious and innovative production of *The Mikado*, for the English National Opera, was greeted with widespread acclaim. As Gilbert boasted to Sullivan in 1887, 'we are world-known, and as much an institution as Westminster Abbey' – a self-satisfied verdict which English-speaking posterity has enthusiastically endorsed.[3]

For many of the Savoy Operas' most ardent and appreciative admirers, this is a state of affairs so self-evidently 'right as right can be' that it requires no detailed explanation. Gilbert and Sullivan, it is argued, were uncommonly gifted individuals, whose latent genius flowered only in their harmonious, if ultimately discordant, collaboration. Together, they produced works which were so original in form and so sparkling in content as to be 'timeless' in their appeal and 'universal' in their significance.[4] But all genius – especially collaborative genius – requires the aid of luck and circumstance to come to full flower. The aim of this chapter is to let a little daylight in on the Savoyards' magic by setting Gilbert and Sullivan in the broader context of nineteenth- and twentieth-century British history. What were the circumstances and conventions of the mid-Victorian theatre, in which Gilbert served his apprenticeship, and against which the Savoy Operas deliberately but indebtedly reacted? How did the operas themselves reflect (or deny) the contemporary concerns of their original, late-Victorian, middle-class audiences? And how was it that they soon established themselves as a British 'tradition', which has survived virtually unaltered almost down to our own time?

I

However venerated and venerable they have since become, the fact remains that in their own day Gilbert and Sullivan were theatrical innovators so deliberate and so successful that they might almost be called revolutionaries. But like all revolutionaries, their achievement was significantly determined by the world they were trying to change: in this case the unrespectable nineteenth-century stage, patronized primarily by members of the working classes, who sought fun, laughter, excitement and escape from the dreary monotony of their humdrum lives.[5] Theatre owners were generally regarded as shady characters, and their living was decidedly precarious. Writers were ill-rewarded, and could only make ends meet by maintaining parallel careers as actors or as journalists. The stage was neither an honourable nor a disciplined profession, and actresses were regarded as being little better than prostitutes. Not surprisingly, the upper and middle classes, who had delighted in the eighteenth-century theatre of Garrick and Sheridan, had effectively withdrawn their patronage altogether. There were occasional attempts to raise the tone and standard, as when Squire Bancroft and his wife staged Thomas Robertson's comedies at their Prince of Wales's Theatre in the 1860s; but this was very much the exception which proved the rule.

For the most part, the works that were produced on the London stage were singularly lacking in distinction or refinement. Tragedy, comedy and satire had effectively disappeared by the early nineteenth century, and had been replaced by a variety of inferior genres. The most popular was melodrama, with its stories of murder, torture, haunted castles and wicked baronets, such as Douglas Jerrold's *Black Ey'd Susan* (1829) and Dion Boucicault's *The Corsican Brothers* (1851). Almost as appealing was burlesque: the deliberate travesty of classical plays and characters, as in the works of James Robinson Planche, which included *Olympic Revels* (1831) and *The Golden Fleece* (1845). Pantomime and extravaganza were also highly popular, with their emphasis on magic, love and the supernatural. And there was ballad opera: a genre which began with John Gay's *The Beggar's Opera* (1728), but which was by this time much debased and was now devoid of satiric edge or musical merit. To this uninspired *mélange* was added imported comic opera: Offenbach's works reached the London stage in the 1860s, and Strauss's *Die Fledermaus* was first performed in 1875. But the libretti were often poorly translated, the music was badly performed and the tone of the productions was vulgar, slapdash and risqué.[6]

It was in this unsavoury theatrical world that W. S. Gilbert learned his craft, appropriately moving, in his early years, between the law, journalism and the stage. Although trained as a barrister, he soon turned to writing, and produced a series of satirical verses eventually published as the *Bab Ballads* (1869), which brought him to the attention of theatre managers. Inevitably, many of his early plays were in the prevailing style of burlesque, pantomime and extravaganza, and these were the forms which were later parodied and mimicked in the Savoy Operas. *Thespis* was actually performed at the Gaiety – a theatre renowned for burlesque – and in its Greek gods and acting troupe contained two essential elements of that genre. *The Sorcerer* was based on *Dulcamara*, Gilbert's earlier burlesque of Donizetti's *L'Elisir d'Amore*. Both *HMS Pinafore* and *The Pirates of Penzance* owed much to nautical melodrama, while *Iolanthe*, with its fairies and final transformation scene, clearly harked back to pantomime. And with *Ruddigore*, Gilbert once more returned to Gothic blood-and-thunder melodrama, complete with haunted house and wicked baronets.[7] Throughout his libretti, Gilbert's delight in disguise and mistaken identity, in topsy-turvydom, and in the last-minute restoration of order by essentially implausible means, showed his indebtedness to this mid-Victorian tradition, just as his ageing and unattractive women – Ruth, Kathisa, Lady Sophy – preserved memories of transvestite dame parts in earlier burlesque.[8]

Even though the Savoy Operas were designed for the middle classes of late-Victorian England, allusions to this older, more vulgar theatrical tradition would have been understood and appreciated – at least during the early years of the collaboration. And it was also from this same mid-Victorian theatrical world that the impresarios emerged who became the midwives to the Gilbert and Sullivan partnership. Thomas German Reed and his wife sought to raise the moral tone of the stage at their euphemistically entitled Royal Gallery of Illustration, where they put on one-act comic operas, imported from France, but shorn of their customary vulgarity, in a large drawing-room, with piano and harmonium, which had more in common with a chapel than with a theatre. Both Gilbert and Sullivan worked for them, writing libretti and scores for comic operas and musical plays, not yet in partnership, but with different collaborators. John Hollingshead, a self-made journalist, opened the Gaiety Theatre in 1868, made it an established home of burlesque, and brought Gilbert and Sullivan together for *Thespis* in 1871. And Richard D'Oyly Carte, who persuaded them to join forces again four years later for *Trial by Jury*, was himself a theatrical agent, manager of the Royalty Theatre and minor composer of operetta.

But Carte's main ambition was 'the staging of English comic opera in a theatre devoted to that alone', and he saw in Gilbert and Sullivan the perfect vehicle for realizing his objective.[9] In 1876, he formed the Comedy Opera Company, which was exclusively devoted to the production of their work, and in 1881 he opened the Savoy, the most modern and glamorous theatre in London and the first to be lit by electricity. He made the first night of a Gilbert and Sullivan opera into one of the social highlights of the 1880s, inviting Oscar Wilde himself to the première of *Patience*, and Captain Shaw to the opening of *Iolanthe*. Also he zealously promoted official performances in the provinces and overseas, especially in the United States. But above all, he enabled Gilbert and Sullivan to establish their own permanent repertory company, which effectively institutionalized the production of their works, and which included principal performers who themselves soon became famous – George Grossmith, Rutland Barrington and Jessie Bond. In short, it was Carte's revolution in theatrical management which made possible Gilbert and Sullivan's revolution in theatrical entertainment.

On the stage of the Savoy, Gilbert and Sullivan were left by Carte in 'absolute control', and they wielded their authority over the company with a dictatorial sway that had been almost entirely absent from the mid-Victorian theatre.[10] Sullivan drilled and disciplined the orchestra, refusing to tolerate slapdash attendance or lacklustre playing, while Gilbert exercised complete dominion over the casting, dressing and staging of the operas. He planned his productions on a model theatre at his home, down to the very last detail. He took endless trouble over the design of the costumes and the scenery. He rehearsed the chorus and the principals until they were exhausted with fatigue. And he insisted that his words and stage directions be followed to the letter: ad libbing, interpolations, slapstick humour and cheap laughs were absolutely forbidden, and offenders were severely reprimanded. The essence of the Savoy style, as Gilbert once explained, was treating 'a thoroughly farcical subject in a thoroughly serious manner', and the success with which he accomplished this meant that he became the first author–producer to dominate the Victorian stage.

In addition to showmanship, glamour and discipline, the Savoy Operas provided wholesome and respectable entertainment. The dialogue was devoid of offence, there was no transvestism and the women's costumes were entirely decent. Men and women changed in rooms on opposite sides of the stage; their morals were expected to be – like the Mikado's – particularly correct; and on more than one occasion, Gilbert came to the defence of female members of the cast whose honour had been wrongly impugned. Not for nothing was D'Oyly Carte's company once rechristened 'The Savoy Boarding School'.[11] Above all, the presence of Sir Arthur Sullivan's illustrious name on the programme conferred unrivalled prestige and reassurance. He had studied music in Leipzig, was the composer of hymn tunes and oratorios and was widely regarded as the greatest English musician since Purcell. He was the close friend of the Prince of Wales and the Duke of Edinburgh, his music was much admired by Queen Victoria, and he was knighted in 1883. That such a paragon should grace the orchestra pit of a theatre was a virtual guarantee of respectability. For all their gaiety and laughter, it was once remarked that the performance of a Gilbert and Sullivan opera at the Savoy, with a rapt audience following every word in their programme, and turning the same page at the same time, was reminiscent of a prayer meeting in a church or chapel.[12]

But it was the content of the operas themselves which most powerfully signalled their departure from earlier theatrical tradition. For Gilbert's libretti were of vastly superior quality to anything that had recently been played on the London stage. His complex plots were carefully and economically crafted. He created a series of memorable, outsize characters: the Lord Chancellor in *Iolanthe*, Poo-Bah in *The Mikado*, Jack Point in *The Yeomen of the Guard*. He brought back political satire, which had been absent from the theatre since the eighteenth century. His dialogue was witty and epigrammatic in a way that had last been heard on the stage in the days of Sheridan. He assumed that his audiences were well educated and well informed: the plots of *Trial by Jury* and *Iolanthe* are unintelligible without some knowledge of the law; *Patience* took for granted an understanding of contemporary developments in the arts; and *Princess Ida* presupposed a familiarity with recent trends in higher education for women. And the word-play in his verses was astonishingly varied in its metre and rhythm, from the profusion of syllables and elaborate rhymes in the patter songs to the genuine vein of poetry which suffuses the verses in *The Yeomen of the Guard*, as in this quatrain, which was later chosen by Gilbert as the inscription for Sullivan's memorial in London:

> Is life a boon?
> If so, it must befall
> That death, when e're he call,
> Must call too soon.

Moreover, Sullivan's music was as clever, as humorous and as versatile as Gilbert's words. When the libretto required it, he composed a hornpipe, a waltz, a march, a gavotte, a cachucha, a madrigal, an aria or a love duet: indeed, Nanki-Poo's opening song in *The Mikado* is, by turns, a sentimental ballad, a patriotic march, a sea shanty and a lullaby. He poured out many memorable melodies, among them 'The sun whose rays' in *The Mikado*, 'Take a pair of sparkling eyes' in *The Gondoliers*. He could illuminate character in a phrase, as with the ponderous double bass passage that introduces the policemen in *The Pirates of Penzance*. He pointed up the contrasts between the different social groups portrayed in the operas: the soldiers and the aesthetes in *Patience*, the Spanish nobility and the Venetian citizens in *The Gondoliers*. And he was unrivalled as a parodist and pasticheur. Mabel's song, 'Poor wand'ring one', in *The Pirates of Penzance* is a Gounodesque waltz, full of coloratura trills and fancy cadences. The finale to Act I of *The Mikado* is strikingly reminiscent of Verdi. 'All hail great judge' (*Trial by Jury*) and 'This helmet I suppose?' (*Princess Ida*) are both exuberant parodies of Handel. And the scene when the banished Iolanthe is raised from the bottom of the stream recalls the opening of Wagner's *Das Rheingold*.

This was the measure of the revolution in theatrical taste for which Carte, Sullivan and Gilbert were jointly responsible. They deliberately sought to make their works appealing to the well-educated middle classes, and they triumphantly succeeded. They created a new form of entertainment, precisely pitched between the music hall and the concert hall, which was intelligent but not intellectual, tasteful but not pretentious, tuneful but not cloying. They took the theatrical conventions of the lower classes, and made them acceptable to the bourgeoisie. As their confidence grew, Gilbert and Sullivan gradually left behind the old traditions of farce, pantomime, melodrama and burlesque, and in their later operas, *The Mikado*, *The Yeomen of the Guard* and *The Gondoliers*, they created self-sufficient dramas and extended scores which seemed to hold out the prospects of limitless creative possibilities. As *The Times* noted in 1887, 'the middle classes, and even the working classes, which had no opportunity of appreciating either art or music fifty years ago, cannot complain that these wholesome enjoyments are now monopolised by a fashionable aristocracy'.[13] And for these developments, the creators of the Savoy Operas themselves were significantly and self-consciously responsible.

Of course, Gilbert, Sullivan and Carte were not alone in bringing about this transformation of the late-Victorian theatre: while they were making comic opera respectable at the Savoy, Henry Irving was achieving very similar results with Shakespeare and melodrama at the Lyceum. And for Gilbert and Sullivan, their very success brought with it its own dangers. In part, this was because, even in their own unrivalled hands, it proved impossible to reproduce comic opera indefinitely. The 'carpet quarrel' of 1890 effectively ended their long run of collaborative triumphs, and neither Gilbert nor Sullivan found another partner with whom he could happily work. But it was also because the new theatre audience which they had done so much to call into being soon began to look elsewhere for less demanding and less cerebral amusement. The long-running successes of Alfred Cellier's *Dorothy* (1886), and Sidney Jones's *A Gaiety Girl* (1893) and *The Geisha* (1896), signalled the arrival of a new form of light entertainment: musical comedy. Its lyrics were less intellectual, there was no satire, the melodies were simpler, the humour was broader and there was a greater stress on romantic entanglement and lavish spectacle.[14] In *The Gondoliers* and *Utopia Limited*, Gilbert and Sullivan made some attempts to adjust their style to this new fashion, with more elaborate staging and greater stress on dancing and display. But by then, they were too old and too disenchanted to change their ways. 'What the public want', Carte lamented, 'is simply "fun" and little else.'[15]

II

Although one essential context for understanding the Savoy Operas is their place in the history of theatrical entertainment, there is a broader perspective that must not be lost sight of. For the years of Gilbert and Sullivan's collaboration, between 1871 and 1896, were for the British among the most crowded, tumultuous and disturbing of the nineteenth century.[16] They saw a deepening economic depression, with well-grounded fears that Britain's industrial pre-eminence was being lost. They saw growing international rivalry between the great powers of Europe, the scramble for colonies in Africa and the murder of Gordon at Khartoum. They saw an unprecedently popular and venerated monarchy, and an increasingly impoverished and insecure aristocracy. And they saw a bourgeoisie bewildered by Irish Home Rule, worried by the depression of prices, profits and interest rates, and concerned about a working class which was better educated and partially enfranchised, yet sometimes seemed ominously discontented. What aspects of this changing world did Gilbert and Sullivan consider fit material for the moral, middle-class audiences of their operas?[17]

In the context of such international and domestic turmoils, it is especially significant that the Savoy Operas were a paean of praise to national pride and to the established order.[18] Whatever their ostensible location, all Gilbert and Sullivan's operas are in fact about England. There is nothing disingenuous about the chorus 'For he is an Englishman' in *HMS Pinafore*. In *Ruddigore*, the Union Jack is described as 'a flag that none dare defy'. The claim, in *Utopia Limited*, that Britain 'occupies a pre-eminent position among civilized nations' is not made ironically. And the prevailing assumption of all the operas is that foreigners – whether Japanese or Spanish or German or Venetian – are mildly comical and profoundly unfortunate. There are schoolboyish satires on the army, the navy and the peerage. But while Sir Joseph Porter, the First Lord of the Admiralty in *HMS Pinafore*, is teased for being a landsman, the skill of Captain Corcoran and the steadfastness of his crew are never doubted – well, 'hardly ever'. In *The Pirates of Penzance*, Major General Stanley may not be the most up-to-date commander in his knowledge of military strategy, but the 'soldiers of the queen' in *Patience* are glamorous, robust, fearless and patriotic. And the most barbed song remaining in *Iolanthe* – 'When Britain really ruled the waves' – was set by Sullivan to a broad, stately, majestic tune, which soothes the simple satire into affectionate mockery.

Within this robustly patriotic setting, the operas were obsessed with the personnel and the rituals of monarchy. 'Because with all our faults we love our Queen' applied as much to Gilbert and to Sullivan personally as it did to the pirates of Penzance. But the image of royalty underwent important changes during the Savoy opera cycle, exactly mirroring the transition in the British monarchy from secluded unpopularity and republican protests in the middle of the queen's reign to popular symbol and ceremonial splend-our by the end.[19] In the early pieces, the pirate king in *The Pirates of Penzance* and the Fairy Queen in *Iolanthe* owe much to the older tradition of melodrama, burlesque and pantomime: they are not credible as real rulers. But the later sovereigns – in *The Mikado, The Gondoliers, Utopia Limited* and *The Grand Duke* – are much more elaborate and individual creations. In the same way, the pageantry surrounding the monarchy reaches its grandiose climax at the gondoliers' court of Barataria, and at the elabor-ately staged Drawing-Room in *Utopia Limited*, which was an almost exact rendition of a royal reception at Windsor Castle or Buckingham Palace. And in *The Gondoliers*, produced only two years after Victoria's Golden Jubilee, and in the centenary year of the French Revolution, it is republican-ism, not monarchy, which is ridiculed and mocked.[20]

In depicting the British aristocracy, Gilbert was no less sensitive to chang-ing circumstances. The pirates of Penzance are 'no members of a common throng; they are all noblemen who have gone wrong' – but who in the end go right again. There are peers and notables in *Iolanthe, The Mikado, The Gondoliers* and *The Grand Duke*. There is a whole dynasty of baronets in *Ruddigore*, and there are titled principals in *The Sorcerer*. In *Patience*, Bunthorne is a landed gentleman (albeit dressed in aesthetic costume), and in the same opera, the Duke of Dunstable is a lieutenant in the Dragoon Guards. In other operas, Major General Stanley, Captain Corcoran and Colonel Fairfax all possess landed estates or patrician relatives. But unlike the monarchy, these 'tremendous swells' are not as secure as they once were. During the early 1880s, the power and composition of the House of Lords were widely attacked by radicals, who were enraged by the way in which the second chamber consistently obstructed Liberal legislation, and this provides the essential background to *Iolanthe*, with its chorus of haughty peers who vainly believe that the upper house 'is not susceptible of improve-ment'. And in the same decade, when landed incomes were hard hit by agricultural depression, many peers were obliged to search for additional income by selling their status for money, and becoming ornamental directors of commercial ventures, in the undignified manner of the Duke of Plaza-Toro in *The Gondoliers*.[21]

In treating the army and the navy, the Savoy Operas were equally up to date and essentially well disposed. Gilbert was the son of a naval man, and adored sailing, and Sullivan's father was a military band conductor: not surprisingly, both were respectfully admiring of the armed services. The Royal Navy – not just in *HMS Pinafore*, but also in *Ruddigore* and *Utopia Limited* – is depicted as the greatest fighting force in the world, 'the bulwark of England's greatness'. At the very time when the era of inexpensive British naval mastery was suddenly drawing to a close, the Savoy Operas offer a robust celebration of the age of unchallenged fighting sail.[22] In the same way, the British Army was very much in vogue. Cardwell's reforms at the War Office, carried out between 1868 and 1870, had abolished the system of purchasing commissions and sought to remedy the inefficiencies and abuses made plain at the time of the Crimean War. And in making fun of Sir Garnett Wolseley as Major General Stanley in *The Pirates of Penzance*, Gilbert was in fact gently mocking one of the most progressive new commanders, who led the British forces in the Ashanti Wars of 1873, and was sent out to relieve Gordon at Khartoum in 1885. Moreover, by giving the army such attention (it also appears in *Patience*, *Ruddigore*, *The Yeomen of the Guard* and *Utopia Limited*), he was also acknowledging its importance in those many late-nineteenth-century imperial conflicts, quaintly known as 'Queen Victoria's little wars'.[23]

The other two professions on which Gilbert lavished his attention were concerned with domestic order rather than international security: the law and the police. Since Gilbert had himself trained for the Bar, it is hardly surprising that *Trial by Jury* was set in a courtroom, and their solicitors, barristers, judges and even the Lord Chancellor himself make repeated appearances in the operas.[24] Moreover, this was the very period that saw extensive legal reform, beginning in the late 1870s with the establishment of the Central Criminal Courts and ending with the creation of the Bar Association in 1894.[25] And it was also at this time that the police force settled itself in the popular imagination as the avuncular representative of state authority. Even as late as the 1870s, the constabulary was still much disliked by the working classes, as licensed snoopers, as symbols of repressive authority, as agents of an intrusive state: they were widely regarded as the 'plague of blue locusts'.[26] Only at the very end of that decade, and during the early 1880s, was the force transformed in the popular imagination into a friendly, familiar and well-disposed organization. The affectionate image so vividly conveyed in *The Pirates of Penzance* was thus not so much a long-established convention but a very recent development. Indeed, Gilbert and Sullivan may not just have reflected this change in popular attitudes: they may actually have helped to create it.

This, in essence, is the social universe of the Savoy Operas: a universe selectively but perceptively modelled on the real and recognizable Britain of the years 1871 to 1896. There is monarchy on the way to apotheosis, and there is aristocracy on the way to decline. There are those great professions most concerned with domestic security and international peace. But, apart from Dr Daly in *The Sorcerer*, there are no clergymen; significantly, Gilbert abandoned his original idea of constructing the plot of *Patience* around two rival curates because both he and Sullivan feared it would offend contemporary sensibility. In the same way, the commercial and entrepreneurial bourgeoisie hardly appears at all, apart form the gentlest references to middle-class social climbing in *The Mikado*. Indeed, Mr Goldbury, the unscrupulous company promotor in *Utopia Limited*, is satirized for not embodying those quintessential middle-class virtues of honesty and decency. As for the working class, they are invariably picturesque and dutiful: rustic maidens, country bumpkins, jolly jack tars. And the settings are almost always pastoral and sylvan: country houses and villages predominate, and apart from Titipu (which is a Japanese town) and the Palace of Westminster (significantly bathed in mellow moonlight in Act II of *Iolanthe*), the press and pace of urban life hardly intrude.

So, in terms of their contemporary resonance, the Savoy Operas were as important for what they left out as for what they put in. The international anxieties generated by Irish Home Rule, the scramble for Africa and economic depression are not just ignored: the patriotic presumptions of Gilbert and Sullivan are that they do not even exist. And the same was true in the domestic sphere. In London, in particular, the 1880s were a decade of real-life melodrama. There were the revelations of appalling poverty contained in Andrew Mearns's book, *The Bitter Cry*, and in Charles Booth's early social surveys; there was 'Bloody Sunday' and the great dock strike; and there were the terrible 'Jack the Ripper' murders.[27] But the only extended and explicit allusions to such contemporary social problems – Strephon's savage song 'Fold your flapping wings' in *Iolanthe* and Princess Zara's final, bitter speech in *Utopia Limited* – were both cut out after adverse public reaction on the first night. At a more refined level, these late-Victorian operas offered essentially the same invitation to the middle classes that the mid-Victorian burlesques and pantomimes had held out to the proletariat: they were encouraged to laugh rather than to think. In so far as there was satire, it was carefully trimmed to the tastes of an increasingly conservative public.[28]

Indeed, it is in this broader context of *fin de siècle* apprehension and dissolving certainties that the ostensibly innocent topsy-turvydom of the

Savoy Operas takes on its real significance.[29] For within their own world of make-believe, they repeatedly hold out the prospect of the established social and political order being overturned and subverted – the very danger which, in reality, so many comfortably off contemporaries genuinely feared. In *The Sorcerer* and *HMS Pinafore*, it is because love may level ranks. In *The Pirates of Penzance*, it is because the police are initially defeated by vagabonds. In *Princess Ida*, it is because the dominance of men is rejected by women. In *Iolanthe*, it is because the fairies subdue the House of Lords, and take over Parliament. And in *The Gondoliers*, it is because the two temporary monarchs are in fact armchair republicans. But in every case – with the exception of *Iolanthe* – order is eventually restored. Of course, the sheer absurdity of the inversion, and the preposterous artificiality of the means whereby everyone lives happily ever after, deliberately invited incredulous laughter. But in the context of the time, the boundary line between humour and anxiety was very narrow indeed.

In all these ways, the Gilbert and Sullivan operas were perfectly judged productions for their targeted audience: the London middle classes, especially of the 1880s. Between them, the court composer and the court jester blended fact and fantasy, realism and escapism, satire and sweetness, 'patriotic sentiment' and 'innocent merriment', comforting reassurance and ludicrous subversion, in a heady and resonant mixture. But their congruence with that particular decade runs even closer. Beginning with the last great fling of Gladstonian reform, it ended with Lord Salisbury's Unionists firmly in power, and witnessed a major shift in middle-class opinion from mid-Victorian Liberalism to late-Victorian Conservatism. Gilbert himself seems to have followed a similar path, from the savagely irreverent versifier of the *Bab Ballads* to the Harrow country gentleman of the 1890s. And the Savoy Operas trace what is recognizably the same trajectory. It is not just that they gradually leave burlesque, pantomime and melodrama behind, and become more self-confident and self-conscious works; it is also that the satire gets weaker, the locations become more exotic, and the importance of spectacle increases.[30] To some extent, these developments may be explained by changing attitudes on the part of the audience and changing theatrical conventions. But they also mirror very closely the broader political patterns of the decade. Far from being 'timeless' creations, they were very much the time-bound products of their own era.

III

Indeed, it was precisely because the Savoy Operas were so much the outcome of this particular theatrical milieu and historical generation that they quickly began to show distinct signs of their age. By the time of *Ruddigore*, Gilbert's continued preoccupation with melodrama and pantomime was clearly anachronistic. The many contemporary allusions in the libretti – to W. H. Smith, Captain Shaw, the aesthetics movement, parliamentary trains and company promoters – inevitably lost their topicality, while Sullivan's references to Offenbach and Gounod, Wagner and Verdi, remained recognizable only to people who knew something of classical music. By the 1890s, the operas seemed altogether too sophisticated and too cerebral, compared with the light musical comedies which George Edwardes was staging at the Gaiety Theatre. And in the early years of the new century, these were followed by the sensational successes of Lehar's *The Merry Widow* (first seen in London in 1907), Frederic Norton's *Chu Chin Chow* (1916) and Harold Fraser Simpson's *The Maid of the Mountains* (1917). When Sullivan died in 1900, his reputation as a serious composer entered a sudden and seemingly irretrievable decline. Gilbert, who lived on until 1911, expected no better: 'Posterity,' he once remarked, 'will know as little of me as I shall know of posterity.'[31] Yet however harshly posterity has dismissed their non-collaborative endeavours, their joint works soon bloomed and blossomed anew. As *The Times* explained in 1948, unconsciously echoing Gilbert's remarks of sixty years before, the Savoy Operas had 'become a national institution'. How, exactly, did this quite unexpected development occur?[32]

Part of the answer undoubtedly lies in the zeal with which the D'Oyly Carte family exploited their exclusive rights of professional performance in Britain – rights which they retained until the 1950s. After Richard D'Oyly Carte's death in 1901, his widow Helen took charge of the company, and she was followed from 1911 to 1948 by her stepson, Rupert. The first major Gilbert and Sullivan revival took place in London between 1906 and 1908, the productions being superintended by W. S. Gilbert himself. Between the wars, Rupert D'Oyly Carte sponsored a succession of London seasons and provincial tours, and gramophone recordings were made of many of the operas. And in the late 1920s and early 1930s, the company returned to the United States once more.[33] The result was that while most of the light operas and musicals that had been staged during the 1880s, 1890s and 1900s disappeared without trace after their initial London run, the sustaining support provided by the D'Oyly Carte Company ensured that Gilbert and Sullivan survived. Moreover, the operas themselves were produced 'precisely in their original form, without any alteration in their words, or any attempt to bring them up to date', and when permission was given to amateur societies to perform them, it was on the same exacting condition that Gilbert's stage directions must be slavishly followed.[34] As a result, the operas soon ceased to be topical, and by firmly resisting any changes, became renowned instead for being unapologetically and proudly (and recently) 'traditional'.

But this deliberate and very successful cultivation of anachronism also suggests a deeper reason for their recovery and survival. For many aspects of British life which by the inter-war years were regarded and revered as 'traditional' had in fact been invented only during the last quarter of the nineteenth century: the splendid public spectacles of monarchy, the Royal Tournament, the Henry Wood Promenade Concerts, the old school tie, the Wimbledon tennis championships, Test Match cricket and Sherlock Holmes, to name but a few.[35] And to some extent at least, the Gilbert and Sullivan operas themselves survived because they had been, and thereafter remained, an integral part of this remarkably enduring late-Victorian cultural cluster. Their pageantry, their stirring marches, their gorgeous costumes, and their robust loyalty to crown and nation made them an essential and appropriate adjunct to the recently apotheosized monarchy. Sullivan's music was regularly played on state occasions at Buckingham Palace; the revived procession of Knights of the Garter, held at Windsor Castle, was a real-life version of the peers' entrance and march from *Iolanthe*; and when Henry Channon noted that there was a 'Gilbert and Sullivan atmosphere' about Queen Elizabeth II's unprecedentedly lavish coronation of 1953, he was essentially describing one invented British tradition in terms of another.[36]

A similar close relationship existed between the evolving reality of aristocratic life and the earlier portrayal in the Savoy Operas. During the 1880s, Gilbert and Sullivan had depicted the gentry and peerage in novel terms, as picturesque yet fading. But it was right for the time, and it became even more valid during the next half century, as they faded still further. In 1909, the peers foolishly behaved as they had threatened to do in *Iolanthe*: they 'interfered in a matter which they did not understand', and threw out Lloyd George's 'People's Budget', with the result that their powers were drastically reduced. Although 'competitive examination' was never suggested, a variety of schemes to reform the composition of the upper house were put forward intermittently from the 1880s to the 1930s. And many noblemen, impoverished by renewed agricultural depression during the 1920s and 1930s and forced to sell some or all of their estates, were compelled to seek remunerative employment in the manner of the Duke of Plaza-Toro.[37] Not surprisingly, P. G. Wodehouse's inter-war aristocratic world is recognizably the same as Gilbert's: indeed, the Duke of Dunstable appears both in the Savoy Operas and in his novels. And Noël Coward's song, 'The Stately Homes of England' is very much the spirit of *Iolanthe*, fifty years further on.[38]

By contrast, the great professions remained as central to British life as they had been in the time of Gilbert and Sullivan. In the case of the armed services, subsequent developments meant that Gilbert's affectionately satirical creations became suffused with an unexpected (and unintended) nostalgic glow. As the cult of Nelson and his flagship *HMS Victory* gathered force, and with the centenary of the Battle of Trafalgar in 1905, *HMS Pinafore* became a worthy sister ship, appropriately anchored nearby, off Portsmouth.[39] In the era of the Dreadnought, the Battle of Jutland and the Washington Treaty, Gilbert's old-fashioned Royal Navy became a comforting reminder of the time when Britannia really had ruled the waves. Admiral Lord Fisher, who had modernized the navy during the 1900s, and was First Sea Lord on the outbreak of the First World War, greatly admired *HMS Pinafore*, and regularly attended D'Oyly Carte performances. And in terms of nautical patriotism, it was a very short step from *HMS Pinafore* to Henry Wood's *Fantasia on British Sea Songs*, and even to Noël Coward's wartime film *In Which We Serve*. In the same way, as the commanders of the British Army became more middle class, and as the humiliations of the Boer War were followed by the horrors of the trenches, Gilbert's 'soldiers of the queen' picturesquely recalled the time when officers had indeed been gentlemen, and when the only wars were (to the British) relatively minor colonial skirmishes.

In similar yet also different ways, Gilbert's portrait of the forces of law and order retained, and even increased, its essential topicality. The structure of the legal profession as reformed during the last quarter of the nineteenth century remained fundamentally unaltered down to the Second World War. British politics were dominated during the ensuing decades as never before by a succession of lawyer–politicians: Asquith, Lloyd George, Lord Reading, Lord Simon and Lord Birkenhead (who knew many of the Lord Chancellor's songs from *Iolanthe* off by heart). And in the lawyer–humorist A. P. Herbert, it almost seemed as if Gilbert himself had been reincarnated. He wrote a succession of articles in *Punch*, entitled 'Misleading Cases', which amusingly satirized the law and its anomalies, and from the 1920s to the 1940s he produced a series of plays, operettas and musical reviews for the London stage. During the same period, crime decreased in Britain, and the police consolidated their position as a force, not just for order, but also for good.[40] Like Gilbert's reluctant heroes in *The Pirates of Penzance*, they were regarded as (and respected for) being decent, dutiful, well-meaning and incorruptible – even if not over-bright. And it was precisely this Gilbertian image of the constabulary that was carried on in the detective stories featuring Sherlock Holmes, Lord Peter Wimsey and Miss Marple, in such songs as 'If you want to know the time, ask a policeman', and in early television programmes like *Dixon of Dock Green*.

The result was that although the Savoy Operas were specifically written for the well-educated middle classes of late-Victorian England, they successfully captivated a much broader national audience during the first half of the twentieth century. As the music halls went into decline during the inter-war years, the unabashed patriotism of Gilbert and Sullivan found a ready response among the many members of the 'flag-saluting, foreigner-hating, peer-respecting' working classes.[41] Their undemanding tunefulness appealed with equal success to the increasingly philistine members of the upper classes, produced by the public schools from the late nineteenth century onwards. Their determined refusal to address social problems, and their light-hearted escapism, which had made them such a tonic during the gloomy decade of the 1880s, were of even greater value at the time of the inter-war depression. And their disdain for 'abroad', their inability to take foreigners seriously, and their determination not to bow down to continental dictators, or endure 'the tang of a tyrant's tongue', gave them a new and reassuring relevance during the First World War – and again during the 1930s. No wonder King George V was a fan.

So, as the specific circumstances of their original performances were gradually forgotten, the Savoy Operas gradually began to acquire all the ahistorical trappings of a national 'tradition'. It was entirely fitting for Englishmen to laugh at themselves in this gentle, self-regarding way, a viewpoint reinforced by the fact that Gilbert's puns, jokes and elaborate rhymes could not be easily translated into foreign languages. The productions of the D'Oyly Carte Company remained essentially unchanging, and the audiences were reassured that this was so. Age could not wither them, nor custom stale their infinite monotony. In 1930, the D'Oyly Carte principal, Henry Lytton, was knighted, specifically for his work in 'Gilbert and Sullivan'. Three years later, he dedicated his autobiography, appropriately entitled *A Wand'ring Minstrel*, 'to Rupert D'Oyly Carte, the worthy upholder of a great tradition'. In 1934, he celebrated his golden jubilee on the stage, and received a national testimonial, signed by past and present prime ministers of all three parties: Ramsay MacDonald, Lloyd George and

Stanley Baldwin.[42] And at almost exactly the same time, the supplement to the *Oxford English Dictionary* officially recognized the adjective 'Gilbertian' as a fully accredited word in the English language. The incorporation of Gilbert and Sullivan into national 'tradition' was complete. In celebrating British institutions, with the gentlest of satire and the greatest of affection, they had become a British institution in themselves.

IV

In an almost Gilbertian fashion, therefore, the Savoy Operas had assumed three very different historical guises: they were the audacious expression of a nineteenth-century theatrical revolution; they were perfectly judged entertainment for the late-Victorian middle class; and they became a national institution, an 'ethnic folk right', during the first half of the twentieth century.[43] Since the Second World War, however, they have gradually been emancipated from the thraldom of British 'tradition', in large part because of the ending of the D'Oyly Carte monopoly. With the expiration of Sullivan's copyright in 1950, and of Gilbert's eleven years later, the family lost its rights of exclusive professional performance, and could no longer insist that Gilbert's stage directions must be precisely followed in all amateur productions. Thereafter, the D'Oyly Carte Opera Company continued to perform, but its finances grew precarious, and its performances seemed increasingly lacklustre and outmoded. In 1982, the Arts Council refused the company a government subsidy because of its staid and unimaginative productions, and after more than one hundred years as the creator, upholder and embodiment of the Savoy 'tradition', the D'Oyly Carte Company closed down.[44] And in 1985, the death of Dame Bridget D'Oyly Carte, who had managed the family business since 1948, and was the last direct descendant of the original impresario, effectively brought to an end this phase in the history of Gilbert and Sullivan opera.[45]

But it is not just that this unique institutional support and controlling influence gradually fell away. For in the radical and confrontational Britain of the 1980s and early 1990s, the operas themselves seemed less comfortingly and relevantly 'traditional' than they had in what appeared by contrast to have been the more emollient and consensual inter-war years. But then, it was Mrs Thatcher rather than Elizabeth II who had more in common with the Fairy Queen in *Iolanthe*. The House of Lords was very largely a political irrelevance, the aristocracy had become the proprietors of safari parks or photographers' studios, and life peerages were given out to members of all social classes. With Britain no longer an imperial power, the army and the navy seemed increasingly tangential to national life. The legal profession was on the brink of the most systematic reform since the time of Gilbert and Sullivan themselves; and with rapidly rising crime rates, and countless allegations of police corruption and brutality, the constabulary were no longer as appreciatively or as affectionately regarded as once they were.

But while traditionalists may have regretted these changes, both institutional and circumstantial, the effect in many ways was both salutary and liberating. There were new and vigorous performances of the operas, both on television and in the theatre. Joseph Papp's production of *The Pirates of Penzance* in New York took many liberties with Sullivan's score, but it also presented the Pirate King as an authentic swashbuckling hero, and in so doing pointed up the close connections between the early Savoy Operas and Victorian melodrama. Even more audaciously, Jonathan Miller's *Mikado* removed Gilbert's Japanese façade altogether, setting the opera in inter-war England, and suggested that its true identity was as a comedy of manners and a satire on social and political ambition. Just as the operas were revitalized by these imaginative new productions, so their creators have become historically credible beings for the first time. Sullivan's recently opened diary shows that he was far from being the pious paragon of popular legend: he loved wine, women and gambling, and there was little sign in his own life of the ponderous religiosity of his sacred music.[46] And the latest interpretation of W. S. Gilbert suggests that he was not so much the crusty but good-humoured uncle so implausibly beloved of Savoyard mythology: on the contrary, his wit and satire were the outward expressions of a coarse, aggressive, ill-tempered and incorrigibly litigious nature.[47]

The result of these recent developments is that the Savoy Operas and their creators have been emancipated from what had increasingly become the stultifying conventions and outmoded encrustations of a hundred-year British 'tradition'. Today, throughout the English-speaking world, the works of Gilbert and Sullivan are being produced with more vigour, freedom, imagination and adventurousness than ever before. And as they are brought alive again, and presented and appreciated in new and different ways, this is also the time to recognize their broader and more lasting impact on popular entertainment, not just in Britain, but on both sides of the Atlantic, during the intervening twentieth century. For, in addition to Coward, Herbert and Wodehouse, any list of those who were influenced by Gilbert's words and Sullivan's tunes would also have to include Cole Porter, Leonard Bernstein and Stephen Sondheim, as well as Lionel Bart, Lerner and Loewe and Rodgers and Hammerstein.[48] The musicals of our own day may seem far removed from the Savoy Operas of the late-Victorian era. But in the longer view of things, it is scarcely more than a step (albeit a step down) from Gilbert and Sullivan to Andrew Lloyd Webber.

10

Conservation: The National Trust and the National Heritage[1]

Without doubt, the National Trust is the most important and successful voluntary society in modern England, and there is no other conservation body remotely like it. Here are some indications of its importance and success. Its present membership is substantially above two million, which is more than the Conservative, Labour and Liberal Democratic Parties combined. This in turn means that *The National Trust Magazine* has a circulation approximately equal to that of the *Daily Telegraph*, *The Times*, the *Guardian* and the *Independent* added together. As the owner of 580,000 acres of land, the Trust's holdings are significantly greater than the Crown Estates, the Duchy of Cornwall and the Church Commissioners, and they are surpassed only by the Forestry Commission and the Ministry of Defence. In addition, the Trust owns 500 miles of coastline, 230 historic houses, sixty villages and hamlets, eight thousand paintings and half a million books. No other national body, private or public, philanthropic or profit-making, is so variously and so virtuously possessed. These are the tangible outcomes of its hundred-year history – a history that has been written several times, most recently in 1995, which was the Trust's centenary year.[2]

Such commemoration at such a time was apt and appropriate. The National Trust has a history that needs to be better known. But it is not an easy task to undertake, for it is a big, complex and difficult subject, which should be carefully framed and broadly conceived. Writing the history of the National Trust is one thing; placing the National Trust in its appropriate historical perspective is quite another. This chapter is a preliminary attempt to locate the Trust in the broader context of modern British history, in the hope of illuminating both subjects.[3] It is divided into four overlapping sections, which correspond to the different phases of the Trust's development and activity: the first, from its foundation in 1895 until 1920, when its main concern was with preserving open spaces; the second, from 1914 until 1949, when it was primarily interested in proclaiming 'spiritual values'; the third, from 1935 to 1970, when it was preoccupied with rescuing country houses; and the fourth, from 1965 to the present, when it has been more broadly committed to safeguarding the environment. Why and how has the National Trust evolved and developed in this way?

I

We begin on by-now familiar ground. 'Nine English traditions out of ten', an ageing academic observes in C. P. Snow's *The Masters*, 'date from the latter half of the nineteenth century.' Indeed, he could have been more precise and narrowed the period down to the years 1875 to 1900. Between those two dates, many now-venerable British traditions were invented or adjusted, among them royal ceremonial, Sherlock Holmes, Gilbert and Sullivan and bacon and eggs.[4] To these should be added a clutch of voluntary associations and publishing ventures, all of which have happily survived: the Society for the Protection of Ancient Buildings (1877); the National Footpaths Preservation Society (1884); the *Dictionary of National Biography* (1885); the Royal Society for the Protection of Birds (1889); *Country Life* (1897); and the Survey of London and the *Victoria History of the Counties of England* (both 1900). As their names suggest, they were a diverse and distinguished group. But they also had much in common. For they were all concerned with recovering, preserving and celebrating various aspects of Britain's cultural and environmental heritage.[5] It is in this context that the foundation of the National Trust in 1895, and the first phase of its existence, need to be set and understood.

Despite the pomp and circumstance of Queen Victoria's Golden and Diamond Jubilees, late-nineteenth-century Britain was in many ways an anxiety-ridden nation, and it was in response to such widespread feelings of uncertainty and concern that these cultural and preservationist initiatives were launched. In an era of agricultural depression, there was a well-grounded fear on the part of landowners and farmers that the countryside was being marginalized and depopulated.[6] At the same time, the revelations of Charles Booth for London, and Seebohm Rowntree for York, exposed a lumpenproletariat impoverished and undernourished, and an easy prey to crime, vice and drink. And the faltering performance of the British economy, compared with the vigour of its German and American rivals, led to a reappraisal of the Industrial Revolution. Instead of being seen as something which had made Britain pre-eminent as the workshop of the world, it was re-evaluated as a regrettable and disastrous phenomenon, which had brought – and was still bringing – human suffering and environmental degradation.[7] Britain may have been the heart of the world's greatest empire, but during the 1880s and 1890s, and on into the Edwardian era, there was growing concern among the educated classes that that heart was neither healthy nor sound.

This anxiety expressed itself in many different ways. Among the most important was a renewed interest in nature and history, which derived from the work of John Ruskin and William Morris.[8] Preservationists began to demand that ancient monuments and venerable buildings must be safeguarded from the builder and the speculator. Defenders of 'the landed interest' urged that the countryside should be given special treatment, and that agriculture must be protected from foreign competition. As the economic importance of the rural world diminished, its cultural importance significantly increased: witness Hardy's novels, Kipling's poems, Elgar's 'Enigma Variations' and Lutyens's early, vernacular houses.[9] These modes of expression differed, but their message was essentially the same: the rural past was preferable to the urban present, and the contemporary English countryside was idyllic yet beleaguered. It was idyllic because, in contrast to the squalor and deprivation of the towns, it was the very embodiment of decency, Englishness, national character and national identity. But it was beleaguered because it was more than ever threatened by the forces of modernity – especially the railway, the motor car and the ever-expanding urban frontier.

Then, as now, environmental politics was a broad church, encompassing as it did Conservative imperialists such as Lord Curzon and Lord Milner, and radical socialists like Henry George. Somewhere between them came the liberal intelligentsia, many of whom played prominent parts in the foundation of the late-nineteenth-century preservationist societies. Among its senior figures, such men as Henry Sidgwick and Leslie Stephen were obsessional walkers and mountaineers, and believed passionately in the transcendent, quasi-religious qualities of nature.[10] Their views were shared by a younger generation which included C. F. G. Masterman, J. L. Hammond, Bertrand Russell – and G. M. Trevelyan and Hugh Dalton, of whom more later. Liberal politicians such as George Shaw-Lefevre and James Bryce were equally committed to the countryside: hence their extended campaign for public access to open spaces in England and Scotland, and their active involvement in the fledgeling National Trust. And among the aristocracy, those who concerned themselves with the Trust in its early years tended to be renegade Whigs, such as the Duke of Westminster and Lord Dufferin, or Liberal survivors like Lord Rosebery. Although it properly presented itself as a 'national' rather than as a partisan organization, the tone of the Trust during this first phase of its history was closer to the left of the political spectrum than to the right.

As such, it merely reflected the outlook of the three founding figures: Canon Rawnsley, Sir Robert Hunter and Octavia Hill.[11] In their social origins, they were quintessentially middle class: Rawnsley had followed his father into the Church; Hunter was the son of a businessman and trained as a solicitor; and Hill was descended from Robert Southwood Smith, one of the great early-Victorian sanitary reformers. In public matters, they had little time for party divisions or Westminster wranglings. But Rawnsley was elected to the first Cumberland County Council as an Independent Liberal; Hunter was described by Rawnsley as 'a sturdy Liberal from first to last'; and Hill's father had been a supporter of parliamentary reform and Corn Law repeal during the 1830s and 1840s.[12] Their conservationist priorities were similar but not identical. Rawnsley sought to preserve and protect the Lake District – where he had a parish for many years – in all its Words-worthian purity. Hunter was an ardent supporter of the Commons Preser-vation Society (of which he was for a time the solicitor), and of the rights of public access against assertive and overbearing landlords. And Hill was the most famous housing reformer of her generation, who was appalled by the squalid conditions of slum life in London, and who saw open spaces as essential for the moral well-being of the working classes.[13]

Together, these three zealots set the tone and the policy of the National Trust during the first phase of its existence. They were decent, disinterested and high-minded, and they were sure they knew what was best for the country and for their social inferiors. They believed in self-help, hard work, individualism and voluntary endeavour. Their concept of the nation was English rather than British (not until 1931 was the National Trust for Scotland established), and with the exception of the Lake District, the properties they took over were more in the south than in the north. They were primarily concerned with preserving open spaces of outstanding natu-ral beauty which were threatened with development or spoliation. They were also interested in safeguarding buildings of historical importance, but this was lower on their list of priorities, and they were not especially concerned with country houses. The national heritage which they sought to preserve was natural rather than man-made, rural rather than urban. Like many of their contemporaries, they believed that the essence of Englishness was to be found in the fields and hedgerows, not in the suburbs and slums.

On all these issues the founding triumvirate was largely in agreement. But in establishing the National Trust in the way they did, they left several questions unresolved, which have since become much debated. Was the Trust primarily concerned with preservation or with access? Rawnsley wanted to save the Lake District from trains and trippers; Hill sought to safeguard open spaces for the enjoyment of city dwellers. Was the Trust anti-landlord or pro-aristocrat? The Commons Preservation Society was by definition hostile to landowners asserting their property rights against the public, and Hunter and Hill were both strongly of the same opinion. But like any late-nineteenth-century voluntary society eager to establish its credentials, the Trust had sought, and secured, the patronage of some of the noblest names in the land. Was the Trust a paternal and oligarchic body, or was it a mass organization? The founding figures had no doubt as to their answer. They ran the Trust as they saw fit, with help from friends and relatives – a substantial proportion of whom, during this initial period, were women. But if membership ever expanded significantly, there might come a time when this restricted way of doing things would no longer seem acceptable.

While Rawnsley, Hunter and Hill were in charge, these questions never surfaced, for they were fully occupied in launching and establishing the Trust. The earliest properties acquired were the cliff at Barmouth and Barras Head, Tintagel. In 1896, the Trust bought – for a mere £10 – its first historic building: the fourteenth-century Clergy House at Alfriston. Four years later, £7,000 was raised to purchase a stretch of land at Brandelhow, on the edge of Derwentwater, and soon after a further £12,000 was collected to safeguard Gowbarrow, on Ullswater. In 1907, the Trust acquired its first country house: Barrington Court in Somerset. But it was only able to do so thanks to a legacy; the building was in a very dilapidated state, and for many years thereafter, no funds were available for restoration work. It was this acquisition which necessitated the passing of the first National Trust Act, which empowered it to preserve 'lands and tenements (including buildings) of beauty or historic interest' for the benefit of the nation. The ordering of priorities is again worth noting. The Act also introduced the concept that the Trust's property was 'inalienable': that it was to be held in perpetuity on behalf of the English people as a whole.[14]

The founding triumvirate were vigorous propagandists and effective fund-raisers, but the National Trust remained a very small-scale organization during the first phase of its existence – a phase that was effectively brought to a close with their deaths: Octavia Hill in 1912, Sir Robert Hunter in the following year and Canon Rawnsley in 1920. By then, the Trust owned 13,200 acres, yielding an annual income of £1,677, and had 713 members, whose subscriptions totalled £532.[15] To put this in perspective, this meant that its entire holdings amounted to little more than one reasonably sized landed estate, and that its total membership was scarcely larger than that of the House of Commons. After twenty-five years, the National Trust had not established itself as an important element in national life, national culture or national identity. It was neither the leading conservationist body of the day, nor a serious influence on the public agenda of the time, and it lacked political connections at the very highest level. 'Of course it might grow,' Octavia Hill had shrewdly observed in 1896, 'But then it might not.' Twenty years on, in the dark days of the First World War, that uncertainty still remained.

II

It did not remain for much longer. In the short run, the First World War was a difficult time for the Trust, and its activities came to a virtual standstill. But in the longer term, the war led to drastic changes in the context in which the Trust operated – changes which proved greatly (and unexpectedly) to its advantage. There was bolshevism and fascism abroad and, from 1918, mass democracy at home. There was the Lloyd George Coalition, which was widely regarded as unprincipled and corrupt. There were two Labour governments, there was serious industrial unrest during the 1920s and serious unemployment during the 1930s. The demise of the Liberal Party and the break-up of the Liberal intelligentsia meant that conservationist endeavour would now be carried on by other political groupings. The 'revolution in landholding' after 1918 saw one quarter of the land put on the market, and meant that the traditional social structure of the shires was irrevocably weakened. And at the same time, the English countryside was subjected to the unprecedented blight of the motor car and the charabanc, the new suburban sprawl and ribbon development, semi-detached houses and seaside bungalows.[16]

In this dramatically altered political and environmental climate, the cult of Englishness and of rural decency became more appealing than ever before, and was now brought to the very centre of public affairs. One reason for this was that the dominant political figure for most of the inter-war period was the Conservative leader, and three times Prime Minister, Stanley Baldwin. Baldwin's politics were built around the avoidance of extremism, the cultivation of consensus, and hostility to Lloyd George, the press Lords and corruption in public life. Although the son of a Worcestershire iron master, Baldwin was deeply attached to the English countryside, which he saw as the repository of everything that was best about the English character.[17] One of Baldwin's greatest admirers was Lord Grey of Fallodon, who had been Liberal Foreign Secretary from 1905 to 1916, but who had fallen out with Lloyd George. Grey was a renowned country-lover and bird-watcher, and came to see Baldwin as the statesman who had delivered the nation from the 'Welsh wizard's' delinquencies. And the same was true of another of Baldwin's closest friends, Lord Halifax, who was Viceroy of India (1926–31) and Foreign Secretary (1938–40). Like Grey, Halifax was a high-minded north-country landowner, who shared his belief in the close connection between rural life and 'spiritual values'.

Between them, these three men set the tone of English public life during the inter-war years, and under their moral and political leadership, the cult of the countryside became more pronounced than ever before. There were renewed protests against urban encroachment and rural spoliation, such as *England and the Octopus* (1928), and *Britain and the Beast* (1937), the one written, the other edited, by the maverick conservationist, Clough Williams-Ellis. The Council for the Preservation of Rural England was established in 1925, and there was a growing demand for the establishment of National Parks.[18] In 1929, Longmans began to publish a series entitled 'English Heritage', with introductions by Stanley Baldwin, and in the following year, Batsford launched another series called 'English Life'. Books with titles such as *The Landscape of England*, *England's Character*, *Heart of England* and *The Beauty of England*, found ready markets. In 1933–4, the BBC broadcast a series of talks on 'National Character', which were primarily concerned with celebrating rural England. And best-selling novelists such as Mary Webb and Francis Brett Young – both much admired by Baldwin – waxed lyrical about the countryside, even as they lamented 'the passing of the squires'.[19]

These Baldwinite sentiments were fully shared by John Bailey, who had been connected with the National Trust from the beginning, and who became the dominant force in its affairs during the 1920s. His father was a Norwich solicitor and Norfolk landowner, and Bailey grew up with a passion for the countryside, strong religious convictions and qualms of guilt about the wealth he would one day inherit. Like many of his generation, he was disturbed by 'the earthquake shock of the war', which meant that 'all established opinions' were now 'attacked or at least questioned'.[20] He was Chairman of the Trust from 1922 until his death in 1931, and during that time he recruited three important new supporters. The first was G. M. Trevelyan, Regius Professor of Modern History at Cambridge from 1927, and a personal friend of Baldwin, Halifax and Grey of Fallodon (whose biography he wrote); he was Chairman of the Estates Committee from 1928 to 1948.[21] The second was R. C. Norman, who was the brother of the Governor of the Bank of England, Chairman of the London County Council (1918–19), and of the BBC (1935–9); he was in charge of the Trust's

Finance Committee from 1923 to 1935. And the third was Oliver Brett, son of Lord Esher, who had been an *éminence grise* in British establishment circles from the reign of Queen Victoria to the time of George V.

Like the founding triumvirate, Bailey, Trevelyan, Norman and Brett were exceptionally public-spirited men. But there were important differences. In the first place, they were much better connected with the highest echelons of public and political life: hence the appointment of Grey of Fallodon as a Vice-President of the Trust, and of both Stanley Baldwin and Ramsay MacDonald as Honorary Vice-Presidents. In the second place, they were non-partisan conservatives rather than non-partisan liberals: Bailey had stood unsuccessfully for Parliament in the 1890s; Norman had been Private Secretary to two Conservative ministers, George Wyndham and Lord Halsbury; Trevelyan gradually evolved from a pre-war Liberal into a Baldwinite Tory; and although Brett remained a lifelong Liberal, he hated Lloyd George and all his coalition stood for.[22] In the third place, they were, by birth or connection, from a higher social stratum than Rawnsley, Hunter and Hill. Norman and Bailey both married into titled families. Trevelyan was a member of the aristocracy of birth as well as the aristocracy of talent. Brett was heir to a peerage. And the most well-connected, Conservative and patrician of them all was the Marquess of Zetland, a grandee and north-country landowner, who was Chairman of the Trust from 1931 to 1945, and Secretary of State for India in the National Government from 1935 to 1940.

Led by these men, the National Trust became, along with the BBC, one of the main props to Baldwin's brand of emollient inter-war decency. It was the Prime Minister's rural nostalgia in action. Although it properly continued to present itself as a 'national' rather than as a partisan organization, the tone of the Trust during this second phase of its history was distinctly more to the right of the political spectrum than to the left. It was not just that the countryside must be preserved as the essential repository of 'spiritual values': it was also that those values were the necessary antidote to the 'base materialism' of the age – telephones, cinemas, Lloyd George, Lord Birkenhead, the *Daily Mail* and the *Daily Express*. It was these concerns which lay behind G. M. Trevelyan's two powerful pieces of propaganda on behalf of the Trust, *Must England's Beauty Perish?* (1926) and *The Calls and Claims of Natural Beauty* (1931). 'Modern inventions', he lamented, the 'inexorable march of bricks and mortar', and the 'full development of motor traffic', were destroying the English countryside at an unprecedented rate. The National Trust was 'an ark of refuge, and a bulwark for the day of trouble'. And how necessary this was. 'Without vision,' Trevelyan concluded, 'the people perish, and without natural beauty, the English people will perish in the spiritual sense.'[23]

These appeals met a ready response among the country-worshippers of inter-war England. As a result of its much higher profile, the Trust expanded at an unprecedented rate, greatly assisted by increasingly enthusiastic editorials in *The Times*, and by the willingness of Baldwin and Grey of Fallodon to lend their names to its efforts.[24] Some land came through benefactions: at Runnymede, at Sugar Loaf in Monmouthshire and at Dovedale in the Peak District. Some came through successful appeals: at Ashridge (for which £80,000 was raised), around Stonehenge (another £35,000) and in the Buttermere valley. Lord Curzon bequeathed Tattershall and Bodiam Castles to the Trust in 1926, and Ernest Cook presented Montacute in 1931. Nor was this the only evidence of expansion. Between 1920 and 1940, membership increased from 713 to 6,800, and subscription income from £532 to £5,772. Over the same period, the total acreage held by the Trust rose from 13,200 to 68,544, and its property income went up from £1,677 to £36,570. This represented progress far beyond the dreams of Rawnsley, Hunter and Hill, and in *England Under Trust* (1937), John Dixon-Scott described a flourishing institution, confident of its mission, and enjoying widespread public support.

For Trevelyan and his generation, the Second World War spelt the end of civilization as they knew it, and the death-knell of 'spiritual values'. But there was a significant growth in acreage if not in membership, and 1945 was not only the year of victory: it was also the Trust's fiftieth anniversary. As the senior survivor of the inter-war quartet, Trevelyan wielded his propagandist's pen once more, contributing an article to *Country Life* (in which he observed that one hundred thousand acres was 'a nice patrimony for a duke, but it is not much for a nation'), and writing the preface to James Lees-Milne's celebratory volume, *The National Trust: A Record of Fifty Years' Achievement* (1945). Trevelyan was also at the centre of the Trust's jubilee appeal, and donated to it the royalties from his *English Social History* – a book which was appropriately suffused with 'spiritual values' and rural nostalgia.[25] In addition, he persuaded Hugh Dalton – like Trevelyan a pre-1914 Liberal, but now Chancellor of the Exchequer in the postwar Labour Government – to match the public subscription pound for pound with a government grant, the first such gift the Trust had ever received. As a result, £120,000 was raised, and by 1950 membership had reached 23,403, and the Trust's holdings stood at 152,500 acres.[26]

The retirement of Zetland as Chairman in 1945, the death of Stanley Baldwin in 1947, and the resignation of Trevelyan as the Chairman of

Estates Committee in 1948, effectively brought this second phase of the National Trust's history to a close. It was a phase which may be described as élitist, paternal and culturally and politically conservative. John Bailey believed that 'a class of cultivated intelligent people' was best able to decide what was good for everybody else, and in insisting that the Trust should put preservation before public access, he was holding fast to that conviction.[27] Whether the founding triumvirate would have expressed their unanimous agreement is a moot point. But during the inter-war years, this Baldwinite view of conservation enjoyed support on the liberal left as well as on the liberal right. Among senior figures in the Labour Party, those with patrician aspirations (Ramsay MacDonald and Hugh Dalton), and those with patrician ancestors (Noel Buxton and Stafford Cripps), were frequently to be found expressing their public support. In 1935, Hugh Dalton had described the Trust as embodying 'practical socialism in action': and he reiterated this opinion in government eleven years later.[28] By then, however, the Trust's priorities had changed decisively and dramatically.

III

It is only in retrospect that the third phase in the Trust's history may be dated as having begun during the mid-1930s. Quite by chance, the very year that Hugh Dalton had written in praise of the Trust's 'practical socialism' saw the beginning of a new and very different policy, concerning the acceptance and preservation of country houses, which for a time would come to be – and would come to be seen – as its prime task and justification. To be sure, the Trust had always been interested in preserving buildings of historical interest and architectural importance. But they had been of varied size and use, and safeguarding places of outstanding natural beauty had always been its highest priority. It was pure coincidence that the National Trust and Death Duties had come into being within a year of each other. By the early 1930s, the Trust possessed only two country houses: Barrington Court, which was dilapidated and let, and Montacute, which had no furniture. And they were both unexpected acquisitions, the result of benefactions which the Trust had felt unable to refuse; there was no endowment in either case, and their acceptance did not reflect a coherent or concerned country house policy. At that time, no such policy existed.

Such a policy tentatively emerged after Lord Lothian had addressed the Trust's annual meeting in 1934, and expressed his fears for the future of country houses in Britain. The matter was taken up by the Trust, which devised a Country House Scheme, and parliamentary legislation passed in 1937 and 1939 made it possible for owners to transfer their properties to the Trust, by gift or bequest, along with appropriate endowment for their upkeep. Provided there was adequate public access, there would be generous tax concessions on transfer, the Trust would maintain the house in perpetuity, and the former owners would be allowed to remain in occupation as tenants.[29] As a result, the Trust set up a Country House Committee, which was to be responsible for vetting potential donors and their properties. Its chairman was Oliver Brett, now third Viscount Esher, and its secretary was the young James Lees-Milne, whose father was a Worcestershire squire. But there was little by way of immediate response. Inconclusive negotiations were begun with Lord Methuen (Corsham Court), Sir Henry Hoare (Stourhead) and Lord Sackville (Knole). But Sir Geoffrey Mander was the only owner to give his house (Wightwick Manor) to the Trust in 1937, and Lord Lothian was the first to bequeath his (Blickling) in the following year.[30]

This was a very small beginning: indeed, from July 1938 to March 1941, the Country House Committee did not meet. But the scheme was given an unexpected impetus by the Second World War. Most country houses were requisitioned, and servants were called up. The aristocratic way of life seemed doomed. Evelyn Waugh wrote *Brideshead Revisited* (1945). And the Labour government of 1945–51 brought high taxes and socialist legislation which seemed to portend 'social revolution'.[31] In fact, it was Hugh Dalton, the Chancellor of the Exchequer, who in 1946 set up the National Land Fund, which was empowered to compensate the Treasury if it accepted land in lieu of Death Duty payments, and these provisions were subsequently extended to cover the historic houses themselves, and also their contents. All this led to a massive increase in the number of houses conveyed to the Trust, some directly transferred by gift or bequest, others passed on by the Treasury. Between 1940 and 1949, there were thirty-one (including Blickling, Wallington and Knole); between 1950 and 1959, there were thirty-four (including Penrhyn Castle, St Michael's Mount and Waddesdon); and between 1960 and 1969, there were thirteen (including Anglesey Abbey, Shugborough and Felbrigg). Within thirty years, the Trust had thus acquired seventy-eight country houses from the old landed élite.

This new activity effectively eclipsed and superseded the Trust's inter-war championship of 'spiritual values'. But as with each phase of its history, there were broader forces at work which also influenced its changing policies. The men who had set the public agenda and dominated the Trust during the 1920s and 1930s had passed from the scene: Baldwin was very much out of fashion and out of favour, and Trevelyan would soon follow him. Dalton and Cripps, both members of the Labour government, were arguably the last two politicians to believe in 'spiritual values' (indeed, Mrs Dalton sat on the Trust's Executive Committee). To be sure, love of the countryside remained strongly felt: this was, after all, the era of *The Archers*, Laura Ashley and R. F. Delderfield. But the postwar world was one of Welfare State experimentation, and of unprecedented material improvement. In Britain, as elsewhere, growth and modernization were high on the political agenda. Neither Harold Macmillan ('you've never had it so good'), nor Harold Wilson ('white-hot technology'), were much concerned with spiritual values. In the era of James Bond, the Profumo scandal, and the 'affluent' and 'permissive' societies, such sentiments were now at a discount.

In a sense, then, the unexpected success of the Country House Scheme gave the postwar National Trust a new purpose and justification, at a time when it very much needed one. And this cause was eagerly taken up by the new men in charge, who were as committed to safeguarding country houses as their predecessors had been to safeguarding the countryside. Lord Crawford, who was chairman from 1945 to 1965, knew about this 'national tragedy' first hand, having been obliged to abandon his mansion at Haigh, near Wigan.[32] Lord Esher, now the senior survivor, found no difficulty in adapting to these changed priorities. They were supported in their work and their views by the Earl of Rosse, who chaired the Historic Buildings Committee from 1954 to 1969, by Earl de la Warr, who became chairman of the Estates Committee in succession to G. M. Trevelyan, and by the Duke of Wellington, Harold Nicolson and Vita Sackville-West.[33] In the long perspective of the Trust's history, this was aristocratic oligarchy at its apogee. Even Nicolson was a touch embarrassed by this blue-blooded excess:

In the morning we had the Historic Buildings Committee of the National Trust. We have a new member, the Earl of Euston. You know I am always rather worried that this committee, which actually decides whether we take a house, is composed almost entirely of peers. Well, we are now to have a man called Mr John Smith. When his name was put up, Esher said, 'Well, it's a good thing to have a proletarian name on the Committee – anybody know the man?' 'Yes', said Lord Euston, 'he is my brother-in-law.'[34]

The fact that there were so many aristocrats involved with the Trust at a time when it was concerned with preserving so many aristocratic houses was hardly coincidence. What did these people think they were doing? Many of them were as public spirited as their predecessors; but their social vision was much narrower, more exclusive. The Duke of Wellington was 'firm, precise, sneery and offensive'. Vita Sackville-West 'hated' the Beveridge Report, 'la populace' in general, and most aspects of the modern world. Harold Nicolson was a self-confessed snob, knew nothing about the lives of ordinary people, was equally ill at ease in the suburbs and the slums, and shared his wife's hostility to the lower orders.[35] Even more reactionary was their friend James Lees-Milne, whose dislikes included Jews, businessmen, politicians and all members of the middle and lower classes. He loathed democracy, had once been (like Nicolson) a supporter of Oswald Mosley, and took pride in being too right wing for the Conservative Party. As Secretary to the Trust's Country House Committee, his mission was to preserve these 'secular shrines' from twentieth-century barbarism. As he candidly admitted, his priorities were the country houses, their traditional owners and then the National Trust – in that order of importance.[36]

Notwithstanding their strong sense of public duty, it seems clear that in running the Trust, these men sought to inflate the sectional interests of their class into the national interests of their country. It is pointless to speculate whether the founding triumvirate or the inter-war Baldwinites would have 'approved' of these changes in the Trust's policies: in the 1890s and 1900s, and even in the 1920s and 1930s, the prospect of country houses disappearing in large numbers was so remote that there is no way of knowing what they would have thought of it. Inevitably, and rightly, the Trust has adjusted its preservationist priorities and redefined the 'national heritage' in every generation. But there was a marked contrast between the anti-landlord feelings of Sir Robert Hunter and Octavia Hill, and the superior sense of class-ridden anxiety of the Lees-Milne generation. In 1881, Lord de la Warr was taken to court by the Commoners of Ashdown Forest, whose customary rights he was infringing.[37] Seventy years later, his successor was a pillar of the National Trust. Here was a measure of how much both the Trust and the aristocracy had changed. The earlier concerns which had animated the leading lights of the Trust – for the well-being of the working classes, or for the well-being of the nation as a whole – were not shared by this new generation of patrician zealots and country house addicts.

Despite the Trust's oft-repeated refusal to accept them, some of the earliest houses were inadequately endowed, and others became so as the costs of upkeep and restoration rose. Opening times were very restricted: sometimes only fifty days a year, and they were 'settled as far as possible to suit the donor's convenience'.[38] And initially, the number of visitors was very small: even at the first opening of Blickling, it was scarcely a handful. For the Trust, the sudden acquisition of so many houses was a massive burden, which required substantial administrative restructuring. But as a proportion of the total country house stock of the nation – variously estimated at between five hundred and five thousand – it was in fact relatively small. Indeed, with the exception of Blickling, Knole, Petworth and Hardwick, few of the nation's greatest houses came the Trust's way.[39] At different times, there were negotiations concerning Longleat, Harewood, Althorp, Holkham, Woburn and Arundel; but nothing resulted from them. Boughton, Chatsworth, Alnwick, Blenheim and Belvoir also remained in private hands. The very grandest aristocrats were usually able to hang on to their mansions (or demolish them). Most of the Trust's country houses came, predictably, from the poorer survivors of the old landed class.

The fact that many of these houses were endowed with land helps explain why the Trust's holdings more than doubled in this period, from 152,500 acres in 1950 to 328,502 in 1965. The growth in membership was even more sensational: from 23,403 to 157,581 during the same time. And after a slow postwar start, the number of visitors, both to beauty spots and to stately homes increased beyond the wildest expectations. As a result, the 'preservation versus access' debate acquired a new intensity. Nor was this the only problem which arose during these years. Despite the sum raised at the Jubilee appeal, and the increase in income from members' subscriptions and visitors' entrance fees, the Trust's finances were far from secure, as expenditure on maintenance and administration consistently outran income.[40] In addition, Harold Wilson's Labour government of 1964–70 was conspicuously less well disposed towards the Trust than that of Clement Attlee.[41] Moreover, the gap was inexorably widening between membership and management. In terms of its size, the Trust had become a mass organization. In terms of its structure, it was a self-perpetuating, aristocratic oligarchy. Sooner or later, these problems were bound to come to the surface, and these contradictions would have to be resolved. In 1965, Lord Antrim succeeded Lord Crawford as Chairman. These problems, and these contradictions, were very soon upon him.

IV

The appointment of Lord Antrim, another hereditary peer who had previously been Chairman of the National Trust for Northern Ireland, was a vote for continuity over change. But the context in which the Trust was operating soon started to shift once more, as proliferating preservationist movements began to assume new forms and espouse new policies, and as the consciousnesses of conservationists were raised, round the world, to unprecedented altitudes.[42] Inspired by books such as Rachel Carson's *Silent Spring* (1962), disillusioned with the obsessive pursuit of economic growth, convinced that small was both better and beautiful, and anxious about world wildlife and the future of the rainforests, a new environmentalist movement came into being, concerned as much with animals as with the countryside, and with global rather than national issues. Hence the advent of radical conservationist politics, involving demonstrations, protest marches and other confrontationalist methods, as espoused by Greenpeace, the Friends of the Earth, the Animal Liberationist Movement and the League Against Cruel Sports. Hence Prince Charles's much-publicized concerns with global warming, the ozone layer and organic farming. Hence the recognition by politicians the world over that they must at least pay lip-service to the environmentalists' agenda. And hence the gradual greening of the British government – changes in outlook which received their official recognition with the appointment of Peter Walker as the first Secretary of State for the Environment in 1970, and of David Mellor as the first Secretary of State for the National Heritage in 1992.

At the same time, there was another development, more British than international, which centred around the increasing cult of the 'national heritage'. This phrase had been around for some time: Canon Rawnsley had used it as the title for his book surveying National Trust properties in 1920. But during the 1970s and 1980s, it became much more widely used in Britain. The preservation of such antique artefacts as the *Mary Rose* became a national obsession.[43] There was an even greater furore over the sale of Mentmore – one of the great Rothschild houses in Buckinghamshire – and the dispersal of its contents. National Heritage Acts were passed in 1980 and 1983, and a National Heritage Memorial Fund was established, to finance further preservationist ventures.[44] The cult of the countryside and of the country house reached epidemic proportions: witness the sensational successes of Mark Girouard's *Life in the English Country House* (1978), of Edith Holden's reprinted *Country Diary of an Edwardian Lady* (1977), and of the television adaptation of *Brideshead Revisited* (1982). Here was unbridled (and often uninformed) nostalgia: something very different from the sentiments which had lain behind the Trust during the first three phases of its existence.

These diverse changes in the public mood, both in Britain and around the world, naturally carried important implications as far as the National Trust was concerned. Indeed, as early as the mid-1960s, there were signs that the Trust was becoming less interested in preserving country houses than it had recently been. As new legislation effectively forbade further demolitions, as postwar austerity receded into the distance, and as the number of visitors to stately homes increased inexorably year by year, country house living underwent a modest revival, and the apocalyptic language of the 1940s and early 1950s became less widespread.[45] And for its part, the Trust became increasingly reluctant to accept any more houses unless they were lavishly endowed with cash, investments or land, and even then, only on condition that they would be opened to the public seven days a week. As a result, the number of country houses which were transferred to the Trust was markedly smaller in the 1960s than it had been in the previous decades, and it has continued to decline still further since then: to thirteen in the 1970s, eleven in the 1980s and only two in the 1990s. In the foreseeable future, there seems no likelihood that this downward trend will be – or should be – reversed.

At the same time, the Trust was gradually moving towards new preservationist interests and also, in some cases, back to its earlier conservationist concerns. In 1963, it was decided to extend its protection to industrial monuments, including machinery, buildings, canals and railways. Here was a very significant change: for the whole of its previous existence, the Trust had embodied the widespread view that the Industrial Revolution had been an unmitigated disaster.[46] Now it was beginning to deem its products worthy of conservation. Meanwhile, there was a renewed emphasis on the Trust's traditional role as the guardian of places of outstanding natural beauty. In 1964, it launched 'Enterprise Neptune', a much-publicized national appeal, initially for two million pounds, for the safeguarding of Britain's remaining 900 miles of unspoiled but threatened coastline. Within twenty-five years, £13.5 million had been raised, and more than 300 miles of coastline was acquired, much of it in Devon and Cornwall.[47] During the same period, the Trust's landholdings also went up dramatically: from 328,500 acres in 1965 to 569,500 in 1990.

As if to emphasize this return to earlier priorities, the appeal director appointed for Enterprise Neptune was Commander Conrad Rawnsley, the grandson of one of the original triumvirate. For reasons which remain a source of controversy, he was dismissed in 1966. His response was to mount a campaign against the Trust, accusing it of being undemocratic and inefficient. Along with his supporters, he alleged that it was too oligarchic and exclusive in its organization, that it did not adequately represent the opinions of its much-enlarged membership, that Enterprise Neptune had been badly bungled, that there was insufficient public access to many of its country houses, and that their former owners had been treated too deferentially. The result was an acrimonious public debate, which coincided with rumours that the Labour government wished to set up an official investigation into the Trust's affairs.[48] To quell the controversy, and to forestall the investigation, Lord Antrim set up a broad-ranging inquiry in August 1967, chaired by an outsider, Sir Henry Benyon, a South African-born accountant, with wide experience in business and government, to investigate the Trust's finances, management, organization and responsibilities. His committee reported within two years, and recommended sweeping reforms, most of which were immediately accepted.[49]

As a result, the Trust was transformed from an amateurish oligarchy into a responsible business enterprise. Budgetary control became more stringent, and much of the administration was devolved on to regional committees. The Historic Buildings Committee and the Estates Committee were merged into a new Properties Committee, and a new post of Director General was created to supervise the day-to-day running of the Trust's affairs. And the patrician oligarchs were replaced by people drawn from very different backgrounds. Lord Antrim, who had himself presided over these momentous changes, was the last aristocratic chairman. In 1977, he was succeeded by Lord Gibson, a life peer, with broad-ranging interests in finance, publishing and the arts, who had himself been a member of the Benyon committee of inquiry. Gibson was followed from 1986 to 1991 by Dame Jennifer Jenkins, the first woman to be in such a prominent position in the Trust's affairs since Octavia Hill herself. In addition, she was the wife of Roy Jenkins, formerly Labour Home Secretary and Chancellor of the Exchequer, and later leader of the SDP, and she had considerable experience of business and conservation. Her successor, Lord Chorley, was another hereditary peer, but in the mould of Gibson rather than Crawford. His father had been a professor and a lawyer, and a member of the Trust's Executive Committee for forty-five years, and he himself moved between the worlds of accountancy, academe, business and government.

In addition, the Benyon Committee had urged that the Trust must become more commercially oriented, and more responsive to, and appreciative of, its membership. Accordingly, a series of new initiatives were launched: National Trust shops were established in big towns and cities; National Trust publications were produced on country houses and country matters; and a North American fund-raising subsidiary was set up, called the Royal Oak Foundation. There was also a concerted drive to increase members, partly to give the Trust a firmer basis of popular support, and partly to raise essential extra funding. As a result, membership grew from 157,581 in 1965 to 539,285 ten years later. In May 1981, membership reached one million, and by October 1990 it had doubled again. On 31 December 1993, it stood at 2,189,386. This was a sensational – almost exponential – increase, and the Trust's campaign must rank as the most successful recruitment drive ever undertaken in Britain in peacetime. The fact that much of it occurred during the years of Mrs Thatcher's pre-eminence was a coincidence deserving further investigation. As is the fact that more people now carry National Trust cards than regularly worship as members of the Church of England.

In the changed and broadened context of the Trust's recent activities, the preservation of country houses no longer bulks as large as it did between 1940 and 1965. To be sure, there have been some important recent acquisitions: Dunster Castle, Erddig and Kingston Lacy by bequest; Belton, Calke Abbey and Kedleston with the assistance of the National Heritage Memorial Fund.[50] And as the exhibition devoted to the 'Treasure Houses of Britain', staged in Washington in 1985–6 made plain, there are still those in the Trust to whom stately homes are sacred objects. But such views carry less weight than they did, and since it now costs in the region of ten million pounds to restore and endow a country house, it seems likely that the rate of transfers will continue to decline. Hence James Lees-Milne's latter-day lament that 'the acquisition of country houses has had its day ... It is', he sadly concluded, 'no use battling against the Zeitgeist.'[51] But this also means that the houses which the Trust does possess are now being treated less deferentially and more historically. Since Merlin Waterson's brilliant and pioneering restoration of Erddig, more attention has been given in other country houses to life below stairs as well as above, and to getting away from the rather formulaic interior decorations – 'sprigged cotton style' – of the John Fowler era. All this is much to be welcomed.[52]

In today's Britain, the conservationists are simultaneously more divided and more determined than ever before. The methods and priorities of the environmentalist pressure groups and of the heritage lobby are significantly different. But together they constitute an unprecedentedly numerous and vociferous movement. And because of the Trust's changed constitution and spectacularly enlarged membership, they can now exert a significant influence on its affairs in ways that would have been unimaginable (and unacceptable) to the founding triumvirate and their successors. At the annual general meeting held in 1933, Lady Corry raised the matter of cruel sports being permitted on the Trust's land. The chairman, Lord Zetland, simply ruled her out of order.[53] In recent years, the same issue has been the subject of heated debate at the Trust's annual general meetings, of a ballot among all members, and of widespread media coverage. And at a time when the Labour government seems uncertain whether to make fox-hunting illegal it continues to be a controversial and divisive subject. Whether it will be possible, in the future, for the Trust to retain the support of both the heritage lobby and the environmentalist pressure groups, only time will tell.[54] Either way, those in charge of the National Trust no longer have the power to define the 'national heritage' that their predecessors possessed in the earlier phases of its existence.

V

This is a very brief survey of a very broad subject, and as such it is inevitably an over-simplified account. But there are several themes which are worth drawing out by way of conclusion. The first is the cumulative impact on the holdings and the structure of the Trust of the changes in preservationist priorities that have been outlined here. In each generation, the Trust has redefined its conservationist policies, but the new acquisitions have been added to those already there, which had been accepted at earlier times when different priorities ruled. Since everything which is transferred to the Trust is inalienable, the result is that over the years the range of its responsibilities has become increasingly diverse, and there is every reason to suppose that it will become more so in the years ahead. At the same time, the bureaucracy required to cope with this expanding and proliferating enterprise has become correspondingly more extensive and elaborate. Whether the Trust should be allowed to continue growing in this rather Topsy-like way, and whether the appropriate administrative structure exists for it, or could be devised for it, are matters which are bound to be increasingly debated in the future.

A further conclusion is that throughout the Trust's existence, those in charge of it have defined and redefined what the 'national heritage' is. Successive generations evolved different definitions: liberal-intellectual, Baldwinite Tory, country-house reactionary, and environmentalist-eclectic. But they were neither arrived at, nor implemented, in a ruthlessly partisan way. In 1913, the liberal-intellectuals appointed Lord Plymouth, a former Conservative cabinet minister, as chairman in succession to Sir Robert Hunter. During the inter-war years, there was support for the Trust from certain sections of the Labour Party. In the postwar period, Lord Esher, a lifelong Liberal, worked successfully with a Catholic reactionary like James Lees-Milne. And since the 1970s, the Trust has sought to negotiate its way between the more extreme views of the heritage and the environmentalist lobbies. These balances, carefully and consciously struck and restruck in each generation, help explain why the Trust has always attracted support throughout the country as a whole. At no stage in its history has it been so partisan that it could not plausibly claim to be national.

Nevertheless, it is also clear that, for many of its dominant figures, the National Trust was indeed the pursuit of politics by other means. To be sure, it has always presented itself as a 'non-political' organization, and its leading figures have rarely been fierce partisans in the conventional sense. But throughout most of its history, there was a general presumption that the few knew what was best for the many that reflected the essentially oligarchic nature of the organization. Moreover, the particular preservationist policies adopted in each generation have invariably been politically charged. For Sir Robert Hunter and Octavia Hill, the desire to preserve open spaces inevitably brought them into conflict with landlords. For G. M. Trevelyan, the conservation of the countryside was a Liberal activity before the First World War, but became a Conservative endeavour afterwards. For James Lees-Milne, the purpose of the Trust was to safeguard country houses and their occupants against the levelling social tendencies of the time. These men were not party-political activists in the normally understood sense: but they did not take up politically neutral positions. Then, as now, the definition and preservation of the 'national heritage' are activities which inescapably carry political messages.

During the most recent phase of the Trust's history, the politicization of conservation has become significantly more pronounced. But it has been a development more noticeable outside the Trust than in. The heritage lobby and the environmentalists are highly organized groups, with their own demands, divisions and debates. The Trust, by contrast, seems to have been less single-minded about its own conservationist agenda since the 1970s than it was in earlier generations. This may partly be explained by the reform of its oligarchic leadership, by the increased influence of its mass membership, and by the sheer range of responsibilities which, thanks to its history, it is now obliged to shoulder. For whatever reason, the environmental eclecticism which has characterized the Trust in recent decades has been the least definite and decisive phase in its history. At a time when conservation has become more popular but more contentious than ever before, it may have been a wise decision for the Trust to try to stay above the battle. In any case, if past experience is a reliable guide, it is highly unlikely that this current phase will endure long beyond its centenary year. Indeed, it may well be that, unknown to its management and its members, a new era in the Trust's history is already beginning.

11

Sentiment:
Noël Coward's Patriotic Ardour[1]

'Mr Coward,' John Osborne once remarked, 'like Miss Dietrich, is his own invention and contribution to this century. Anyone who cannot see that should keep well away from the theatre.' So, indeed, he was, and so, indeed, they should have. But what, exactly, *was* that 'invention'? Most famously and enduringly, it was of the sleek, precocious, sophisticated young man, effortlessly dashing off a brittle drama or a flippant song before breakfast. 'Every play you appear in is exactly the same,' Roland Maule tells Garry Essendine, Coward's thinly disguised self-portrait in *Present Laughter* (1939), 'frivolous and without the slightest intellectual significance . . . All you do with your talent is to wear dressing gowns and make witty remarks.'[2] Indeed, this invention was so appealing and so convincing that it powerfully influenced contemporary evaluation of Noël Coward's work, which was regularly dismissed as trivial, superficial and irrelevant. And this was exactly what he wanted: partly in self-defence (as a homosexual, he was throwing 'predatory' and 'greedy' people off the scent), and partly in self-disguise (in fact, like the true late-Victorian that he *just* was, he worked hard all his life). 'I have', he once wrote, 'no deep thoughts about the human race'; the stage, he insisted, 'is primarily a place of entertainment . . . Political or social propaganda in the theatre . . . is a cracking bore'; and anyone who argued to the contrary would merely be contributing to the 'nonsense' which he was sure would be 'written about me and my works and my motives' after his death.[3]

But even while his subject was still alive and still saying this, Sheridan Morley's pioneering biography urged an alternative and more plausible view, namely that in Coward 'a social historian, a moralist and a philosopher were forever asking to be let out'.[4] For all its apparent frivolity, a substantial slice of his work was concerned, as befitted a homosexual, and as the titles of his plays often suggest, to explore the complexities, ironies, deceptions and hypocrisies of personal relationships: in *The Vortex* (1923), *Fallen Angels* (1923), *Easy Virtue* (1924), *Semi-Monde* (1926), *Private Lives* (1930) and *Design for Living* (1932), during the first phase of his career, and in *Volcano* (1956) and *Suite in Three Keys* (1965) towards the end. And in between, much of Coward's large and varied output was devoted to telling the English (and it was very much the *English*, not the British) about themselves, their country and their Empire – so much so that one explanation for the ups and downs in his reputation is the degree to which his patriotic vision did (or did not) resonate with the mood and circumstances of the time. Accordingly, one essential element of that necessary posthumous 'nonsense', which Coward anticipated and deplored, involves taking him seriously as the ardent patriot, imperial laureate, naval romantic and fervent monarchist that he certainly became in his mature years, and probably had been for the whole of his life. How did he come to love his country so much? What vision of his country did he have? And why did he feel his patriotic ardour was insufficiently requited?

I

These are pertinent questions: for the dressing-gown-wearing, cigarette-smoking, cocktail-drinking Noël Coward of the 1920s seemed very much a rebel – part angry young man, part bright young thing, the self-appointed scourge of conventional behaviour, establishment attitudes and theatrical conservatism. And that persona was itself a combination of unavoidable circumstance and self-conscious creation. He was born (hence his name) in December 1899, and was thus a very late Victorian, who also belonged to the younger end of that doomed generation, many of whose finest flowers fell on the fields of Flanders. Among them were his own friends, Philip Streatfield and John Ekins.[5] For someone with so sensitive and highly strung a temperament, these were traumatic losses to endure in mid-adolescence, and they left Coward with an abiding distrust of politicians – 'the old gang' and 'the men at the top' who had sent his friends to their deaths. To add to his discomfiture, his own involvement in the First World War was brief and inglorious. As a child-actor, eager to make his way in the theatre, he did all he could to avoid conscription; he was neither physically nor psychologically robust enough for military life; and after a few months he was invalided out, having suffered some sort of nervous breakdown. 'I was too young', he later recalled, 'and ambitious and filled with my own concerns for it to have much significance for me.' At this time, all Coward cared about was getting back to the theatre, which reinforced his view that the war had been mistaken and futile – pent-up feelings which he finally poured out, angrily and unsuccessfully, in *Post-Mortem* (1930).[6]

Accordingly, much of Coward's work in the 1920s was concerned with experimentation and rebellion, and this in two senses. For Coward was addressing a variety of (what seemed to an older generation) decadent, confused, aberrant and selfish forms of human behaviour – drugs, alcohol, infidelity and sexual deviance – and he did so in works whose forms were as experimental as their contents were novel, combining clipped dialogue and jazz-age jaggedness with new dramatic structures and effects. *The Vortex* lurches from a conventional opening to a dream-like middle and a big-bang finale; *Easy Virtue* turned Victorian melodrama upside down and inside out; and *Hay Fever* (1924) has no plot whatsoever, its last act a nonsensical denial of every dramatic convention of narrative, suspense and climax.[7] This was theatrical revolution projecting (and celebrating?) social anarchy. 'I think very few people are completely normal, really, deep down in their private lives,' Amanda tells Victor, in the most quoted line from his most famous play. 'Let's be superficial', Elyot later responds, 'and pity the poor philosophers. Let's blow trumpets and squeakers and enjoy the party as much as we can . . . Let's savour the delight of the moment. Come and kiss me darling, before your body rots and worms pop in and out of your eye sockets.' Here was the authentic voice of the twenties generation, stridently in revolt against their parents: small wonder that Virginia Woolf and Bloomsbury were attracted to Coward's early work.[8]

As a young man with a career and a reputation to make, Coward was determined to shock, and shock he did. 'I am never out of opium dens, cocaine dens, and other evil places,' he teasingly told the *Evening Standard* in 1925. 'My mind is a mass of corruption.' 'I am hopelessly depraved, vicious and decadent,' he informed the *Sunday Chronicle*, for good measure. Such remarks scarcely endeared him to the establishment – of the British theatre or of the British nation. He made it plain that he had no time for the 'high-toned drawing room histrionics' of the old guard of playwrights, among them Pinero and Somerset Maugham, and he was in open rebellion against their 'false sentiments and hypocrisy'.[9] Inevitably, his work fell foul of the theatrical censorship which then prevailed, for no play could be produced on the London stage without a licence, which could only be granted by the Lord Chamberlain, who also happened to be the senior figure at the royal court, responsible for overseeing the smooth functioning of the British monarchy. With *The Vortex* and *Private Lives*, Coward had real difficulties in getting past the censor, *Semi-Monde* was not produced until well after his death, and *Design for Living* had to wait seven years after its New York première before it reached the London stage. For most of his life, Coward railed against this regime of legalized intolerance, which was not ended until 1968, and which denied 'all one really minds about – creative instinct, freedom of thought and expression, individualism'; while on the other side, there were many in official circles who, after these early encounters, never liked him, trusted him or took him seriously (indeed George V, the ultimate official, thought *The Vortex* 'disgusting').[10]

But this was not the only form of government interference with freedom of expression against which the young Coward ineffectually protested. For as a homosexual, he lived in shame and fear – and, again, in anger. In inter-war Britain, homosexuality was a criminal offence, punishable by prison and/or social ostracism. The trial, conviction and ruination of Oscar Wilde had taken place only four years before Coward was born; and in the early thirties, Lord Beauchamp, a former Liberal cabinet minister, a Knight of the Garter and Lord Warden of the Cinque Ports, was forced to leave England rather than face prosecution.[11] 'I thought', George V once observed, 'men like that shot themselves.' Some did. Coward was reticent about his private life, but was far from sexually inactive, which meant he was constantly at risk from scandal, exposure and blackmail. In such an environment, where homosexuals were marginalized, vulnerable and persecuted figures, the theatre was an ideal career, with its relaxed tolerance and easy camaraderie. But for all his nineteenth-century work-ethic, Coward detested the 'barbarous' Victorian moral (and legal) code of the British establishment and of the Church of England, and he rightly feared this was an additional reason why he had enemies in high places. Inevitably, this made him a rebel. 'Being a sexual outsider', Philip Hoare rightly observes, 'gave his work its edge.' 'Had [Coward] not been homosexual,' he further suggests, 'he might have been a conservative, run-of-the-mill playwright.'[12]

This is a shrewd observation – in more senses than one. For despite his dislike of war, his theatrical innovativeness, and his 'decadent' life-style, even the early Coward's rebelliousness had its limits. After all, he had grown up in lower-middle-class south London, classic 'villa Tory' country, and although he later escaped that world sociologically, he never rejected it politically. Moreover, he was born into the age of high imperialism, just in time for the Relief of Mafeking, for the great Queen's death and funeral, and for Edward VII's coronation. This was the era of 'Land of Hope and Glory', and Coward's family had appropriately glorious imperial connections and hopeful social aspirations. Among his ancestors were naval captains and military men, and among his earliest memories was the sight of great grey British warships lying off Spithead.[13] Coward's father was an unprepossessing figure and an ineffectual piano salesman. By contrast, his domineering and ambitious mother was 'brought up in the tradition of being a gentlewoman', and she vainly sought permission to use the coat of arms of one of her forebears; but this request was refused, in part because the Cowards were seriously impoverished. Until his plays began to make money in the mid-1920s, their finances were always uncertain, Mrs Coward had to take in lodgers, and there were constant fears about falling (rather than rising) in the social scale. Here, glimpsed from a lowly, insecure, but aspiring, vantage-point, were subjects which would later loom large in her son's work: the Empire, the monarchy, the navy, the aristocracy and class.[14]

And so, despite his genuine rebelliousness and sense of not belonging, Coward was never a thoroughgoing nonconformist: for his aim, like many ostensibly angry outsiders, was to rise up the social ladder, rather than overturn it. Like Disraeli, whom he in some ways closely resembles, Coward was not only flippant, cynical and irreverent, he was also emotional, sentimental and romantic. (Hence *Bitter Sweet* (1929) where these two cultures confront each other, and reach an uncertain accommodation.) He wanted money, success and recognition, and he wanted to conquer the great world beyond Teddington. As soon as he could, he escaped from suburbia, and by the mid-1920s he was settling into a society which was limited, both geographically and sociologically, and to which he would return again and again in his writings: England not Britain; country mansions and Mayfair; the upper-middle-class Home Counties; and the embassies, government houses and officers' messes of greater Britain overseas.[15] For the young Coward was a remorseless social climber, cultivating his aristocratic connections, and befriending Lord and Lady Mountbatten, and the Duke of Kent (with whom he had an affair). He may have been a theatrical and sexual revolutionary, but he was already a social and political conservative, as one of his characters observes in *The Queen was in the Parlour* (1922): 'the air is full of voices of cheap people crying out against the existing order of things, trying to tear down kings and queens and loyalties, and establish themselves on the throne in their shirt sleeves with their feet on the mantelpiece.' The bolsheviks were not for him.[16]

This veneration for the established order, for keeping things as they were, for good manners and good behaviour, was further reinforced by Coward's lack of education. As befitted the son of poor parents, who was a stage-struck show-off from an early age, his formal schooling was minimal, and he never acquired any well-informed understanding of history or politics or government, let alone an informed appreciation of great art. On all these subjects, his opinions rarely rose above the dogmatic clichés of *Daily Mail* conservatism. As St John Irvine put it in a searing review of the first volume of Coward's autobiography in 1937:

I am amazed and disturbed at the slenderness of his intellectual resources ... We might well wonder whether he had ever read a good book, seen a fine picture or a notable play, listened to music of worth, observed a piece of sculpture, or taken any interest in even the commonplaces of a cultured man's life ... His political, social and religious interests are negligible or non-existent.[17]

In his more flippant moments, Coward would agree, once admitting, in words which, for those in the know, gave a great deal away: 'My body has certainly wandered a good deal, but I have the uneasy suspicion that my mind has not wandered nearly enough.' His lack of education clearly embarrassed him, and left him with an abiding distrust of ideas and a deep dislike of intellectuals (whom he regarded as left-wing subversives), bordering on the philistine:

> I wish the intellectuals,
> The clever ones,
> Would go to Russia.
> Those who have University Degrees,
> Those 'Leftist' boys and girls
> Who argue so well
> About the 'Workers Rights'
> And 'Man's True Destiny' and the delights
> Of equal independence, State controlled.
> Let them leave England please ...
> To go to Russia.[18]

Distrust of 'too much education and intellectualism' certainly strengthened Coward's innate conservatism; and so, in one important way, did his homosexuality. For Coward *adored* (the word is not too strong) men in uniform. He liked generals and admirals, who combined glamorous masculinity with high rank; and also the ordinary soldiers and sailors, in whose able bodies he took an obvious erotic delight. Again, for those in the know, he gave himself away. In *Middle East Diary*, he described a 'rating on the Bridge who is really magnificent. He is about six foot, youngish, and dressed in an abbreviated pair of faded blue shorts.' And in *Ace of Clubs*, he wrote a song about a sailor, celebrating 'His devil-may-care, his nautical air, of brawn and brine'.[19] From adolescence onwards, Coward seems to have enjoyed close relations with officers such as Sydney Lormer, Leo Charlton and Jeffrey Amherst, as well as more passing flings with the lower decks. And these individual liaisons served to reinforce his liking for the armed services in general, those all-male bastions of British greatness, and for their traditions, pageantry and ceremony. Like many homosexuals, Coward was radical and rebellious in his private life, but reticent, conservative and conformist in his public life. 'Of course,' one such Tory recently remarked, 'gays are Conservatives. We believe in freedom and individual responsibility and low tax – and we love patriotism and pomp and circumstance.' This description summarizes Coward's 'apolitical' attitudes and 'commonsense' opinions precisely.[20]

By the late 1920s, Coward was completing an astonishingly innovative, productive and controversial decade as a playwright, in which he had shown real insight into the human heart and the human condition, and he was on the brink of beginning the second great enterprise of his creative life, the sentimental celebration of England. In so doing, he would be true to his own conservatism, and propound commonplace opinions which, if the circumstances were right, would be well received. But he would also face difficulties in projecting this new identity. It was not easy for someone to play the patriotic card whose record in the First World War was distinctly inglorious, and which caused him genuine embarrassment. At a time when Britain was governed by the 'respectable tendency' of Stanley Baldwin, Lord Halifax and Cosmo Lang, there were many in government who regarded him as little more than a pampered pansy and perfumed playboy on the make.[21] In associating with the more raffish members of the royal family, and in falling foul of the Lord Chamberlain, he had made powerful enemies. And as his work became more conservative and lost its edge, the critics (and Bloomsbury) would also turn against him, sneering at his lack of education and at his commonplace opinions in ways that irritated, wounded, enraged and ultimately embittered him. It was easy for Coward to be a patriot, and it would be easy for him to be a patriotic writer during the thirties and the Second World War. But thereafter, he rather lost his way, and the approval he craved was a long time in coming.[22]

II

The 1930s were Coward's most successful era in the theatre, ushered in by the still long-running *Bitter Sweet*, and with the production of *Private Lives*. But it turned out to be a very different decade from the 1920s, as the brittle glitter of the bright young things (which he had so brilliantly caught and articulated) faded away, to be replaced by an altogether more sombre scene and cast of characters. For the slump of 1929–31 brought with it unprecedented unemployment, and widespread hardship in those industrial regions of the nation which lay far beyond the confines of Coward's cocktail world. It brought a sharp turn to the right in politics, with the disintegration of Ramsay MacDonald's Labour government in 1931, and the establishment of a National Government, dominated by the Conservatives, which would govern Britain uninterruptedly until 1945. And it also witnessed the apotheosis of George V, with his Silver Jubilee in 1935; the trauma of Edward VIII's brief reign and abdication; and the failure of appeasement and the drift to war. Against this darkening background, it is scarcely surprising that someone of Coward's outlook and attitudes began to move away from jagged comedies exploring indulgent modes of behaviour: to escapist fantasies prefigured in *Bitter Sweet*, and realized in *Conversation Piece* (1933) and *Operette* (1937); and to works addressing the more serious matters of national character and imperial presence.

It was the production of *Cavalcade*, in October 1931, which established Coward in a new (and to many) unexpected guise – as a patriotic writer, by turns resonant, rousing and sentimental. Alternating between intimate domestic scenes and large-scale crowd tableaux, this massive production surveyed the great moments of recent English history from the time of his own birth – the Relief of Mafeking, Queen Victoria's funeral, the sinking of the *Titanic*, Armistice Night – through the eyes of one ordinary, decent middle-class family, the Marryots, and their no-less ordinary and decent servants, the Harrises. Towards the end of Act III, the moral of the work was pointed in Jane Marryot's New Year's Eve toast, which was 'as deeply sincere and true' as Coward could make it:

Let's couple the future of England with the past of England. The glories and victories and triumphs that are over, and the sorrows that are over, too. Let's drink to our sons who made part of the pattern, and to our hearts that died with them. Let's drink to the spirit and gallantry and courage that made a strange heaven out of an unbelievable hell, and let's drink to the hope that one day, this country of ours, which we love so much, will find dignity and greatness and peace again.[23]

This was immediately followed by a chaotic, anomic nightclub scene, in which 'Twentieth-century Blues' ('What is there to strive for, Love or keep alive for?') was sung. Then the theatre was darkened, 'the lights slowly come up, and the whole stage is composed of massive tiers, upon which stand the entire company. The Union Jack flies over their heads, as they sing "God Save the King".' The robust, reassuring message was clear, and it was reiterated by Coward himself in his first-night curtain speech: 'I hope that this play has made you feel that, in spite of the troublous times we are living in, it is still a pretty exciting thing to be English.'[24]

'Coward's call to arms' was how the press interpreted his show and his words, and this view was made yet more plausible by the coincidental return of the National Government, with an overwhelming majority, at the general election two weeks after the first night. On the following evening, George V and Queen Mary attended, the king received a great ovation, and Coward was delighted: 'He stood there, looking a little tired, and epitomising that quality which English people have always deeply valued: unassailable dignity.' With this ultimate seal of royal approval, *Cavalcade* was launched on its way: a story-book version of the nation's past, peopled by simplistic, two-dimensional, upstairs-downstairs characters, and expressing its author's fondness for pageantry, tradition and ceremonial.[25] But as Coward later explained, the 'love of England' which *Cavalcade* contained was also 'a certain pride in some of our very typical characteristics', as exemplified by Jane Marryot: 'ordinary, kind and unobtrusively heroic, capable of deep suffering and incapable of cheap complaint.' And it was traits such as these which led him to conclude that 'I belonged to a most remarkable race': 'I loved its basic integrity, an integrity formed over hundreds of years by indigenous humour, courage and common sense.' Thus it was that, seemingly overnight, Coward the playboy had transformed himself into Coward the patriot.[26]

By this time, he was making two other important discoveries about greater England, the first of which was the British Empire. In the winter of 1929–30, Coward had travelled across the Pacific to Tokyo, China, Hong Kong, Indo-China, Singapore, Malaya and Colombo, and returned to England on a P. & O. liner. Two years later, he went on another lengthy tour to South America, and in 1935 he returned to the Far East, visiting Tokyo, Shanghai, Singapore and Bali. For Coward, these journeys were not merely a way of escaping from the pressures of theatrical and personal life, powerful and overbearing though he found them: they also meant the discovery of Grand Hotels, British Embassies and Government Houses – a world which was to loom so large in his later work. As Cole Lesley explained:

He belonged to a time when people – and his fame placed him in that class of person – went automatically on arrival at their destination to sign the book at Government House or British Embassy, and he delighted in the subsequent invitations, the luxury and the grandeur.[27]

In later years, Coward himself always denied this. But he protested too much: his picture of the Empire was as narrow as his image of England.

There was no room in this imperial vision for power or prejudice or exploitation, for poverty, famine or riot. The natives were colourful (in more senses than one), contented, happy, grateful and quiescent – a picturesque backdrop to imperial pageantry, but nothing more.[28]

Coward's second discovery was the British Navy, no longer merely glimpsed from afar, but enjoyed from close-up. In the spring of 1930, when on his first extended visit to the Far East, he sailed from Shanghai to Hong Kong aboard HMS *Suffolk*, and thus began his lifelong love affair with the senior service. Again, his image was blinkered: it was the discipline, the traditions, the glamorous officers and the worthy men he saw, rather than the loneliness, the boredom, the fears, or the professional expertise. Like the British Empire, the Royal Navy was for Coward essentially a happy holiday:

To me, the life of guest in a warship is deeply satisfactory. I have passed some of the happiest hours of my life in various wardrooms. The secret of naval good manners is hard to define; perhaps discipline has a lot to do with it, and prolonged contact with the sea; perhaps a permanent background of such dignity makes for simplicity of mind.[29]

Thereafter, Coward became a frequent 'guest of the Royal Navy in all parts of the world and in every type of ship'. He spent many summers in the 1930s in the Mediterranean, as the guest of sea-dogs such as Admiral Sir Dudley Pound and Admiral Sir Philip Vian, and the Mountbattens were especial friends. 'Whenever I wanted a holiday,' Coward later recalled, somewhat breezily, 'I went to wherever his ship happened to be.'[30]

These discoveries powerfully affected Coward's outlook during the 1930s, well illustrated in 'P-&-O 1930', a later poem based on these journeys.[31] The heroine is 'the Governor's Lady', 'inwardly timorous and shy' but also 'indestructibly self-possessed', exemplifying that stern sense of duty that made the Empire great:

> Bugles blowing, deafening, insistent,
> The Governor's Lady, amiable but distant
> Returning home for six months' leave
> A necessary, all too brief reprieve
> From State Receptions, Women's Federations,
> Official visits to remote plantations,
> From garden parties under alien trees
> And mocking, inefficient ADCs.

She and her fellow passengers return home along the lifeline of Empire: each port of call a hallowed name – Hong Kong, Singapore, Colombo, Bombay, Aden and Suez, and eventually reach the rock:

> Gibraltar rose, impressive, dignified,
> Knowing no rising sun could ever set
> On such a symbol of imperial pride,
> On such invulnerable majesty.

And so, finally, to the citadel of Empire itself, endowed by long years of absence with a singular and magical attractiveness:

> England at last . . .
> Passengers crowd the rails, eager to catch
> The first glimpse, after months and years away,
> Of their beloved and inalienable home.
> This is the moment that must be remembered.

Such was Coward's vision of the British Empire: ardent, appreciative, mandarin, and not especially well informed. But during the 1930s, he generally concealed this sentimental admiration behind his trade-mark façade of gentle mockery and 'irreverent flippancy', most memorably displayed in 'Mad Dogs and Englishmen'.[32] Like 'P-&-O 1930', this song was inspired by his Far Eastern travels, and like that poem again, it reads like an itinerary of the places he visited: Malaya, Burma, Bengal, Hong Kong. It was written while journeying from Hanoi to Saigon in February 1930, it was presented two years later in the review *Words and Music*, and it was Coward's most famous effort at imperial evocation. In its form (and attitudes), it is a patter song of almost Gilbertian complexity; in atmosphere it is suffused with the steam and heat of the Orient; and in content it ostensibly mocks the British for their inflexibility:

> It's such a surprise for the Eastern eyes to see
> That though the English are effete,
> They're quite impervious to heat . . .
> It seems such a shame
> When the English claim
> The earth
> That they give rise to such hilarity and mirth.

But beneath the gentle teasing is unaffected pride in the greatness and swagger and permanence of Empire, and a genuine appreciation of the fortitude with which the White Man's Burden is borne.[33]

Much of Coward's work during the 1930s was preoccupied with exploring and evoking the British Empire and the Royal Navy. In *Point Valaine* (1934), he wrote his first play in a colonial setting, where the characters 'sit on the verandah and talk very sentimentally about skies and fogs in Piccadilly'. 'Planters' Wives' repeated the approach of 'Mad Dogs and Englishmen', as did 'The Stately Homes of England', which treated the aristocracy in the same manner as the proconsuls. 'Half-Caste Woman', as its title implies, was a rare attempt to say something deeper.[34] Several of the plays in *Tonight at 8.30* (1935) were equally imperial in their settings and stories: *We Were Dancing* was a tale of love and infidelity set in the mythical Pacific island of Samolo; and in *Hands Across the Sea*, a naval-cum-society couple (clearly modelled on the Mountbattens) are embarrassed by the arrival in London of two planter friends from the same island. Both plays exude an imperial atmosphere – the Indian Army, the Royal Navy, the P. & O.; retired admirals, worthy planters, colonial gossip; and Hong Kong, Burma, Penang and Singapore. Likewise, *Red Peppers* contained the number 'Has Anybody Seen Our Ship?', which was an appreciative pastiche of Edwardian music-hall songs about the navy; and in *Fumed Oak*, Henry Gow muses on 'a sea with whacking great waves and water spouts and typhoons and flying fish, and phosphorus making the foam look as though it was lit up'.[35]

Finally, at the close of the decade, Coward looked again at the state of England itself. In *This Happy Breed* (written in 1939 but not produced until 1943), he wrote an exclusively domestic *Cavalcade*, another story of middle-class life, once more pinned on the great events of twentieth-century English history – this time the end of the Great War, the General Strike, the return of the National Government, the abdication of Edward VIII and the Munich agreement. As in *Cavalcade*, the play celebrated the solid virtues of the English middle classes, as the Gibbons family bear, with tight-lipped, understated fortitude, the inevitable bereavements and unexpected sorrows of family life. Again, there is the familiar distrust of politicians ('The old men at the top'), and of left-wing intellectuals ('I don't want to have anything to do with a man who listens to a lot of dirty foreigners and goes against his own country'). Once more, the values which are acclaimed are those of common decency ('There are worst things than being ordinary and respectable and living the way you've been brought up to live'), and a political, consensual conservatism ('The country suddenly got tired . . . and it's up to us ordinary people to keep things steady').[36]

As Coward later explained, this was a play written 'with sincerity, affection and the inherent understanding that is the result of personal experience', for he drew on his own memories of lower-middle-class life in the suburbs of south London. But he had long since abandoned that world, which explains why Frank Gibbons – the hero who was played by Coward in the original production – is so unconvincing. He was another wooden character, expressing views which Coward believed the lower middle classes should have, regardless of whether they did or not, and doing so with an implausible articulacy and coherence.[37] He serves in the Great War, drives a bus in the General Strike, prefers hotch-potch British progress to utopian socialist revolutions, is in favour of the National Government, has a low opinion of Edward VIII for giving up his job, and is sceptical of the Munich settlement and of the politicians who made it. And, again using the toast technique from *Cavalcade*, the play concludes with Gibbons explaining the facts of life to his grandson:

You belong to a race that's been bossy for years, and one reason it's held on so long as it has is that nine times out of ten it's behaved decently and treated people right. Just lately, I'll admit, we've been giving at the knees a bit, and letting down people who trusted us, and allowing noisy little men to bully us with a lot of guns and bombs and aeroplanes. But don't worry – that won't last – the people themselves, the ordinary people like you and me, know something better than all the fussy old politicians put together – we know what we belong to, where we come from, and where we're going. We may not know it with our brains, but we know it with our roots. And we know another thing, too, and it's this. We 'aven't lived and died and struggled all these hundreds of years to get decency and justice and freedom for ourselves without being prepared to fight fifty wars if need be – to keep 'em.[38]

This image of England and her empire in which Coward believed so fervently remained essentially unaltered for the rest of his life, regardless of how far it did – or did not – correspond to later reality. Essentially, it was a blend of romantic imperialism, which was usually disguised by a façade of affectionate mockery, and a consensual, apolitical conservatism, which conflated the domestic rhetoric of Stanley Baldwin with the anti-appeasement attitudes of Winston Churchill. To Coward, the essential wisdom of these views was self-evident. As he said of Lord Lloyd, in words equally applicable to himself, 'he was an imperialist in the best sense, because his passionate love of England and his unshakeable belief in the British

Empire were based on common sense.'[39] In fact, this ostensibly apolitical vision unthinkingly accepted a certain social, political and imperial order as axiomatic and God-given, and where there should be no change whatsoever. But it was well suited to the mood of the 1930s: for in a dark and difficult decade, it presented the English with an agreeable, comforting picture of themselves as decent people who treated others right, and who only wanted to be left alone to live good and virtuous and dutiful lives.

III

During the Second World War, they were not left alone, and Coward's response was a powerful and sincere patriotic avowal, which strongly contrasted with his attitude in 1914–18:

> I was a flagrant unabashed sentimentalist, and likely to remain so until the end of my days. I did love England and all it stood for. I loved its follies and apathies and curious streak of genius; I loved standing to attention for 'God Save the King'; I loved British courage, British humour, and British understatement; I loved the justice, efficiency and even the dullness of British colonial administration. I loved the people – the old, the extraordinary, the good, the bad, the indifferent, and what is more, I belonged to that exasperating, weather-sodden little island, with its uninspired cooking, its muddled thinking, and its unregenerate pride, and it belonged to me, whether I liked it or not.[40]

It is a revealing (and unsurprising) catalogue of the national characteristics and institutions which Coward deemed to be important and, as always with him, it moved with effortless and unselfconscious ease from the English people to the British Empire. All that is missing is the disapproval of politicians and party politics: but that, too, is well attested in a wartime letter to his mother, where he explained that by England he meant 'the ordinary people who belong to it', who were entitled to 'grumble about governments as much as we like'.[41]

Here were the classic Coward patriotic sentiments: simple, ardent, unaffected, well-meaning – and naïve. But while Coward was an *emotional* patriot, he also wanted to be an *active* patriot, and to be recognized (and rewarded?) as such – in part to atone for having nothing done in 1918, in part (as he would later claim) to prove himself to himself. But his expectations were unrealistic, and so, to his great disappointment and frustration, he found it difficult to convert these aspirations into action. In the light of his war record, there was no prospect of a military job (in this connection, his name was also something of a handicap). He wanted to undertake undercover work: but as a celebrity and a homosexual this was patently unrealistic. He wanted to go on morale-raising tours: but why should this pampered playboy be subsidized to travel abroad when most Britons were enduring the Blitz uncomplainingly? Churchill, in particular, took a dim view of Coward, as someone who was not serious, and whose best prospects lay in singing 'Mad Dogs and Englishmen' to the troops.[42] Coward could not understand why he was treated as a lightweight, and greatly resented it. In the end, his wartime contribution was considerable, but it was (as Churchill had urged) in the realm of entertainment; he spent a great deal of time out of the country; and he got into trouble more than once.

But there can be no doubt that he was supremely moved by the valiant efforts of ordinary English men and women, as they rose to the ultimate challenge of defending their island and their freedom from Hitler. Here, in the second volume of Coward's autobiography, is his panegyric on blitzed and war-torn London:

London as a city in the past had never attracted me much. It was my home, of course, and I knew it intimately, perhaps too intimately. Now, suddenly, in my early forties, I saw it for the first time as somewhere where I belonged. This sentimental revelation was made clearer to me by the fact that I was staying in a London hotel for the first time in my life. It was a strange sensation to step out of the comfortable impersonality of the Savoy into the personal, familiar streets of my childhood. I felt a sudden urge to visit the Tower, the Abbey, Madam Tussaud's and go to the zoo. The move from Gerald Road to the Strand had transformed me overnight into a tourist in my own home, and as such it seemed to me more attractive and more genuinely gay than it had ever been before ... In 1941, the real lights of London shone through the blackout with a steady brilliance that I shall never forget.[43]

The admission that he was now 'a tourist in my own home', and that it was because of this that the city seemed so attractive, is revealing. From now on, Coward increasingly saw London and England from the same vantage point that he viewed the Empire – through the windows of Grand Hotels. And his response in both cases would be the same: a brief encounter with a colonial governor, or a chance episode witnessed in a city street, and there would be a sincere yet superficial patriotic response. During the war, it generally suited the popular mood; but thereafter it would not be so easy for him.

The best example of what Coward could achieve was 'London Pride', a popular patriotic lyric, inspired by just such a combination of circumstance and feeling, as he watched Londoners in an underground station after a night of particularly heavy bombing:

They all seemed to me to be gay and determined and wholly admirable, and for a moment or two I was overwhelmed by a wave of sentimental pride. A tune started in my head, then and there, and was finished in a couple of days. The tune was an age-old English melody that had been appropriated by the Germans and used as a foundation for *Deutschland über alles*, and I considered that the time had come for us to have it back in London, where it belonged. I am proud of the words of this song; they express what I felt then, and what I still feel:

> In our city darkened now, street and square and crescent,
> We can feel our living past in our shadowed present.
> Ghosts beside our starlit Thames
> Who lived and loved and died,
> Keep throughout the ages London Pride.[44]

Here, Coward caught and articulated exactly the mood of the Blitz, perhaps as it was, and certainly as people wished to believe it was, telling Londoners more about themselves than they would ever have been able to say. The feelings of understated pride and bravery were generously judged; the sense of history and the evocation of the city were vivid and warm; and the consensual flavour ('from the Ritz to the Anchor and Crown') was exactly appropriate. As an outsider, Coward was presenting Londoners with an image of themselves which described, heightened and idealized their wartime feelings and heroic endurance. Another song, 'Could You Please Oblige Us with a Bren Gun?', paid tribute to the Home Guard and to its talent for imaginative improvisation, in the same affectionately teasing manner that he had perfected in 'Mad Dogs and Englishmen'. But Coward's judgement did sometimes err. 'Don't Let's Be Beastly to the Germans' attacked with savage mockery the appeasers of the 1930s, and the high-minded critics during the war, who urged that Germany be treated leniently. But so many misconstrued its ironic appeal – 'Let's help the dirty swine again to occupy the Rhine again' – as a genuine plea for forgiveness that there was an outcry in the press, and for a time the song was suppressed.[45]

But writing patriotic, morale-raising songs was not enough, and with no prospect of an official appointment, Coward set off on propaganda tours to the United States, the Antipodes and South Africa, and entertained the troops in the Middle East and India. It was, doubtless, hard, exacting and sometimes dangerous work; but he was scarcely in the front line, and he spent much of his time in the company (and the houses) of governors, admirals and viceroys, which he greatly (and perhaps unwisely) enjoyed. 'I felt strongly', he later wrote in describing these travels, 'that my name, my reputation and my friends would get me wherever I wanted to go within reason, an assumption which I am bound to say was abundantly justified.'[46] So, in the pages of his autobiography, we can follow him on his proconsular progress from Australia ('I spent Christmas with Lord and Lady Gowrie at Canberra'), to New Zealand ('Lunch with Lord Galway, the Governor General'), to Cairo ('Sitting on the terrace at Shepherds'), to Beirut ('My hosts were General and Lady Spears'), to Trinidad ('I was weatherbound for three days, and stayed with Sir Bede Clifford at Government House'), to Accra ('Lord Swinton's ADC met me'), to Kandy ('Dickie Mountbatten and I dined quietly'), to Delhi ('We stayed in the Viceroy's House, with Lord and Lady Wavell'), and to Madras ('We stayed in Government House with Lady Hope').[47]

This was scarcely empire – or war – as most Britons were experiencing it at the time. And, as this account of a stop-off in Northern Nigeria suggests, these travels did nothing to broaden or deepen Coward's imperial vision: the natives were still there to provide a picturesque background for the British; and the British were there to give him stiff-upper-lipped hospitality:

The resident came to meet me, and drive me back to his house. On the way we stopped off for a drink at the club, which as an example of the 'outpost of Empire' tradition was accurate to the last detail. There were bead curtains, faded chintz covers, and a rack full of month-old English newspapers and magazines. There was a mixed tennis foursome going on which might have been lifted bodily, court and players, from Cheltenham, and set down in one piece in this savage, alien land. 'Well played', 'yours, partner', 'love fifteen'. Clear English voices echoed across the dusty grass separating the verandah from the edge of the court, while from the village nearby came the thud of native drums and the thin wail of reed instruments. The natives in Maiduguri move beautifully and wear robes of the most lovely shades of blue which they dye themselves. The resident British moved perhaps less beautifully, and their apparel was nondescript, but their quality was unmistakable. That small club, so very far away from home, was touching and curiously impressive.[48]

As always, when it came to the Empire, Coward was easily moved and easily impressed. Sometimes, as in his 'Mad Dogs and Englishmen' mode, he concealed this behind his mandarin façade of affectionate irreverence – as in 'I Wonder What Happened to Him', a gently mocking evocation of the military men of the Raj:

The India that one read about
And may have been misled about
In one respect has kept itself intact.
Though 'Pukka Sahib' traditions may have cracked
And thinned
That good old Indian army's still a fact.
That famous monumental man
The Officer and the Gentleman
Still lives and breathes and functions from Bombay to Katmandu.
At any moment one may glimpse
Matured or embryonic 'Blimps'
Vivaciously speculating as to what became of who.[49]

But he was often more overtly sentimental, as in his short story, *Mr and Mrs Edgehill*, where he celebrated the understated fortitude of the British Resident and his wife on Cowrie Island, set against a background of the daily raising and lowering of the Union Jack, and their wish to obtain an appropriately regal picture of the king and queen. It was based on his experience when, in 1941, he landed at Canton Island on his way from Australia to America. 'Typically English,' he wrote of them, 'in the best possible way – simple, unpretentious and getting on with the job.'[50]

However demanding and well-intended they may have been, these highly publicized imperial tours did not go down well in blitzed and beleaguered Britain, as even war itself seemed to provide yet another opportunity for Coward to enjoy a holiday as the privileged guest of the British overseas establishment. As he himself later admitted, 'I behaved through most of the war with gallantry tinged, I suspect, by a strong urge to show off.' There was criticism in the press, questions were asked in Parliament, and in 1941 he was summonsed for being in breach of wartime currency regulations. He was fined £200, and for many years this episode was cited as the reason for denying him an honour.[51] Three years later, in ill-judged self-justification, he published his *Middle East Diary*, a name-dropping chronicle, in which the comfort of his life was only matched by the shallowness of his analysis, and seemed to confirm his critics' complaints. Ivor Brown's comment, reminiscent of St John Ervine's earlier remarks, caught its tone well:

He sees so much – and so little. He has travelled far more than most men of his age, and yet, when he writes, it always has to be of the same little world. Dump him anywhere, on any island of the seven seas, and he would certainly at once run into somebody known as Tim or Tiny, Boodles or Bims, and be dining with an excellency or an admiral twenty minutes later. If there were natives on the island, he would hardly notice. God put them there, no doubt, to serve dinners to Excellencies.[52]

Coward's wartime touch was surer when it came to the Royal Navy. Many of his journeys were accomplished on His Majesty's ships, and he was made godfather to HMS *Charybdis*. As always, he was overwhelmed by naval hospitality, and by the 'impeccable manners' of both the officers and the lower deck. But his great opportunity to do something for them came when he learned from Lord Mountbatten the details of the loss of his own destroyer:

After dinner, he told me the whole story of the sinking of the *Kelly* off Crete. He told it without apparent emotion, but the emotion was there poignantly behind every word he uttered . . . I was profoundly moved and impressed. The Royal Navy . . . means a great deal to me, and here, in this odyssey of one destroyer, was the very essence of it. All the true sentiment, the comedy, the tragedy, the casual valiance, the unvaunted heroism, the sadness without tears, the pride without end.[53]

For those in high places, this whole episode was merely further evidence that Mountbatten was a foolhardy and medal-chasing sailor: there was nothing epic or heroic about it. But Coward did not see things that way. Instead, he took it as the raw material out of which he fashioned the film *In Which We Serve* (1941), which lauded, even in defeat, the invincibility of the navy, and paid tribute to the heroism of the men who made up the 'stratified unity' of the ship's community.[54]

As such, it was, essentially, a nautical version of *Cavalcade* and *This Happy Breed* – a patriotic pageant celebrating ordinary (and, as usual, rather two-dimensional) people caught up in great events, but never failing to rise to the stern and testing demands of the occasion. And in paying this emotional tribute to his much-loved senior service, Coward scored an unequivocal popular and creative triumph. He wrote it, starred in it and directed it; the king and queen visited the studio to watch the filming; and there were rumours that Coward's knighthood could not now be long delayed.[55] At last he had got himself into uniform, delivering rousing speeches to the assembled men, and ending with this stirringly patriotic message:

Here ends the story of a ship, but there will always be other ships, for we are an island race. Through all our centuries, the sea has ruled our destiny. There will always be other ships and men to sail in them. It is these men, in peace or war, to whom we owe so much. Above all victories, beyond all loss, in spite of changing values in a changing world, they give, to us, their countrymen, eternal and indomitable pride. God bless our ships and all who sail in them.

Or, as he put it in his *Middle East Diary*, 'Britannia still rules the waves all right.' Truly, he had travelled a long way from the brittle, self-indulgent flippancies of *Hay Fever* and *Private Lives* – all the way back to those early, childhood memories of the Royal Navy at Spithead.[56]

As a writer and an Englishman, Coward's war was thus both good and bad. He was bitterly disappointed that none of his friends in high places took him seriously enough to get him an important official job; he suffered much adverse publicity, often through his own naïvety; and the knighthood for which he had hoped did not materialize.[57] In retrospect, too, the war accentuated that loss of contact with Britain, and the growing obsession with empire, already present by the late 1930s, and which would become even more marked after 1945, with serious consequences for his reputation. But he had also written two cheerful comedies (*Present Laughter* and *Blithe Spirit* (1941)), had composeed several memorable patriotic songs, and had created the best morale-raising film of the war. At a time when political issues were simplified and national emotions were heightened, Coward's talents and feeling were often well suited to the occasion, telling the English what they wanted to believe (and perhaps briefly believed) about themselves, their country and their Empire. And few would have argued with his description of VE-Day itself: 'I suppose this is the greatest day in our history.'[58]

IV

So, perhaps, it was. But the twenty years after the war were no more happy for Britain as a great power than they were for Coward as a great star. Postwar austerity, recurrent economic difficulties, the loss of the Indian and African empires, and the fiasco of Suez, all suggested a nation whose greatest days were past, which even the euphoria of the queen's coronation and the unexampled prosperity of the 1950s and 1960s could not entirely conceal. By the time 'I Wonder What Happened to Him' was sung in *Sigh No More* (1945), the 'good old Indian Army' would only be 'still a fact' for two brief years. Britain was in eclipse, and in his wartime travels to America, even Coward had been reluctantly obliged to face this unhappy reality:

There seemed already to be an assumption in the champagne American air that Britain had muddled through for the last time, that her former greatness together with her die-hard imperialistic pretensions were flaking off her as dried old paint flakes off a decrepit building. Economically we were done for, and in the general, and in particular the American, view, to be economically done for was the end, or at least the beginning of the end. I do not subscribe to this view any more now than I did in 1943. If, in the next fifty years of wars and revolutions, Great Britain should sink wearily into being economically a third-rate power, so much the worse; but I cannot believe that the quality of its people nor the curious tenacity of its traditions will change.[59]

Or, as the Countess of Marshwood explains to Don Lucas, an American visitor in *Relative Values* (1950), 'I am afraid that with one thing and another you haven't chosen the best time to come, but we still have quite a lot to be proud of.'[60]

At the same time, Coward's own reputation went into a sharp and protracted critical decline. In part, this was because his work rarely reached the high levels of his best pre-1945 efforts. His musicals – *Pacific 1860* (1946) and *Ace of Clubs* (1949) – were 'not up to standard': slight, dated, romantic, escapist confections, which could not compete with the more accomplished and fabulously successful works by Rodgers and Hammerstein and Lerner and Loewe.[61] His comedies – *Relative Values, Quadrille* (1951) and *Nude With Violin* (1954) – were neither as carefully plotted nor as economically written as their pre-war predecessors, and they were built around single ideas which soon palled. His more serious plays – *Peace in Our Time* (1946) and *Waiting in the Wings* (1959) – were not serious enough. And the second volume of his autobiography, *Future Indefinite*, was a laboured and not altogether convincing justification of his wartime activities. More than that, Coward also lost his ability to tell the British public what they wanted to hear about themselves. As the spectacular success of the James Bond novels showed, the patriotic, flag-waving, navy-loving, imperial card could still be played with great popular appeal if suitably presented and updated. But Coward found himself so alienated by developments in postwar England that by the late 1950s he had clearly lost his balance, and seemed 'an irrelevant survival from a bygone era'.[62]

Part cause, part consequence of these developments, was that it proved very difficult for him to find a niche for himself in British life after 1945. Having spent so much time out of the country, both before and during the war, he had become a stranger in his own land, out of touch and out of date – cocooned in the drawing-room in what would soon become the era of the council house. In theatrical terms, he was hard to place: at forty-five, he was too senior to be still a bright young thing; but he was too young to be revered as a grand old man. And in politics, he was more adrift than ever. As a homosexual and the friend of Lord Mountbatten, he was scarcely *persona grata* with the Conservative Party, and Lord Beaverbrook continued a personal vendetta against him through his *Express* newspapers, which had begun during the Second World War.[63] But as someone who also flaunted his royal connections, venerated the Empire, disliked the manual working class, and detested the Welfare State, he was even less acceptable to the Labour Party, whose socialistic politics he loathed, and whose landslide victory in 1945 he found 'too horrible to contemplate'. As Beverley Baxter had the temerity to remark: Noël Coward may have survived the war, but how would he survive the peace? For a long time, he did not do so easily or convincingly.[64]

In the aftermath of victory in Europe, Churchill's departure, Labour's triumph, revived party politics, protracted austerity and socialist legislation all displeased him greatly. 'The rigours of peace and postwar party-politics have done much to dim its glow,' he noted at the end of his panegyric on wartime London, and 'the general decline in standards and the crushing down of initiative, originality and ambition, the lack of incentive' also offended him. Several of his immediate postwar songs reflected this sense that 'the present government is the worst that this country has ever had'.[65] 'The Burchells of Battersea Rise' lampooned socialism, bureaucracy and state control; 'There are Bad Times Just Around the Corner' sent up the press, the politicians and the BBC, and protested against social revolution and the Cold War; and in 'Don't Let's Make Fun of the Fair', he did just that, portraying the Festival of Britain as pretentious, expensive and bound to be unpopular. Two couplets in particular expressed his contemporary disillusionment:

> Labour leaders lead us all
> Though we know they bleed us all.

> Cheer our new Decline and Fall
> Gibbon might have dreamed it all.[66]

Accordingly, and in marked contrast to his wartime work, a large part of Coward's output after 1945 was devoted to telling the English what was *wrong* with them: for unlike him, they themselves were 'too stupid and complacent to grasp what is happening'. What, if anything, remained for him to admire? Of course, there was always the Empire, increasingly embodied in the mythical island of Samolo, which he had originally invented for *Tonight at 8.30*, and which had reappeared in *Mr and Mrs Edgehill* during the war. At that time, it was merely one of Britain's many tropical possessions. But after 1945, Coward became engrossed in this fantasy island, he gave it an exact location in the Pacific, provided information about its flora, fauna and rainfall, drew maps of its terrain, and even devised a history of the colony.[67] Accordingly, Samolo was the setting for *Pacific 1860*, the musical with which Drury Lane was reopened in 1946. It was an unsuccessful effort which flopped badly – light, escapist and old-fashioned. 'His Excellency Regrets' was another attempt at gentle mockery in Coward's 'Mad Dogs and Englishmen' vein, this time directed at those polished ADCs who smoothed the Governor's social path, and there were some familiar but by now dated expressions of imperial pride:

> Make way for their Excellencies
> Kindly step aside.
> They are symbols representing
> Sceptre, Crown and mighty race
> Gently but firmly ornamenting
> This remote but pleasant place.

But at a time when the British were beginning to feel guilty about their empire, and were on the brink of beginning to dismantle it, such sentiments seemed more inappropriate than amusing.[68]

Coward then turned his attention to a domestic drama – but with no more success. In *Peace in Our Time*, he speculated on the British reaction had Hitler invaded successfully in 1940. Predictably, it was yet another reworking of the themes and characters of *Cavalcade* and *This Happy Breed*, but much less convincing. The setting was a London pub, presided over by Fred Shattock, another Frank Gibbons figure ('your age-old character, your kindness and firmness and stubborn humour could never let us down'), and the play is a paean of praise to British bravery, humour, fortitude, understatement, and to their capacity for muddling through.[69] The climax is the confrontation between Chorley Bannister, a pretentious intellectual who has sold out to the nazis, and Janet Braid, an ordinary working woman whose son was killed in the Battle of Britain. He ridicules her patriotic sentiments as 'a series of outworn slogans'. She replies in an impassioned and unanswerable oration, denouncing left-wing thinkers, thirties appeasers and forties collaborators, reaffirming her faith in England and freedom, cursing Hitler, and giving Chorley 'two ringing slaps in the face'.[70]

The play did not do well – partly because it was a depressing fictionalization of a subject still too close for comfort, which many people now wished to put behind them, but also because the national image it conveyed was too comfortable and too condescending for the brave new postwar world. It was the last time Coward attempted a serious play about his country. 'England', he concluded, reluctantly and pompously, 'does not deserve my work.' Thereafter, he turned to period-piece musicals, *Ace of Clubs* and *After the Ball* (1954), for which he wrote new songs in praise of London, once again harking back to the social solidarity of wartime:

> Low class and high class
> Contrive to defy class
> And brightly, politely unite
> In London at night.[71]

But the mood of 'London Pride' could not be so easily recaptured. Even less in touch with the welfare-state era was a song from *After the Ball*, sung by 'Ladies and Gentlemen, pillars of London society', who were 'never in doubt that our blood is impeccably blue':

> Nature selected us,
> Perfected us,
> Expected us to be
> Ladies and Gentlemen, born to eternal prosperity,
> Firmly convinced our position is really unique,
> We believe in the status quo
> Because deep in our hearts we know
> That though social reformers try to queer our pitch
> God's on the side of the rich.[72]

Thus was anachronism piled on escapism. For by this time, Coward was deeply unhappy about what he saw as the socialistic levelling down of England, to which both Labour and the Conservatives seemed wedded. As he saw it, the trend towards equality spelt the end of the world in which he had thrived – a world of style, wit and elegance; of charm, good manners and fashionable clothes; and of the established social order whose heights he had so successfully scaled. It received short shrift in *Future Indefinite*:

I have always believed more in quality than quantity, and nothing will convince me that the levelling of class and rank distinctions and the contemptuous dismissal of breeding as an important factor in life can lead to anything but a dismal mediocrity.[73]

This was also the theme of *Relative Values*, in which the intended second wife of the Earl of Marshwood is discovered to be the sister of the family's most devoted servant. The play thus becomes an extended discussion on the regretted decline in hierarchy and social distinctions. 'Comedies of manners', we are told with evident regret, 'swiftly become obsolete when there are no longer any manners.' The most powerful character in the play (Crestwell, the butler) cynically regards the whole idea of equality as nothing but 'a spiritually hygenic abstraction'. And, using the familiar Coward technique, it is he who closes the play by proposing this toast: 'I drink to the final, glorious disintegration of the most unlikely dream that ever troubled the foolish heart of man – Social Equality.'[74]

Coward was equally hostile to 'the so-called high-brows, the artsy-craftsy and the intellectual do-gooders', those handmaids and hangers-on of socialism, who he was sure would have been Hitler's most willing collaborators, and who he thought would be better off in Stalin's Russia; and in *Nude With Violin*, he wrote an entire comedy mocking and ridiculing them, not in the gently affectionate manner of 'Mad Dogs and Englishmen', but with real anger and scorn.[75] The play opened with the death of a great modern artist, Paul Sorodin, whose much-acclaimed and very expensive paintings turn out to have been the works of three totally unaccomplished adults and a young boy. An art dealer is savagely criticized as 'a pompous, plausible, double-crossing weasel'; 'cant, jargon, intellectual snobbism, and the commercializing of creative talent' are also condemned; and in the conclusion, another butler makes another moralizing speech, as he considers what might happen if it ever became generally known that Sorodin was a complete and utter fraud.

The whole world of modern painting will be humiliated and impoverished . . . Thousands of up and coming young artists will starve . . . If the news leaks out that the great Sorodin's masterpieces were painted by a Russian tart, an ex-Jackson girl, a Negro Eleventh-Hour Immersionist, and a boy of fourteen, the rot will spread like wildfire. Modern sculpture, music, drama and poetry will all shrivel in the holocaust. Tens of thousands of industrious people who today are earning a comfortable livelihood by writing without grammar, composing without harmony, and painting without form, will be flung into abject poverty, or forced really to learn their jobs. Reputations will wither overnight. No one will be spared.[76]

So, for Coward, it was back to the Empire again, and in the same year, he produced *South Sea Bubble* (1956), a light comedy set in contemporary Samolo, which merged the mandarin escapism of *Pacific 1860* with the social satire of *Relative Values*. It was not a successful combination. The natives still live in childhood Eden:

They sing from morning till night. They weave away and make the most lovely waste paper baskets and never stop having scores of entrancing children . . . And whenever they feel a bit peckish, all they have to do is to nip a breadfruit off a tree or snatch a yam out of the ground.

Naturally, this 'far-flung outpost of empire' remains a 'conservative stronghold'. Even though the pro-independence party is actively supported by a socialist governor, the majority of the population remain unswervingly loyal to Britain:

There are some subversive elements, of course, but most Samolans are still Empire minded. You see, they've been happy and contented under British rule for so many years that they just don't understand when they're suddenly told that it's been nothing but a corrupt capitalistic racket from the word go.[77]

In short, the Samolans are 'too young yet' for the 'brave experiment' of independence, and they prefer their 'old nanny' to enduring 'unprotected the fearful discomforts of state-controlled democracy which are wrecking western civilisation'. Even the attempts by the governor to introduce free public conveniences for all are derided as romantic, Western, utopian folly. 'Your conviction', the governor is told, 'that extreme socialism necessarily implies progress is romantic to the point of fantasy.' Coward thought it 'typically English and topical': such was his view of the Empire in the year that Nasser and the 'idiotic Egyptians', making 'beasts of themselves', nationalized the Suez Canal.[78]

It was, then, still not yet clear that Coward had successfully survived the war. He had endured a decade of critical failure, his finances were depleted, and in 1956 two events crystallized his national disenchantment and professional alienation. First came the Suez disaster, in which Britain failed to regain control of the Canal, and was humiliated in the eyes of the world, as its once-proud Empire was denounced for being toothless, immoral and anachronistic. Coward was appalled. 'The good old imperialism', he confided to his diary, 'was a bloody sight wiser and healthier than all this woolly-headed, muddled, "all men are equal" humanitarianism, which has lost us so much pride and dignity and prestige in the modern world.'[79] The second significant event that year was the sensational opening of John Osborne's play *Look Back in Anger*, announcing the arrival on the London stage of a new generation of 'angry young men' who, in both the substance and the form of their dramas, were as much theatrical revolutionaries in their day as Coward himself had been forty years before. But the one-time rebel was now the old-guard reactionary, the drawing-room has-been, against whom the new men were in their turn rebelling, and his later diaries are littered with bewildered, uncomprehending denunciations of Albee ('a chaotic mess of sex and symbolism'), Pinter ('completely incomprehensible and insultingly boring'), Ionesco ('amateur, pseudo-intellectual scribblings') and Beckett ('pretentious gibberish').[80]

It was these feelings of political and professional alienation which drove him to make a momentous decision: to leave England for good, sell all his property there, and re-establish himself overseas. As he put it in a song in *Ace of Clubs*: 'when the storm clouds are riding through a winter sky, sail away – sail away'.[81] In a sense, this was the logical end to what had become an increasingly peripatetic existence. Ever since the late 1920s, Coward had been spending more and more of his time abroad; he had often been absent during the Second World War; and he never settled down in England again thereafter. In 1944, he had visited Jamaica for the first time, and fallen in love with it; four years later, he rented 'Goldeneye', Ian Fleming's property on the island; shortly after, he built his own house, and became a regular winter resident. In 1956, he sold his London home and his country house in England, and thereafter divided his time between Jamaica and Bermuda, both of them British colonies. But it made little sense to have two residences on the western side of the Atlantic, so he soon parted with his Bermuda house (which he had named 'Spithead Lodge') and, when not in Jamaica, lived at 'Chalet Coward' near Les Avants in Switzerland.[82]

V

It is easy to see why Coward chose to leave a country which, for all his genuine patriotic ardour, had become critically unsympathetic, financially unrewarding and politically unappealing.[83] Indeed, many similarly disenchanted Britons left in the fifteen years after the Second World War, disappointed that the fruits of victory had been so meagre, and settled in the Antipodes, South Africa, Southern Rhodesia, Kenya, and parts of the Caribbean, where they made new lives, free from English taxes, English weather and the Welfare State. But for Coward, who had become so associated in the public mind with patriotic celebration, the decision to abandon ship only added to his unpopularity. It was hard to appear as the loyal and lifelong Englishman when he had decided to quit the country; and those who dismissed his patriotism as a self-advertising sham felt themselves amply vindicated. Although he was and would remain 'a Britisher', his decision 'brought a torrent of envy and malice' from almost every newspaper in the country. 'There was something rather sad', noted one more restrained commentator, 'that the brilliant author of *Cavalcade*, *This Happy Breed* and *In Which We Serve* – all tributes to Britain and the British – should be in a self-imposed exile from his own country.' Indeed, according to John Gielgud, Coward 'was never the same after leaving England, though he wouldn't have admitted it. I think that tax business, and the way people reacted to it, shocked him . . . He wasn't much good as a tax exile.'[84]

It certainly did not bring about an improvement in the quality of his work. On the contrary, his departure for colonial climes, where he enjoyed the reassuring company of such true-blue Tories as Ian and Ann Fleming, merely reinforced his disdain for contemporary England and encouraged his preoccupation with empire and the past. This was vividly illustrated in the aptly named *Pomp and Circumstance*, a light-fictional sequel to *South Sea Bubble*, which was published in 1960, and in which Coward's absorption in the colonial periphery reached its self-indulgent climax. The novel begins at Government House, Somolo, ends with the arrival of the Queen and Prince Philip on a state visit to the island, and in between is largely concerned with the misdemeanours of an English duchess who arrives incognito.[85] Once more, it is Coward's planter society, peopled with admirals and retired civil servants, and figures named Bunny and Bimbo, who spend their time drinking at the club, and the natives are still happy, friendly and entirely contented under British rule:

The Samolans are a mild and temperamentally cheerful people; they are uninterested in politics and sensible enough to realise that they are perfectly happy under the aegis of the British . . . The present agitation, by the Labour party at home, the Russians in Moscow, the Americans in Washington, and the Samolan Socialist National Party here, for Samolo to break free from British rule, and achieve dominion status has very few supporters in the whole Samolan archipelago.

For many, this novel was merely proof that Coward had 'signed off from the real world around him', and taken refuge in an imperial fantasy land, a view which this fervent affirmation of loyalty to the British throne tended to reinforce:

The crown is a symbol, and as such is, or should be, of tremendous importance. We are used to the tradition of royalty, and have been brought up to believe in it and respect it and love it. I, being thoroughly British and sentimental to the core, would hate to live in a country in which there was no royal pageantry and no chance of seeing the queen pass by . . . I want the symbol to go on shining, to go on being out of reach, and I am thankful to say that in our country and its colonies and dominions, it still does, in spite of efforts to belittle it.[86]

As these words imply, Coward was, by now, a fully fledged Windsor-worshipper. Indeed, he always had been from the time he began to climb into high society, and like many would-be courtiers, especially gay single men, he had often made more of his royal connections than circumstances warranted. But by the 1950s, by which time his work presented no problems to the Lord Chamberlain, he was very well in at court. In addition to the Mountbattens and the Duchess of Kent, he was friends with the Queen Mother, the Queen and Princess Margaret, with all of whom he lunched, dined and stayed. Even after leaving the country, he was a frequent attender at great royal occasions, and this account of the wedding of Princess Margaret, with its echoes of his first-night speech from *Cavalcade*, is typical of his 'Hurrah for England' view of the crown:

Nowhere in the world could such Pomp and Circumstance and Pageantry be handled with such dignity . . . It was gay, lusty, charming, romantic, splendid, and conducted without a false note. It is still a pretty exciting thing to be English.[87]

And if he could not get to see them, they could always come to him. In March 1965, he entertained the Queen Mother to lunch in Jamaica. Once again, the breathless excitement of his diary says it all:

The Queen Mother arrived at 1.20 and was gayer and more enchanting than ever . . . Lunch was a great success . . . She was supposed to leave at three o'clock . . . but . . . she didn't actually leave until ten to four . . . As for me, I am at her feet. She has infinite grace of mind, charm, humour and deep-down kindness, in addition to which she looks enchanting. She puts everyone at ease immediately without condescention or apparent effort . . . It was all tremendous fun, and she leaves behind her five gibbering worshippers.[88]

Ensconced in his Swiss chalet, exiled in his colonial retreat, delighting in receiving royalty, and increasingly living in the past, much of Coward's later work was suffused with a lazy escapist nostalgia which his audiences were less and less inclined to share. In his last musical, *The Girl Who Came to Supper* (1962), he once again reworked the themes of 'London Pride': the basic decency of all cockneys, and the easy camaraderie of the metropolis. But by now the Blitz was twenty-three years ago:

> Watch our lads in the Palace Yard
> Troop the Colour and Change the Guard
>
> . . .
>
> Saturday night at the Rose and Crown,
> That's just the place to be,
>
> . . .
>
> You can stray through any neighbourhood,
> If you haven't a swanky club
> Just pop into the nearest pub
> A little of what you fancy does you good . . .[89]

Or, as he put it on another occasion, with the sort of clichéd breeziness that concealed neither his ignorance nor his concerns:

No people in the world have a better time than the English . . . They're merry as grigs, all of them. Obviously, there is a certain amount of poverty and disease and unhappiness, but not nearly as much as in other countries. The Welfare State is doing very nicely, thank you.[90]

But in his innermost heart, and in the privacy of his diary, Coward did not believe this. In a poem aptly entitled 'Not Yet the Dodo', he revisited the upper-middle-class, Home Counties world, that had once been so happily and so certainly his own. But the ex-colonial governors, the retired bishops, the former diplomats and the superannuated admirals were now as much on the shelf as he was:

> In the countryside of England
> Tucked snugly beneath the Sussex Downs
> Or perhaps a mile or two away
> From gentle cathedral towns
> There still exist today
> A diminishing few
> A residue
> Of unregenerate characters who
> Despite two world wars and the Welfare State

And incomes sadly inadequate
Still, summoned by Sunday morning chimes,
Walk briskly to church to say their prayers
And later, in faded chinz arm-chairs,
Read of divorces, wars and crimes
And, shocked by the trend of world affairs,
Compose,
In a cozy, post-prandial doze,
Tart letters of protest to *The Times*.[91]

But the present kept impinging, and Coward did not like it at all. On 14 September 1963, he attended a 'Battle of Britain' dinner in New York, 'given in remembrance of those young men who saved, temporarily, the world'. 'It was', he recorded in his diary, 'simple, dignified, sparsely attended, and, to me, almost intolerably sad.' 'The atmosphere', he noted, 'was thick with dreadful nostalgia. The Battle of Britain was twenty-three years ago, and the world has forgotten it.' Those gallant young men, 'so incredibly brave, so beautiful and true', had died in vain. 'Nobody knows or cares if they ever existed ... Their enemy, the German nation, is now flourishing ... The peace we are enduring', he concluded, 'is not worth their deaths. England has become a third-rate power, economically and morally.'[92] He left 'that gentle, touching, tatty little party' with 'a heavy and sad heart', and wrote another poem of age and disenchantment, contrasting the tight-lipped heroism of 'the few' with the strident degeneracy of the younger generation:

Today in our country, it is the young men who are frightened.
They write shrill plays about defeat and are hailed as progressives.
They disdain our great heritage. They have been labelled by their dull
Facile contemporaries as Angry Young Men.
But they are not angry, merely scared and ignorant.
Many of them are not even English,
But humourless refugees from alien lands,
Seeking protection in our English sanity
And spitting on the valiant centuries
That made sanity possible.[93]

What, then, if anything, did Coward have left to say that was 'serious' about contemporary England? The answer was, not very much. He achieved a certain amount of notoriety with three articles he wrote for the *Sunday Times* in January 1961, which purported to be analysing the contemporary

British theatre, but which were primarily the vehicle for venting his pent-up feelings of hurt, anger, disappointment and incomprehension – at his own recent failures, at the 'bitter persecution' he felt he had received from the press, and at the dominance of the detested Roland Maules, in the theatre as well as in the country.[94] The new wave of writers, he insisted, were 'obsessed with left-wing socialism and the grievances of the underprivileged', and ignored the public. The actors belonged to the 'scratch and mumble school', which meant that 'wit, charm and elegance have been forced into political eclipse'. As for the critics: they merely over-praised those play-wrights and actors whose left-wing political views agreed with their own. This was not theatre, he insisted, it was squalor; it was not entertainment, but propaganda. The replies from the likes of Kenneth Tynan and Robert Bolt were withering: Coward had once been an innovative, rule-breaking rebel; now he was a bitter, out-of-date reactionary. And who was *he* to claim to know what theatre audiences wanted, when his 'brazenly old-fashioned' plays were no longer pulling in the crowds?[95]

This was a shrewd and cruel riposte. Of Coward's later serious work, *Volcano* (again set in Samolo) went unproduced in his lifetime: it could scarcely have been otherwise, since it was a study of the infidelities of the Flemings and other British ex-patriots in Jamaica.[96] In *Waiting in the Wings*, on which he 'worked hard' and took 'great pains', and which he thought 'strong and well-constructed', he sought to retrieve his reputation by writing about theatre people in old age, a subject which was, understandably, now beginning to preoccupy him. But although well acted by a distinguished cast, it was savaged by the critics, and closed after only three months, leaving a chastened Coward feeling 'repeatedly slashed in the face':

It is perfectly possible that I am out of touch with the times. I don't care for present trends in literature or the theatre. Pornography bores me. Squalor disgusts me. Garishness, vulgarity, and commonness of mind offend me, and problems of social significance on the stage, unless superbly well-presented, to me are the negation of entertainment. Subtlety, discretion, restraint, finesse, charm, intelligence, good manners, talent and glamour still enchant me ... Have I really or at least nearly reached the crucial moment when I should retire from the fray?[97]

He probably had, and very soon he would. But there was one more curtain-call, *Suite in Three Keys* (1966), his last appearance on the London stage, where Coward made his only attempt to address openly the issue of homo-sexuality. The critics greeted his valedictory appearance with unexpected generosity. But it was tame stuff by the changed standards of the time, he sometimes forgot his own lines, and the dialogue was windy and verbose in a manner that would have been inconceivable in his early, economical, tightly worded plays.[98]

That was the end of Coward's serious *oeuvre*; all that were left were his poems and a few short stories, in many of which he again sought refuge in the past. By the time 'P-&-O 1930' was published in 1967, it was a period piece; and 'Not Yet the Dodo' was a domestic lament for the same imperial and national demise. Even Jamaica was no longer the place it had been, but was full of domestic trouble and American tourists, and his last encounter with Samolo was a short story of double murder, in which the sun-lit and contented colony which had basked so innocently happy under British rule had been transformed since independence into a nightmare island, where the old colonial society has vanished, and the natives have become restless, discontented, cruel and violent.[99] In his last years, Coward made valedictory visits to the Middle East, the Seychelles, India, Australia, Singapore and Hong Kong where, as befitted the author of 'Mad Dogs and Englishmen', he fired off the noonday gun, and where he again delighted in the 'impeccable' manners of the Royal Navy. But these were the dying embers of departing imperial greatness. 'The Welfare State', he opined, when Ian Smith's Southern Rhodesia declared its independence, 'may be all right for improving the living conditions of the mediocre, but it isn't dazzlingly successful in dealing with foreign affairs and colonial administration . . . I don't see why it should be, really,' he concluded, 'as few of its leaders have been further than Blackpool.'[100]

Amidst what he lamented as this 'universal decay of values', when the world was 'coming to complete moral and mental disintegration', when 'our history, except for stupid, squalid social scandals, is over', and when the mood of the times was 'down with pageantry . . . up with mediocrity', all that was left was the thrill of the British monarchy and the matchless glamour of its ceremonial:

> The slow decline of our island race
> Alien prophets had long foreseen.
> But still, to symbolise English grace
> We go to London to look at the Queen.
>
> Our far-flung Empire imposed new rules
> And lasted a century or so.
> Until, engrossed in our football pools
> We shrugged our shoulders and let it go.

> But old traditions are hard to kill
> However battered about they've been,
> And it's still for some an authentic thrill
> To go to London to see the Queen.[101]

But even Coward recognized, in one sad, bleak speech he had intruded into *Waiting in the Wings*, that this was no longer enough:

I'm thankful that I'm old and near the end of my time. All the standards are lowered, all the values have changed. There is no elegance, reticence or dignity left.

> Milton thou shoudst be living at this hour
> England hath need of thee.[102]

VI

By the last decade of his life, Noël Coward had thus evolved into a figure far removed from the flippant, brittle, dressing-gowned persona he had created for himself during the 1920s. For he was in many ways a sad, bitter, disillusioned old man – lamenting the decline, both domestically and imperially, of the British world he had conquered and celebrated, known and loved; despising 'the young, who see no quality in our great past, and who spit, with phony, left-wing disdain on all that we, as a race, have contributed to the living world'; and even asserting, despite his earlier, unhappy encounters with the Lord Chamberlain, that censorship was 'a very, very good thing indeed'.[103] Thus had the ardour and ambition of youth given way to the regrets and resentments of old age – resentment at the Welfare State, resentment at the decline of Britain, resentment at the 1960s. By then, indeed, such pent-up feelings of disappointment and frustration were widespread on the right and, within less than a decade of Coward's death, Margaret Thatcher (whom he would surely have admired, and probably *adored*) would recognize their existence and their force, and would exploit them to great political effect.

But his final years were not all bitterness and disappointment: there was a happy ending – of sorts. For as his sense of national gloom intensified, his own reputation suddenly recovered – not on the basis of any work he was still doing, but in renewed recognition of the things he had written long ago. During the mid-1960s, Coward's early comedies were revised to great critical acclaim, and the author of *Hay Fever, Private Lives, Present*

Laughter and *Blithe Spirit* found himself applauded as the worthy successor to Sheridan and Wilde. And his seventieth birthday, in the final month of the much-disliked 1960s, inspired unprecedented interest in his life and work, with a 'Holy Week' of events, culminating with a gala dinner at the Savoy, including tributes from Sir Laurence Olivier and Lord Mountbatten. Thus was the embittered exile transformed into Grand Old Man of the English theatre; the belated knighthood was finally bestowed as a seventieth-birthday gift; and on his death three years later, Coward was mourned as one of the great figures of the twentieth-century stage.[104] His memorial service was held in St Martin-in-the-Fields, appropriately enough on Empire Day; a plaque was placed in the Actors' Church at Covent Garden; and a stone was later unveiled in Poets' Corner in Westminster Abbey by the Queen Mother.

There were many ironies to this late-flowering apotheosis, or 'Dad's Renaissance', as Coward called it.[105] For while he regretted the decline of Great Britain, and loathed the unrestrained vulgarity of its 'permissive society', it was these very changes in national circumstances and public mood which had effectively permitted his own theatrical rehabilitation. In an era when class barriers were tumbling, his comedies of manners no longer seemed trite and out of date, but were revived and relished as authentic period pieces. The decriminalizing of homosexual activity between consenting adults in private opened the way for his own belated knighthood, which was proposed by Roy Jenkins, the liberal and reforming Home Secretary. And so a fundamentally reactionary figure emerged as an acclaimed icon in a permissive age; the lover of empire was fêted in the decade when the colonies vanished; and the once-derided tax exile was welcomed back home as a national treasure. For Coward, these were, at best, mixed blessings. The 1960s made Britain a better place for homosexuals; they did not make it a better place for imperial patriots.[106] For someone in whom there was both a touch of Oscar Wilde, and also of Edward Elgar, this meant some rejoicing – but even more regret.

12

Fantasy: Ian Fleming and the
Realities of Escapism

In 1953, Richard Usborne published a book entitled *Clubland Heroes*, which explored the writings of three authors who had been best sellers for his generation (he was born in 1910) in the days of his youth: Sapper, Dornford Yates and John Buchan. 'I suppose', he lamented, 'no one reads them now. We are not as cavalier about race, nor so certain about the greatness of Britain as we once were; and the moral code of [Richard] Hannay and Bulldog Drummond is singularly unfashionable.' In the postwar era of Attlee, austerity and Indian independence, he went on, England was no longer governor of half the globe; the *ius Britannicum* did not apply to so many lands of palm and pine; and the Englishman's traditional mistrust of foreigners could not be as frankly expressed as in the days of Pax Britannica. Inevitably, this meant that history had 'not been kind to my authors and their heroes', and in this book Usborne wrote what he assumed would be their requiem.[1] Yet in the very same year that he composed his affectionate obituary notice for these patriotic thrillers and thrilling patriots, a neophyte novelist inaugurated what would become a long-running series which, in 'a souped up model with a sexy Italian body', reasserted many (though significantly, and as this quotation implies, not all) of the values and attitudes articulated in these earlier works, and did so with unrivalled popular appeal and unprecedented commercial success.[2]

The author in question was Usborne's near-contemporary, Ian Fleming, who wrote *Casino Royale*, his first James Bond novel, in 1952, ostensibly to take his mind off the shock of his impending marriage at the relatively advanced age of forty-four. He went on to produce a further thirteen Bond books, which meant that by the time of his death in 1964, at the relatively early age of fifty-six, he was one of the best-known men in England, and James Bond was established in his own right as an international celebrity, 'perhaps the most famous and popular hero in the history of literature' since Conan Doyle's Sherlock Holmes.[3] Although the Bond novels were stylishly produced by Jonathan Cape, one of London's most reputable publishers, and were favourably reviewed in journals such as *The Times Literary Supplement* and the *Spectator*, the early books did not sell particularly well, and it was only with the appearance of *From Russia With Love* that Fleming emphatically entered the best-seller lists. Thereafter, the Bond boom was not just a literary but also a social phenomenon, as his secret agent became 'a fictional character unrivalled in modern publishing history'. In 1963, royalties were in excess of £100,000; and in the following year, by which time some forty million Bond books had been sold, they had more than doubled. But it was 1965 which was *annus mirabilis* for 007 (though too late for Fleming), with no fewer than twenty-seven million copies sold, and revenue in excess of £350,000.[4]

The period during which the Bond novels appeared, and made such a cumulative impact on popular culture, from 1953 to 1966, was one in which Britain was often described as being a nation 'in decline'. At home, a 'loosening' of 'conventional' morality was accompanied by an unprecedented rise in living standards, which encouraged puritanical critics to liken the affluent England of the Welfare State to the degenerate days of the later Roman Empire or early seventeenth-century Spain – obsessed with sex, violence, materialism and self-indulgence, and turning its back on the more Spartan mode of life which they believed had been the foundation of former greatness. And moral 'decline' at home was mirrored in – indeed, may have helped bring about – international 'decline' abroad, as the tropical African empire was wound up, the Commonwealth was severely shaken by the departure of South Africa, and Britain's standing in the eyes of the world was irretrievably damaged as a result of the Suez fiasco. Thereafter, Harold Macmillan, the Conservative Prime Minister from 1957 to 1963, sought to make much more of the 'special relationship' with the United States than either Presidents Eisenhower or Kennedy were minded to do, and he vainly tried to turn his country and his party away from the Empire towards Europe. But with General de Gaulle's resounding veto on Britain's application to join the Common Market, Macmillan's foreign policy was in tatters. 'Great Britain', Dean Acheson woundingly but rightly observed, in harsh words from an ally, 'has lost an empire but not yet found a role in the world.'[5]

These changes, in both the substance of British power and in the perception of that power, took place very quickly, and were symbolized by two very different national events which were less than fifteen years apart. Queen Elizabeth II's coronation, which coincided with the publication of the first Bond novel, was a retrospectively unconvincing reaffirmation of Britain's continued great-power status and imperial amplitude. But Winston Churchill's state funeral, which took place no less coincidentally in the same year as the publication of the last, was not only the obsequies of the great man himself, but was also self-consciously recognized as being a requiem for Britain as a great world power and an empire state.[6] International downsizing is never easy (and never voluntary), which meant these were traumatic and on occasions humiliating changes. They may have been less traumatic and humiliating than the impact of the end of empire was on, say, France or Belgium (or, later, the USSR), but they were scarcely insignificant. During the first half of the twentieth century, the British Empire was part of the indissoluble order of things, and it had emerged triumphant from the wars with Germany, Italy and Japan in 1945. But in the second half of the century, between Indian independence in 1947 and the return of Hong Kong to China exactly fifty years later, it disappeared with astonishing rapidity and completeness. Thus was Sir John Seeley's expansionist dictum put smartly and suddenly into reverse, as England underwent a contraction of power that was monumental, unprecedented and irreversible.[7]

Yet it was against this unpromising background of imperial recession and global retreat, which his friend Noël Coward also felt so deeply but was unable to turn into something popular and resonant in his work, that Ian Fleming created James Bond – a character who, in his romantic daring, ardent patriotism and unalloyed success, owed much to the clubland heroes of his youth, even as Usborne believed their world and their values were visibly vanishing. From one perspective, then, these were unpropitious – even perverse – circumstances in which to bring into being an action-man British hero, flying the flag, confounding the enemy, committed to queen and country and empire, and saving the world from conspiracy and catastrophe in the nick of time. But from another vantage point, and as the sales figures suggest, they turned out to be the *ideal* circumstances in which to offer just this fictional brand of great-power nostalgia, imperial escapism and national reassurance. To complicate matters further, Bond's creator was himself an enigmatic and contradictory character – the product of his time and of his class, but not fully at ease with either. To understand the agent, we must understand the author. But to understand Ian Fleming, we must begin with his forebears and his family.[8]

I

Like Robert Louis Stevenson and John Buchan (and also like James Bond), the Flemings were Scottish. To say this is to say a great deal, for since the Act of Union with England of 1707, the Scots had become a formidable trading, military and governing force throughout and beyond the British Empire, and often in a clandestine way. 'Why', John le Carré's eponymous hero wonders in *Smiley's People*, and 'not for the first time in his career', were 'Scots so attracted to the secret world? Ships engineers, colonial administrators, spies.'[9] The Flemings originated in Dundee, not as engineers, but in the (appropriately imperial) jute business. The family fortune was founded by Robert Fleming in the late nineteenth century, when he launched the Investment Trust Corporation in London, and he soon established himself as the doyen of what we would now call unit trust managers. In 1906 he was described by Gaspard Farrer of Barings as the best judge of American securities in Britain, who was 'a rich man with a very large following and straight as a die'; and soon after he established the merchant bank which always bore his name. All his life, Robert Fleming remained a dour, respectable and puritanical Scotsman, but by this time the family had acquired many of the trappings of the 'gentlemanly capitalists' whose ranks they had now joined: there was a town house in Grosvenor Square, there were broad acres at Nettlebed in Oxfordshire, and there was a (rented) shooting estate in Scotland.[10]

Robert Fleming's eldest son, Valentine, was born in 1882, and received an appropriately exclusive education at Eton and Magdalen College, Oxford. In 1906, he married Evelyn St Croix Rose, by whom he fathered four sons, of whom Ian Fleming, born in 1908, was the second. Valentine Fleming trained as a lawyer, was devoted to country pursuits and the Territorial Army, was a close friend of Winston Churchill, and in 1910 was elected (and re-elected) Conservative MP for the Henley Division of Oxfordshire.[11] There seemed every prospect that he would spend (and end) his days as a country gentleman and knight of the shire. So, indeed, he did; but the end came much sooner than anyone expected. Like most members of his class and generation, he volunteered on the outbreak of the First World War, and he was almost immediately on active service as a major in the Oxfordshire Hussars. But in May 1917, Valentine Fleming was killed. He was awarded a posthumous DSO, and Winston Churchill wrote a moving obituary, lamenting the demise of a fine officer and gallant gentleman. The complexities of the Fleming family financial arrangements meant Valentine's children were left less well off than they might have hoped, and the emotional consequences of his death were even more marked. All his life, Ian Fleming felt himself in the shadow of a father whom he had scarcely known, but whom he and his family venerated as a patriot and martyr, and his framed version of Churchill's obituary notice was among his most prized possessions.

The widowed Evelyn Fleming was a stern and dominant matriarch, who ruled her children with a rod of iron, and was simultaneously critical of them, protective of them and ambitious for them. Yet she also brought to the puritan Scottish Flemings a more raffish and capricious moral code which, more than any of his siblings, her son Ian would later embrace and enjoy. Her two brothers were notorious rakes and philanderers, she herself was frivolous, vain, snobbish and extravagant, and after her husband's death, she took a succession of lovers, culminating in Augustus John, the most renowned (or notorious) Lothario of his generation.[12] The result of this liaison was an illegitimate daughter, Amaryllis Fleming, who became a gifted cellist, and who would be mentioned by her half-brother in the Bond short story 'The Living Daylights'. Much later in her life, 'Mrs Val' embarked on an affair with the ninety-year-old Marquess of Hastings, one of the more disreputable members of the British aristocracy, and she eventually took up residence with him in Monte Carlo. There was much gossip and scandal, culminating in a sensational court case in which Hastings's estranged wife accused Eve Fleming of 'stealing' her husband. This episode caused her sons great embarrassment, especially Ian, whom she predeceased by scarcely a month, and in whose life she remained a dominant figure to the end.

In addition to his mother and father, the third significant family influence on Ian Fleming was his elder brother, Peter, who had been born in 1907. Throughout their lives, the two elder Fleming brothers were very close, and they remained fiercely loyal to each other. But Peter's influence on Ian, like that of their parents, was in many ways more overbearing than enabling. Val Fleming was an officer, gentleman and war hero; Eve Fleming was an ambitious matriarch and a headstrong man-hunter; Peter Fleming was a paragon, widely regarded as the most handsome, accomplished and charismatic man of his generation. At Eton, he was Member of Pop, editor of the school magazine and Captain of Oppidans; and at Christ Church, Oxford, he was a stalwart of the (very smart) Bullingdon Club, editor of *Isis* and took an effortless first in English. He was a traveller and explorer of resource and renown; he soon established close and life-long contacts at *The Times* and the *Spectator*; and he wrote articles, essays and books with an assured ease and witty brilliance that, for many years, deterred his younger brother from daring to compete. As the squire of Nettlebed, Peter Fleming devoted himself to country pursuits and, in 1935, he married Celia Johnson, one of the most beautiful and talented actresses of her day. As befitted a status-conscious dowager in a parvenu family, Mrs Val did not approve: the only thing Peter ever did to upset his mother was to marry someone who earned her living by appearing *on the stage*.

Such was Ian Fleming's family background, by turns upstart and establishment, puritan and unrespectable, privileged and deprived; and with a martyred father, a dominant mother and a glittering brother, he grew up very conscious of his own limitations, inadequacies and shortcomings. All his life, there was about him an aura of wounded and solitary melancholy, of deep but usually latent romanticism that would also characterize the Bond books and give them much of their unique tone, conviction and appeal. At Eton he was not a success: his elder brother was an impossible act to follow and, apart from excelling at athletics, Ian Fleming did not try. He left early, and lived for a time in Austria, Germany and Switzerland, perfecting his skills with languages – and with women. On his return to Britain, the family bank would not accept him, so his mother shamelessly engineered a succession of career openings she deemed appropriate for a man of his status; but they came to nothing. In rapid succession, Fleming left Sandhurst under a cloud, failed to get into the Foreign Office, briefly worked for Reuters, and joined the stockbroking firm of Rowe and Pitman. In equally rapid succession, women came and went, attracted by his good looks, Etonian drawl, animal magnetism, cultivated air of mystery and (at least initially) rather cruel and arrogant charm. As a dynasty, the Flemings were quintessential gentlemanly capitalists, but in truth Ian Fleming was no capitalist – and no gentleman either.[13]

The most that could be said of him at this stage was that through his family, his Etonian friends and his (by now) many professional contacts, he was becoming very well connected, and it was thanks to the old-boy network that he was recruited, in the summer of 1939, to work for the secret service, over an appropriately epicurean meal at the Carlton Grill. He was soon appointed to be Personal Staff Officer to Admiral Sir John Godfrey, the Director of Naval Intelligence, and he was a member of the famed Room 39 team at Bletchley Park.[14] This job not only gave Fleming direct experience of spying and espionage and of covert operations in distant lands: it also left him with an abiding love of the British Navy. Although he was dubbed a 'chocolate sailor', who never served at sea or saw action on a ship, he relished his rank of Commander in the RNVR, and he delighted in showing off his uniform to his family – and his girlfriends. For the first time in his life, Ian Fleming was fully engaged in a job at which he was a considerable success. As such, he had (in William Plomer's words) 'youth, health, strength, money, general eligibility, a social status taken for granted, work that interested him, and a consciousness of his powers'.[15] And it was out of these experiences, memories and sensations that he would later create and elaborate the world of James Bond – who was himself, like Fleming, a Commander in the RNVR.

At the end of the war, Fleming returned to civilian life, and became foreign manager of Kemsley newspapers, where he was responsible for gathering what he liked to call 'intelligence' from around the world. His contract made provision for two months' annual leave, and he spent January and February in Jamaica, where he built his house, 'Goldeneye', fraternized with expatriate friends like Noël Coward, worked on the Bond novels and set several of them. In the aftermath of the Suez fiasco, Sir Anthony Eden convalesced at Goldeneye, a sojourn which did nothing for Eden's reputation but a great deal for Fleming's. Meanwhile, he was a frequent *habitué* of White's and Boodle's Clubs, he regularly wrote the 'Atticus' column of the *Sunday Times*, and he took on overseas assignments which resulted in two books, *The Diamond Smugglers* and *Thrilling Cities*. In the second of these, he revealed much of himself, giving vent to his dislike of the Middle East, India and Japan, expressing his opposition to international agencies, high taxes and mass tourism, and relishing both the fleshpots of Hamburg and Macao, and the many delights of colonial Hong Kong.[16] But his wayward private life was not appreciated at Kemsley House, and in 1959 Fleming resigned to devote himself fulltime to writing. By then he could well afford to do so, as the Bond boom was about to begin, and he would soon (but briefly) enjoy a world-wide audience of admirers ranging from Raymond Chandler to John F. Kennedy.

In 1952, Fleming had married Lady Ann Rothermere, with whom he had enjoyed an on-off liaison for the best part of a decade. Their union began happily enough, but soon turned sour, in part because neither of them was suited to a long-term and monogamous relationship, and in part because, by birth and upbringing, she was very much his social superior. Her grand-father was the eleventh Earl of Wemyss, and her cousin was Martin Char-teris, who would soon become Private Secretary to Queen Elizabeth II. Her first husband, Lord O'Neill, was an Irish grandee of exceptionally ancient lineage, who was killed on active service in 1940; her second, Viscount Rothermere, was a newspaper tycoon and proprietor of the *Daily Mail*, whom she divorced in 1951. Throughout her multifarious marriages, Ann Fleming retained the outlook of a traditional aristocrat, and was 'a Tory of the deepest blue'.[17] But in 1956 she began an affair with Hugh Gaitskell, the Labour leader, which lasted until his death in 1963. She was also (much to her husband's annoyance and regret) an accomplished hostess, regularly entertaining leading politicians from both parties at their London house in Victoria Square and in the country at Sevenhampton Place in Wiltshire. She also numbered Evelyn Waugh, Maurice Bowra, Isaiah Berlin, Noël Annan, Lucien Freud, Frederick Ashton and Francis Bacon among her friends.

Notwithstanding their increasing incompatibilities, 'Mr and Mrs Ian Fleming' were, as befitted the creator of James Bond and his aristocratic wife, a very fashionable couple indeed.[18]

II

Such was Ian Fleming's family background and personal history – a background and a history which explain a great deal about the content and values of his Bond books, since he put so much of his complex and contradictory self into them that they were in many ways a kind of autobiographical wish-fulfilment. Brought up, like most male members of his class and generation, on a fictional diet of Robert Louis Stevenson and Usborne's clubland heroes, it is scarcely surprising that his own novels show a strong and appreciative indebtedness to them.[19] Far from being the first in a brand of new, space-age thrillers, Fleming's work might be better placed in what was by then the half-century tradition of British 'shockers' going back to the 'invasion scare' literature which flourished in the years before the First World War at the hands of Erskine Childers, Le Queux and E. Phillips Oppenheim.[20] 'The exoticism, the fisticuffs, the ingenious hardware, the sinister flora and fauna', all of them defining characteristics of 007's world are, as Colin Wilson notes, 'variations on traditional themes'. Indeed, the Bond books have rightly been described as being 'astonishingly derivative', and from no author did they derive more than John Buchan. Even their titles are similar in their cadences and their inventiveness: for *Greenmantle* read *Goldfinger*, for *Huntingtower* read *Moonraker*, for *Prester John* read *Dr No* and for *Sick-Heart River* read *You Only Live Twice*.[21]

More substantially, many of the people who flit through the Bond books are recognizably these 'top of the form' characters, labelled solely by their larger-than-life successes and achievements, that were earlier to be found in Buchan's pages.[22] When Bond takes his place at the table in the casino at Royale-les-Eaux, his fellow-gamblers include 'a wealthy Belgian with metal interests in the Congo', a young Italian 'who possibly had plenty of money from rackrents in Milan', Lord Danvers 'whose francs were presumably provided by his rich American wife', an 'American film star with alimony from three husbands', the 'Maharajah of a small Indian State' who has 'all his wartime sterling balances to play with', and a 'well-known Greek gambler . . . who owned a profitable shipping line'.[23] Later novels are peopled with similar figures. In *Moonraker*, Sir Hugo Drax is 'a millionaire, a public hero, a man with a unique position in the country', and his chief scientist,

Professor Train, is 'one of the greatest experts on guided missiles in the world'. In *Dr No*, we encounter Major Boothroyd, 'the greatest small-arms expert in the world'; in *You Only Live Twice* we meet Sir James Molony, 'the greatest neurologist in England', who has recently won a Nobel Prize; and when, in *The Man with the Golden Gun*, M avails himself of academic advice, no ordinary scholar will do: it has to be the 'retired Regius Professor of History [*sic*] at Oxford'.

But it is with Bond's opponents that this element of excessive accomplishment becomes most pronounced, as the reader is bludgeoned by remorseless hammer-blows of sinister superlatives. Le Chiffre is 'a powerful Soviet agent', and 'a faultless and lucky gambler'. Mr Big is 'probably the most powerful negro criminal in the world', who is 'pre-eminent in his chosen profession'. The Spangled Mob are 'one of the most powerful gangs in the United States', who are running 'the biggest smuggling operation in the world'. Dr No is 'one of the most remarkable men in the world', who boasts on his Caribbean island 'the most valuable technical intelligence centre in the world'. Emilio Largo 'had fought for Italy in the Olympic foils, was almost an Olympic class swimmer', and possesses 'nerves of steel, a heart of ice, and the ruthlessness of a Himmler'. Goldfinger is the 'richest man in England' and, by planning 'one of the greatest conspiracies of all time', hopes to become 'the richest man in the world, the richest in history'. And Ernst Stavro Blofeld is 'the biggest crook in the world', whose enterprises are 'on the scale of a Caligula, of a Nero, of a Hitler, of any of the great enemies of mankind'. After such overwhelming criminal grandeur, the fact that Bond's last adversary, Scaramanga, is 'possibly the fastest gun in the world' seems almost a disappointment.

Inevitably, this means that Bond himself, as their adversary and nemesis, is himself a figure of superhuman talents and attainments. He knows everything there is to know about food and wine and cars – and women. According to the Russians, he is 'the most famous British spy', and a 'danger to the state'; and he is also 'the finest gambler' and the 'best shot' in the service. Like many of Buchan's clubland characters, Bond's chief challenge is to avoid boredom ('the only vice he utterly condemned'): he finds desk and paper work tedious, he thirsts for action and excitement, and the 'only assignments he enjoyed' were 'the dangerous ones'. And he undertakes them with controlled and calculating ruthlessness: his features are 'ironical, brutal and cold', and he 'walks alone and keeps his heart to himself'. Yet in a manner further reminiscent of Buchan's heroes, Bond is not so much devoid of emotions as constantly striving to control and conceal them: for, 'like all harsh, cold men, he was easily tipped over into sentiment'. 'It is surprising',

Sir James Molony later tells M, 'what soft centres, the so-called tough men always have.' As with 'all the silly bastards who get mixed up with the service', Bond is 'a romantic at heart'. And he pays a high price for it. When rejected by Gala Brand at the end of *Moonraker* (the only time this happens in the whole series), he steels himself 'to play the role she expected of him. The tough man of the world. The Secret Agent.' And by the later books, 007 has become the quintessential wounded, silent hero bearing, after the murder of his wife Tracy on the day of their wedding, 'a secret sorrow over a woman, aggravated, as it should be, by self-reproach'.[24]

From villains to heroes, Fleming's characters are essentially Buchan's characters, and so is the world in which they operate, as places, objects and events are constantly transformed from the humdrum into the splendid, the prosaic into the exciting, the commonplace into the glamorous, and the ordinary into the fantastic. Accordingly, Bond drinks Taittinger '45, which is 'the finest champagne in the world', and Blue Mountain coffee, which is 'the most delicious in the world'. In Jamaica, which is naturally 'one of the most fertile islands in the world', he encounters the humming-bird, the 'most beautiful bird in the world', and (of all things!) guano, 'the greatest natural fertiliser in the world'. When Bond visits Istanbul, the panorama he enjoys from his hotel room is 'one of the most famous views in the world', and when he smokes local, Turkish tobacco, it is 'the most wonderful cigarette he had ever tasted'. Everything in the Bond books is the biggest, loveliest, best, fastest (or most horrible and sinister) on the planet. Nothing is mundane, and there are no half measures. When Bond and Solitaire take the 'Silver Phantom' express from New York to Florida, it is no ordinary journey, but partakes of 'the romance of American railroads'. They do not travel in a long train, but in 'a quarter of a mile of gleaming carriages'. The company livery is not so much painted on the engine, but 'glows regally on the streamlined locomotive'. And when they alight at five o'clock in the morning at Jacksonville, it is not at a sleepy station in the middle of nowhere, but at 'the great Florida junction'.

By consistently empurpling his prose, inflating his rhetoric and heightening his style, Fleming, like Buchan before him, established and intensified the mood of drama and tension, excitement and anticipation, conspiracy and menace which characterizes and pervades his thrillers. They also share with Buchan the schoolboy sense that the best way to handle such tensions and anxieties is to regard life and work as being primarily concerned with playing up to win the game. For Fleming's language is frequently that of the sports ground, the cricket pitch and the hunting field. In *Casino Royale*, SMERSH is 'on the scent', Bond's cover is not blown but 'bowled out', and his relationship with Vesper Lynd has fewer 'hurdles' than he expected, so they soon become 'a team'. In *Live and Let Die*, Bond informs Leiter that 'Solitaire's on our side now', when he has successfully extricated her from the clutches of Mr Big. There is, then, much to cheer at as the home team plays hard, sticks at it and wins through in the end. 'Splendid show! What a lark!', Bond recalls of one earlier adventure. 'Once more into the breach, dear friends!' he exclaims at a crisis point in another. And in *The Man with the Golden Gun*, we are further reassured that 'the enemy's fire was not going unanswered'. Throughout Fleming's pages, we can almost hear Buchan's Sandy Arbuthnot exclaiming, 'Oh, well done our side!'[25]

As this suggests, Fleming's novels were, like Buchan's, essentially school-boy stories dressed up for adults, and in case there is any doubt about this, he makes it plain that he and his characters know it. Towards the end of *Casino Royale*, Le Chiffre informs Bond that the children's game of cowboys and Indians is now over, and that the grown-ups have taken charge: but of course it is Bond who eventually wins. When on missions in the Caribbean, 007 is regularly reminded of Captain Morgan, of pirates and of sunken galleons, and he often senses a '*Treasure Island* atmosphere of excitement and conspiracy'. And when M regails Bond with his naval stories, he concludes: 'perhaps it was all just the stuff of boys' adventure books, but it was all true'. One way in which it was all true was that the mental universe of the books is simple and straightforward, with a clear demarcation between right and wrong. When upbraiding Bond, Le Chiffre notes that 'This is not a romantic adventure story in which the villain is finally routed and the hero is given a medal and marries the girl. Unfortunately these things don't happen in real life.' Maybe not. But they all happened in Buchan; and, with the exception of marrying (as distinct from bedding) the girl, they all happen in Fleming. *Dr No* provides a classic instance of this, so it is scarcely surprising that when Bond fills in Honeychile Rider on the background, he (like Fleming) tells 'the story in simple terms, with good men and bad men, like an adventure story out of a book'.

III

In all these ways, the Bond novels were closely modelled on the Buchan books; but this is not the sum total of their many resemblances. For Fleming, like Buchan, vividly evoked the sights and smells and atmosphere of the far-off places where 007 went on his missions: the birds and beaches of the Caribbean in several novels, the August race meetings at Saratoga Springs in *Diamonds Are Forever*, the idyllic late summer at Royale Les Eaux at the opening of *On Her Majesty's Secret Service*, and the flora and fauna of Japan in *You Only Live Twice*. Indeed, the resemblances between them were so close, and in so many ways, that this summary of the Buchan 'shockers' would apply equally well to Fleming's thrillers:

They were essentially juvenile fantasies, artfully embellished for adults, which comforted rather than jolted: virtue wins out over evil in the end, the subversive conspiracies . . . are thwarted, those who live a healthy, open-air life vanquish . . . ruthless plutocrats, and the natural order of things is safely and successfully re-asserted.[26]

Thus described, Fleming's novels were, like Buchan's, the product of what Gertrude Himmelfarb has called a 'Tory imagination', preoccupied with physical fitness and individual action, more concerned with success than with sagacity, fascinated by race and class, nation and empire, and pervaded by a sense of 'evil, violence and apocalypse'.[27]

As befitted a man of his class, background and outlook, Fleming's fiction also shared with Buchan's an abiding belief in the greatness and innate moral superiority of his own country. From the first Bond book to the last, foreigners in general are disliked, distrusted and regarded with scorn. Bulgarians are 'stupid but obedient'. Negroes are 'clumsy black apes', whose women 'don't know anything about birth control'. The Russians are 'among the cruellest people in the world' – 'cold, dedicated and chess-playing'. But they are far surpassed, both by the Koreans, who are 'the cruellest, most ruthless people on earth', and by the Japanese, 'who have only been playing at civilised people for fifty, at the most a hundred years'. Even America is only a 'civilised country. More or less'; and the western Europeans fare little better. Berlin is 'a glum, inimical city, varnished on the western side with a brittle veneer of gimcrack polish, rather like the chromium trim on American motor cars', and Paris has sold its heart to the 'Russians, Rumanians and Bulgarians', 'the scum of the world who had gradually taken the town over'. In the same way, none of the major villains is English and several are probably Jewish. Even Sir Hugo Drax and Goldfinger, both of whom are British citizens, turn out be of German and Baltic origin.[28]

Consistent with this general view of British superiority over the lesser breeds, Bond himself is described as 'a patriotic sort of chap'. Assuredly, in *Casino Royale*, he had briefly suggested that 'this country right or wrong business is getting a little out of date'. But he never expresses that subversive opinion again. When Vesper Lynd (whom he has befriended and bedded) is found dead and discovered to have been a double agent, Bond does not feel sorrow for her: it is 'her treachery to the Service and to her country and . . . the damage it had done' that most stirs him. In the title story of *For Your Eyes Only*, Bond agrees to assassinate a villain, despite the fact that he dislikes killing in cold blood, because it is necessary in the interests of the state:

'I suppose I can stand most things if I have to and if I think it's right, sir. I mean . . . if the cause is, er sort of just . . . Of course, it's not easy to know what is just and what isn't. I suppose I assume that when I'm given an unpleasant job in the Service, the cause is a just one.'[29]

And when M is wondering, at the beginning of *You Only Live Twice*, what can be done to shake Bond out of his bereaved lethargy, his medical adviser, Sir James Molony, urges: 'Give him something that really matters to his country.' How appropriate, then, is M's obituary notice of Bond at the end of that novel, where he declares that

Commander Bond's last mission was one of supreme importance to the state . . . It is no exaggeration to pronounce unequivocally that, through the recent valorous efforts of this one man, the Safety of the Realm has received mighty reassurance.[30]

More generally, the novels are pervaded by an omnipresent tone of national pride and patriotic sentiment. Bond believes (surely, quite implausibly), that 'the best English cooking is the best in the world', and (with rather more substance) that the old British currency was 'the most beautiful money in the world'. And in *Moonraker*, when 007 and Gala Brand go for a walk atop the cliffs of Kent, Fleming describes the view before them in one of his most effortless and effective pieces of purple prose, vibrant with history, atmosphere and national pride:

It was a wonderful afternoon of blue and green and gold . . . They stopped for a moment on the edge of the great chalk cliff and stood gazing over the whole corner of England where Caesar had first landed two thousand years before. To their left, the carpet of green turf, bright with small wildflowers, sloped gradually down to the long pebble beaches of Walmer and Deal, which curved off towards Sandwich and the bay . . . As far as the eye could reach, the Eastern Approaches of England were dotted with traffic plying towards near or distant horizons, towards a home port or towards the other side of the world. It was a panorama full of colour and excitement and romance, and the two people on the edge of the cliff were silent as they stood for a time and watched it all.[31]

But if Bond was so patriotic, what sort of Britain was it which he lived to serve and fought to save? It is, superficially, as apolitical as was his creator. 'I am', Fleming once explained, in his teasing essay in the *Spectator* entitled 'If I Were Prime Minister',

a totally non-political animal. I prefer the name of the Liberal Party to the name of any other, and I vote Conservative rather than Labour mainly because the Conservatives have bigger bottoms, and I believe that big bottoms make for better government than scrawny ones . . . My own particular hero is Sir Alan Herbert . . . And of course I have the affectionate reverence for Sir Winston Churchill that most of us share.[32]

All his life, Fleming, like his elder brother, Peter, had no serious interest in politics or politicians, beyond voting Conservative for the good of the country, and the same attitude pervades the Bond books. M, for instance, declares emphatically that he is 'not a politician', and fears 'getting all balled up in high politics. Not my line of country at all.' The Prime Minister is occasionally at the other end of his telephone, but remains aloof, Olympian and supreme – the steward of Her Majesty's affairs, rather than a calculating, partisan politician, temporarily enjoying the fruits of office. Only once is his identity revealed, and that is in *Moonraker* where he must be Churchill, whom Gala Brand reveres as 'the voice of all the great occasions of her life'.

So, for all the lack of strong, party-political commitment, Bond's England, like Fleming's England, is located, in the words of Kingsley Amis, 'substantially right of centre'.[33] May, 007's housekeeper and 'Scottish treasure', will only call Churchill and the king 'sir', and she (like Fleming?) believes that the Electricians' Union is full of communists. 'The cheap, bungaloid world of the holiday lands' holds no allure for Bond, who prefers the Bank of England, with its 'heavy, grave atmosphere of immense riches', *The Times*, which was 'the only newspaper Bond ever read', and the British Empire, with its governors 'solid, loyal, competent, sober and just: the best type of colonial civil servant'. When 007 dreams of his native land towards the end of *Dr No*, having completed a testing but triumphant mission, it is not the England of trade unions and factory workers and council house estates, or of television or pubs, but a 'world of tennis courts and lily ponds and kings and queens. Of London. Of people being photographed with pigeons on their heads in Trafalgar Square.' It is, in short, the Establishment England of the Conservative governments of 1951–64, just as Buchan's England was that of the Conservative (and Coalition) governments of 1922–40. In such consistently Tory times, it was scarcely surprising that two writers possessing an essentially 'Tory imagination' should blossom and flourish.

Of all great British institutions, Fleming most adored the Royal Navy. Bond himself, like his creator, is a former naval person; and so, too, is M, Admiral Sir Miles Messervy, with his 'keen sailor's face, with the clear, sharp sailor's eyes', whose 'jaw stuck out like the prow of a ship', who 'thinks in the language of battleships', and who gave up the certain prospect of becoming Fifth Sea Lord to become Head of the Secret Service. Naturally, M believes that the Senior is 'the greatest of all Services' clubs in the world', and his house, 'Quarterdeck', is full of maritime mementoes, with its 'treasured collection of naval prints. Everywhere there were mountainous seas, crashing cannon, bellying sails, tattered battle pennants.' There M entertains 007 with his 'stories about the Navy, to which Bond could listen all day – stories of battles, tornados, bizarre happenings, courts-martial, eccentric officers, neatly worded signals'.[34] Gunmetal and battleship grey are Fleming's two favourite colours; Strangeways, the Secret Service agent in the West Indies, has 'the sort of aquiline good looks that are associated with the bridges of destroyers'; and in *Thunderball*, the narrative is held up while Domino tells a Maugh-amesque fable about the sailor pictured on a packet of Players cigarettes.[35] Most revealing of all is M's obituary notice of Bond at the end of *You Only Live Twice*, where he credits 007 with possessing 'what almost amounted to "The Nelson touch" in moments of highest emergency'.

IV

In his daring patriotism, his lack of doubt or complexity, and his disdain for introversion, Bond was a quintessential clubland hero, flourishing in the very era when they were deemed to be doomed. But 007, like his creator, was not wholly at ease in the post-Buchan world of domestic change and international decline. One reason for this was that Fleming was the sort of Tory who did not like the Welfare State, and thought it had done the nation great harm.[36] 'There had been', he noted in *Thrilling Cities*, 'periods when the liberal spirit got a little out of hand', and that was how he saw Butskellite Britain. For he deplored what he regarded as 'the increasing emphasis of our society upon not only materialism, but upon materialism *without effort*'; and in 'If I Were Prime Minister', he mounted a more sustained assault:

In the United Kingdom we have a basically nonconformist conscience, and the fact that taxation, controls and certain features of the Welfare State have turned the majority of us into petty criminals, liars and work-dodgers is, I am sure, having a bad effect on the psyche of the kingdom.[37]

Naturally enough, Bond took the same view, regretting that 'carrots for all are the fashion', and venting his wrath on a working-class taxi-driver early in the pages of *Thunderball*:

It was typical of the cheap, self-assertiveness of young labour since the war. This youth, thought Bond, makes about twenty pounds a week, despises his parents, and would like to be Tommy Steele. It's not his fault. He was born into the buyers' market of the Welfare State . . . For him life is easy and meaningless.[38]

Faced with such unwelcome evidence of what he saw as domestic moral decline, Fleming urged a return to what he regarded as the earlier, more robust values of the Victorian era. For, as he opined in *Thrilling Cities*, the slide towards decadence could be halted 'only, I think, if the spirit of adventure which opened the Orient to us can be re-kindled, and our youth can heave itself off its featherbed and steam out and off across the world again'.[39] As Fleming saw things, the most important pre-condition for this much-needed national revival was to bring back those competitive, tough, masculine qualities which he and his generation had learned in public school; and that, of course, was precisely what he made happen in his thrillers. For in the person of James Bond, the 'spirit of adventure' *is* 're-kindled', and 'our youth' *does* 'heave itself off its featherbed and steam out and off across the world'. Of course, 007 had been educated at Eton and Fettes and enjoyed the comfort and security of a private income. Yet (as Simon Raven pointed out) Bond is not a 'pampered and privileged' figure, but something of a latter-day Smilesian character. He has to work for his triumphs, which come as a result of careful preparation, tireless effort, supreme professionalism and sheer grit. While Fleming fervently believed that Bond was in the right, his hero does not win because he is in the right, but because he works harder and fights tougher than his enemies.[40]

Hence, in the Bond novels, there is the same veneration for Spartan living, fortitude, bravery and physical courage found in Buchan; the same celebration of sturdy independence and individual self-reliance; and the same belief in personal redemption through valorous deeds on the imperial frontier and in the far corners of the world. Here, again, the 'Tory imagination' was hard at work. As a 'man of action and resource', Bond takes pride in being 'one hundred per cent' fit for his work in the double-O section; and when he over-indulges at the beginning of *Goldfinger* with Mr du Pont, 'the puritan in him' (that powerful Scottish Fleming trait) is revolted. Even cold showers are as much a part of his life as cold baths were for the clubland heroes, and when, in *Live and Let Die*, Bond trains so as to be supremely fit for action, his sense of self-satisfaction is extreme:

By the end of the week, Bond was sunburned and hard. He had cut his cigarettes down to ten a day, and had not had a single drink. He could swim two miles without tiring . . . and all the scales of big-city life had fallen from him.[41]

In the course of his adventures, Bond is frequently tortured, but he never betrays his secrets, his friends or his country: his upper lip remains stiff on all occasions. As he explains to Tiger Tanaka, in *You Only Live Twice*, when criticizing the Japanese custom of atoning for failure by committing suicide, that is not how the British do things: 'it would be cowardly – a refusal to stand up to reverses, to life'.

For Fleming as for Buchan, this casual, understated bravery was an essentially masculine characteristic, and there was a special camaraderie among those men on the same side who shared it. 'Affection' is the word Fleming constantly uses to describe 007's attitude towards 'the half dozen of those real friends whom Bond, who had no "acquaintances", would be ready to take to his heart'.[42] They are an exclusive group, both socially and sociologically, and (as Ann Fleming would have wished) there is no one from the slums or the suburbs. There is M, Bond's superior, modelled on Admiral Godfrey, 'who held a great deal of his affection and all of his loyalty and obedience', to whom he is 'almost married', and whom he 'loves, honours and obeys'. Indeed, there is a sense in which M is the real hero of the books. He is the product of a 'Victorian upbringing' and he possesses 'a Victorian soul'. He is dutiful, high-minded and incorruptible, and regrets that 'nowadays, softness was everywhere'. He treats Bond with a firm but fatherly hand, always sees the men from the lower ranks right, and invariably backs up his staff. He is, in short, both the repository and the embodiment of those characteristics that make for British greatness, and is also responsible for maintaining that greatness in an increasingly hostile and unsympathetic world.

Among those men friends who are Bond's professional equals, pride of place goes to Felix Leiter, the American agent whom he meets in *Casino Royale*, and who appears in five further novels. 'Good Americans were fine people', 007 notes on their first encounter, 'and most of them seemed to come from Texas.' As befits two men of action, their dialogue is continually that style of light-hearted banter and casual badinage which covers deeper feelings – feelings which surface in *Live and Let Die*, when Leiter is horribly injured by a shark, and Bond observes the bruised, broken, bandaged body of his friend:

He saw again the straw-coloured mop that used to hang down in disarray over the right eye, grey and humorous, and below it the wry, hawk-like face of the Texan, with whom he had shared so many adventures. He thought of him for a moment, as he had been. Then he tucked the lock of hair back into the bandages, and sat on the edge of the other bed, and quietly watched over the body of his friend, and wondered how much of it could be saved.[43]

Reunited with Leiter in *Diamonds Are Forever* ('the grey eyes were undefeated, the shock of straw-coloured hair had no hint of grey in it'), their parting is again the cause of stiff-upper-lipped sorrow:

Leiter drove them [Bond and Tiffany Case] out to the airport and dropped them there. Bond felt a lump in his throat when the lanky figure limped off to his car . . .
    'You got yourself a good pal there', said the girl . . .
    'Yes,' said Bond, 'Felix is all right.'[44]

'Bond treasured his men friends', Fleming later tells us in *The Man with the Golden Gun*, 'and Felix was a great slice of his past.'
    There are other manly figures with whom Bond feels the same sense of easy equality and trusting camaraderie: Dako Kerim, who is Britain's staunchest ally in Istanbul; Marc-Ange Draco, who is boss of the Union Corse, and briefly Bond's father-in-law; and Tiger Tanaka, the head of the Japanese Secret Service. They all have appropriately 'firm dry handshakes', and evoke 007's deepest feelings of 'respect' and 'affection'. And so, lower down the social scale, does Quarrell, the Cayman Islander, who helps Bond in his early Caribbean adventures. He belongs to 'the most famous race of seamen in the world', and boasts 'the blood of Cromwellian soldiers and buccaneers'. Bond's relationship with him is 'that of a Scots laird with his head stalker: authority was unspoken and there was no room for servility'. As befits his subordinate (but unservile) status, Quarrell 'followed Bond unquestioningly'; but he is killed in action in *Dr No*, and when he views Quarrell's body, 007 feels deep remorse for having let him down:

He had to say goodbye . . . He said softly, 'I'm sorry Quarrell.' . . . He remembered the soft ways of the big body, the innocence in the grey, horizon-seeking eyes, the simple lusts and desires, the reverence for superstition and instincts, and childish faults, the loyalty and even the love that Quarrell had given him – the warmth, that was the only word for it, of the man.[45]

For all its soft and sentimental centre, Bond's world is thus very much an action man's place. To be sure, it is being undermined by the Welfare State, by 'giving votes to women and "sexual equality"', and by 'fifty years of emancipation' which meant men wanted to be 'nannied' and women wanted to 'dominate', with the result that 'pansies of both sexes were everywhere'. But like most men of their generation, Fleming and Bond regarded 'masculine domination' as the 'natural state of affairs'.[46] The only women at headquarters are pliant secretaries, who fantasize about going out with him: Loelia Ponsonby, Miss Moneypenny and Mary Goodnight. As a group, Bond believes women are indifferent drivers, unable to do a man's work, and essentially 'for recreation'. Early in *Casino Royale*, he is faced with the prospect of working with Vesper Lynd, and he responds as follows: 'On the job they got in the way and fogged things up with sex and hurt feelings and all the emotional baggage they carried around.' Later on, she is abducted by Le Chiffre, and Bond's fury knows no bounds:

These blithering women, who thought they could do a man's work. Why the hell couldn't they stay at home and mind their pots and pans and stick to their frocks and their gossip, and leave men's work for the men.[47]

As one commentator rightly notes, Fleming, like Buchan, regarded women 'as a kind of permanent second eleven, one or two of whom might in an emergency be allowed to field as substitutes'. But for the most part, their prime duty was to be 'always smiling and wanting to please'.[48]

Yet there was another side to Bond's belief in the permanent subordination and immutable inferiority of women, which also derived from the code of the clubland heroes. For even in his most exasperated moments, Bond admits that 'one had to look out for them, and take care of them', and he frequently does precisely that, often treating his 'girls' with a chivalrous mixture of kindness, affection, warmth and understanding. He 'makes up his own mind' about women, as about men, does not want girls who are 'in any way public property', and regularly behaves 'like a prince in the fairy tales', rescuing 'a damsel in distress' and giving her 'Tender Loving Care'.[49] When hearing of their troubles or shattered pasts, he listens with empathy and imagination, and tries to help them build a new life. This description would certainly apply to his treatment of Solitaire in *Live and Let Die*,

Tatiana Romanova in *From Russian With Love*, Honeychile Rider in *Dr No*, Pussy Galore in *Goldfinger*, Judy Havelock and Mrs Krest in *For Your Eyes Only*, Vivienne Mitchel in *The Spy Who Loved Me*, Dominetta Vitali in *Thunderball* and Tracy in *On Her Majesty's Secret Service*. Like many Bond heroines, Tracy is described (a very Buchan phrase, this) as 'a bird with a wing down and needed his help'. She was; she did; and she got it, as Bond feels 'a wave of affection for her, a sweeping urge to protect her, to solve her problems, make her happy'.

Here are paraded what seemed, by the 1950s and 1960s, to be the unfashionable qualities of chivalry and gallantry, and they are allied to the no-less unfashionable qualities of patriotism, bravery and a clear sense of right and wrong. Small wonder that Fleming's defenders described his novels as being 'entirely wholesome', for in many ways they *are* traditional morality tales about courage, fidelity and duty, about generosity towards the weak, hostility towards the wicked, and loyalty towards one's friends.[50] These were the values and virtues of the clubland heroes, and they lived on and thrived in the person of James Bond. Here he is, contemplating his mission in *Live and Let Die*:

Bond had gone out on the verandah and was gazing at the stars. Never before in his life had there been so much to play for. The secret of the treasure, the defeat of a great criminal, the smashing of a great Communist spy ring, and the destruction of a tentacle of SMERSH, the cruel machine that was his own private target. And now Solitaire, the ultimate personal prize.[51]

And here is a similar passage in *Dr No*: Bond 'admitted to himself that this adventure excited him. It had all the right ingredients – physical exertion, mystery, and a ruthless enemy. He had a good companion. His cause was just.'[52] As the author himself conceded on one occasion, borrowing one of his own phrases from his own novels, 'Bond is really a latter-day Saint George. He does kill wicked dragons after all.'[53]

All this helps explain why, soon after Ian Fleming's death, his friend William Plomer noted that his books were 'brilliant romantic fairytales, in which a dragon-slaying, maiden-rescuing hero wins battle after battle against devilish forces of destruction, and yet is indestructible himself.' And the result was the successful re-creation of what has rightly been called a 'world of high Buchanesque adventure'. Appropriately enough, John F. Kennedy admired both Fleming and Buchan, for their skilful blending of overt romance and latent emotion, and in *The Man with the Golden Gun*, Fleming returned the compliment.[54] For Bond sets out to read Kennedy's book, *Profiles in Courage*, where he is thrilled by 'the high endeavours of great men'. This was a very nineteenth-century view of the world, in which individual heroes changed the course of history, and there was much that was very nineteenth century about Fleming's outlook. In *Thrilling Cities*, he had quoted the Chief of Police in Los Angeles, who deplored 'the decline and fall of mid-Victorian values in Anglo-American civilization, leaving the individual to mature in a society that fails to establish a clear moral definition of right and wrong'. 'These are strong words,' Fleming adds. 'I dare say we in Britain would second them.'[55] Not everyone would; but the author of James Bond certainly did; and he did so in his novels at the very time when Richard Usborne had pronounced such Victorian values to be dead.

V

Thus understood, Ian Fleming was the champion and successor of the club-land heroes in a degenerate age who, like M, was opposed to the domestic decline, and to the softening of the national backbone, which he believed had been ushered in by the postwar Labour governments, the Welfare State and the emancipation of women. But that was not how all his contemporaries regarded Fleming, or received his novels. For his critics believed that his work did not deplore Britain's decline at all: on the contrary, it seemed to them to depict it graphically, and to welcome it eagerly. According to such self-appointed guardians of national standards as Bernard Bergonzi, Paul Johnson, James Price and Mordecai Richler, the Bond books were not 'entirely wholesome' but 'morally repugnant': they lacked 'any ethical frame of reference', they were as anti-humanist as they were anti-Christian, and they were thus 'the completest possible contrast' to Buchan's work and world. Far from being a conservative writer with a 'Tory imagination', Fleming deserved the blame for encouraging the very trend he affected to lament, namely that 'the liberal spirit was getting out of hand'.[56] How was it that the Bond books, which were in so many ways so derivative of Buchan, were seen by Fleming's critics as being the denial of everything that they believed Buchan had stood for?

Part of the answer lay in what was termed the 'affective superstructure' of the Bond books, the detailed descriptions of places and gadgets and meals, which seemed to parade and endorse the very materialism that, elsewhere in his writings, Fleming claimed to abhor and condemn.[57] And there can be no doubt that, even allowing for the rising living standards of the

1950s and early 1960s, Bond lived exceptionally well. 'There are moments of great luxury in the life of a secret agent,' Fleming writes at the outset of *Live and Let Die*, and throughout the books 007 had plenty of them. He stays in five-star hotels (where the room service is invariably impeccable), dines in expensive restaurants (where the food and wine are of the highest quality), and golfs and gambles in exclusive clubs (with other people of exceptional worldly distinction). He flies in Stratocruisers and Constellations, Viscounts and Comets, and this in the days when air travel was much more glamorous and exclusive than it is now. He returns from one mission to the United States in the 'great safe, black belly' of the *Queen Elizabeth*, and from another to Istanbul on the Orient Express, 'one of the most romantic [trains] in the world'. In Europe, he drives a Bentley or an Aston Martin, in America a Studebaker or a Thunderbird. His favourite meal is an almost unlimited supply of scrambled eggs, he smokes sixty to seventy cigarettes a day, washed down with half a bottle of spirits, and with additional (and abundant) wine and champagne when he is eating and drinking on the job.

This was scarcely the restrained, understated world of John Buchan's gentlemanly heroes. For all his Scottish puritanism and delight in being fit, Bond is (like Fleming) also an exceptionally self-indulgent man and, with his arteries clogged with cholesterol, his lungs damaged by nicotine and his liver injured by alcohol, it is almost inconceivable that he could have undertaken the physically demanding tasks he was regularly called upon by M to perform. Yet it was not so much Bond's manifest unfittedness for his work which irked the critics as the vulgar and detailed relish with which Fleming described his material circumstances. For the resulting 'fantasies of upper class life' glorified consumer spending and consumer culture in ways they did not like, and confirmed their worst forebodings that, in the era of the 'affluent society', the whole British population was now living (as Bernard Levin put it) 'in a haze of Drambuie, After Eight chocolates, Kosset carpets, Swedish glass, Viyella blankets, Lanvin perfume and king-sized cigarettes'. By thus glamorizing the possession and accumulation of worldly goods, Fleming seemed to his critics to be encouraging individual greed and personal gain – shallow and selfish (and godless) activities which were incompatible with the sterner imperatives of national greatness, and were, indeed, inimical to them.[58]

It was bad enough that the Bond books celebrated the 'affluent society': it was even worse that they prefigured the sexual liberation of the 'permissive society'. For notwithstanding his admiration of M's 'Victorian upbringing' and 'Victorian soul', Fleming had no time for 'Victorian morality', as he made clear in 'If I Were Prime Minister':

I should proceed to a complete reform of our sex and gambling laws, and endeavour to cleanse the country of the hypocrisy with which we so unattractively clothe our vices . . . I would consult with my Minister of Leisure about the possibility of turning the Isle of Wight into one vast pleasuredome . . . This would be a world where the frustrated citizen of every class could give rein to those basic instincts for sex and gambling which have been crushed through the ages . . . Since it is impossible to suppress the weaknesses of mankind, I would at least put an honest face on the problem, and do something to release the *homme moyen sensuel*, or *femme* for the matter of that, from some of their burden of shame and sin.[59]

He ventured the same opinion in *Thrilling Cities*. Hamburg was 'one of my favourite cities in the world', largely because 'normal heterosexual "vice" is permitted to exist in appropriate "reservations" and on condition that it remains local and light-hearted. How very different', he added, 'from the prudish and hypocritic manner in which we so disgracefully mismanage these things in England.' And in the Orient, things were even better, for there sex was 'a delightful pastime, totally unconnected with sin – a much lighter, airier affair than in the West.'[60]

Thus Fleming: and thus 007. For Bond's chivalrous treatment of women has its limits – and they are limits which he often transgresses. In one guise, he may be a knight-errant, helping damsels in distress; but he is also a promiscuous predator, who lusts after women, provided they are beautiful, with no subtlety, or reticence or shame or guilt.[61] In *Casino Royale*, Fleming introduced Vesper Lynd as the prototypical available-and-ultimately-disposable 'girl': Bond is 'excited by her beauty'; her dress is 'lasciviously tight across her fine breasts'; and he 'wants to sleep with her, but only when the job was done'. Thus perceived, Lynd and her successors are essentially sex objects, animated pin-ups, with exotic names, wide mouths, firm breasts and pert behinds; they all 'love semi-rape. They love to be taken'; and Bond duly takes them – and then throws them away. For he has no wish to establish, and no capacity to sustain, a long-term relationship. Instead, his liaisons (like Fleming's) follow a 'conventional parabola': 'sentiment, the touch of the hand, the kiss, the passionate kiss, the feel of the body, the climax in the bed, then more bed, then less bed, then the boredom, the tears and the final bitterness.' This is not chivalry; it is lechery. Unlike Buchan's heroes, but like his creator, Bond is (as his critics alleged) no gentleman.[62]

Vulgar materialism and sexual licence did not form the code of the clubland heroes. Nor did they spend time in casinos. But Bond frequently does, sharing with his creator the view that the desire to gamble – like the desire for sex – was innate, and that the activity was both harmless and pleasurable. So it is that in *Casino Royale, Moonraker, Diamonds Are Forever, Thunderball* and *On Her Majesty's Secret Service* Fleming's prose lights up when he describes the atmosphere, the action and the excitement of the gaming-tables. This was especially the case in *Moonraker*, where his luxuriant descriptions of Blades Club drove his sternest critics to paroxysms of rage. Naturally, Blades is 'the most famous private cards club in the world', and the scene of 'the highest polite gambling in the world'. Of necessity, 'the food and wine are the best in London', and the servants 'have no equal'. When Bond dines there as M's guest, prior to the famous bridge game with Sir Hugo Drax, he looks around:

It was a sparkling scene. There were perhaps fifty men in the room, the majority in dinner jackets, all at ease with themselves and their surroundings, all stimulated by the peerless food and drink, all animated by common interest – the prospect of high gambling, the grand slam, the ace pot, the key throw in a 64 game at backgammon. There might be cheats or possible cheats among them, men who beat their wives, men with perverse instincts, greedy men, cowardly men, lying men; but the elegance of the room invested each one with a kind of aristocracy.[63]

For Fleming, gambling was, like sex, a 'basic instinct', a harmless enjoyment; but to his critics (including his wife), this description had 'an air of vulgarity and display', which they found reprehensible.[64] Indeed, the glorification of gambling, sex and high living, which was so characteristic of the Bond books, seemed to them to mirror all that was rotten in contemporary British life: the introduction of the Premium Bond, the sensational and sordid revelations of the Profumo affair, and the 'you've-never-had-it-so-good' philosophy of Harold Macmillan. This was a country and an establishment (to which, as the critics did not hesitate to point out, the Flemings belonged) that was going rapidly to the dogs; and the Bond novels were helping speed it on its way. Add to their general tone of indulgent and amoral decadence, the violent torture scene in *Casino Royale*, the fight between gipsy women in *From Russia With Love*, and the squalid seduction and abortion in *The Spy Who Loved Me*, and it was easy to see why Paul Johnson dismissed the books as being 'obsessed with the sadism of the schoolboy bully, the mechanical, two-dimensional longings of a frustrated adolescent, and the crude snob-cravings of the suburban adult'. Instead of upholding the admirable values of the clubland heroes, the Bond novels were thus a 'systematic onslaught on everything decent and sensible in modern life'.[65]

VI

It should by now be clear that, as befitted the son of a puritan father and a promiscuous mother, Fleming's attitude towards Britain's domestic decline was genuinely equivocal. At one level, his books *did* urge a return to the stern Victorian values of his youth, which were becoming increasingly unfashionable in the 'softer' world in which he wrote and Bond worked. But they also approved and celebrated the more relaxed sexual ethos of a postwar generation in revolt against conventional Victorian morality, as Fleming himself had always been. So it was scarcely surprising that the books were praised by some for being 'entirely wholesome', and condemned by others for being 'morally repugnant', with equal conviction and plausibility. There is a similar ambiguity in Fleming's treatment of international decline, although this was more a response to contemporary circumstances than a sign of the contradictions of his character. He had grown up when Britain was the greatest power in the world; but, as foreign manager of Kemsley Newspapers, he was fully aware of Britain's lessened standing after 1945; and this tension between past glories and present uncertainties was never resolved in the novels. In the early Bond books, Fleming paid scarcely any attention to Britain's weakened international position; halfway through the series, he was obliged to recognize that Bond was operating against the 'canvas of a diminishing England'; yet to the very end, he also tried to pretend that the British nation and Empire were still strong.[66]

The first seven novels, from *Casino Royale* (1953) to *Goldfinger* (1959), depict England in general and Bond in particular as being in the front line of the Cold War against the Russians, just as Richard Hannay had once been against the Germans. The enemy may have changed; but the struggle among the Great Powers remains. In *Casino Royale*, Bond is helped by 'our French friends' and 'our American colleagues' in his attempt to discredit Le Chiffre, the communist trade unionist who would be a powerful fifth columnist in France 'in the event of a war with redland'. But in attacking the Russians in this way, Bond and the British Secret Service are in fact asserting their primacy within the Western alliance. For the job is one which the French should have done, and which the Americans wanted to do. But the British get there first. 'Washington's pretty sick we're not running the show . . .', Leiter explains to Bond. 'Anyway, I'm under your orders, and I'm to give you any help you ask for.' Of course, the United States does give help, to the tune of thirty-two million francs, which bail Bond out at the gaming-tables; but this timely example of Marshall Aid is not allowed to detract from the fact that it is the British who are essentially in charge.

There is, then, little trace in these early books of the reality of that 'special relationship' by which Britain became increasingly dependent on America in the postwar period. On the contrary, the situation depicted in the Bond novels is often the exact reverse. In *Live and Let Die*, Bond is ostensibly subordinate to the American Secret Service while in the United States, but he inflicts far greater injury on Mr Big's organization than does the relatively inept Leiter. And, later in the novel, while Leiter bungles his attack on the villain and is injured by the shark, it is Bond who successfully avenges him. In the same way, although *Diamonds Are Forever* is set entirely in the United States, it is Bond who takes on and defeats the Spangled Mob; something which the Americans are too timid or inept to accomplish for themselves. Once again, as Leiter enviously and admiringly notes, 007 is playing 'in a bigger league' than he is. Accordingly, as Bond explains to Leiter in *Thunderball*, it is the United Kingdom rather than the United States which still carries the burden of defending the West. Peace may be 'bustin' out all over' in the Great American Republic, but for Britain, circumstances are different:

Perhaps it's just that in England we don't feel quite as secure as you do in America. The war just doesn't seem to have ended for us. Berlin, Cyprus, Kenya, Suez . . . There always seems to be something boiling up somewhere.[67]

Thus (in the manner of Churchill's image of FDR in his wartime memoirs) the worldly-wise representative of a great power explains the facts of international life to the naïve and provincial American.

This comforting theme of Britain's continued pre-eminence among the great powers of the West is most elaborately developed in *From Russia With Love*. For in the early chapters, the Soviet Secret Service, anxious to attack 'the heart of the intelligence apparatus of the West', assesses the relative military and political strengths of their Western opponents. Norway, Holland, Belgium and Portugal are instantly written off: 'we need not worry about these smaller countries'. As for the Italians and the Spanish, they, too, 'can be dismissed . . . They are clever and active, but they do us no harm.' Recent political gains by the communists also mean that France is 'looking after itself '. Even the Americans, although possessing 'the biggest and richest service', have 'no understanding for the work. Good spies will not work for money alone – only bad spies; of which the Americans have several divisions.' Which leaves the British as the 'best of an indifferent lot':

Their security service is excellent. England, being an island, has great security advantages, and their so-called MI5 employs men with good education and good brains. Their secret service is still better. They have notable successes. In certain types of operation, we are constantly finding that they have been there before us. Their agents are good. They pay them little money . . . but they serve with devotion. Yet these agents have no special privileges in England, no relief from taxation, and no special shops such as we have, from which they can buy cheap foods. Their social standing abroad is not high, and their wives have to pass as wives of secretaries. They are rarely awarded a decoration until they retire. And yet those men and women continue to do this dangerous work. It is curious. It is perhaps the public school and university tradition. The love of adventure.[68]

So, in Russian eyes, the British Secret Service is incomparably the most impressive, against which 'an act of terrorism' is the best way of damaging the Western alliance.

But this buoyant depiction of Britain's place in the world was becoming increasingly difficult to maintain by the late 1950s, in the aftermath of Suez and with decolonization gathering momentum. For Fleming himself, the single most important lesson which he learned from his world tour collecting material for *Thrilling Cities* was 'the fantastically rapid contraction in our influence, commercial and cultural, over half the globe'; and the later Bond novels vividly convey this intensified sense of contraction and retreat.[69] In the title story of *For Your Eyes Only*, a book which marks this fundamental turning-point in the series, Bond urged the need to assassinate the villain because 'if foreign gangsters find they can get away with this sort of thing, they'll decide the English are as soft as some other people seem to think we are'. In 'Quantum of Solace', the British Empire is described as 'crumbling'; and in 'The Hildebrand Rarity', Milton Krest, the obnoxious American millionaire, makes the same point:

'Nowadays,' said Mr. Krest, 'there were only three powers – America, Russia and China. That was the big poker game, and no other country had either the chips or the cards to come into it. Occasionally some pleasant little country – like England – would be lent some money so that they could take a hand with the grown-ups. But that was just being polite, like one sometimes had to be – to a chum in one's club who's gone broke. No. England – nice people, mind you, good sports – was a place to see the old buildings and the Queen and so on.'[70]

Thereafter, further evidence of Britain's national decline is inescapable. In *On Her Majesty's Secret Service*, the College of Arms is preoccupied with designing the flags, arms, stamps and currency of the newly independent African nations; and even Bond himself is nostalgic for past glories. M's naval stories, he realizes, are 'about a great navy that was no more, and a great breed of seamen and officers that would never be seen again'. And by 1964, M is pictured as the head of a service recently discredited by scandal, so that the Americans are now 'worried about our security'. 'He probably doesn't think much of us,' M tells Bond when describing Tiger Tanaka, head of the Japanese Secret Service. 'People don't these days.' Indeed, the whole plot of *You Only Live Twice* centres on the attempt by Bond to obtain important secret information from the Japanese to which the Americans will no longer allow Britain access. For by this time, the theme of Anglo-American co-operation which was so pronounced in the earlier novels is more muted. In the first seven books, Leiter appears as Bond's ally on four occasions. In the remaining seven books, he, too, only lives twice. Even the Russians have come to feel that 'America will not risk a nuclear war . . . for the sake of rescuing a now more or less valueless ally – an ally now openly regarded in Washington as of little more account than Belgium or Italy' – a stark contrast to the ready and robust power that had so worried the Soviets in *From Russia With Love*.[71]

How then did Fleming, romantic, patriotic, but all too well aware of the evidence of Britain's global withdrawal, adapt his later novels to this decline in Britain's international position? One solution was to recognize what had happened and change the plots to take account of it. So, from the time of *Thunderball*, and on the pretext that 'with the cold war wearing off, it was not like old days', Britain is no longer located in the forefront of the battle against Soviet Russia. SMERSH and the Russian Secret Service take a back seat, to be replaced as the main enemy by Blofeld, and SPECTRE, which is, significantly, described as 'freelance . . . an independent gang working for whoever was willing to pay for them'. Accordingly, *Thunderball*, *On Her Majesty's Secret Service* and *You Only Live Twice* are dominated by SPECTRE and, after the murder of Tracy, Bond's personal vendetta against Blofeld replaces the machinations of the great powers as the centre of attention. Even in those novels where SPECTRE is absent, the setting of the Cold War, with Britain in the front line, is not revived. In *The Spy Who Loved Me*, the villains are relatively small-time American gangsters. Only two of the short stories in *For Your Eyes Only* are in any way connected with Soviet Russia. And even though Scaramanga in *The Man with the Golden Gun* has communist affiliations, he is almost a small-time crook compared with those whom Bond has previously taken on.

But although the later books are appropriately set in a more confined world of imperial retreat and eroded national confidence, they also try to perpetuate the comfortable illusion that despite everything that has happened, nothing has really altered. Notwithstanding the Suez débâcle, the Americans are still playing second string to the British. In *Thunderball* and *The Man with the Golden Gun*, Leiter again bungles things, has to be rescued by Bond, and is then helped to safety while the British hero carries on to complete the mission. Cricket, we are assured, 'is a much more difficult and skilful game than baseball'. And although the American nuclear submarines are fitted with the Mark B reactor, Bond disparagingly describes that as 'Steam-age stuff – our navy's got the Mark C'. In the same way, when crime and violence in Toronto get too much for the local police to sort out, 'the mounties even went so far as to call in two top CID sleuths from Scotland Yard to help them out'. And Blofeld's defeat at the hands of Bond only boosts Britain's position further: 'when they were pushed, the British could do this sort of thing supremely well'. Finally, in *The Man with the Golden Gun*, the escapist theme reaches its fullest development. For while independence may have come to Jamaica and the imperial flag been hauled down, in practice, Fleming reassures us, nothing has changed:

For all her new-found independence, he could bet his bottom dollar that the statue of Queen Victoria in the centre of Kingston had not been destroyed or removed to a museum as similar relics of an historic infancy had been in resurgent African states.[72]

In such an agreeable outpost of empire, the regrettable reality of change can be ignored, and Fleming successfully takes us with him into this world fantasy where the Pax Britannica has never ended.

While in one sense, therefore, the later Bond novels recognize the reality of Britain's decline, they also try to pretend it has never happened, and in *You Only Live Twice* this ambiguity is vividly encapsulated in an exchange between Bond and Tiger Tanaka. Initially, Bond is taunted by Tiger with the enfeebled state of his country:

'You have not only lost an empire, you have seemed almost anxious to throw it away with both hands . . . When you apparently sought to arrest this slide into impotence at Suez, you succeeded only in stage-managing one of the most pitiful bungles in the history of the world . . . Your governments have shown themselves successively incapable of ruling, and have handed over effective control of the country to the trade unions, who appear to be dedicated to the principle of doing less and less work for more money. This feather-bedding, this shirking of an honest day's work, is sapping at ever-increasing speed the moral fibre of the British, a quality the world once so admired. In its place, we now see a vacuous, aimless horde of seekers after pleasure.'

Thus Tanaka: and thus, in their heart of hearts, Fleming and Coward, and M and Bond. But our hero replies with spirit:

'England may have been bled pretty thin by a couple of world wars, our Welfare State policies may have made us expect too much for free, and the liberation of our Colonies may have gone too fast, but we still climb Everest and beat plenty of the world at sports, and win plenty of Nobel Prizes . . . There's nothing wrong with the British people.'

And to make us feel even more comforted, Tiger then admits that this is really his view too. 'Those are', he explains, 'very similar to the words I addressed to my Prime Minister.' So, once more, reality may have broken in briefly; but it is soon forgotten.[73]

VII

As befitted an admirer of the clubland heroes of his youth, who was also thought by many people to be something of a cad, Ian Fleming's attitude towards his country 'in decline' was by turns varied and equivocal, ambiguous and contradictory.[74] In the era of Churchill and Attlee, Macmillan and Gaitskell, Charles Clore and Hughie Green, Lord Longford and John Profumo, he certainly recognized 'decline' was happening, socially and politically, internally and internationally. And in so far as he welcomed increasing sexual freedom and the accompanying shift in moral values, he found such 'decline' congenial, and was anxious that it should proceed more rapidly. But to its other manifestations, Fleming's response was far less enthusiastic. For he profoundly regretted the passing of those stern, upright (Scottish?) qualities which he was sure had made his country great, and he feared that Britain's once pre-eminent global position had been irretrievably weakened because of the easy living and material excesses of the Welfare State, which he believed had sapped the fibre and will of the people. In such unhappy times, he took refuge in an international world of make-believe, where imperial decline never happened, or where its consequences were minimal, and where it was possible to pretend that the clubland heroes were still playing, and winning, the great game.

Awareness and approval, recognition and regret, denial and delusion:

such were Fleming's responses to the national retreat which was happening all around him. This was partly because Britain's decline *was* a genuinely complex thing, and partly because Fleming was a genuinely complex character, which meant he was both an admirer of the Victorians and an enemy of the Victorians, a conservative in politics and a liberal in morality. And so he wanted, simultaneously and contradictorily, to be more permissive and more puritanical, more self-indulgent and more self-denying. Had he been prime minister, he would have encouraged sexual freedom, made gambling easier, dismantled the Welfare State, and he would (above all) have reasserted Britain's place in the world. But Fleming never became prime minister, and events did not unfold in this way. For while he would have applauded the sexual revolution which had scarcely begun by the time of his death, he would have been appalled by the pop culture and the rebellious youth of the late 1960s and early 1970s. And although he would have appreciated the efforts by Margaret Thatcher to tame the trade unions, to roll back the Welfare State, to revive the nation's spirit of enterprise and adventure, to re-establish Victorian values, and to wave the flag and bang the drum, he would never have been socially at ease in the corner-shop world of the Grantham grocerocracy.

Nor would Fleming have been able to conceal from himself the continued evidence of Britain's inexorable decline, aptly symbolized by the sale of the family bank to Chase Manhattan in 2000.[75] Indeed, by the time of his death, that retreat had already become so marked that a whole new genre of post-Bond spy fiction was coming into being, which made Fleming's romantic patriotism, schoolboy adventures, easy certainties and assured victories look naïve, unsophisticated and hopelessly out of date. In 1962, Len Deighton's *The Ipcress File* signalled the arrival of a new sort of spy and a new sort of story: the anti-hero, Harry Palmer, living in bedsit-land, drinking Nescafé and watching the rain fall on damp and drab and dismal pavements. The following year, John le Carré scored his first sensational success with *The Spy Who Came in from the Cold* and, for the next two decades, his very different style of thriller dominated the genre. For in le Carré's world, the British Secret Service seems in almost terminal decay, uncertain of its mission and riddled by moles and double agents. There is no élan, no romance, no confidence, no high living: only treachery, betrayal, squalor, greyness, despair and an enfeebled and senescent *esprit de corps*. And while George Smiley's patriotism is absolute, he is emphatically no James Bond, no Richard Hannay, no clubland hero. On the contrary, he is subtle, cerebral and reflective; he is clever but not charismatic; he is unsuccessful with women and a cuckolded husband; and he is used to failure and unexhilarated by triumph.[76]

So, by the last quarter of the twentieth century, the great power certainties and heroic simplicities that had (albeit increasingly implausibly) underlain Fleming's books had vanished, and were no longer sustainable, even in the fantasy of fiction. Indeed, if James Bond had been a real-life, flesh-and-blood being, he would long since have despaired of his native land, and given it up as a lost cause, no longer worth living for, fighting for, killing for, or dying for. Angry and embittered at Britain's continued and seemingly irreversible decline, and bewildered and dismayed by women's liberation and the revolution in gender relations, the ageing Bond would eventually have settled into a retirement home at Royale-les-Eaux, the scene of his first great triumph, consoling himself with the novels of Frederick Forsyth, receiving occasional visitors, with whom he reminisced about the good bad old days, and drinking and chain-smoking his way to a grave not far from that of Vesper Lynd. All of which helps explain why, in the early twenty-first century, it is easy to condemn the Bond books for being racist and imperialist, sexist and misogynist, élitist and sadistic.[77] But this is merely another way of saying that we cannot understand the Bond books without reference to the personality, the outlook and the 'Tory imagination' of the man who wrote them, and to the time in which he wrote them; and that we cannot understand the 1950s and 1960s without some reference to them – and to him.

But while Fleming's world, and his hero's world, have long since vanished, James Bond still lives. Indeed, he has been a near-permanent fixture in popular culture, as an international celebrity and public property, for fifty years. Initially, this was because of the sensational success of the books; but since Fleming's death, it has been because of the long-running series of films.[78] The earliest adaptations – *Dr No*, *From Russia With Love*, *Goldfinger*, *Thunderball*, *Diamonds Are Forever* – kept faith with the substance and spirit of the novels; and Sean Connery was a convincing Bond, not only because of his ruthless good looks, but also on account of his Scottish background (although Fleming thought Connery's working-class Edinburgh accent made him inappropriate for the part).[79] But thereafter, the films took on a momentum and developed an identity all their own, which have projected and perpetuated Bond in a post-Fleming world. This was partly because the original stories eventually ran out; partly because later actors played Bond their way rather than Fleming's; partly because the films assumed a tone of cute flippancy and amused self-parody which is wholly absent from the books; partly because the end of the Cold War, the proliferation of nuclear weapons and the rise of international terrorism brought into being a wholly new geopolitical world; and partly because the producers had to recognize that there might be intelligent and well-educated women who would be immune to Bond's unsubtle and lustful blandishments. Indeed, in the most recent films, M is played by a woman. What would Bond, or Fleming, or any of Usborne's clubland heroes, have made of *that*? Or of *her*?

Acknowledgements

I am grateful to the editors and publishers of the journals and books in which these essays first appeared for permission to reproduce them here. The original locations and dates of publication were as follows:

1. *The Houses of Parliament: History, Art and Architecture*, ed. C. Riding and J. Riding (London, 2000).
2. *Understanding Decline: Perceptions and Realities of Britain's Economic Performance*, ed. P. Clarke and C. Trebilcock (Cambridge, 1997).
3. *Transactions of the Royal Historical Society*, 6th Series, xii (2002).
4. *'Blood, Toil, Tears and Sweat': Winston Churchill's Famous Speeches*, ed. D. Cannadine (London, 1989).
5. *Enlightenment, Passion and Modernity: Historical Essays in European Culture and Thought*, ed. M. S. Micale and R. Dietle (Stanford, 2000), copyright © 2000 by the Board of Trustees of the Leland Stanford Jr University, by permission of Stanford University Press.
6. *Staffordshire Studies*, xi (1999).
7. *Midland History*, iv (1978 for 1977).
8. *The New England Quarterly*, lxxii (1999).
9. *Myths of the English*, ed. R. Porter (Oxford, 1992).
10. *The National Trust: The Next Hundred Years*, ed. H. Newby (London, 1995).
11. *Encounter*, lx (March 1983).
12. *Encounter*, liii (September 1979).

The author and publishers would like to thank Glidrose Productions Ltd for permission to quote from the works of Ian Fleming, and William Heinemann for permission to quote from the works of Francis Brett Young. Extracts from the works of Noël Coward are published by kind permission of Methuen Publishing Ltd, copyright © the Estate of Noël Coward.

A Note on Sources

The following archival collections have been consulted in preparing the essays that have gone into this book:

Baldwin MSS: Stanley Baldwin Papers, University Library, Cambridge.

Brett Young MSS: Francis Brett Young Papers, Birmingham University Library, Birmingham.

BRL MSS: Local Collection, Birmingham Reference Library, Birmingham.

Bryant MSS: Arthur Bryant Papers, Liddell Hart Centre for Military Archives, King's College, London.

Harvard University MSS: Harvard University Archives, Harvard University, Cambridge, Mass.

HoP [W] MSS: Lord Wedgwood Papers, History of Parliament, Wedgwood House, London.

Jones MSS: Jones Archive, Beineke Library, Yale University, New Haven, Conn.

Lewis MSS: W. S. Lewis Papers, Lewis Walpole Library, Yale University, New Haven, Conn.

Merriman MSS: Merriman Family Papers, Massachusetts Historical Society, Boston Mass.

Nevins MSS: Allan Nevins Papers, Special Collections, Columbia University, New York, NY.

Notestein MSS: Wallace Notestein Papers, Sterling Library, Yale University, New Haven, Conn.

Pollard MSS: A. F. Pollard Papers, London University Library, Senate House, London.

PRO FO: Foreign Office Papers, Public Record Office, Kew.

Roosevelt MSS: Franklin Delano Roosevelt Papers, Presidential Library, Hyde Park, NY.

Yale Review MSS: *Yale Review* Papers, Beineke Library, Yale University, New Haven, Conn.

List of Abbreviations

The following abbreviations are used throughout the notes:

2 WW i–vi	W. S. Churchill, *The Second World War* (6 vols., London, 1948–54)
AHR	*American Historical Review*
Autobiography	S. Morley (ed.), *Noël Coward: Autobiography*, consisting of *Present Indicative, Future Indefinite and the uncompleted Past Conditional* (London, 1986)
BDP	*Birmingham Daily Post*
BP	*Birmingham Post*
Churchill i–viii	R. S. Churchill and M. Gilbert, *Winston S. Churchill* (8 vols., London, 1966–88)
CV i–v	R. S. Churchill and M. Gilbert, *Winston S. Churchill, Companion Volumes* (5 vols., London, 1966–82)
Diaries	G. Payn and S. Morley (eds.), *The Noël Coward Diaries* (London, 1982)
DNB	*Dictionary of National Biography*
Econ. Hist. Rev.	*Economic History Review*
ESP i–iv	W. S. Churchill, *A History of the English-Speaking Peoples* (4 vols., London, 1956–58)
Essays i–ii	*The Collected Essays of J. H. Plumb* (2 vols., London, 1988–89), vol. i, *The Making of an Historian*; vol. ii, *The American Experience*
FBY	Francis Brett Young
FDR	Franklin Delano Roosevelt
GMT	George Macaulay Trevelyan
HC	House of Commons
IF	Ian Fleming
JBY	Jessica Brett Young, *Francis Brett Young: A Biography* (London, 1962)
JCW	Josiah Wedgwood
Lyrics	*The Lyrics of Noël Coward* (London, 1965)

Marlborough i–ii	W. S. Churchill, *Marlborough: His Life and Times* (2 vol. edn, London, 1947). The original edition was in four volumes, published between 1933 and 1938
PP i–vi	Noël Coward, *Play Parade* (6 vols., London, 1934–62)
RBM	Roger Bigelow Merriman
SB	Stanley Baldwin
Speeches i–viii	R. Rhodes James (ed.), *Winston S. Churchill: His Complete Speeches, 1897–1963* (8 vols., London, 1974) – see note 7, chapter 4, for the original editions' titles and dates
TLS	*Times Literary Supplement*
Trevelyan	D. Cannadine, *G. M. Trevelyan: A Life in History* (London, 1992)
TWC	W. S. Churchill, *The World Crisis* (6 vols., London, 1923–31): *1911–14* (1923) *1915* (1923) *1916–18*, part i (1927) *1916–18*, part ii (1927) *The Aftermath* (1929) *The Eastern Front* (1931)
VCH	*Victoria History of the Counties of England*
Verse	G. Payn and M. Tickner (eds.), *Noël Coward: Collected Verse* (London, 1984)
WP i–ii	M. Gilbert, *The Churchill War Papers* (2 vols., London, 1993–4)
WSC	Winston Spencer Churchill

Notes

1 Parliament:
The Palace of Westminster as the Palace of Varieties

1. I am most grateful to Dr D. Birch, Ms C. Pearson, Ms C. Riding, Sir John Sainty and Mr E. P. Silk for their help, advice and encouragement during the preparation of this essay.

2. R. Quinault, 'Westminster and the Victorian Constitution', *Transactions of the Royal Historical Society*, 6th Series, ii (1992), p. 79.

3. For a fuller discussion of this contextual approach to the 'meaning' of buildings and ceremonial, see D. Cannadine, 'The Context, Performance and Meaning of Ritual: The British Monarchy and the "Invention of Tradition", *c.* 1820–1977', in E. Hobsbawm and T. Ranger (eds.), *The Invention of Tradition* (Cambridge, 1983), pp. 103–8, and the further references cited there.

4. T. S. R. Boase, 'The Decoration of the New Palace of Westminster, 1841–1863', *Journal of the Warburg and Courtauld Institute*, xvii (1954), p. 319; K. Solender, *Dreadful Fire! Burning of the Houses of Parliament* (Cleveland, 1984), pp. 27–30, 33.

5. R. J. B. Walker, 'The Palace of Westminster after the Fire of October 1834', *Walpole Society*, xliv (1972–4), p. 100; L. J. Colley, *Britons: Forging the Nation, 1707–1837* (London, 1992), p. 325.

6. The two most authoritative accounts of the design and construction of the New Palace of Westminster are M. H. Port (ed.), *The Houses of Parliament* (London, 1976); and M. H. Port, 'The New Houses of Parliament', in J. Mordaunt Crook and M. H. Port, *The History of the King's Works*, vol. vi, *1782–1851* (London, 1973), pp. 573–626, on both of which I have freely and frequently drawn in subsequent paragraphs.

7. F. M. L. Thompson, *The Rise of Respectable Society: A Social History of Victorian Britain, 1830–1900* (London, 1988), pp. 13–22; W. J. Rorabaugh, 'Politics and the Architectural Competition for the Houses of Parliament, 1834–1837', *Victorian Studies*, xviii (1973), p. 155.

8. K. Clark, *The Gothic Revival* (London, 1928), pp. 141–3; M. Girouard, *The Return to Camelot: Chivalry and the English Gentleman* (London, 1981), pp. 40–54; J. Mordaunt Crook, 'Introduction' to C. L. Eastlake, *A History of the Gothic Revival* (Leicester, 1970), pp. 50–57; C. L. Eastlake, *John Carter and the Mind of the Gothic*

Revival (London, 1995 edn), pp. 1, 4, 7–8, 11, 31–2; J. M. Frew, 'Gothic is English: John Carter and the Revival of Gothic as England's National Style', *Art Bulletin*, lxiv (1982), pp. 315–19; Port, *Houses of Parliament*, pp. 6–7, 30–32; J. Mordaunt Crook, *The Rise of the Nouveaux Riches: Style and Status in Victorian and Edwardian Architecture* (London, 1999), p. 235.

9. Port, *Houses of Parliament*, pp. 24–8; Rorabaugh, 'Architectural Competition', pp. 166–8.

10. Port, *Houses of Parliament*, p. 23.

11. Quinault, 'Victorian Constitution', p. 96; N. Pevsner, *The Buildings of England, London*, vol. i, *The Cities of London and Westminster* (Harmondsworth, 1957), p. 95; Rorabaugh, 'Architectural Competition', pp. 164, 173; Port, *Houses of Parliament*, pp. 71, 232.

12. Ibid., pp. 232–6.

13. Quinault, 'Victorian Constitution', pp. 81–6; Girouard, *Return to Camelot*, pp. 116–24, 179–81; M. Bond (ed.), *Works of Art in the House of Lords* (London, 1980), pp. 44–59, 66–83.

14. S. Sawyer, 'Sir John Soane's Symbolic Westminster: The Apotheosis of George IV', *Architectural History*, xlix (1996), pp. 60–61, 68–72; Port, *Houses of Parliament*, pp. 203–5.

15. P. Stanton, 'The Sources of Pugin's *Contrasts*', in J. Summerson (ed.), *Concerning Architecture: Essays on Architectural Writers and Writing presented to Nikolaus Pevsner* (London, 1968), pp. 128–39; P. Stanton, *Pugin* (London, 1971), pp. 81–4, 91–2, 170–71; D. Meara, 'The Catholic Context', and A. Saint, 'Pugin's Architecture in Context', both in P. Atterbury (ed.), *A. W. N. Pugin: Master of Gothic Revival* (London, 1995), pp. 45–61, 79–101; A. Wedgwood, 'Domestic Architecture', R. O'Donnell, 'Pugin as a Church Architect', M. Belcher, 'Pugin's Writing', and A. Wedgwood, 'The New Palace of Westminster', all in P. Atterbury and C. Wainwright (eds.), *Pugin: A Gothic Passion* (London, 1994), pp. 43–61, 63–89, 105–16, 219–36; Girouard, *Return to Camelot*, pp. 30–38, 56–66; Port, *Houses of Parliament*, pp. 256–7.

16. Quinault, 'Victorian Constitution', pp. 82, 86–91; C. Wainwright, 'Ceramics', in Atterbury and Wainwright, *Pugin: A Gothic Passion*, pp. 127–42; Boase, 'Decoration of the New Palace', p. 332; Bond, *Works of Art in the House of Lords*, pp. 84–91; Port, *Houses of Parliament*, pp. 187, 245–53.

17. C. Wainwright, 'A. W. N. Pugin and France', and P. Atterbury, 'Pugin and Interior Design', both in Atterbury, *Pugin: Master of Gothic Revival*, pp. 63–71, 177–99; A. Wedgwood, 'The Early Years', and L. Lambourne, 'Pugin and the Theatre', both in Atterbury and Wainwright, *Pugin: A Gothic Passion*, pp. 26–30, 35–41. According to one contemporary, 'the true bent of Pugin's mind was towards the theatre': Clark, *Gothic Revival*, p. 174.

18. Quinault, 'Victorian Constitution', pp. 82–5; W. L. Arnstein, 'Queen Victoria Opens Parliament: The Disinvention of Tradition', *Historical Research*, lxiii (1990), pp. 184–5.

19. Quinault, 'Victorian Constitution', pp. 86–7, 103–4; D. Cannadine, 'The Last Hanoverian Sovereign? The Victorian Monarchy in Historical Perspective,

1688–1988', in A. L. Beier, D. Cannadine and J. Rosenheim (eds.), *The First Modern Society: Essays in English History in Honour of Lawrence Stone* (Cambridge, 1989), pp. 139–46; G. H. L. Le May, *The Victorian Constitution: Conventions, Usages and Contingencies* (London, 1979), pp. 22–96; G. E. Buckle (ed.), *The Letters of Queen Victoria*, 2nd Series, *1862–85* (3 vols., London, 1926), vol. ii, pp. 165–6.

20. J. H. Plumb, 'The Growth of the Electorate in England from 1600 to 1715', *Past & Present*, no. 45 (1969), p. 116; G. Holmes, *The Electorate and the National Will in the First Age of Party* (Kendal, 1976), pp. 9–24; Colley, *Britons*, pp. 349–50; D. E. D. Beales, 'The Electorate Before and After 1832: the Right to Vote, and the Opportunity', *Parliamentary History*, xi (1992), pp. 139–50; F. O'Gorman, 'The Electorate Before and After 1832', *Parliamentary History*, xii (1993), pp. 171–83.

21. Boase, 'Decoration of the New Palace', p. 341; M. Hay and J. Riding, *Art in Parliament: The Permanent Collection of the House of Commons* (London, 1996), pp. 104–6. Pugin himself designed many churches and chapels for Ireland: see R. O'Donnell, 'The Pugins in Ireland', in Atterbury, *Pugin: Master of Gothic Revival*, pp. 137–59.

22. G. W. Martin: 'Empire Federalism and Imperial Parliamentary Union, 1820–1870', *Historical Journal*, xvi (1973), pp. 65–92; and 'The Idea of "Imperial Federation"', in R. Hyam and G. Martin, *Reappraisals in British Imperial History* (London, 1975), pp. 125–9; Bond, *Works of Art in the House of Lords*, pp. 11, 95. It was originally planned to commission a series of paintings referring to 'the acquisition of the countries, colonies and important places constituting the British Empire', but these were never proceeded with: Boase, 'Decoration of the New Palace of Westminster', p. 342.

23. N. Gash, *Reaction and Reconstruction in English Politics, 1832–1852* (Oxford, 1965), pp. 1–59; Arnstein, 'Disinvention of Tradition', pp. 185–7.

24. F. W. S. Craig, *British Electoral Facts, 1832–1987* (5th edn, Aldershot, 1989), p. 67.

25. Port, *Houses of Parliament*, pp. 50–51, 73–80, 97–121; Rorabaugh, 'Architectural Competition', pp. 155–75.

26. Ibid., pp. 1, 53, 142–94, 298.

27. Ibid., pp. 119, 232, 268–79; Boase, 'Decoration of the New Palace', pp. 343–58; Hay and Riding, *Art in Parliament*, p. 10; Bond, *Houses of Parliament*, pp. 39–42.

28. Stanton, *Pugin*, p. 33; Meara, 'The Catholic Context', p. 60; Saint, 'Pugin's Architecture in Context', p. 92.

29. R. Blake, *Disraeli* (London, 1998 edn), pp. 167–73, 190–202, 208–11, 270–78, 545–9, 562–9; Meara, 'The Catholic Context', p. 55; O'Donnell, 'Pugin as a Church Architect', p. 64; Girouard, *Return to Camelot*, pp. 80–86, 200. For a more nuanced account of Disraeli's attitude to the peerage and the upper house see D. Slater, 'Beaconsfield: or Disraeli in the Elysian Fields', in H. S. Cobb (ed.), *Parliamentary History, Libraries and Records: Essays Presented to Maurice Bond* (London, 1981), pp. 66–76.

30. Port, *Houses of Parliament*, pp. 94–6.

31. See ch. 9.

32. Cannadine, 'Invention of Tradition', pp. 133–4; J. Lant, *Insubstantial Pageant: Ceremony and Confusion at Queen Victoria's Court* (London, 1979).

33. Cannadine, 'Invention of Tradition', pp. 120–21, 139; C. C. Weston, 'The Royal Mediation in 1884', *English Historical Review*, lxxxii (1967), pp. 296–322; V. Bogdanor, *The Monarchy and the Constitution* (Oxford, 1995), pp. 113–44.

34. D. Cannadine, *The Decline and Fall of the British Aristocracy* (London, 1990), pp. 37–54, 195–206, 308–25, 458–72.

35. D. Butler, *The Electoral System in Britain Since 1918* (2nd edn, Oxford, 1963), pp. 7–57; N. Blewett, 'The Franchise in the United Kingdom, 1885–1918', *Past & Present*, no. 32 (1965), pp. 27–56; H. C. G. Matthew et al., 'The Franchise Factor and the Rise of the Labour Party', *English Historical Review*, xci (1982), pp. 820–31; D. M. Tanner, 'The Parliamentary Electoral System, the "Fourth" Reform Act and the Rise of Labour in England and Wales', *Bulletin of the Institute of Historical Research*, lvi (1983), pp. 205–19.

36. P. Hunting, *Royal Westminster* (London, 1981), p. 125; Cannadine, *Decline and Fall*, pp. 184–95.

37. A. F. Pollard, *The Evolution of Parliament* (2nd edn, London, 1926), pp. 16–17; N. Wilding and P. Laundy, *An Encyclopaedia of Parliament* (3rd edn, London, 1968), p. 791.

38. G. D. Phillips, *The Diehards: Aristocratic Society and Politics in Edwardian England* (London, 1979), pp. 82–110; A. Adonis, *Making Aristocracy Work: The Peerage and the Political System in Britain, 1884–1914* (Oxford, 1993), pp. 210–39; Cannadine, *Decline and Fall*, pp. 588–602.

39. D. Cannadine, *Aspects of Aristocracy: Grandeur and Decline in Modern Britain* (London, 1994), pp. 121–7.

40. Lord Meath, 'Shall Indian Princes Sit in the House of Lords?', *Nineteenth Century*, xxxv (1894), pp. 710–16; J. A. R. Marriott, 'The House of Lords as an Imperial Senate', *Fortnightly Review*, lxxxvii (1907), pp. 1003–17; S. M. Mitra, 'The House of Lords and the Indian Princes', *Fortnightly Review*, xciii (1910), pp. 1090–99; Cannadine, *Aspects of Aristocracy*, pp. 109–10.

41. Pollard, *Evolution of Parliament*, pp. 360, 369–73; Martin, 'Idea of "Imperial Federation"', pp. 131–4.

42. J. W. Lowther, *A Speaker's Commentaries* (2 vols., London, 1925), vol. i, pp. 306–7; Sir S. Lee, *King Edward VII: A Biography*, vol. ii, *The Reign* (London, 1927), pp. 21–23; M. V. Brett (ed.), *Journals and Letters of Reginald Viscount Esher* (4 vols., London, 1934–8), vol. i, pp. 284–5; Cannadine, 'Invention of Tradition', pp. 135–6.

43. For descriptions of state openings in the reigns of George V and Edward VIII, see R. Rhodes James (ed.), *'Chips': The Diaries of Sir Henry Channon* (London, 1967), pp. 74–5, 139; K. Rose, *King George V* (London, 1983), pp. 101–5, 131; F. Donaldson, *Edward VIII* (London, 1976), pp. 233–4; P. Ziegler, *King Edward VIII: The Official Biography* (London, 1990), pp. 264–5.

44. Port, *Houses of Parliament*, p. 280; Hay and Riding, *Art in Parliament*, pp. 26, 90–93, 98–101.

45. Pollard, *Evolution of Parliament*, pp. vi, 3, 9, 11; *Trevelyan*, pp. 110–26; L. J. Colley, *Namier* (London, 1989), pp. 74–7. See also M. MacDonagh, *The Pageant of Parliament*, vol. i (London, 1921), p. 7: 'Parliament . . . is, perhaps, as

fine and perfect an instrument of democratic government as can humanely be devised ... It is the fabric of the life of the people ... It is the country's chief political instrument of progressive civilisation.'

46. *Interim Report of the Committee on House of Commons Personnel and Politics, 1264–1832* (Cmd 4130, 1932), pp. 52–3; J. C. Wedgwood: 'The History of Parliament', *Fortnightly Review*, cxxxviii (1935), p. 173; and *History of Parliament: Biographies of the Members of the Commons House, 1439–1509* (London, 1936), pp. lii–liii; J. E. Neale, *Essays in Elizabethan History* (London, 1958), pp. 202–3. I am grateful to Dr Peter Mandler for this reference. See also ch. 6.

47. H. Boardman, *The Glory of Parliament* (London, 1960), p. 87.

48. *Surveys: A Publication of the Ideal Press Technical Group*, vol. i, no. 3 (March 1951), p. 70; *Speeches* viii, pp. 8108–10.

49. Rhodes James, *Diaries of Sir Henry Channon*, p. 75.

50. Cannadine, *Aspects of Aristocracy*, p. 129; D. W. Thomson, 'The Fate of Titles in Canada', *Canadian Historical Review*, x (1929), pp. 236–46; G. W. Martin: *Bunyip Aristocracy: The New South Wales Constitutional Debates and Hereditary Institutions in the British Colonies* (London, 1986), pp. 182–8; and 'Idea of "Imperial Federation"', p. 136.

51. F. Barker and R. Hyde, *London as it Might Have Been* (London, 1982), pp. 150–53; Port, *Houses of Parliament*, p. 281.

52. J. E. Kendle: 'The Round Table Movement and "Home Rule All Round"', *Historical Journal*, xi (1968), pp. 332–53; and *Federal Britain: A History* (London, 1997), pp. 58–78; P. Jalland, 'United Kingdom Devolution, 1910–14: Political Panacea or Tactical Diversion?', *English Historical Review*, xciv (1979), pp. 757–85; *Speeches* ii, pp. 2021–3.

53. Hay and Riding, *Art in Parliament*, pp. 106–7; Quinault, 'Victorian Constitution', p. 93; J. E. Kendle, 'Federalism and the Irish Problem in 1918', *History*, lvi (1971), pp. 207–30.

54. H. W. Lucy, *Memories of Eight Parliaments* (London, 1908), pp. 322–34; R. F. Foster, *Lord Randolph Churchill: A Political Life* (Oxford, 1981), pp. 101–2, 222–4, 243–4, 350.

55. Cannadine: *Aspects of Aristocracy*, pp. 156–60; and *Decline and Fall*, pp. 547–50.

56. M. H. Port, *Imperial London: Civil Government Building in London, 1851–1914* (London, 1995), pp. 233–51; R. G. Irving, *Indian Summer: Lutyens, Baker and Imperial Delhi* (London, 1981), pp. 89–90, 166–70; T. R. Metcalf, *An Imperial Vision: Indian Architecture and Britain's Raj* (London, 1989), pp. 176–210. The only British imperial legislature which the New Palace seems to have influenced was that in Ottawa (1859–67): Port, *Houses of Parliament*, pp. 298–308.

57. A. Bowness (ed.), *The Impressionists in London* (London, 1973), pp. 24–5, 33–8; P. H. Tucker, 'The Revolution in the Garden: Monet in the Twentieth Century', and G. T. M. Shackleford and M. A. Stevens, 'Series of Views of the Thames in London, 1899–1904', both in P. H. Tucker (ed.), *Monet in the Twentieth Century* (London, 1998), pp. 26–32, 128–47.

58. Pevsner, *Cities of London and Westminster*, pp. 461–2; Boardman, *Glory of*

Parliament, pp. 100–107. For two very well-disposed works, see K. Mackenzie, *The English Parliament* (Harmondsworth, 1950); R. Rhodes James, *An Introduction to the House of Commons* (London, 1961).

59. Boardman, *Glory of Parliament*, p. 198; Hansard, 5th Series, vol. 705, HC col. 668. See also ch. 4.

60. For a vivid account of Queen Elizabeth II's first state opening, see Boardman, *Glory of Parliament*, pp. 109–13.

61. D. Dimbleby, *Richard Dimbleby: a Biography* (London, 1975), pp. 340–43.

62. Martin: 'Empire Federalism', p. 66; and 'Idea of "Imperial Federation"', p. 135.

63. Cannadine, 'Invention of Tradition', p. 157.

64. E. Taylor, *The House of Commons at Work* (9th edn, London, 1979), pp. 176–8; H. Young, *This Blessed Plot: Britain and Europe from Churchill to Blair* (London, 1998), pp. 325–38, 422–34; K. Robbins, *The Eclipse of a Great Power: Modern Britain, 1870–1992* (2nd edn, London, 1994), pp. 376–86; P. Giddings and G. Drewery (eds.), *Westminster and Europe: The Impact of the European Union on the Westminster Parliament* (London, 1996).

65. H. Young, 'Why I'm so glad to be European', *Guardian*, 2 January 1999.

66. B. Lenman, *The Eclipse of Parliament: Appearance and Reality since 1914* (London, 1992); T. Nairn, *The Break-Up of Britain* (London, 1977); V. Bogdanor, *Devolution* (Oxford, 1979); Robbins, *Eclipse of a Great Power*, pp. 277–85, 396–400.

67. V. Bogdanor, 'Speaking up for stubborn England', *Independent*, 4 February 1999.

68. Wilding and Laundy, *Encyclopaedia of Parliament*, p. 434.

69. Cannadine, *Decline and Fall*, pp. 663, 674–5, 680–83; B. Crick, *The Reform of Parliament* (2nd edn, London, 1968), pp. 124–38.

70. The Hansard Society, *Parliamentary Reform, 1933–1958* (London, 1959), esp. pp. 61–127, 157–91, 214–23; N. Nicolson, *People and Parliament* (London, 1958), pp. 12, 21, 27, 169; J. Morgan, *The House of Lords and the Labour Government, 1964–1970* (Oxford, 1975).

71. P. Baines, 'History and Rationale of the 1979 Reforms'; P. Giddings, 'What Has Been Achieved?'; G. Drewery, 'The 1979 Reforms – New Labels on Old Bottles?': all in G. Drewery (ed.), *The New Select Committees: A Study of the 1979 Reforms* (Oxford, 1985), pp. 13–36, 367–81, 382–93.

72. For a recent discussion of many of the issues touched on in this and the preceding paragraphs, see P. Riddell, *Parliament Under Pressure* (London, 1998).

73. Pevsner, *Cities of London and Westminster*, p. 95.

74. R. J. B. Walker, *Catalogue of Paintings, Drawings, Sculpture and Engravings in the Palace of Westminster* (7 vols., London, 1959–67; 10-vol. supplement, London, 1965–76); Parliamentary Works Directorate: *The Victorian Tower Restored* (London, 1993), and *Five Years of Restoration and Improved Facilities, 1992–1997* (London, 1998). See also the following volumes of the *History of Parliament*: J. S. Roskell, L. Clark and C. Rawcliffe (eds.), *The House of Commons, 1386–1421* (4 vols., London, 1992); S. T. Bindoff (ed.), *The House of Commons, 1509–1558* (3 vols., London, 1982); P. W. Hasler (ed.), *The House of Commons, 1558–1603*

(3 vols., London, 1981); B. D. Henning (ed.), *The House of Commons, 1660–1690* (3 vols., London, 1983); R. Sedgwick (ed.), *The House of Commons, 1715–1754* (2 vols., London, 1970); Sir L. Namier and J. Brooke, *The House of Commons, 1754–1790* (3 vols., London, 1964); R. G. Thorne (ed.), *The House of Commons, 1790–1820* (5 vols., London, 1986).

75. Dimbleby, *Dimbleby*, pp. 340–43; R. Day, 'The State Opening of Parliament', in L. Miall (ed.), *Richard Dimbleby: Broadcaster* (London, 1966), pp. 110–14. For a recent re-articulation of this view, see M. Leonard, 'The Empire's new clothes', *Guardian*, 21 November 1998.

76. Hay and Riding, *Art in Parliament*, p. 79. For recent reaffirmations of the Pugin-cum-Dimbleby view of the state opening, see M. Brentnall, *Old Customs and Ceremonies of London* (London, 1975), pp. 132–4; J. Brooke-Little, *Royal Ceremonies of State* (London, 1980), pp. 75–81.

77. A. Parker, 'The ermine has to go, says Lady with an eye for reform of the Lords', *Financial Times*, 23 January 1999.

2 Statecraft:
The Haunting Fear of National Decline

1. The concept of national decline as explored here owes much to J. H. Elliott, 'The Decline of Spain', *Past & Present*, no. 20 (1961), pp. 52–75; J. H. Elliott, 'Self-Perception and Decline in Early Seventeenth-Century Spain', *Past & Present*, no. 74 (1977), pp. 41–61.

2. This paradox is suggestively explored in B. Supple, 'Fear of Failing: Economic History and the Decline of Britain', *Econ. Hist. Rev.*, 2nd Series, xlvii (1994), pp. 441–58.

3. K. Robbins, *The Eclipse of a Great Power: Modern Britain, 1875–1975* (London, 1983); D. A. Low, *The Contraction of England* (Cambridge, 1985); D. Reynolds, *Britannia Overruled: British Policy and World Power in the Twentieth Century* (London, 1991).

4. Sir J. Seeley, *The Expansion of England* (London, 1883), p. 8; J. G. Darwin, 'The Fear of Falling: British Politicians and Imperial Decline since 1900', *Transactions of the Royal Historical Society*, 5th Series, xxxvi (1986), pp. 29, 39–43.

5. A. Ramm (ed.), *The Political Correspondence of Mr. Gladstone and Lord Granville, 1876–86* (2 vols., London, 1962), vol. i, p. 85; H. C. G. Matthew, *Gladstone, 1875–1898* (Oxford, 1995), p. 24; P. Marsh, *The Discipline of Popular Government: Lord Salisbury's Domestic Statecraft, 1881–1902* (Hassocks, 1978), pp. 10–11, 276–7; J. H. Elliott, *The Count-Duke of Olivares: The Statesman in an Age of Decline* (London, 1986), esp. pp. 89–94, 116–19, 230–31, 394–5.

6. In addition to the works of J. H. Elliott, cited above, I have been much helped by the following: R. Starn, 'Meaning-Levels in the Theory of Historical Decline', *History and Theory*, xiv (1975), pp. 1–29; P. Burke, 'Tradition and Experience: The Idea of Decline from Bruni to Gibbon', *Daedalus*, no. 105 (1976), pp. 137–52; C. M. Cipolla (ed.), *The Economic Decline of Empires* (London, 1970); M. Olson, *The*

Rise and Decline of Nations: Economic Growth, Stagflation and Social Rigidities (London, 1982); S. Friedlander et al., *Visions of Apocalypse: End or Rebirth?* (London, 1985); P. M. Kennedy, *The Rise and Fall of the Great Powers: Economic Change and Military Conflict from 1500 to 2000* (London, 1988).

7. P. F. Clarke, *A Question of Leadership: Gladstone to Thatcher* (London, 1991), pp. 75–6. The essential books for Chamberlain's life are: J. Boyd (ed.), *Mr. Chamberlain's Speeches* (2 vols., London, 1914); J. L. Garvin and J. Amery, *The Life of Joseph Chamberlain* (6 vols., London, 1932–69); P. Fraser, *Joseph Chamberlain: Radicalism and Empire, 1868–1914* (London, 1966); R. Jay, *Joseph Chamberlain: A Political Study* (Oxford, 1981); M. Balfour, *Britain and Joseph Chamberlain* (London, 1985); P. Marsh, *Joseph Chamberlain: Entrepreneur in Politics* (London, 1994).

8. The Venetian iconography of Chamberlain's Birmingham still awaits its historian. For some suggestive hints, see: Marsh, *Chamberlain*, pp. 87, 97, 100, 102, 139–40; N. Pevsner and A. Wedgwood, *The Buildings of England: Warwickshire* (Harmondsworth, 1966), p. 170; A. P. D. Thomson, 'The Chamberlain Memorial Tower, University of Birmingham', *University of Birmingham Historical Journal*, iv (1954), pp. 174–9. See also chapter 5.

9. R. Quinault, 'John Bright and Joseph Chamberlain', *Historical Journal*, xxviii (1985), pp. 623–46.

10. Boyd, *Chamberlain's Speeches*, vol. ii, p. 181.

11. Marsh, *Chamberlain*, pp. 10, 74–6, 104, 181–2; B. Semmel, *Imperialism and Social Reform: English Social-Imperial Thought, 1895–1914* (London, 1960), pp. 84–90.

12. R. Hyam, *Britain's Imperial Century, 1815–1914: A Study of Empire and Expansion* (London, 1976), pp. 92–102; B. Porter, *The Lion's Share: A Short History of British Imperialism, 1850–1983* (2nd edn, London, 1985), pp. 75–151.

13. Marsh, *Chamberlain*, p. 164.

14. J. Chamberlain, 'A Bill for the Weakening of Great Britain', *Nineteenth Century*, xxxiii (1893), pp. 545–58; J. Loughlin, 'Joseph Chamberlain, English Nationalism and the Ulster Question', *History*, lxxvii (1992), pp. 202–19; N. M. Marris, *The Rt. Hon. Joseph Chamberlain: The Man and the Statesman* (London, 1900), p. 263; Boyd, *Chamberlain's Speeches*, vol. ii, pp. 272, 335.

15. Garvin and Amery, *Chamberlain*, vol. i, p. 498; Marsh, *Chamberlain*, pp. 176–78; Seeley, *Expansion of England*, pp. 15–16, 39–44, 51–5, 72–6, 133–4, 157–9, 293–308. See also: D. Wormell, *Sir John Seeley and the Uses of History* (Cambridge, 1980), pp. 95–6, 154–6, 162–3; P. Burroughs, 'John Robert Seeley and British Imperial History', *Journal of Imperial and Commonwealth History*, i (1973), pp. 191–212; P. M. Kennedy, *Strategy and Diplomacy, 1870–1945* (London, 1989), pp. 41–86.

16. Marris, *Chamberlain*, pp. 249, 318; Marsh, *Chamberlain*, p. 521; P. M. Kennedy, *The Rise and Fall of British Naval Mastery* (London, 1976), p. 220. See also A. L. Friedberg, *The Weary Titan: Britain and the Experience of Relative Decline, 1895–1905* (Princeton, 1988), pp. 21–88; G. R. Searle, *The Quest for National Efficiency: A Study in British Politics and Political Thought, 1899–1914* (Oxford, 1971), pp. 5–13; P. J. Cain and A. G. Hopkins, *British Imperialism*, vol. i, *Innovation*

and Expansion, 1688–1914 (London, 1993), pp. 202–25; E. H. H. Green, *The Crisis of Conservatism: The Politics, Economics and Ideology of the British Conservative Party, 1880–1914* (London, 1995), pp. 11–18, 27–56, 59–77, 194–206, 223–41.

17. Boyd, *Chamberlain's Speeches*, vol. ii, pp. 5, 108, 144–8, 177, 217, 267–8, 368; Garvin and Amery, *Chamberlain*, vol. iv, p. 177; Green, *Crisis of Conservatism*, pp. 35, 53–4.

18. Boyd, *Chamberlain's Speeches*, vol. i, pp. 238–9, 244–6, 255.

19. For the broader background, see J. E. Tyler, *The Struggle for Imperial Unity, 1868–95* (London, 1938); B. H. Brown, *The Tariff Reform Movement in Great Britain, 1881–95* (New York, 1943).

20. Marris, *Chamberlain*, pp. v, 4, 320, 374, 378–80, 383–6; Boyd, *Chamberlain's Speeches*, vol. i, pp. 322–3; vol. ii, pp. 67–72, 110, 366–9; R. Quinault, 'Joseph Chamberlain: A Reassessment', in T. R. Gourvish and A. O'Day (eds.), *Later Victorian Britain, 1876–1900* (London, 1988), pp. 84–5.

21. Boyd, *Chamberlain's Speeches*, vol. i, pp. 365–72.

22. There is a large literature on this subject. In addition to the biographies of Chamberlain, see: J. H. Zebel, 'Joseph Chamberlain and the Genesis of the Tariff Reform Controversy', *Journal of British Studies*, vii (1967), pp. 131–57; R. A. Rempel, *Unionists Divided: Arthur Balfour, Joseph Chamberlain and the Unionist Free Traders* (Newton Abbott, 1972); A. Sykes, *Tariff Reform in British Politics, 1903–13* (Oxford, 1979).

23. Marsh, *Chamberlain*, p. 661; Darwin, 'Fear of Falling', p. 32; A. Chamberlain, *Politics from the Inside* (London, 1936), p. 508.

24. L. S. Amery, *My Political Life* (3 vols., London, 1953–5), vol. iii, p. 225.

25. Marsh, *Chamberlain*, pp. 668–72; Hyam, *Britain's Imperial Century*, pp. 114–18; Green, *Crisis of Conservatism*, pp. 230–38; P. J. Cain, 'Political Economy in Edwardian England: The Tariff Reform Controversy', in A. O'Day (ed.), *The Edwardian Age: Conflict and Stability, 1900–1914* (London, 1979), pp. 48–59.

26. For comparisons between Chamberlain and Thatcher, see: P. Jenkins, *Mrs. Thatcher's Revolution: The Ending of the Socialist Era* (Cambridge, Mass., 1988), p. 53; H. Young, *Iron Lady: A Biography of Margaret Thatcher* (New York, 1990), p. 100.

27. P. F. Clarke, 'Churchill's Economic Ideas, 1900–30', in R. Blake and W. R. Louis (eds.), *Churchill* (Oxford, 1994), pp. 84–8; P. Addison, 'The Political Beliefs of Winston Churchill', *Transactions of the Royal Historical Society*, 5th Series, xxx (1980), pp. 28–30; J. R. Colville, *The Fringes of Power: 10 Downing Street Diaries, 1939–1955* (London, 1985), p. 345.

28. *Speeches* vii, p. 7802.

29. Clarke, 'Churchill's Economic Ideas', pp. 88–95; Addison, 'Political Beliefs of Winston Churchill', p. 46; *Churchill* iv, pp. 914–15.

30. D. Cannadine, *Aspects of Aristocracy: Grandeur and Decline in Modern Britain* (1994), pp. 156–60; M. Cowling, *Religion and Public Doctrine in Modern England* (Cambridge, 1980), pp. 284, 305; P. Addison, *Churchill on the Home Front, 1900–55* (London, 1992), pp. 329–33.

31. Colville, *Fringes of Power*, p. 278; *Speeches* vi, p. 5809.

32. Hyam, *Britain's Imperial Century*, p. 118; S. Gopal, 'Churchill and India', in Blake and Louis, *Churchill*, p. 459; W. R. Louis, *'In The Name of God, Go!'*, Leo Amery and the British Empire in the Age of Churchill (New York, 1992), p. 20.

33. Addison, 'Political Beliefs of Winston Churchill', pp. 37–41; R. Rhodes James, *Churchill: A Study in Failure, 1900–1939* (London, 1970), pp. 217–23; *Speeches* v, p. 4990.

34. Rhodes James, *Study in Failure*, p. 224; 2 WW i, p. 257.

35. Rhodes James, *Study in Failure*, p. 355; *Speeches* vi, p. 6013.

36. Rhodes James, *Study in Failure*, pp. 237, 273, 354.

37. Ibid., pp. 235, 265; Louis, *'In the Name of God, Go!'*, pp. 109–10; D. Cameron Watt, 'Churchill and Appeasement', in Blake and Louis, *Churchill*, pp. 199–214.

38. Clarke, *A Question of Leadership*, p. 143.

39. Louis, *'In the Name of God, Go!'*, pp. 123–78; Gopal, 'Churchill and India', pp. 461–6; R. J. Moore, *Churchill, Cripps, and India* (Oxford, 1979); W. R. Louis, *Imperialism at Bay: The United States and the Decolonization of the British Empire* (Oxford, 1970), esp. pp. 147–58, 198–210, 349–54, 433–60.

40. Kennedy, *Rise and Fall of the Great Powers*, pp. 347–437; Colville, *Fringes of Power*, p. 564.

41. *Speeches* viii, pp. 8213, 8262–3.

42. *Speeches* vii, pp. 7447–8, 7462, 7554, 7669–74.

43. *Speeches* viii, p. 7950.

44. Darwin, 'Fear of Falling', pp. 37–8; W. R. Louis, 'Churchill and Egypt, 1946–1956', in Blake and Louis, *Churchill*, pp. 473–90.

45. Colville, *Fringes of Power*, pp. 259, 709; Addison, *Churchill on the Home Front*, p. 359.

46. J. Morris, *Farewell the Trumpets: An Imperial Retreat* (Harmondsworth, 1978), pp. 545–57; J. Dimbleby, *Richard Dimbleby* (London, 1977), pp. 370–75; B. Levin, *The Pendulum Years: Britain and the Sixties* (London, 1972), pp. 399–411.

47. The fullest accounts of Thatcher's early years are: Young, *Iron Lady*, pp. 3–80; and J. Campbell, *Margaret Thatcher*, vol. i, *The Grocer's Daughter* (London, 2000).

48. B. Harrison, 'Thatcher and the Intellectuals', *Twentieth Century British History*, v (1994), esp. pp. 209–17.

49. M. Wiener, *English Culture and the Decline of the Industrial Spirit, 1850–1980* (Harmondsworth, 1992); C. Barnett: *The Collapse of British Power* (London, 1972); and *The Audit of War: The Illusion and Reality of Britain as a Great Nation* (London, 1986). For a critique of these views, see: B. Collins and K. Robbins (eds.), *British Culture and Economic Decline* (London, 1991); J. Harris, 'Enterprise and Welfare States: A Comparative Perspective', *Transactions of the Royal Historical Society*, 5th Series, xl (1990), pp. 175–95; D. Edgerton, 'The Prophet Militant and Industrial: The Peculiarities of Corelli Barnett', *Twentieth Century British History*, ii (1991), pp. 360–79. There is also a Marxist account of British decline which develops a very similar argument, albeit with a different vocabulary: A. Gamble, *The Decline of Britain* (London, 1981); S. Hall and M. Jacques (eds.), *The Politics of Thatcherism* (London, 1983); H. Overbeck, *Global Capitalism and National*

Decline: The Thatcher Decade in Perspective (London, 1990). For a helpful discussion, see P. Warwick, 'Did Britain Change? An Inquiry into the Causes of National Decline', *Journal of Contemporary History*, xx (1985), pp. 99–133.

50. M. Thatcher, *The Downing Street Years* (London, 1993), pp. 4–15, 30, 38, 42. See also D. Young: *Enterprise Regained* (London, 1985), pp. 5–8; and *The Enterprise Years* (London, 1990), pp. 25–9; Harrison, 'Thatcher and the Intellectuals', p. 237; B. Porter, ' "Though Not Myself an Historian . . .": Margaret Thatcher and the Historians', *Twentieth Century British History*, v (1994), pp. 252–5. For a discussion of Thatcher's preoccupation with national decline, see: Jenkins, *Thatcher's Revolution*, pp. xiii–xviii, 30–49; P. Riddell, *The Thatcher Era and its Legacy* (Oxford, 1991), pp. 6–7, 70–71.

51. Young, *Iron Lady*, p. 130; Riddell, *Thatcher Era*, p. 7; M. Thatcher: *Let Our Children Grow Tall* (London, 1977), pp. 43–4, 77, 88, 93; and *The Revival of Britain* (London, 1989), pp. 22, 57–8, 84–95.

52. Thatcher, *Downing Street Years*, pp. 10, 46; Jenkins, *Thatcher's Revolution*, p. 173; D. Kavanagh, *Thatcherism and British Politics: The End of Consensus?* (2nd edn, Oxford, 1990), p. 194.

53. Thatcher, *Revival of Britain*, p. 158; Riddell, *Thatcher Era*, p. 7; I. Gilmour, 'The Thatcher Memoirs', *Twentieth Century British History*, v (1994), p. 274.

54. Jenkins, *Thatcher's Revolution*, pp. 66–77; Riddell, *Thatcher Era*, p. 8; S. R. Letwin, *The Anatomy of Thatcherism* (London, 1992), pp. 22–3.

55. Young, *Iron Lady*, p. 6; Riddell, *Thatcher Era*, p. 3; Thatcher, *Downing Street Years*, p. 627; N. Ridley, *'My Style of Government': The Thatcher Years* (London, 1991), pp. 18–19.

56. J. Walvin, *Victorian Values* (London, 1988); E. M. Sigsworth (ed.), *In Search of Victorian Values* (Manchester, 1988); G. Marsden (ed.), *Victorian Values* (London, 1990), T. C. Smout (ed.), *Victorian Values, Proceedings of the British Academy*, lxxviii (1992).

57. Thatcher, *Downing Street Years*, pp. 8, 173, 264, 340–41, 377, 645; Jenkins, *Thatcher's Revolution*, pp. 161, 225; Gilmour, 'Thatcher's Memoirs', p. 274.

58. Thatcher, *Renewal of Britain*, pp. 164, 225, 235; and *Downing Street Years*, pp. 235, 254–5, 320; Young, *Iron Lady*, pp. 280–81, 371.

59. Sir A. Parsons, 'Britain and the World', in D. Kavanagh and A. Seldon (eds.), *The Thatcher Effect* (Oxford, 1989), p. 158; Riddell, *Thatcher Era*, pp. 184–5, 203; Jenkins, *Thatcher's Revolution*, p. 165.

60. Reynolds, *Britannia Overruled*, pp. 256–89; Thatcher, *Downing Street Years*, pp. 789–96, 813–15.

61. I. Gilmour, *Dancing with Dogma: Britain Under Thatcherism* (London, 1992), pp. 9–29, 45–75; N. Lawson, *The View from Number 11: Memoirs of a Tory Radical* (London, 1992), p. 339.

62. Riddell, *Thatcher Era*, pp. 69–86, 171, 214–15, 244–5; I. Crewe, 'Values: The Crusade that Failed', in Kavanagh and Seldon, *Thatcher Effect*, pp. 239–50; D. Willetts, 'The Family', in Kavanagh and Seldon, *Thatcher Effect*, p. 267.

63. Thatcher, *Downing Street Years*, pp. 719, 721, 724, 757, 832, 861; and 'Don't Undo My Work', *Newsweek*, 27 April 1992, pp. 36–7.

64. Thatcher, *Downing Street Years*, pp. 676, 755; Jenkins, *Thatcher Revolution*, p. xviii; Riddell, *Thatcher Era*, pp. 206, 245.

65. This was a comparison which Thatcher greatly liked: Thatcher, *Downing Street Years*, p. 82.

66. Reynolds, *Britannia Overruled*, pp. 5–35.

67. Supple, 'Fear of Failing', pp. 445–6.

3 Thrones:
Churchill and Monarchy in Britain and Beyond

1. This is, despite the overwhelming mass of pertinent material, a strangely neglected subject, with the honourable exception of P. Ziegler, 'Churchill and Monarchy', in R. Blake and W. R. Louis (eds.), *Churchill* (Oxford, 1994), pp. 187–98, to whose pioneeringly perceptive essay this account is much indebted. The original, and much shorter, version of this essay was presented at a conference on 'Churchill in the Twenty-First Century' jointly sponsored by the Royal Historical Society and the Institute of Historical Research in January 2001.

2. J. R. Colville, *The Fringes of Power: 10 Downing Street Diaries, 1939–1955* (London, 1985), p. 708; *Churchill* viii, pp. 1120–24; B. Pimlott, *Harold Wilson* (London, 1992), p. 685.

3. *Speeches* viii, pp. 8645–6.

4. N. Frankland, *Witness of a Century: The Life and Times of Prince Arthur, Duke of Connaught, 1850–1942* (London, 1993), pp. 1–2.

5. *Churchill* viii, p. 570; Colville, *Fringes of Power*, p. 128. By agreeable coincidence, the first Sir Winston Churchill, father of the great Duke of Marlborough, published a book entitled *Divi Britannici*, exploring 'those principles of the divine right of kings for which he had fought and suffered' in the Civil War: *Marlborough* i, p. 28.

6. *Churchill* viii, p. 371; D. Cannadine, *Aspects of Aristocracy: Grandeur and Decline in Modern Britain* (London, 1994), p. 156.

7. V. Bonham Carter, *Winston Churchill as I Knew Him* (London, 1965), p. 161; Lord Butler, *The Art of the Possible* (London, 1971), p. 156; P. Addison, *Churchill on the Home Front, 1900–1955* (London, 1992), pp. 47, 52–3, 211, 311–15, 439; *Marlborough* i, pp. 915–16.

8. I. Berlin, *Mr Churchill in 1940* (London, nd), pp. 12, 17, 36–7. The origins of the kingly and hierarchical social order were sketched out by Churchill in *ESP* i, pp. 53, 122, 136–8.

9. Lord Moran, *Churchill: The Struggle for Survival, 1940–1965* (London, 1966), p. 192.

10. *Essays* i, pp. 240–43.

11. *ESP* i, pp. xiii–xiv, 92–6, 131–40, 157–69, 178–89, 224–43, 315–24; ii, pp. 13–21, 82–95, 106-15; iii, pp. 3–22.

12. *ESP* i, pp. 152–3, 190–202, 289–307, 378–95; ii, p. 76–81, 304–13; iii, pp. 131–2, 135–43, 193; iv, pp. 12–15, 32–3.

13. R. Rhodes James, *Churchill: A Study in Failure, 1900–1939* (London, 1970), p. 312: 'Churchill's histories are populated with the Good and the Bad.'

14. Moran, *Struggle for Survival*, p. 399.

15. *Essays* i, pp. 227–9; *ESP* ii, pp. 166, 178, 190, 219, 261–3, 271, 293–303, 314–24; iii, p. viii.

16. *ESP* iv, pp. 45, 225.

17. *ESP* iv, pp. 43–5, 224–5, 230–31, 298–9.

18. D. Cannadine, 'The Context, Performance and Meaning of Ritual: The British Monarchy and the "Invention of Tradition"', *c.* 1820–1977', in E. J. Hobsbawm and T. O. Ranger (eds.), *The Invention of Tradition* (Cambridge, 1983), pp. 120–60.

19. *Speeches* vii, p. 7743; viii, p. 8337.

20. *Churchill* ii, p. 327; v, p. 1037.

21. *Churchill* viii, p. 366; *ESP* ii, p. 267.

22. *Marlborough* i, pp. 889–92; ii, pp. 48–50, 82.

23. *Essays* i, pp. 226–7.

24. K. D. Reynolds, *Aristocratic Women and Political Society in Victorian Britain* (Oxford, 1998), p. 201.

25. *Marlborough* i, p. 38.

26. Cannadine, *Aspects of Aristocracy*, pp. 132–3.

27. *Churchill* i, p. 17.

28. *Churchill* i, pp. 25–34, 41–2; CV i, part i, pp. 23–75; P. Magnus, *King Edward the Seventh* (Harmondsworth, 1967), pp. 185–93; R. F. Foster, *Lord Randolph Churchill: A Political Life* (Oxford, 1981), pp. 30–32, 46–7, 63, 66, 159.

29. Frankland, *Witness of a Century*, pp. 137–8; Foster, *Randolph Churchill*, pp. 191–3, 305–10, 318–21, 341–2.

30. Magnus, *Edward the Seventh*, pp. 89–91; Ziegler, 'Churchill and the Monarchy', p. 187.

31. Cannadine, *Aspects of Aristocracy*, pp. 134–8.

32. D. Cannadine: *The Decline and Fall of the British Aristocracy* (London, 1990), pp. 416–17; and *Aspects of Aristocracy*, p. 140; Viscount Churchill, *Be All My Sins Remembered* (New York, 1965), pp. 11, 40–43, 85–126.

33. Frankland, *Witness of Century*, pp. 215–22, 283, 354–5, 362–3, 372; Magnus, *Edward the Seventh*, p. 497; CV ii, part ii, pp. 1082–3.

34. *Churchill* i, pp. 75, 147–50, 205, 227, 242–3, 336.

35. *Speeches* vi, p. 6552; *Churchill* i, pp. 381–2, 420–21; CV i, part ii, pp. 763, 1231–2; Magnus, *Edward the Seventh*, pp. 330–31.

36. WSC, *My Early Life* (London, 1944 edn), pp. 166–7; *Churchill* i, pp. 336, 545–6.

37. *Churchill* ii, pp. 52, 158–9, 160–61, 211, 271, 274; Magnus, *Edward the Seventh*, p. 432.

38. *Churchill* i, p. 25; WSC, *Lord Randolph Churchill* (London, 1951 edn), pp. 68–69, 383–94; Foster, *Randolph Churchill*, p. 395; *Essays* i, p. 237.

39. J. Vincent (ed.), *The Crawford Papers* (Manchester, 1984), p. 83; K. Rose, *King George V* (London, 1983), p. 112; Magnus, *Edward the Seventh*, p. 432.

40. Cannadine, *Aspects of Aristocracy*, p. 138; *Churchill* ii, pp. 94, 107, 184–5.

41. Magnus, *Edward the Seventh*, pp. 473, 506; *Churchill* ii, pp. 326–7, 338–9.

42. H. Nicolson, *King George V: His Life and Reign* (London, 1967), p. 71; Rose, *George V*, pp. 83–4; *Churchill* ii, pp. 373–5, 382–3, 418–23, 426, 436.

43. Rose, *George V*, pp. 106–7; Nicolson, *George V*, p. 258; *CV* ii, part ii, pp. 1257–60; part iii, p. 1781.

44. *Churchill* ii, pp. 670–71; iii, p. 87; Nicolson, *George V*, p. 138; Rose, *George V*, p. 71.

45. *Churchill* ii, pp. 433–9; Rose, *George V*, pp. 76, 111–12.

46. *Churchill* ii, pp. 646–54; *CV* ii, part iii, p. 1764; Rose, *George V*, pp. 160–61.

47. *Churchill* iii, pp. 87–8; Rose, *George V*, p. 160.

48. *Churchill* ii, pp. 195–7, 312, 353–4; *CV* ii, part ii, pp. 910–11, 1091–2; part iii, p. 1492.

49. *Churchill* ii, pp. 706, 710; iii, p. 10; *CV* ii, part ii, pp. 1102–3; part iii, pp. 1984–5; *CV* iii, part i, pp. 12–13, 423–4.

50. *Churchill* iii, pp. 86–7, 120, 150–51, 383–4.

51. *Churchill* iii, pp. 454, 473; iii, part ii, p. 939; Rose, *George V*, p. 189; P. Ziegler, *King Edward VIII: The Official Biography* (London, 1990), p. 78.

52. Cannadine, *Aspects of Aristocracy*, pp. 156–7; M. Cowling, *Religion and Public Doctrine in Modern England* (Cambridge, 1980), pp. 320–28; *Churchill* iv, pp. 914–15; *TWC, 1915*, p. 17; *TWC, The Eastern Front*, p. 82; *Speeches* v, p. 5291.

53. *TWC, The Aftermath*, pp. 18, 31; *TWC, The Eastern Front*, p. 17.

54. *TWC, 1915*, pp. 201–2; *1916–18*, part i, pp. 102, 223–4; *The Aftermath*, pp. 70–86; *The Eastern Front*, pp. 348–53; Rhodes James, *Study in Failure*, pp. 105–6.

55. *TWC, 1916–18*, part i, pp. 87–8; part ii, pp. 492–93; *The Aftermath*, pp. 42–4, 158–9, 223–9, 442; *The Eastern Front*, pp. 17–32, 344–6.

56. *TWC, 1915*, pp. 455–80; *1916–18*, part i, pp. 197–212; part ii, pp. 537–8; *The Aftermath*, pp. 226–30, 378–89; *The Eastern Front*, p. 17.

57. *Churchill* iv, pp. 665, 702, 870, 891; v, pp. 143, 233; *CV* iv, part iii, p. 1845; *CV* v, part i, pp. 463–8, 979–83, 1267–70, 1459–60.

58. Rose, *George V*, p. 337; Rhodes James, *Study in Failure*, p. 120; *Churchill* iv, pp. 790–91; v, pp. 244, 303, 700–701.

59. *CV* iv, part ii, pp. 919, 1203, 1391–1400; Rhodes James, *Study in Failure*, p. 120; Addison, *Home Front*, p. 211; *Churchill* iv, pp. 166, 278, 502, 551–3, 560.

60. WSC, 'Will the world swing back to monarchies?', in M. Wolff (ed.), *The Collected Essays of Sir Winston Churchill*, vol. iv, *Churchill at Large* (London, 1976), pp. 268–72. The essay was originally published in *Pearson's Magazine* in February 1934. Churchill clearly blamed Woodrow Wilson, as a misguided American liberal, for much of this. There are very unflattering portraits of Wilson in *TWC, 1916–18*, part i, pp. 228–34; *The Aftermath*, pp. 120–40.

61. *Churchill* iv, p. 108; *CV* v, part ii, pp. 274, 285, 300; WSC, *Great Contemporaries* (London, 1942 edn), pp. 21–32, 149–60; WSC, *Thoughts and Adventures* (London, 1947 edn), pp. 49–57.

62. *Marlborough* i, pp. 16, 40–41, 65–78, 228–9, 322–3, 427, 444–5, 466–7, 494, 510, 555–68, 619, 632–49; ii, pp. 127, 135, 550–55, 628; Rhodes James, *Study in Failure*, p. 312.

63. *Marlborough* i, pp. 498–511, 528–9, 703, 736; ii, p. 285, 315–16, 407–8, 472–3.

64. Rose, *George V*, p. 190; *CV* v, part ii, pp. 668, 670–71.

65. *Marlborough* i, p. 509; *ESP* iv, p. 299.

66. *Speeches* v, pp. 5097–5108; Rhodes James, *Study in Failure*, p. 199.

67. This was not the first time Churchill had written appreciatively about the king, having earlier produced a film script for Alexander Korda to commemorate George V's Silver Jubilee: *CV* v, part ii, pp. 962–4, 989–1031.

68. WSC, *Great Contemporaries*, pp. 245–56.

69. *CV* v, part iii, p. 809.

70. *CV* ii, part ii, p. 1099; *CV* v, part iii, p. 1781; Ziegler, *Edward VIII*, p. 46.

71. *Churchill* iv, pp. 525, 682–3; v, pp. 7, 809; *CV* v, part i, pp. 42–3, 1065–6; *CV* v, part iii, pp. 34–5; *Speeches* v, p. 5291.

72. *Churchill* v, pp. 809–31; Rhodes James, *Study in Failure*, pp. 269–77; Vincent, *Crawford Papers*, pp. 573–7, 580.

73. *Churchill* v, pp. 810–11; *CV* v, part iii, pp. 450–54; Vincent, *Crawford Papers*, p. 577; Colville, *Fringes of Power*, p. 716; Ziegler, *Edward VIII*, pp. 302–27.

74. Colville, *Fringes of Power*, p. 196; *Speeches* vi, pp. 5820–22.

75. *Churchill* v, pp. 828, 831; *CV* v, part iii, pp. 489, 493–4.

76. R. Rhodes James (ed.), *'Chips': The Diaries of Sir Henry Channon* (London, 1967), p. 128.

77. *Speeches* vi, pp. 5847–9.

78. Ziegler, 'Churchill and the Monarchy', p. 194; *CV* v, part iii, pp. 519, 651–3, 1530; *Speeches* vi, p. 6017.

79. *Churchill* v, p. 853, 855–6, 1035, 1037; vi, pp. 12–13, 154; *CV* v, part iii, pp. 634–5; *WP* i, pp. 369–70, 376–7, 776, 1070; Vincent, *Crawford Papers*, p. 604; Rhodes James, *Diaries of Henry Channon*, p. 122.

80. *CV* v, part iii, pp. 673–4; 2 *WW* i, p. 172; Rhodes James, *Diaries of Henry Channon*, pp. 60–61, 80–83, 90–91.

81. *Churchill* vi, pp. 313; J. W. Wheeler-Bennett, *King George VI: His Life and Reign* (London, 1965), pp. 443–4; S. Bradford, *The Reluctant King: The Life & Reign of George VI, 1895–1962* (New York, 1989), pp. 274–9; A. Roberts, *Eminent Churchillians* (London, 1994), pp. 10–40.

82. Cannadine, *Aspects of Aristocracy*, p. 161, and references cited there.

83. Colville, *Fringes of Power*, pp. 29, 121–3, 130.

84. Roberts, *Eminent Churchillians*, pp. 14–15, 38–41; Colville, *Fringes of Power*, p. 145; Ziegler, 'Churchill and the Monarchy', p. 194; R. Blake, 'How Churchill Became Prime Minister', in Blake and Louis, *Churchill*, p. 273; *Churchill* vi, pp. 316, 453–4; Bradford, *Reluctant King*, pp. 312–14.

85. Ziegler, 'Churchill and the Monarchy', p. 195; Colville, *Fringes of Power*, pp. 160, 211; *Churchill* vi, pp. 560, 716; vii, p. 655.

86. Rhodes James, *Diaries of Henry Channon*, p. 272; Colville, *Fringes of Power*, pp. 211, 467; Bradford, *Reluctant King*, p. 340.

87. Colville, *Fringes of Power*, pp. 211, 323; *Churchill* vi, pp. 961, 1148; Wheeler-Bennett, *George VI*, pp. 446–7, 525–6.

88. 2 *WW* ii, p. 335; Colville, *Fringes of Power*, pp. 439–40.

89. B. Pimlott, *The Queen: A Biography of Queen Elizabeth II* (London, 1996), pp. 81, 173.

90. 2 WW ii, pp. 554–5; Wheeler-Bennett, *George VI*, p. 467. For another, similar letter from Churchill to the king in 1943, see ibid., pp. 564–5.

91. Wheeler-Bennett, *George VI*, pp. 553–4; *Churchill* vii, pp. 249–51.

92. Bradford, *Reluctant King*, p. 305.

93. *Churchill* vii, pp. 530–31.

94. 2 WW v, pp. 546–51; Wheeler-Bennett, *George VI*, pp. 600–606.

95. P. Dixon, *Double Diploma* (London, 1968), p. 115.

96. *Churchill* vi, pp. 613–14, 698–709; Colville, *Fringes of Power*, p. 197; Roberts, *Eminent Churchillians*, pp. 47–8.

97. Colville, *Fringes of Power*, pp. 183–4, 211; Bradford, *Reluctant King*, pp. 434–9.

98. *Churchill* ii, pp. 551–2, 631–2; iii, pp. 147–53; Nicolson, *George V*, p. 333; *TWC*, *1911–14*, pp. 400–401.

99. P. Ziegler, *Mountbatten: The Official Biography* (London, 1985), pp. 49, 132–3, 165–9, 176–8, 216–24, 299; Colville, *Fringes of Power*, p. 127; *Churchill* viii, p. 100.

100. Colville, *Fringes of Power*, pp. 148–9; *Churchill* vi, pp. 407, 414–15, 464; vii, p. 781; *WP* ii, pp. 177, 690; *Speeches* vi, p. 6227; *TWC*, *1911–14*, pp. 350–51. The case in defence of the king of Belgium, namely that Churchill made him scapegoat for British and French military failure, is put in: R. Keyes, *Outrageous Fortune: The Tragedy of King Leopold III of the Belgians, 1901–1941* (London, 1984), esp. pp. 308–10; Bradford, *Reluctant King*, pp. 316–19.

101. WSC, 'Will the world swing back to monarchies?', p. 272; Colville, *Fringes of Power*, pp. 163, 210; *Churchill* vi, pp. 694–5.

102. Wheeler-Bennett, *George VI*, pp. 496–8; Rhodes James, *Diaries of Henry Channon*, pp. 295, 299; *Churchill* vi, pp. 1042–3; W. R. Louis, *The British Empire in the Middle East, 1941–1951: Arab Nationalism, the United States, and Post-war Imperialism* (Oxford, 1984), pp. 226–8; M. Kolinsky, 'Lampson and the Wartime Control of Egypt', in M. J. Cohn and M. Kolinsky (eds.), *Demise of the British Empire in the Middle East: Britain's Response to Nationalist Movements, 1943–55* (London, 1998), pp. 96–111.

103. *WP* i, p. 1277; *Marlborough* i, p. 512; *Churchill* vi, p. 472.

104. Moran, *Struggle for Survival*, pp. 240–41; *Churchill* vi, p. 1082; vii, pp. 1225–6; 2 WW vi, pp. 348–9.

105. M. Glenny, *The Balkans: Nationalism, War and the Great Powers, 1804–1999* (London, 1999), pp. 393–478.

106. 2 WW vi, pp. 342–3; Moran, *Struggle for Survival*, p. 208; Colville, *Fringes of Power*, p. 533; F. Loewenheim, H. D. Langley and M. Jonas (eds.), *Roosevelt and Churchill: Their Secret Wartime Correspondence* (London, 1975), pp. 60–61. The disagreements between the Prime Minister and the President may be followed in W. F. Kimball (ed.), *Churchill & Roosevelt: The Complete Correspondence* (3 vols., Princeton, 1984), esp. vol. ii, pp. 365–8, 660–61, 679–81; vol. iii, pp. 274–5, 450–61.

107. Moran, *Struggle for Survival*, p. 192; Colville, *Fringes of Power*, p. 534.

108. *Churchill* vii, pp. 453–7, 650, 710–11; Colville, *Fringes of Power*, p. 478; H.

Macmillan, *War Diaries: Politics and War in the Mediterranean, January 1943–May 1945* (London, 1984), p. 361.

109. Dixon, *Double Diploma*, p. 115; 2 WW v, p. 455; vi, p. 103; D. Mack Smith, *Italy and its Monarchy* (London, 1989), pp. 330–36.

110. *Churchill* iii, pp. 221, 287, 329, 336.

111. *Churchill* vii, p. 1135; Macmillan, *War Diaries*, p. 544.

112. *Churchill* vii, pp. 513, 640–41; *Speeches* vii, p. 6821; Colville, *Fringes of Power*, p. 464.

113. *Churchill* vii, p. 921; 2 WW vi, p. 83; Moran, *Struggle for Survival*, p. 165; Dixon, *Double Diploma*, p. 115.

114. *Churchill* vii, pp. 993–4, 999–1001.

115. Colville, *Fringes of Power*, p. 550; *Churchill* vii, p. 1005; Kimball, *Churchill & Roosevelt*, vol. iii, pp. 274–5.

116. *Churchill* vii, pp. 1000–1001, 1146–7.

117. *Churchill* vii, p. 911; 2 WW vi, pp. 368–9; H. Pakula, *The Last Romantic: A Biography of Queen Marie of Roumania* (London, 1996), p. 423.

118. *Churchill* viii, p. 174; *Speeches* vii, pp. 7164–5.

119. *Churchill* viii, pp. 109, 114–15, 177–8; Wheeler-Bennett, *George VI*, pp. 635–7, 645, 650; Bradford, *Reluctant King*, pp. 377–8.

120. *Marlborough* ii, pp. 912–13; Moran, *Struggle for Survival*, p. 312; *Churchill* viii, pp. 390–91, 446–7, 491, 760–61; *Speeches* vii, pp. 7632–3.

121. *Speeches* vii, p. 7541; *Churchill* viii, pp. 340–41; Rhodes James, *Diaries of Henry Channon*, p. 418. The full list of foreign royalty attending is given in Wheeler-Bennett, *George VI*, p. 754.

122. Ziegler, *Edward VIII*, p. 505; *Churchill* viii, pp. 174, 207, 232–5, 267–8, 409–10, 431, 450; *Marlborough* i, pp. 906–11.

123. Moran, *Struggle for Survival*, pp. 352, 369; Colville, *Fringes of Power*, p. 593; *Churchill* vii, p. 1314; 2 WW i, pp. 8–9, 49; vi, p. 640.

124. 2 WW i, p. 172; iii, p. 521; v, pp. 40–60, 88–104, 166–79, 408–23, 470–88; vi, pp. 82–6, 247–83. Harold Macmillan wrote in a similiar vein about Italy and Greece in his memoirs: *The Blast of War, 1939–1945* (London, 1967), esp. chs. 15, 17, 20–23.

125. *Churchill* viii, pp. 422–3; Ziegler, *Mountbatten*, pp. 358, 385, 461.

126. *Churchill* viii, pp. 264, 396, 450; Pakula, *Last Romantic*, pp. 423–4.

127. Pimlott, *The Queen*, p. 173; Moran, *Struggle for Survival*, pp. 414, 421.

128. Moran, *Struggle for Survival*, pp. 341, 372–4; Colville, *Fringes of Power*, p. 640; *Churchill* viii, pp. 696–701; *Speeches* viii, pp. 8336–7.

129. For Churchill's letter of condolence to Queen Mary on the death of George V, see CV v, part iii, p. 36.

130. Colville, *Fringes of Power*, p. 211; *Speeches* viii, pp. 8463–4.

131. Rhodes James, *Diaries of Henry Channon*, p. 473; J. Pope-Hennessy, *Queen Mary, 1867–1953* (London, 1959), pp. 496, 609.

132. *Churchill* v, p. 303; CV v, part i, p. 1349; Rhodes James, *Diaries of Henry Channon*, p. 474; *Marlborough* i, p. 167; ii, p. 312; Moran, *Struggle for Survival*, pp. 403, 484, 607; Pimlott, *The Queen*, pp. 193–4; S. Bradford, *Elizabeth: A Biography of Her Majesty the Queen* (London, 1996), pp. 220–22, 226–7.

133. Moran, *Struggle for Survival*, pp. 404, 414, 450–51, 472, 547; *Churchill* viii, pp. 763–5, 770–71, 822–4, 852, 874, 884, 886–7, 914, 942, 993.

134. *Speeches* viii, pp. 8487, 8567.

135. *Churchill* viii, pp. 1072–6.

136. *Churchill* viii, p. 979; Ziegler, *Edward VIII*, pp. 539–40, 549, 551; Bradford, *Elizabeth*, pp. 184, 310–11, 343–4; Colville, *Fringes of Power*, pp. 670, 675.

137. *Churchill* viii, pp. 672–3; Ziegler, *Mountbatten*, pp. 502–3, 512, 523–4, 681–2; Pimlott, *The Queen*, pp. 183–6; Bradford, *Elizabeth*, pp. 176–8; Colville, *Fringes of Power*, pp. 637, 641–2, 760.

138. Pimlott, *The Queen*, pp. 205–7, 218–20; Bradford, *Elizabeth*, pp. 182–3, 204–5.

139. *Churchill* viii, p. 722; Colville, *Fringes of Power*, p. 646; Bradford, *Elizabeth*, p. 275.

140. *Churchill* viii, pp. 449, 558, 623; *Speeches* vii, p. 8229.

141. *Churchill* viii, pp. 371, 747, 1270–72, 1283.

142. *Churchill* vii, p. 125; viii, pp. 1123–8; Colville, *Fringes of Power*, p. 709; Bradford, *Elizabeth*, p. 228; Moran, *Struggle for Survival*, p. 653.

143. Moran, *Struggle for Survival*, p. 710; Pimlott, *The Queen*, p. 258; Bradford, *Elizabeth*, p. 236; *Churchill* viii, pp. 1177–8, 1193–4, 1223, 1227, 1313, 1330–31, 1333.

144. H. C. G. Matthew, 'Gladstone's Death and Funeral', *Historian*, no. 57 (Spring 1998), pp. 20–24; Hansard: 4th Series, vol. lviii, HC cols. 69, 80, 123–6, 265, 415; 5th Series, vol. 705, HC cols. 667, 679.

145. *Sunday Telegraph*, 31 January 1965.

146. *Marlborough* i, p. 298.

147. *Speeches* vi, p. 5821; *ESP* ii, p. 262.

148. *Speeches* vi, p. 5821; Ziegler, 'Churchill and the Monarchy', p. 198.

149. *Speeches* viii, p. 8338.

150. Vincent, *Crawford Papers*, p. 319.

151. *Churchill* vii, p. 1314; Moran, *Struggle for Survival*, p. 699.

152. *Churchill* viii, pp. 366, 1364; Moran, *Struggle for Survival*, p. 372.

4 Language:
Churchill as the Voice of Destiny

1. A. L. Rowse, *The Later Churchills* (Harmondsworth, 1971), pp. 529, 533–4.

2. *Speeches* viii, p. 8608; *Churchill* viii, p. 1075; R. Rhodes James, 'The Parliamentarian, Orator and Statesman', in R. Blake and W. R. Louis (eds.), *Churchill* (Oxford, 1994), p. 516.

3. Earl of Oxford and Asquith, *Memories and Reflections* (2 vols., London, 1928), vol. ii, p. 46.

4. *The Memoirs of Lord Chandos* (London, 1962), p. 183; Lord Moran, *Churchill: The Struggle for Survival, 1940–1965* (London, 1966), pp. 449, 713.

5. Moran, *Struggle for Survival*, p. 123.

6. L. Strachey, *Eminent Victorians* (London, 1918), p. 308; *Essays* i, p. 233; J. Meisel, 'Words by the Numbers: A Quantitative Analysis and Comparison of the Oratorical Careers of William Ewart Gladstone and Winston Spencer Churchill', *Historical Research*, lxxiii (2000), p. 290.

7. *Speeches* i, p. 905. For brief anthologies including many of the most memorable Churchill phrases, see: *The Concise Oxford Dictionary of Quotations* (Oxford, 1964), pp. 62–3; J. M. and M. J. Cohen (eds.), *The Penguin Dictionary of Modern Quotations* (Harmondsworth, 1971), pp. 43–7; R. Stewart (ed.), *A Dictionary of Political Quotations* (London, 1984), pp. 35–6. The original editions of Churchill's speeches were as follows: *Arms and the Covenant* (London, 1938); *Into Battle* (London, 1941); *The Unrelenting Struggle* (London, 1942); *The End of the Beginning* (London, 1943); *Onwards to Victory* (London, 1944); *The Dawn of Liberation* (London, 1945); *Victory* (London, 1946); *Secret Session Speeches* (London, 1946); *The Sinews of Peace* (London, 1948); *Europe Unite* (London, 1950); *In The Balance* (London, 1951); *Stemming the Tide* (London, 1953); *The Unwritten Alliance* (London, 1961). Among Churchill's near contemporaries, only Stanley Baldwin merits comparison: *On England* (London, 1926); *Our Inheritance* (London, 1928); *This Torch of Freedom* (London, 1935); *Service of Our Lives* (London, 1937). For Baldwin's (very un-Churchillian) oratory, see ch. 7.

8. *CV* i, part ii, pp. 816–21.

9. P. Addison, 'The Political Beliefs of Winston Churchill', *Transactions of the Royal Historical Society*, 5th Series, xxx (1980), p. 31.

10. WSC, *Savrola* (London, 1900), pp. 88–9.

11. Ibid., pp. 146–53.

12. Ibid., pp. 153–4, 344.

13. Moran, *Struggle for Survival*, p. 123; WSC, *My Early Life* (London, 1930), p. 18.

14. R. Rhodes James, *Churchill: A Study in Failure, 1900–1939* (London, 1970), pp. 23, 197.

15. N. Nicolson (ed.), *Harold Nicolson: Diaries and Letters, 1939–1945* (London, 1967), p. 259; Moran, *Struggle for Survival*, pp. 123, 346; J. Campbell, *Aneurin Bevan and the Mirage of British Socialism* (New York, 1987), p. 8.

16. J. Colville, in J. Wheeler-Bennett (ed.), *Action This Day: Working with Churchill* (London, 1968), p. 70; Moran, *Struggle for Survival*, pp. 18, 118, 254, 780.

17. Rhodes James, *Study in Failure*, p. 25; Hansard, 5th Series, vol. lxxx, HC col. 1571.

18. Meisel, 'Words by the Numbers', p. 269; *Memoirs of Lord Chandos*, p. 183; Moran, *Struggle for Survival*, p. 633; Rhodes James, *Study in Failure*, p. 24.

19. Nicolson, *Diaries and Letters, 1939–1945*, p. 321; Rhodes James, *Study in Failure*, p. 25.

20. *Speeches* vi, pp. 6007, 6220, 6268.

21. *Churchill* v, p. 174; *Speeches* vi, p. 6161.

22. *Speeches* vi, p. 6266.

23. R. Hyam, 'Winston Churchill Before 1914', *Historical Journal*, xii (1969), pp. 172–3. 'Blood, toil, tears and sweat' had also been anticipated nearly a decade

before in *TWC, The Eastern Front*, p. 17: 'their sweat, their tears, their blood bedewed the endless plain'.

24. V. Bonham Carter, *Winston Churchill as I Knew Him* (London, 1967), p. 18; Nicolson, *Diaries and Letters, 1939–1945*, p. 93.

25. Rhodes James, *Study in Failure*, p. 185; Moran, *Struggle for Survival*, p. 123.

26. I. Berlin, *Mr Churchill in 1940* (London, nd), p. 39.

27. Rhodes James, *Study in Failure*, p. 247.

28. R. Hyam, *Elgin and Churchill at the Colonial Office, 1905–1908: The Watershed of Empire-Commonwealth* (London, 1968), pp. 500–501; J. A. Spender, *Life, Journalism and Politics* (2 vols., London, 1927), vol. i, p. 163; M. V. Brett (ed.), *Journals and Letters of Viscount Esher* (4 vols., London, 1934–8), vol. ii, p. 344.

29. Rhodes James, *Study in Failure*, p. 26; W. F. Moneypenny and G. E. Buckle, *The Life of Benjamin Disraeli, Earl of Beaconsfield* (6 vols., London, 1910–20), vol. vi, pp. 356–7.

30. Rhodes James, *Study in Failure*, p. 40; Brett, *Viscount Esher*, vol. iv, pp. 120–21.

31. Nicolson, *Diaries and Letters, 1939–1945*, p. 21; *Speeches* vi, p. 6702.

32. Moran, *Struggle for Survival*, pp. 429, 701.

33. R. Rhodes James, *An Introduction to the House of Commons* (London, 1966 edn), pp. 33–4, 55.

34. *Memoirs of Lord Chandos*, p. 184; Rhodes James, *Study in Failure*, p. 279.

35. Meisel, 'Words by the Numbers', pp. 282–3.

36. *Churchill* v, pp. 606, 613.

37. Bonham Carter, *Churchill As I Knew Him*, p. 127; Moran, *Struggle for Survival*, p. 253.

38. *Speeches* i, pp. 598–9; ii, p. 2042; Hyam, *Elgin and Churchill*, p. 85.

39. *Speeches* v, pp. 4966, 4985; Lord Butler, *The Art of the Possible* (London, 1971), p. 40.

40. *Speeches* vi, pp. 7172, 7851–2; R. Jenkins, *Nine Men of Power* (London, 1974), pp. 102–3.

41. *Speeches* v, p. 5067; Addison, 'Political Beliefs of Winston Churchill', pp. 46–7; Rhodes James, *Study in Failure*, p. 214; Hyam, 'Churchill Before 1914', p. 172.

42. Rhodes James, *Study in Failure*, pp. 212–14, 321–2; Butler, *Art of the Possible*, p. 40; V. Cowles, *Winston Churchill: The Era and the Man* (London, 1953), pp. 308–9.

43. Berlin, *Churchill in 1940*, p. 9; Rhodes James, *Study in Failure*, p. 153.

44. Moran, *Struggle for Survival*, p. 780. Churchill's experience of broadcasting before 1939 was distinctly limited: Meisel, 'Words by the Numbers', pp. 286–8.

45. R. Jenkins, *Asquith* (London, 1964), pp. 339–40.

46. Rhodes James, *Study in Failure*, pp. 310, 322.

47. *Speeches* i, p. 276; Moran, *Struggle for Survival*, p. 124.

48. Rhodes James, *Study in Failure*, pp. 21, 29; Bonham Carter, *Churchill As I Knew Him*, p. 127.

49. *Speeches* i, pp. 274–6, 594–601; Rhodes James: *Study in Failure*, pp. 30–31; and 'Parliamentarian, Orator, and Statesman', pp. 510–11; J. L. Garvin and J. Amery, *The Life of Joseph Chamberlain* (6 vols., London, 1932–69), vol. vi, p. 876.

50. Rhodes James, *Study in Failure*, p. 29; *Speeches* i, p. 562; Hyam, 'Churchill Before 1914', p. 172.

51. Rhodes James, *Study in Failure*, p. 21.

52. *Speeches* i, p. 662.

53. *Speeches* i, p. 562; iii, pp. 2233–62.

54. *Speeches* ii, p. 1424; Rhodes James, *Study in Failure*, p. 27.

55. *Speeches* iii, pp. 3040–58, 3242–55; Rhodes James, *Study in Failure*, p. 159; P. F. Clarke, 'Churchill's Economic Ideas, 1900–1930', in Blake and Louis, *Churchill*, p. 89.

56. Meisel, 'Words by the Numbers', p. 291; *Churchill* v, p. 116; H. Macmillan, *Winds of Change, 1914–1939* (London, 1966), p. 176.

57. H. C. G. Matthew, 'Rhetoric and Politics in Great Britain, 1860–1950', in P. J. Waller (ed.), *Politics and Social Change: Essays Presented to A. F. Thompson* (London, 1987), pp. 34–58; *Essays* i, p. 234.

58. *Speeches* iii, pp. 2919–20.

59. Rhodes James, *Study in Failure*, p. 121; *Churchill* v, pp. 180–81.

60. Butler, *Art of the Possible*, p. 40; Rhodes James, *Study in Failure*, pp. 200, 212.

61. *Churchill* v, p. 613; *Speeches* v, pp. 4955–6.

62. *CV* i, part ii, p. 816.

63. *Speeches* vi, p. 6013; Rhodes James, *Study in Failure*, pp. 278, 322; *Churchill* v, pp. 926–7.

64. Rhodes James, *Study in Failure*, p. 214; Hansard, HC, 27 March 1933, col. 736.

65. Butler, *Art of the Possible*, pp. 48–9; Rhodes James, *Study in Failure*, p. 265; T. Jones, *A Diary with Letters, 1931–1950* (Oxford, 1954), p. 204.

66. Moran, *Struggle for Survival*, p. 782; A. Storr, 'The Man', in A. J. P. Taylor et al., *Churchill: Four Faces and the Man* (Harmondsworth, 1969), p. 245.

67. Moran, *Struggle for Survival*, p. 782; *Speeches* vi, p. 6231.

68. Moran, *Struggle for Survival*, p. 13.

69. *Speeches* vi, p. 6238.

70. *Speeches* vi, p. 6268.

71. D. J. Reynolds, 'Churchill and the British "Decision" to Fight On in 1940: Right Policy, Wrong Reasons', in R. T. B. Langhorne (ed.), *Diplomacy and Intelligence During the Second World War* (Cambridge, 1985), pp. 147–67; D. J. Reynolds, 'Churchill in 1940: The Worst and Finest Hour', in Blake and Louis, *Churchill*, pp. 241–55.

72. Nicolson, *Diaries and Letters, 1939–1945*, p. 93; *Churchill* vi, p. 742, note 1; J. Colville, *The Fringes of Power: 10 Downing Street Diaries, 1939–1955* (London, 1985), p. 292; E. Bliss (ed.), *In Search of Light: The Broadcasts of Edward R. Murrow* (London, 1968), p. 237.

73. *Speeches* vi, p. 6536; Campbell, *Bevan*, p. 113.

74. *Speeches* vi, p. 6506.

75. Moran, *Struggle for Survival*, p. 292.

76. *Speeches* vi, pp. 6350, 6540, 6578, 6695.

77. *Speeches* vii, pp. 7138, 7141, 7163.

78. Nicolson, *Diaries and Letters, 1939–1945*, pp. 472–4; Moran, *Struggle for Survival*, pp. 253, 783; *Speeches* vii, p. 7174.

79. Moran, *Struggle for Survival*, p. 313; Campbell, *Bevan*, pp. 208–9; *Speeches* vii, pp. 7438–48, 7541–54, 7717–30, 7731–42, 7844–57.

80. *Speeches* vii, p. 7219.

81. *Speeches* vii, pp. 7285–93, 7379–82.

82. Colville, in Wheeler-Bennett, *Action This Day*, p. 72; Colville, *Fringes of Power*, pp. 367, 553, 695; Moran, *Struggle for Survival*, pp. 364–8.

83. Moran, *Struggle for Survival*, pp. 571, 608; E. Shuckburgh, *Descent to Suez: Diaries, 1951–56* (London, 1986), p. 157.

84. *Speeches* viii, pp. 8551–8; Moran, *Struggle for Survival*, pp. 459, 474, 534–8, 571, 609, 644; Shuckburgh, *Descent to Suez*, pp. 158–60.

85. Moran, *Struggle for Survival*, pp. 601–4, 609–11, 622–3; *Speeches* viii, pp. 8593–8601, 8604–5.

86. R. Jenkins, 'Churchill: The Government of 1951–55', in Blake and Louis, *Churchill*, p. 493; *Speeches* viii, pp. 8323–9, 8337.

87. R. Rhodes James (ed.), *'Chips': The Diaries of Sir Henry Channon* (London, 1967), p. 479; Moran, *Struggle for Survival*, pp. 477, 492–4, 633–7; *Speeches* viii, pp. 8489–97, 8495–8505, 8625–33.

88. Moran, *Struggle for Survival*, pp. 637, 669–73, 686, 723.

89. Moran, *Struggle for Survival*, pp. 429, 537; for one particular late example, see *Speeches* vii, pp. 7538–40.

90. D. Healey, *The Time of My Life* (Harmondsworth, 1990), p. 147.

91. Meisel, 'Words by the Numbers', p. 291.

92. WSC, *Savrola*, pp. 88–9; *Speeches* vi, p. 6238.

93. *Speeches* viii, p. 8633; Rhodes James, 'Parliamentarian, Orator and Statesman', p. 516.

5 Locality:
The 'Chamberlain Tradition' and Birmingham

1. Earlier versions of this essay were presented to the seminars in modern British history at Cambridge University, and to the Institute of Historical Research in London. I am most grateful to the participants for their many helpful comments and constructive suggestions. My thanks also to Chuck Abdella and Ian Bennett for essential research assistance.

2. The standard lives are as follows: J. L. Garvin and Julian Amery, *The Life of Joseph Chamberlain* (6 vols., London, 1932–69); P. Marsh, *Joseph Chamberlain: Entrepreneur in Politics* (London, 1994); Sir Charles Petrie, *The Life and Letters of the Rt. Hon. Sir Austen Chamberlain* (2 vols., London, 1939–40); D. Dutton, *Austen Chamberlain: Gentleman in Politics* (London, 1987); Sir K. Feiling, *Neville Chamberlain* (London, 1947); D. Dilks, *Neville Chamberlain*, vol. i, *Pioneering and*

Reform, 1869–1929 (Cambridge, 1984). See also R. C. Self (ed.), *The Austen Chamberlain Diary Letters: The Correspondence of Sir Austen Chamberlain with his Sisters Hilda and Ida, 1916–1937* (Cambridge, 1995).

3. B. S. Benediktz, *Guide to the Chamberlain Collection* (Birmingham, 1978), p. 6. For three examples of family pride, see: Arthur Chamberlain, *The Book of Business* (privately printed, 1899), dedicated to 'my children in particular and to all my descendants in general'; Austen Chamberlain, *Notes on the Families of Chamberlain and Harben* (privately printed, 1915); Neville Chamberlain, *Norman Chamberlain: A Memoir* (privately printed, 1923). See also D. H. Elletson, *The Chamberlains* (London, 1966).

4. A. Briggs: *History of Birmingham*, vol. ii, *Borough and City, 1865–1938* (Oxford, 1952), esp. pp. 67–134, 164–99; and *Victorian Cities* (Harmondsworth, 1968), pp. 184–240; D. Fraser, *Power and Authority in the Victorian City* (Oxford, 1979), pp. 101–10, 151–73; E. P. Hennock, *Fit and Proper Persons: Ideal and Reality in Nineteenth-Century Urban Government* (London, 1973), pp. 17–57; L. V. Jones, 'Public Pursuit or Private Profit? Liberal Businessmen and Municipal Politics in Birmingham, 1865–1900', *Business History*, xxv (1983), pp. 240–59.

5. E. V. Hiley, 'Birmingham City Government', in J. H. Muirhead (ed.), *Birmingham Institutions* (Birmingham, 1910), p. 138; *BDP*, 30 November 1888; 1 February 1889; 10 November 1905; 20 June 1911.

6. J. Chamberlain, 'The Caucus', *Fortnightly Review*, new series, xxiv (1878), pp. 721–41; P. Auspos, 'Radicalism, Pressure Groups and Party Politics: From the National Education League to the National Liberal Federation', *Journal of British Studies*, xx (1980), pp. 184–204; F. H. Herrick, 'The Origins of the National Liberal Federation', *Journal of Modern History*, xvii (1945), pp. 116–29; T. R. Tholfsen, 'The Origins of the Birmingham Caucus', *Historical Journal*, ii (1959), pp. 161–84.

7. F. W. S. Craig, *British Parliamentary Election Results, 1885–1918* (2nd edn, Aldershot, 1989), p. 75. Chamberlain was returned unopposed in 1886, 1900 and (twice) 1910.

8. *BDP*, 18 and 19 January 1906; Dilks, *Neville Chamberlain*, pp. 7, 15; D. Cannadine, *Lords and Landlords: The Aristocracy and the Towns, 1774–1967* (Leicester, 1980), pp. 190–94; C. Green, 'Birmingham's Politics, 1873–1891: The Local Basis of Change', *Midland History*, ii (1973), pp. 84–88; F. W. S. Craig, *British Parliamentary Election Results, 1832–1885* (2nd edn, Aldershot, 1989), p. 46. For one contemporary example of local anti-Chamberlain propaganda, see BRL MSS 89151, Anon, 'Joseph and His Brethren' [1880].

9. R. Quinault, 'John Bright and Joseph Chamberlain', *Historical Journal*, xxviii (1985), pp. 623–46. H. Pelling, *Popular Politics and Society in Late Victorian Britain* (London, 1968), p. 3, describes Chamberlain's improvement scheme as 'Municipal Stalinism': 'Municipal Haussmannism' might be a better phrase. For the conditions of life for ordinary people, see R. Woods, 'Mortality and Sanitary Conditions in the "Best-Governed City in the World" – Birmingham, 1870–1910', *Journal of Historical Geography*, iv (1978), pp. 35–56.

10. R. Quinault, 'Joseph Chamberlain: A Reappraisal', in T. R. Gourvish and A. O'Day (eds.), *Later Victorian Britain, 1867–1900* (London, 1988), pp. 76–81.

11. M. C. Hurst: *Joseph Chamberlain and West Midland Politics, 1886–1895* (Dugdale Society Occasional Papers, no. 5, 1962); and 'Joseph Chamberlain, the Conservatives and the Succession to John Bright, 1886–89', *Historical Journal*, vii (1964), pp. 64–93; K. W. D. Rolf, 'Tories, Tariffs and Elections: The West Midlands in English Politics, 1918–1935' (Ph.D. dissertation, Cambridge University, 1974), pp. 65–7; H. Pelling, *Social Geography of British Elections, 1885–1910* (London, 1967), pp. 175–203.

12. J. Pemble, *Venice Rediscovered* (Oxford, 1995), esp. pp. 87–109; E. Muir, *Civic Ritual in Renaissance Venice* (Princeton, 1981), pp. 13–23. See also Feiling, *Neville Chamberlain*, p. 3: 'If Manchester might think of itself as the Florence, the Venice of this second Renaissance was Birmingham.' All the Chamberlains were frequent visitors to Venice.

13. *The Times*, 4 and 7 July 1914; R. Hartnell, 'Art and Civic Culture in Birmingham in the Late Nineteenth Century', *Urban History*, xxii (1995), pp. 229–37.

14. C. Schorske, *Fin-de-Siècle Vienna: Politics and Culture* (New York, 1980), pp. 24–7, 62.

15. J. T. Bunce, 'Art in the Community', *Fortnightly Review*, new series, xxii (1877), pp. 340–54; C. Cunningham, *Victorian and Edwardian Town Halls* (London, 1981), pp. 5–6, 8–10, 18–19, 83–5, 208–9; R. Dixon and S. Muthesius, *Victorian Architecture* (London, 1978), p. 149.

16. Metropolitan opinion considered Birmingham's buildings from this period extravagantly over-ornamented: *Builder*, 27 November 1897, p. 440; *Builder's Journal*, 2 October 1907, p. 163.

17. T. Anderton, *A Tale of One City: The New Birmingham* (Birmingham, 1900), pp. 95–6; B. Morris, 'The Harborne Room', *Victoria and Albert Museum Bulletin*, iv (1968), pp. 82–95; *VCH Warwickshire*, vol. vii (London, 1964), pp. 44–5; N. Pevsner and A. Wedgwood, *The Buildings of England: Warwickshire* (Harmondsworth, 1966), pp. 100, 118–19, 121, 124, 140–41, 145, 187, 207; Marsh, *Joseph Chamberlain*, pp. 75, 87, 102, 139–40.

18. Pemble, *Venice Rediscovered*, pp. 122–4, 131–6; M. W. Brooks, *John Ruskin and Victorian Architecture* (London, 1987), pp. 233–53; J. Mordaunt Crook, 'Ruskinian Gothic', in J. Dixon Hunt and F. M. Holland (eds.), *The Ruskin Polygon* (Manchester, 1982), pp. 65–93; J. Mordaunt Crook, *The Dilemma of Style: Architectural Ideas from the Picturesque to the Post Modern* (London, 1987), pp. 69–97, 133–60; BRL MSS 78126, 'A Catalogue of the Works of Mr John Ruskin', as collected by J. H. Chamberlain [1878].

19. J. H. Chamberlain: *On the Office and Duties of Architecture* (Birmingham [1858]); and *Exotic Art* (Birmingham [1883]); J. T. Bunce, *In Memoriam, John Henry Chamberlain* (Birmingham [1884]); BRL MSS 382842, Newspaper Cuttings relating to J. H. Chamberlain [1883–84], esp. *BDP*, 23 and 24 October 1883.

20. *BDP*, 6 October 1881; 21 September 1885; 2 October 1885.

21. *VCH Warwickshire*, vol. vii, frontispiece; *BDP*, 24 April 1880.

22. *BDP*, 22 July 1891; Dixon and Muthesius, *Victorian Architecture*, pp. 176–7; *VCH Warwickshire*, vol. vii, p. 45; Pevsner and Wedgwood, *Warwickshire*, pp. 117–19.

23. A. P. D. Thomson, 'The Chamberlain Memorial Tower, University of Birmingham', *University of Birmingham Historical Journal*, iv (1954), pp. 167–79; E. W. Ives, *Image of a University: The Great Hall at Edgbaston, 1900–1909* (Birmingham, 1988); Pevsner and Wedgwood, *Warwickshire*, pp. 169–70.

24. Muir, *Renaissance Venice*, pp. 4, 60, 74–5, 183, 250, 300; Marsh, *Joseph Chamberlain*, pp. 641–2. The 'Chamberlain tradition' in Birmingham is but one example, albeit perhaps the most famous and well developed, of the close relationship between urban ceremonial, civic power and local politics in Britain from the last quarter of the nineteenth century to the outbreak of the Second World War. For some other examples, see D. Cannadine: 'The Brief Flowering of a Civic Religion', *Listener*, 26 July 1984, pp. 14–15; and 'The Transformation of Civic Ritual in Modern Britain: The Colchester Oyster Feast', *Past & Present*, no. 94 (1982), pp. 107–30; D. Cannadine and E. Hammerton, 'Conflict and Consensus on a Ceremonial Occasion: The Diamond Jubilee in Cambridge', *Historical Journal*, xxiv (1981), pp. 111–46; T. B. Smith, 'In Defence of Privilege: The City of London and the Challenge of Municipal Reform, 1875–1890', *Journal of Social History*, xxvii (1993–4), pp. 59–83.

25. *BDP*, 17 and 18 June 1874; 24 February 1875; 10 November 1879; 2, 26 and 27 October 1880; 20 July 1881; 2 June 1882; 8 May and 4, 6, 12, 14, 15 and 16 June 1883; 6, 7, 8, 12 and 29 March 1888; 9 January 1889; *Pall Mall Gazette 'Extra', The Bright Celebration*, 18 June 1883.

26. *BDP*, 4 November 1874; 5 August 1885; 23 and 24 March 1887.

27. Briggs, *History of Birmingham*, pp. 336–7; W. Corfield, 'Birmingham Statues and Memorials', in W. Corfield (ed.), *Extracts from 'Notes and Queries', March 14 to May 9 1914* (London, 1914), p. 332; *BDP*, 11 January 1901; 15 March, 24 April 1913.

28. BRL MSS 174049, 'Mr Chamberlain's Visit to South Africa: Newspaper Cuttings on his Farewell and Return to Birmingham' [1902–03], esp. *Birmingham Daily Gazette, BDP, Birmingham Daily Mail*, all for 18 November 1902. On Chamberlain's return from South Africa to Birmingham, a memorial clock was unveiled in his constituency: *BDP*, 1 February 1904.

29. BRL MSS 243171, 'The Chamberlain Celebrations, July 7 & 9 1906: Official Programme'; BRL MSS 194741, 'Chamberlain Souvenir, 1836 to 1906' [1906]; BRL MSS 199541, 'Chamberlain Celebration, 1906, Programme of the Congratulatory Meeting, Bingley Hall, Birmingham, 9 July 1906' [1906]; *BDP*, 7 and 9 July 1906; BRL MSS 202060, 'Commemoration of Mr Joseph Chamberlain's Seventieth Birthday, Newspaper Cuttings, etc.' [1906]; Garvin and Amery, *Joseph Chamberlain*, vol. vi, pp. 897–907; Marsh, *Joseph Chamberlain*, pp. 641–7.

30. *BDP*, 11 and 27 June, 21 and 22 July 1904; 27 September 1889, 6 and 25 February, 3 March 1905. For the background see P. J. Morrish, 'The Struggle to Create an Anglican Diocese of Birmingham', *Journal of Ecclesiastical History*, xxxi (1980), pp. 59–88.

31. BRL MSS 218653, 'City of Birmingham, Authorised Programme of the Royal Visit to Birmingham for the Opening of Birmingham University' [1909]; *BDP*, 17 and 29 May; 5, 8, 9, 11, 15, 22, 24 and 30 June; 7, 8 and 9 July 1909.

32. *BDP*, 1 February 1904.

33. Marsh, *Joseph Chamberlain*, p. 278; D. Dutton: 'Life Beyond the Grave: Joseph Chamberlain, 1906–14', *History Today*, May 1984, p. 26; and *Austen Chamberlain*, p. 49.

34. Rolf, 'Tories, Tariffs and Elections', pp. 135–6; Elletson, *The Chamberlains*, pp. 202–10; N. Chamberlain, 'Municipal Government in Birmingham', *Political Quarterly*, i (1914), pp. 89–119; *BDP*, 12 February 1912; 3 November 1913.

35. Feiling, *Neville Chamberlain*, pp. 52, 62; Dilks, *Neville Chamberlain*, pp. 76–9, 105–8, 123–80; *BDP*, 10 November 1916.

36. *BDP*, 4, 6 and 7 July 1914; *The Times*, 4, 7 July 1914; Marsh, *Joseph Chamberlain*, pp. 666–7.

37. Ibid., pp. 667–8; BRL MSS 259694, 'A Catalogue of the Collection of Orchids formed by the Late Right Hon. Joseph Chamberlain . . . to be sold on 15 and 16 April 1915'; BRL MSS 259695, 'A Catalogue of the Collection of Stove and Greenhouse Plants, formed by the late the Right Hon. Joseph Chamberlain . . . to be sold on 22 April 1915'; BRL MSS 259773, Highbury, Moor Green, Birmingham, 'Catalogue of Surplus Household Furniture . . . to be sold 28 and 29 April 1915'; BRL MSS 626472, Correspondence between Sir Austen Chamberlain and others concerning the disposal of part of the Highbury Estate, 1923–4; D. Ayhurst, *Garvin of the Observer* (London, 1985), pp. 51–5, 235; Self, *Austen Chamberlain Diary Letters*, pp. 136, 397; Dutton, *Austen Chamberlain*, p. 4.

38. Hurst, *Joseph Chamberlain and West Midland Politics*, p. 3; Rolf, 'Tories, Tariffs and Elections', p. 86; Self, *Austen Chamberlain Diary Letters*, p. 201; *BP*, 23 February 1926; BRL MSS 325935, Presentation of the Freedom of the City to the Rt. Hon. Sir Austen Chamberlain, Monday 22 February 1926.

39. Rolf, 'Tories, Tariffs and Elections', p. 87; BRL MSS 384453, 'City of Birmingham Gas Department, Proceedings at the Unveiling of the Bust of the Late Mr Joseph Chamberlain . . . on 8th December 1925'.

40. Dutton, *Austen Chamberlain*, p. 165; Self, *Austen Chamberlain Diary Letters*, pp. 14–15, 198–99; H. Macmillan, *The Past Masters: Politics and Politicians, 1906–1939* (London, 1975), p. 128.

41. Dilks, *Neville Chamberlain*, p. 397; Rolf, 'Tories, Tariffs and Elections', pp. 88, 145; Self, *Austen Chamberlain Diary Letters*, pp. 259–60.

42. Elletson, *The Chamberlains*, pp. 218, 265, 271–5. Neville wrote his cousin's memoir (*Norman Chamberlain*, p. v), so 'that future generations of the family should realise how greatly Norman had contributed to the family fame'.

43. Rolf, 'Tories, Tariffs and Elections', p. 48; E. Hopkins, 'Working Class Life in Birmingham Between the Wars, 1918–1939', *Midland History*, xv (1990), pp. 129–50.

44. *BP*, 11 November 1924, 10 November 1925; R. P. Hastings: 'The General Strike in Birmingham, 1926', *Midland History*, ii (1974), pp. 250–73; and 'The Birmingham Labour Movement, 1918–1945', *Midland History*, v (1979–80), pp. 78–84; F. W. S. Craig (ed.), *British Parliamentary Election Results, 1918–1949* (Glasgow, 1969), pp. 80–91.

45. E. J. Hobsbawm, 'Mass-Producing Traditions', in E. J. Hobsbawm and T. Ranger

(eds.), *The Invention of Tradition* (Cambridge, 1983), pp. 303–4; Hartnell, 'Art and Culture in Birmingham', pp. 236–7.

46. Briggs, *History of Birmingham*, pp. 336–7; *BP*, 31 January, 10 and 21 February, 28 March, 14 and 17 October 1919; 1 July 1920; 12 June 1923; 15 May, 6 July 1925.

47. W. H. Bidlake, 'Birmingham as it Might Be', in Muirhead, *Birmingham Institutions*, pp. 598–601; *BP*, 1 April 1922, 12 June 1923.

48. *BP*, 12 October 1926, 15 August 1927; Anon, 'Birmingham Civic Centre Competition', *The Architect and Building News*, cxviii (1927), pp. 297–301; W. Dougill, 'Birmingham Civic Centre Competition: A Criticism of the Designs', *The Town Planning Review*, xiii (1928), pp. 19–29.

49. Craig, *British Parliamentary Election Results, 1918–1949*, pp. 83, 90. Hastings, 'Birmingham Labour Movement', pp. 82, 84–7.

50. Self, *Austen Chamberlain Diary Letters*, p. 493; Hastings, 'Birmingham Labour Movement', p. 80; *Observer*, 3 November 1935.

51. Ayerst, *Garvin*, pp. 235–8; Rolf, 'Tories, Tariffs and Elections', pp. 418, 420, 425.

52. L. S. Amery, *My Political Life* (3 vols., London, 1953–5), vol. iii, p. 201; *BP*, 17 March, 8 and 9 July 1936; E. M. Rudland, *Three Poems* (Birmingham, 1937), unpaginated, 'Centenary of the Right Honourable Joseph Chamberlain, 1836–1936'.

53. Sir Austen Chamberlain: *Down the Years* (London, 1935), p. 5; and *Politics from Inside: An Epistolary Chronicle, 1906–1914* (London, 1936), p. 15; *BP*, 12 November 1936.

54. Self, *Austen Chamberlain Diary Letters*, p. 520; *BP*, 17, 18 and 20 March 1937; E. M. Rudland, 'The Rt. Hon. Sir Austen Chamberlain, died 16 March 1937', in his *Three Poems*.

55. Self, *Austen Chamberlain Diary Letters*, pp. 399–400, 405–6; *BP*, 5 February 1932, 20 March 1937.

56. BRL MSS 391766, 'Special Council Meeting to be held in the Town Hall, to admit to the Hon. Freedom of the City Barrow Cadbury, the Rt. Hon. Neville Chamberlain, Alderman John Henry Lloyd, Friday 6 May 1932'; *BP*, 7 May 1932; 28 November 1933; 29 May 1937; 5 July 1937; N. Chamberlain, *The Struggle for Peace* (London, 1939), pp. 19–20; Feiling, *Neville Chamberlain*, p. 306.

57. *BP*, 11 July 1935; 17 July 1935; 23 May 1936; 28 June 1938; Sir Reginald Blomfield, 'Birmingham Civic Centre Competition', *The Architect and Building News*, 19 July 1935, p. 75; W. T. Benslyn, 'Birmingham Municipal Offices Competition', *The Builder*, 19 July 1935, p. 99; Cadbury Brothers, *Our Birmingham* (2nd edn, Birmingham, 1950), p. 56; Pevsner and Wedgwood, *Warwickshire*, pp. 116–17.

58. *BP*, 24 January 1930; 24 October 1934; 24 June 1938; *Birmingham Mail*, 14 July 1938.

59. C. Gill and C. Grant Robertson, *A Short History of Birmingham* (Birmingham, 1938), esp. pp. 53–63; BRL MSS 496108, *Birmingham Gazette, Centenary Supplement*, 11–16 July 1938, esp. pp. 18–19; BRL MSS 484281, 'Birmingham, 1838–1938: Centenary Souvenir and Guide to the City' [1938]; BRL MSS 489614, ' "Build us a City": A Programme in Celebration of the Birmingham Charter Centen-

ary' (BBC Radio, devised and produced by Robin Whitworth); BRL MSS 493289, 'City of Birmingham, Centenary Celebrations, 1838–1938, Visit of their Majesties the King and Queen, Thursday 14th July 1939'. In the event, the king and queen were unable to attend, and their place was taken by the Duke and Duchess of Gloucester.

60. BRL MSS 506373, 'City of Birmingham: Centenary Celebrations: Pageant Committee: Notices of Meetings, Agendas etc., 1937–8; BRL MSS 486185, 'Pageant of Birmingham, 1938: Costume Designs Drawn Under the Direction of Jean Campbell' (4 vols.); BRL MSS 493287, 'Pageant Progress: The News Bulletin of the Pageant of Birmingham', nos. 1–4, 1 April to 1 July 1938; BRL MSS 83218 Birmingham, '1838–1938: Charter Centenary Celebrations: Official Programme, July 11–16 1938'; BRL MSS 494493, Newspaper Cuttings Relating to the Pageant of Birmingham, 1938; BRL MSS F920.008 K113, Gwen Lally, 'Autobiography of a Pageant Master', Newspaper Cuttings from the *Birmingham Weekly Post*, 17 February to 31 March 1939.

61. *BP*, 30 September and 1 October 1938; E. M. Rudland, 'To Mrs Neville Chamberlain' and 'The Rt. Hon. Neville Chamberlain', both in his *Mrs Neville Chamberlain and other Poems* (Birmingham, 1938), pp. 3, 5. The poem about Neville Chamberlain was originally published in the *Daily Express* on 29 September 1938.

62. Sir Charles Petrie, *The Chamberlain Tradition* (London, 1938), esp. pp. v, 32, 275–7. For his later, and rather less effusive, views of the family, see Sir Charles Petrie, *A Historian Looks at His World* (London, 1972), pp. 64–5.

63. Amery, *The Unforgiving Years*, pp. 358–65; Chamberlain, *The Struggle for Peace*, p. 381.

64. Chamberlain, *The Struggle for Peace*, pp. 381, 413–20; *BP*, 4 September 1939, 10 and 11 May 1940.

65. A Sutcliffe and R. Smith, *History of Birmingham*, vol. iii, *Birmingham, 1939–1970* (Oxford, 1974), p. 14.

66. For some useful hints, see: C. Behagg, 'Myths of Cohesion: Capital and Compromise in the Historiography of Nineteenth-Century Birmingham', *Social History*, xi (1986), pp. 375–84; D. P. Leighton, 'Municipal Progress, Democracy and Radical Identity in Birmingham, 1838–1886', *Midland History*, xxv (2000), pp. 115–42; A. Sutcliffe, 'The "Midland Metropolis": Birmingham, 1890–1980', in G. Gordon (ed.), *Regional Cities in the UK, 1890–1980* (London, 1986), pp. 25–39; D. Smith, *Conflict and Compromise: Class Formation in English Society, 1830–1914: A Comparative Study of Birmingham and Sheffield* (London, 1982); H. Berghoff, 'Regional Variations in Provincial Business Biography: The Case of Birmingham, Bristol and Manchester, 1870–1914', *Business History*, xxxvii (1995), pp. 64–85.

67. Hastings, 'Birmingham Labour Movement', pp. 87–9; R. B. McCallum and A. Readman, *The British General Election of 1945* (Oxford, 1947), p. 265; Sutcliffe and Smith, *Birmingham*, p. 82. For the later history, see R. Waller and B. Criddle, *The Almanac of British Politics* (5th edn, London, 1996), pp. 77–92.

68. Rolf, 'Tories, Tariffs and Elections', pp. 135–6.

69. *VCH Warwickshire*, vii, p. 46; Hartnell, 'Art and Culture in Birmingham', p. 237; *BP*, 14 July 1986.

6 Piety:
Josiah Wedgwood and the History of Parliament

1. This essay originated as the Earle Lecture, delivered at Keele University in 1999, and it was subsequently read to the Modern British History Seminar at Cambridge University, and to the History of Parliament Seminar at the Institute of Historical Research in London. My thanks to the participants, to Dr Joseph Meisel and Dr James Thompson for research assistance, and to Lord Jenkins of Hillhead and Sir John Sainty for their help and advice. I am especially grateful to Valerie Cromwell, then Director of the History of Parliament, for her sustained assistance and encouragement, and for allowing me to read and benefit from her unpublished paper, 'Concern for the History of Parliament: Twentieth-Century Initiatives'. The chief published sources for Lord Wedgwood's life are: *The Times*, 27 July 1943; *DNB*, *1941–1950* (Oxford, 1959), pp. 941–3; JCW, *Memoirs of a Fighting Life* (London, 1940); and C. V. Wedgwood, *The Last of the Radicals: Josiah Wedgwood MP* (London, 1951).

2. Wedgwood, *Last of the Radicals*, p. 78.

3. E. J. D. Warrillow, *A Sociological History of the City of Stoke-on-Trent* (Hanley, 1960), p. 225; *VCH Staffordshire*, vol. viii (Oxford, 1963), p. 7, JCW, *Memoirs*, pp. 209–10.

4. *The Ceramic Society's Celebration of the Bicentenary of Josiah Wedgwood, 21st to 23rd May, 1930* (Stoke-on-Trent, 1930); *Stoke-on-Trent Historical Pageant, Hanley Park, Monday May 19th to Saturday May 24th, 1930* (Stoke-on-Trent, 1930).

5. *Daily Express*, 19 May 1930; JCW, *Memoirs*, pp. 210–11; Wedgwood, *Last of the Radicals*, pp. 208–9.

6. Ibid., pp. 53–68, 102–24; JCW, *Memoirs*, pp. 43–58, 88–114.

7. JCW, *History of Parliament: Register of the Ministers and of the Members of Both Houses, 1439–1509* (London, 1938), p. cxliv; JCW, 'Wedgwood's', in his *Essays and Adventures of a Labour MP* (London, 1924), pp. 31–8; JCW, *Memoirs*, p. 212; Wedgwood, *Last of the Radicals*, pp. 224–5.

8. Wedgwood, *Last of the Radicals*, pp. 224–5; JCW, *A History of the Wedgwood Family* (London, 1908), p. 207; JCW, *Memoirs*, pp. 17, 29–30, 35, 210.

9. N. Annan, 'The Intellectual Aristocracy', in J. H. Plumb (ed.), *Studies in Social History: A Tribute to G. M. Trevelyan* (London, 1955), pp. 246, 260–65.

10. Wedgwood, *Last of the Radicals*, pp. 22–8, 31–4, 41, 50, 243; JCW, *Memoirs*, pp. 16, 24–5, 40–41, 60, 96, 229.

11. Wedgwood, *Last of The Radicals*, p. 60; JCW, *Memoirs*, pp. 30, 34.

12. M. W. Greenslade, *The Staffordshire Historians: Collections for a History of Staffordshire*, 4th Series, xi (1982), pp. 139–45.

13. Ibid., pp. 146–8; *DNB*, 2nd supplement, vol. iii (London, 1912), pp. 714–15;

JCW, *Memoirs*, p. 213. See also the reference to Wrottesley in JCW, *History of Parliament: Biographies of the Members of the Commons House, 1439–1509* (London, 1936), p. xii.

14. JCW, *Wedgwood Family*, pp. x–xi, 169–73; JCW and J. G. E. Wedgwood, *Wedgwood Pedigrees* (London, 1925), pp. 116–22, 125–7; JCW, *Staffordshire Pottery and its History* (London, 1913), pp. 83–106.

15. Wedgwood, *Last of the Radicals*, pp. 126–36; JCW, *Memoirs*, pp. 117, 134.

16. F. W. S. Craig: *British Parliamentary Election Results, 1885–1918* (2nd edn, Dartmouth, 1989), p. 156, and *British Parliamentary Election Results, 1918–1949* (Glasgow, 1969), p. 200; H. Pelling, *Social Geography of British Elections, 1885–1910* (London, 1967), pp. 270–74; F. Bealey, J. Blondel and W. P. McCann, *Constituency Politics* (London, 1965), esp. ch. 3.

17. JCW, *Staffordshire Parliamentary History from the Earliest Times to the Present Day*: vol. i, *1213 to 1603*, in *Collections for a History of Staffordshire* (1917); vol. ii, part i, *1603 to 1715*, in ibid. (1920); vol. ii, part ii, *1715–1832*, in ibid. (1922); vol. iii, *1780–1841*, in ibid. (1933).

18. JCW, *1213–1603*, p. xxii, and *1780–1841*, p. 82; JCW, *Memoirs*, p. 213.

19. JCW, *1213–1603*, p. liii.

20. JCW, *1213–1603*, p. xxix, *1603–1715*, p. xiii, and *1715–1832*, pp. xxiv–xxvi.

21. Wedgwood, *Last of the Radicals*, p. 139; JCW, *Memoirs*, pp. 146–7; JCW, 'Introduction', 'Land Values – How They Should Be Taxed' and 'The Professor and the Politician', in his *Essays and Adventures*, pp. 7, 71–115, 212–30.

22. Wedgwood, *Last of the Radicals*, pp. 149–61; JCW, *Memoirs*, pp. 29, 144, 176–7.

23. JCW, 'Native Lands and Crown Colonies' and 'Indian Home Rule', in his *Essays and Adventures*, pp. 116–29, 136–44; JCW, *The Future of the Indo-British Commonwealth* (London, 1921); JCW, *The Seventh Dominion* (London, 1928); Wedgwood, *Last of the Radicals*, pp. 140–48, 181–203.

24. Wedgwood, *Last of the Radicals*, pp. 209–17, 226–36; JCW, 'Under the Red Flag', in his *Essays and Adventures*, pp. 11–30; JCW, *Memoirs*, pp. 224–38.

25. JCW, *1213–1603*, p. xix.

26. Ibid., p. xxix; Wedgwood, *Last of the Radicals*, p. 176.

27. JCW, *1213–1603*, pp. xxi–xxii.

28. JCW, *Essays and Adventures*, p. 12; JCW, *Testament to Democracy* (London, 1942), pp. 42–4. He dedicated the first volume of his *History of Parliament* to those MPs who had been killed on active service between 1914 and 1918.

29. Wedgwood, *Last of the Radicals*, p. 167.

30. JCW, *1780–1841*, pp. 108–9.

31. For this early phase in the history of the History of Parliament, see JCW, *Memoirs*, pp. 213–23; Wedgwood, *Last of the Radicals*, pp. 163–81; A. Sandall, 'The History of Parliament', *The Table*, liv (1986), pp. 80–84.

32. L. Stone, 'Prosopography', in his *The Past and the Present* (London, 1981), pp. 45–73; E. L. C. Mullins, 'The Making of the "Return of Members"', *Bulletin of the Institute of Historical Research*, lviii (1985), pp. 189–209.

33. JCW, *Memoirs*, pp. 213–14; R. S. Ferguson, *Cumberland and Westmorland MPs, 1660–1867* (London, 1871); J. Foster, *Members of Parliament, Scotland,*

1357–1882 (2nd edn, London, 1882); G. R. Park, *Parliamentary Representation of Yorkshire* (Hull, 1886); W. D. Pink and A. B. Bevan, *Parliamentary Representation of Lancashire, 1258–1885* (London, 1889); W. W. Bean, *Parliamentary Representation of the Six Northern Counties of England, 1603–1886* (Hull, 1890); W. P. Courtney, *Parliamentary History of Cornwall* (1893); W. R. Williams, *Parliamentary History of the Principality of Wales, 1541–1895* (Brecknock, 1895).

34. Trevelyan, pp. 110–26; H. A. L. Fisher, 'The Whig Historians', *Proceedings of the British Academy*, xiv (1928), pp. 304–36.

35. JCW, *Memoirs*, p. 134; D. Cannadine, *Aspects of Aristocracy: Grandeur and Decline in Modern Britain* (London, 1994), pp. 155–60; *Essays* i, pp. 226–30.

36. JCW, *Memoirs*, p. 214; *The Times*, 24 May, 18 and 19 July 1928; Pollard MSS, Pollard to JCW, 14 July 1928.

37. Hansard, 5th Series, vol. 223, HC col. 2805, 18 December 1928; Wedgwood, *Last of the Radicals*, p. 168; JCW, *Memoirs*, p. 214.

38. Notestein MSS, Neale to Notestein, 1 January 1929, 19 November 1929.

39. *The Times*, 1 July 1929, 28 January 1930; *Interim Report of the Committee on House of Commons Personnel and Politics, 1264–1832* (Cmd 4130, 1932); HoP [W] MSS, Box A-44, Buchach to JCW, 15 January 1931.

40. *Interim Report*, p. 50.

41. Ibid., pp. 52–3.

42. *The Times*, 4 January, 9 June 1932; 13 and 18 July 1933; 11 May 1934; 6 December 1935; [A. F. Pollard,] 'Parliamentary History', *TLS*, 13 October 1932.

43. JCW, *Memoirs*, p. 216; Notestein MSS: JCW to Notestein, 18 April 1930; Notestein to JCW, 1 July 1930; Pollard MSS, JCW to Pollard, 2 March 1934.

44. H. Butterfield, *The Whig Interpretation of History* (Harmondsworth, 1973 edn), pp. 9, 11, 13, 24, 71, 79, 83–5; Trevelyan, pp. 208–9.

45. G. Lapsley, 'Some Recent Advances in English Constitutional History (Before 1485)', *Cambridge Historical Journal*, v (1936), pp. 119–61; G. Templeman, 'The History of Parliament in the Light of Modern Research', *University of Birmingham Historical Journal*, i (1948), pp. 202–31.

46. L. B. Namier: *England in the Age of the American Revolution* (London, 1930); and 'The Biography of Ordinary Men', in *Nation & Athenaeum*, 14 July 1928, reprinted in *idem, Crossroads of Power* (London, 1962), pp. 1–6; *The Structure of Politics at the Accession of George III* (London, 1929); J. Namier, *Namier: A Biography* (London, 1971), pp. 199–200; L. J. Colley, *Namier* (London, 1989), pp. 74–7.

47. Lewis MSS, Namier to JCW, 19 June 1929 (copy); Pollard MSS, Pollard to JCW, 20 June 1929; HoP [W] MSS, Box A-44, Astor to JCW, 16 August 1929.

48. M. Lawrence, 'The History of Parliament Trust', *Parliamentary Affairs*, xviii (1964), p. 458; Sandall, 'History of Parliament', pp. 82–3.

49. JCW, *Memoirs*, p. 216; *The Times*, 8 June 1933.

50. Hansard, 5th Series, vol. 292, HC cols. 1255–6, 19 July 1934; Wedgwood, *Last of the Radicals*, pp. 169–70; JCW, *Memoirs*, p. 218; 871; Lawrence, 'History of Parliament Trust', p. 459; CV v, part ii, p. 871; Pollard MSS, JCW to Pollard, 8 September 1934.

51. JCW, 'The History of Parliament', *Fortnightly Review*, cxxxviii (1935), pp. 164–73, with quotation at p. 173. See also *The Times*, 6 December 1935; JCW, 'A History of Parliament and of Public Opinion', *Political Quarterly*, v (1934), pp. 506–16.

52. JCW, *Memoirs*, p. 215.

53. Namier, *Namier*, p. 284.

54. Wedgwood, *Last of the Radicals*, p. 171; JCW, *Memoirs*, pp. 215, 218.

55. Pollard MSS, JCW to Pollard, 30 July 1935, enclosing minutes of meeting of History of Parliament Sub-Committee, 23 July 1935; Notestein MSS, Pollard to Notestein, 11 August 1935; *The Times*, 31 October 1938.

56. Pollard MSS, Notestein to Pollard, 9 August 1935; Powicke to Pollard, 15 November 1935, enclosing memorandum of meeting between Powicke and JCW, 25 September 1935; JCW to Pollard, 13 August 1935 and 11, 14, 16 July 1936; GMT to Pollard, 22, 23, 25 July 1936; Notestein MSS, Neale to Notestein, 24 October and 10 November 1935; Namier to Notestein, 7 November 1935; Powicke to Notestein, 31 January 1936 with enclosure dated January 1936; HoP [W] MSS, GMT to JCW, 27 November 1936.

57. Notestein MSS, JCW to Notestein, 31 January and 11 July 1935; Pollard MSS, JCW to Pollard, 14 July 1936, Neale to Notestein, 17 February 1937; Wedgwood, *Last of the Radicals*, p. 219; JCW, *Memoirs*, p. 218.

58. *CV* v, part ii, pp. 871–2, 878–9, 916–17; E. M. Johnston, 'Managing an Inheritance: Colonel J. C. Wedgwood, the *History of Parliament*, and the Lost History of the Irish Parliament', *Proceedings of the Royal Irish Academy*, vol. lxxxix, C, no. 7 (1989), pp. 167–86.

59. JCW, *Parliament, Biographies*, pp. viii, ix–xi, liv.

60. Ibid., pp. iv, vi, xxviii; JCW, *Parliament, Register*, p. cxxii.

61. JCW, *Parliament, Biographies*, pp. xlv, lii–liii; JCW, *Parliament, Register*, pp. cxxxiv–cxxxviii, cxlv.

62. JCW, *Parliament, Biographies*, pp. vi, xvii–xviii; JCW, *Parliament, Register*, p. lxxxi.

63. JCW, *Parliament, Biographies*, pp. xi–xiv, xx, xli; JCW, *Parliament, Register*, pp. xxxviii, lxxxii, xciv–xcv.

64. *The Times*, 5 and 26 November 1936, 28 October 1938.

65. [A. F. Pollard], 'The Mother of Parliaments: English Democracy in the Making', *TLS*, 5 December 1936; M. McKisack, review of JCW, *Parliament, Biographies*, in *English Historical Review*, liii (1938), pp. 503–6; *Guardian*, 11 November 1938; J. A. R. Marriott, 'Parliament in the Fifteenth Century', *Quarterly Review*, no. 540 (April 1939), pp. 195–6.

66. *TLS*, 19 December 1936; Pollard MSS, B. C. Richmond to Pollard, 11 August and 12 November 1936. See also HoP [W] MSS, Box A-50, JCW to J. G. Edwards, 5 August 1938, complaining about the treatment of the first volume in the *English Historical Review*.

67. JCW, *Parliament, Register*, pp. xi–xxv.

68. *TLS*, 12, 19, 26 November and 3 December 1938; HoP [W] Box A-84, Pollard to JCW, 16 November 1938.

69. Pollard MSS, JCW to Pollard, 18 November and 6 December 1938; JCW to Astor, 12 November 1938, 18 December 1940 (copies).

70. *The Times*, 31 October and 2, 7 November 1938.

71. Wedgwood, *Last of the Radicals*, p. 219; JCW, *Parliament, Biographies*, pp. lii, lv; JCW, *Parliament, Register*, p. lxxxii.

72. *The Times*, 3, 15 November 1938; JCW, *Memoirs*, p. 222.

73. *The Times*, 5 November 1936; JCW, *Memoirs*, p. 222; Lawrence, 'History of Parliament', p. 460.

74. Wedgwood, *Last of the Radicals*, p. 172; Lord Macmillan, *A Man of Law's Tale* (London, 1952), pp. 228, 304; History of Parliament, *Report by the Trustees* (30 July 1942).

75. JCW, *Memoirs*, pp. 222–3; Lawrence, 'History of Parliament Trust', pp. 460–61; Sandall, 'History of Parliament', p. 85; *The Times*, 21 December 1943.

76. *CV* v, part iii, pp. 487, 491, 941, 1158–9; *WP* i, p. 15.

77. *WP* ii, pp. 248, 457, 478, 554–5; JCW, *Memoirs*, pp. 239–49.

78. *WP* ii, p. 970; Wedgwood, *Last of the Radicals*, pp. 174–5; JCW, *Memoirs*, pp. 4–5, 223.

79. Ibid., p. 249; Wedgwood, *Last of the Radicals*, p. 245.

80. Pollard MSS, JCW to Pollard, 15 August 1941.

81. L. B. Namier, *Avenues of History* (London, 1952), p. 171; Namier, *Namier*, pp. 284–5; Wedgwood, *Last of the Radicals*, pp. 140, 178–9.

82. Namier, *Namier*, p. 285; Sandall, 'History of Parliament', p. 85; Lawrence, 'History of Parliament Trust', p. 461.

83. See the reminiscences of J. H. Plumb in *Essays* i, pp. 97–100.

84. Colley, *Namier*, pp. 77–9; Sir L. Namier and J. Brooke, *The History of Parliament: The House of Commons, 1754–1790* (3 vols., London, 1964). The remaining volumes published as *The History of Parliament* thus far are as follows: J. S. Roskell, L. Clark and C. Rawcliffe (eds.), *The House of Commons, 1386–1421* (4 vols., London, 1992); S. T. Bindoff (ed.), *The House of Commons, 1509–1558* (3 vols., London, 1982); P. W. Hasler (ed.), *The House of Commons, 1558–1603* (3 vols., London, 1981); B. D. Henning (ed.), *The House of Commons, 1660–1690* (3 vols., London, 1983); R. Sedgwick (ed.), *The House of Commons, 1715–1754* (2 vols., London, 1970); R. G. Thorne (ed.), *The House of Commons, 1790–1820* (5 vols., London, 1986).

85. Namier, *Namier*, pp. 289–91; Colley, *Namier*, pp. 79–89.

86. See, for example: A. J. P. Taylor, *Observer*, 3 May 1964; J. H. Plumb, *Spectator*, 22 May 1964; H. Butterfield, *Listener*, 8 October 1964; J. Sainty, 'The History of Parliament: The House of Commons, 1754–1790', *Parliamentary Affairs*, xvii (1964), pp. 453–7. See also Sandall, 'History of Parliament', pp. 86–8.

7 Emollience:
Stanley Baldwin and Francis Brett Young

1. R. Blake, *The Unknown Prime Minister: The Life and Times of Andrew Bonar Law (1858–1923)* (London, 1955), p. 519; N. Nicolson (ed.), *Harold Nicolson: Diaries and Letters, 1930–1939* (London, 1966), p. 301.

2. For the growing size of the electorate between 1906 and 1935, the years in which Baldwin contested his first and last general elections, see D. E. Butler, *The Electoral System in Britain since 1918* (2nd edn, Oxford, 1963), p. 172; D. Cannadine, *Class in Britain* (London, 1998), p. 106, and references cited there.

3. This case is most persuasively made in P. Williamson: 'The Doctrinal Politics of Stanley Baldwin', in M. Bentley (ed.), *Public and Private Doctrines: Essays in British History Presented to Maurice Cowling* (Cambridge, 1993), pp. 184–208; *Stanley Baldwin: Conservative Leadership and National Values* (Cambridge, 1999). See also Cannadine, *Class in Britain*, pp. 137–40.

4. H. Macmillan, *The Past Masters: Politics and Politicians, 1906–1939* (London, 1975), pp. 107–8; H. J. Laski, *Parliamentary Government in England: A Commentary* (London, 1938), p. 242; G. M. Young, *Stanley Baldwin* (London, 1952), pp. 56–7.

5. Nicolson, *Diaries and Letters, 1930–1939*, pp. 228; A. Boyle, *Montagu Norman: A Biography* (London, 1967), p. 155; A. J. P. Taylor (ed.), *W. P. Crozier Off the Record: Political Interviews, 1933–1943* (London, 1973), pp. 24–5; R. Rhodes James (ed.), *Memoirs of a Conservative: J. C. C. Davidson's Memoirs and Papers, 1910–1937* (London, 1969), p. 105; A. W. Baldwin, *My Father: The True Story* (London, 1955), pp. 50–51, 100–101, 305.

6. See chapter 10.

7. *Trevelyan*, pp. 151–67; Williamson, *Baldwin*, p. 244; W. J. Keith, *Regions of the Imagination: The Development of British Rural Fiction* (Toronto, 1988), pp. 129–40.

8. Laski, *Parliamentary Government*, p. 161. The chief sources for this section, in addition to the Baldwin MSS and the many biographical studies, are the published volumes of SB's speeches: *On England* (London, 1926); *Our Inheritance* (London, 1928); *This Torch of Freedom* (London, 1935); *Service of Our Lives* (London, 1937); *An Interpreter of England* (London, 1939).

9. A. J. P. Taylor, *English History, 1914–1945* (Harmondsworth, 1970), p. 74; J. Campbell, *Lloyd George* (London, 1977), pp. 3, 234, 242; K. O. Morgan, *Consensus and Disunity: The Lloyd George Coalition, 1918–1922* (Oxford, 1979), pp. 1–6, 363–6.

10. SB, *On England*, pp. 101–2; SB, *Torch of Freedom*, p. 184. In his famous memorandum on the disputed succession to Bonar Law, J. C. C. Davidson stressed Baldwin's 'honesty, simplicity and balance': Rhodes James, *Memoirs of a Conservative*, p. 154.

11. SB, *On England*, pp. 19, 56; Williamson, *Baldwin*, pp. 206–8.

12. C. L. Mowat, *Britain Between the Wars, 1918–1940* (Boston, 1971), p. 196;

SB, *On England*, pp. 62, 101–2, 108, 133, 144–5, 158, 160, 163, 267; SB, *Our Inheritance*, pp. 60, 124, 210, 256, 268, 295; SB, *This Torch of Freedom*, pp. 15, 78, 239, 255; *The Times*, 16 March 1923.

13. K. Young, *Stanley Baldwin* (London, 1976), p. 45; the Earl of Birkenhead, *F. E.: The Life of F. E. Smith, First Earl of Birkenhead* (London, 1959), pp. 334, 554; H. Pelling, *Winston Churchill* (London, 1974), pp. 417–18; R. Blake, 'Baldwin and the Right', in J. Raymond (ed.), *The Baldwin Age* (London, 1960), pp. 35–6; K. Middlemas and J. Barnes, *Baldwin: A Biography* (London, 1969), p. 499; SB, *Our Inheritance*, pp. 284, 307; SB, *Torch of Freedom*, pp. 6, 197, 224; SB, *Service of Our Lives*, pp. 47, 94.

14. Williamson, 'Doctrinal Politics of Stanley Baldwin', pp. 201–2, 205; SB, *On England*, 52, 60. For the impact of these speeches on the Commons, see Middlemas and Barnes, *Baldwin*, pp. 151–2, 296–8.

15. A. J. P. Taylor: *Beaverbrook* (Harmondsworth, 1974), p. 840; and *English History, 1914–1945*, p. 74; Middlemas and Barnes, *Baldwin*, pp. 27, 95–9, 208; Rhodes James, *Memoirs of a Conservative*, pp. 79, 94, 103, 170, 238–9, 243–5, 278–88; M. Cowling, *The Impact of Labour, 1920–1924* (Cambridge, 1971), p. 415; SB, *On England*, p. 16.

16. *Morning Post*, 4 January 1926.

17. Young, *Baldwin*, p. 106; H. Montgomery Hyde, *Baldwin: The Unexpected Prime Minister* (London, 1973), p. 291. See note 8 above for details of SB's volumes of speeches.

18. SB, *Torch of Freedom*, p. v.

19. T. Jones, *A Diary with Letters, 1931–1950* (London, 1954), p. 157.

20. SB, *On England*, pp. 93–7, 114, 155; SB, *Torch of Freedom*, p. 271; Rhodes James, *Memoirs of a Conservative*, p. 171.

21. SB, *Torch of Freedom*, p. 155.

22. SB, *Service of Our Lives*, p. 65; Mowat, *Britain Between the Wars*, p. 586; Hyde, *Baldwin*, p. 504; Nicolson, *Diaries and Letters, 1930–1939*, pp. 285–6.

23. *Northern Whig*, 30 July 1923. For the distrust with which Churchill's over-polished oratory was widely regarded, see chapter 4.

24. *Manchester Guardian*, 14 October 1931; Young, *Baldwin*, p. 83; Rhodes James *Memoirs of a Conservative*, pp. 253–4.

25. A. Briggs, *The History of Broadcasting in the United Kingdom*, vol. i, *The Birth of Broadcasting* (London, 1961), pp. 268, 271; vol. ii, *The Golden Age of Wireless* (London, 1965), pp. 5, 133, 135, 139, 141; Taylor, *English History, 1914–1945*, pp. 301, 594; Pelling, *Churchill*, pp. 341–2.

26. C. E. Bechofer Roberts, *Stanley Baldwin: Man or Miracle?* (London, 1936), p. 109. A. Bryant, *Stanley Baldwin: A Tribute* (London, 1937), p. 101; Middlemas and Barnes, *Baldwin*, p. 171.

27. Sir David Low, *Low's Autobiography* (London, 1956), p. 162; Baldwin, *My Father*, p. 102; Young, *Baldwin*, pp. 56–7; S. Salvidge, *Salvidge of Liverpool* (London, 1934), p. 255; Bechofer Roberts, *Baldwin*, p. 110.

28. *The Times*, 30 April 1923; Taylor, *English History*, p. 288; Bryant, *Baldwin*, p. 100.

29. Baldwin, *My Father*, pp. 69–70.

30. Lord Butler, *The Art of the Possible* (London, 1971), p. 30; K. Middlemas (ed.), *Thomas Jones: Whitehall Diary* (2 vols., London, 1969–71), vol. i, p. 243; Rhodes James, *Memoirs of a Conservative*, p. 105.

31. SB, *On England*, pp. 6–7; Hyde, *Baldwin*, pp. 66, 81; Rhodes James, *Memoirs of a Conservative*, pp. 82, 112.

32. SB, *Service of Our Lives*, pp. 91–2.

33. SB, *On England*, p. 6.

34. SB, *The Preservation of Ancient Cottages: An Appeal* (London, n.d.), p. 6.

35. SB, *Our Inheritance*, pp. 304–5; SB, *Torch of Freedom*, pp. 116, 120. For a more fully coherent articulation of this view of the countryside, see: A. Bryant: *The Spirit of Conservatism* (London, 1929), pp. 3–4, 74–80; and *Humanity in Politics* (London, 1938), pp. 61–4, 177–80.

36. SB, *On England*, p. 19; SB, *Service of Our Lives*, p. 99.

37. SB, *On England*, p. 14.

38. For his speeches to the Association, see SB, *Torch of Freedom*, p. 119; *Worcestershire Echo*, 9 October 1926; *Worcestershire Daily Times*, 20 February 1930; *Kidderminster Times*, 20 February 1932; *The Times*, 27 February 1929, 27 October 1938.

39. *Worcestershire Echo*, 9 October 1926.

40. *Daily Telegraph*, 24 February 1927.

41. *The Times*, 27 October 1938.

42. R. Blake, *The Conservative Party from Peel to Churchill* (London, 1972), p. 216.

43. R. G. G. Price, *A History of Punch* (London, 1957), pp. 160–63, 225–6, 232–3, 248, 285; Low, *Low's Autobiography*, pp. 208–12.

44. *The Times*, 22 February 1934. In addition to the Brett Young MSS and *JBY*, this section quotes extensively from FBY's novels. Because they went through so many editions and reprintings, I have only given references for the most extended quotations, which are to chapters rather than pages.

45. 'The Master Touch of Francis Brett Young', *Daily Mail*, 24 February 1933; Pamela Hansford Johnson, 'Literature', in Raymond, *Baldwin Age*, pp. 186–8.

46. For FBY's early years, see: *JBY*, ch. 1, and FBY's early autobiographical novel, *The Young Physician* (London, 1919).

47. Brett Young MSS: 23, Notes for an autobiography, pp. 9–10; 2770, FBY to E. G. Twitchett, 30 January 1935; Baldwin MSS vol. 169, f. 378, FBY to Baldwin, 21 July 1934.

48. Brett Young MSS, 276, FBY to Jessica Brett Young, 8 October 1906.

49. FBY, *The Young Physician*, preface.

50. Brett Young MSS 2270, FBY to E. G. Twitchett, 30 January 1935; E. G. Twitchett, *Francis Brett Young* (London, 1935), pp. 18–19; L. J. Jay, 'The Black Country of Francis Brett Young', *Transactions of the Institute of British Geographers*, lxvi (1975), pp. 57–72.

51. Brett Young MSS, 781, FBY to J. B. Pinker, 10 December 1919.

52. FBY, *The Iron Age*, ch. 1; FBY, *The Young Physician*, book ii, ch. 1.

53. R. Williams, *The Country and the City* (London, 1973), p. 253.

54. FBY, *The Young Physician*, book 1, ch. 10; FBY, *The Black Diamond*, ch. 8.

55. *The Times*, 29 March 1954.

56. FBY, *Portrait of Clare*, preface.

57. Brett Young MSS: 1953, SB to FBY, 23 April 1927; 1954, SB to FBY, 17 October 1928; SB, *Our Inheritance*, p. 82.

58. Baldwin MSS, vol. 165, f. 382, FBY to SB, 25 October 1930; Brett Young MSS, 1619 and 1920, A. Gyde to FBY, 20 December 1932, 4 January 1933.

59. Jones, *Diary with Letters*, p. 65; Baldwin MSS, vol. 169, f. 378, FBY to SB, 21 July 1934; FBY MSS 1962, SB to FBY, 31 August 1936.

60. *JBY*, pp. 235, 249, 250; Jones, *Diary with Letters*, p. 78; Brett Young MSS: 1957, 1963, 2531, SB to FBY, 3 February 1933, 28 August 1936, 7 December 1939; 1623, FBY to A. Gyde, 27 July 1937; 2535, Windham Baldwin to FBY, 23 July 1951.

61. Baldwin MSS, vol. 167, f. 132, FBY to SB, 28 September 1932; Brett Young MSS, 2833, FBY to A. P. Herbert, 10 February 1933.

62. *JBY*, pp. 189, 193, 209–10; A. Gyde, article on FBY in *DNB, 1951–1960* (London, 1971), p. 1091; Brett Young MSS: 1851, Statement of account of alterations made at Craycombe, 1934 (the bill was £2,850); 2554, Lord Beauchamp to FBY, 28 June 1938; 61, MS speech on behalf of the Council for the Preservation of Rural England, 5 October 1938; 2478, FBY to Hugh Walpole, 16 March 1939; 2486, FBY to C. S. L. Alford, 24 March 1951.

63. Williamson, 'Doctrinal Politics of Stanley Baldwin', p. 195; Brett Young MSS: 56A, Typescript for speech in the USA, 1927, pp. 5, 10; 2181, FBY to K. Nirschl, 4 December 1934; *Mr Lucton's Freedom*, part ii, ch. 9; *This Little World*, chs. 5, 9.

64. FBY, *Mr Lucton's Freedom*, part i, ch. 4; FBY, *Far Forest*, part iii, ch. 2; FBY, *Dr Bradley Remembers*, ch. 6; FBY, *My Brother Jonathan*, book iii, ch. 3.

65. FBY, *Portrait of a Village*, ch. 2; FBY, *This Little World*, Prelude, chs. 10, 12.

66. FBY, *Mr Lucton's Freedom*, part ii, ch. 2.

67. FBY, *Portrait of a Village*, ch. 3.

68. FBY, *This Little World*, chs. 1, 20.

69. Twitchett, *Francis Brett Young*, p. 261.

70. FBY, *This Little World*, chs. 1, 22.

71. Baldwin MSS, vol. 152, f. 72, FBY to SB, 7 July 1937.

72. A. Roberts, *'The Holy Fox': A Biography of Lord Halifax* (London, 1991), p. 305.

73. R. I. McKibbin, *The Ideologies of Class: Social Relations in Britain, 1880–1950* (Oxford, 1990), pp. 270–300.

74. D. Cannadine, *Aspects of Aristocracy: Grandeur and Decline in Modern Britain* (London, 1994), pp. 158–60.

75. FBY, 'Craycombe House, Worcestershire', *Country Life*, 6 July 1940, pp. 10–14.

76. 'Cato', *Guilty Men* (London, 1940), esp. pp. 15–35.

77. Jones, *Dairy with Letters*, p. 491; Young, *Baldwin*, p. 251.

78. Brett Young MSS, 1941, FBY to Mr Clemens, 24 April 1948.

79. Brett Young MSS: 3035, FBY to Sir Compton Mackenzie, 20 October 1948; 3003, FBY to Viscount Cobham, 19 December 1950; 2536, FBY to Windham Baldwin, 10 September 1951; 2976, FBY to Lady Frances Lloyd George, 13 January 1948.

80. Brett Young MSS: 3365, FBY to Austin Strong, 20 June 1947; 3164, FBY to H. V. Morton, 22 October 1947; 2626, FBY to Edwin Cerio, 29 October 1947; 2509, FBY to William Armstrong, 10 February 1948; R. Church, 'Fashion Passed Him By', *Books and Bookmen* i (1955), p. 13.

81. 2 *WW* i, pp. 169–70, 615; Taylor, *Beaverbrook*, pp. 275–8, 520–21, 575, 658; M. J. Wiener, *English Culture and the Decline of the Industrial Spirit, 1850–1980* (Harmondsworth, 1992), pp. 101–2, 108–9.

82. P. Ziegler, *Wilson: The Authorized Life of Lord Wilson of Riveaux* (London, 1993), pp. 436, 518; A. Seldon, *Major: A Political Life* (London, 1997), pp. 370, 587, 744.

83. E. Chitham, *The Black Country* (London, 1972), p. 162, describes his characters as 'cardboard dodos who lacked depth'. For a more sympathetic treatment, see G. Cavaliero, *The Rural Tradition in the English Novel, 1900–1939* (London, 1977), pp. 81–92.

8 Diplomacy:
G. M. Trevelyan and R. B. Merriman

1. This essay began life as a lecture delivered to the Colonial Society of Massachusets, and it was subsequently given to the annual conference of the Historical Association in Cambridge. I am most grateful to Dr Kevin Van Anglen, Professor John M. Blum, Professor Sir John Elliott, Professor Paul Kennedy, Dr David Reynolds, Professor Arthur M. Schlesinger, jr. and Dr James Thompson for their help in preparing this essay. And a special word of thanks to Roger Merriman's daughter, Mrs Helen Merriman Fernald, for her many kindnesses. For GMT's side of this story, I have drawn heavily on *Trevelyan*, to which the reader is referred for fuller documentation.

2. D. Reynolds, *The Creation of the Anglo-American Alliance, 1937–41: A Study in Competitive Co-operation* (London, 1981), pp. 37–62, provides much the best and fullest account.

3. Ibid., p. 7.

4. K. S. Davis, *FDR: Into the Storm, 1937–1940: A History* (New York, 1993), pp. 403–4; F. Freidel, *Franklin D. Roosevelt: A Rendezvous with Destiny* (Boston, 1990), pp. 312–13; W. R. Rock, *Chamberlain and Roosevelt: British Foreign Policy and the United States, 1937–1940* (Columbus, Ohio, 1988), p. 144; D. Reynolds: 'FDR on the British: A Postscript', *Proceedings of the Massachusetts Historical Society*, xc (1978), pp. 106–10; and *Lord Lothian and Anglo-American Relations, 1939–1940*, in *Transactions of the American Philosophical Society*, lxxiii, part ii (1983), pp. 7–8.

5. I. M. Calder, *The New Haven Colony* (reprinted, Hamden, Conn., 1970), p. 74; *Reunion of Descendants of Nathaniel Merriman at Wallingford, Conn., June 4, 1913* (New Haven, 1914); *The Merriman Bulletin*, 4 March 1915, p. 4.

6. G. Bigelow Howe, *Report of the Bigelow Family Reunion at Lincoln Park, Thursday June 2 1887* (Buffalo, 1887); and *Genealogy of the Bigelow Family of America* (Worcester, Mass., 1890); *Dictionary of American Biography*, vol. ii (New York, 1929), pp. 254–61; J. S. Ewing and N. P. Norton, *Broadlooms and Businessmen: A History of the Bigelow-Sanford Carpet Company* (Cambridge, Mass., 1955), pp. 15–20, 61–6, 143–4; P. D. Hall, 'What the Merchants Did with Their Money: Charitable and Testamentary Trusts in Massachusetts, 1780–1880', in C. E. Wright and K. P. Viens (eds.), *Entrepreneurs: The Boston Business Community, 1700–1850* (Boston, 1997), pp. 413–14.

7. N. Godwin, *The Foote Family: or, the descendants of Nathaniel Foote, one of the first settlers in Wethersfield, Connecticut, with general notes of Pasco Foote, who settled in Salem, Massachusetts, and John Foote, and others of the name, who settled more recently in New York* (Hartford, 1849); M. Wilder Tileston, *Caleb and Mary Wilder Foote: Reminiscences and Letters* (New York, 1918).

8. R. Story, *The Forging of an Aristocracy: Harvard and the Boston Upper Class, 1800–1870* (Middletown, Conn., 1980), pp. 175–9; R. Norton Smith, *The Harvard Century: The Making of a University to a Nation* (New York, 1986), p. 27; J. Finley, 'Roger Bigelow Merriman '96, First Master of Eliot House', article in possession of Mrs Helen Merriman Fernald. Merriman's son, Daniel, would go on to be Master of Davenport College at Yale University, 1946–66: *The Installation of Daniel Merriman, Second Master of Davenport College, 14 May 1946* (New Haven, privately printed for the Fellows of Davenport College, 1946).

9. GMT, *Sir George Otto Trevelyan: A Memoir* (London, 1932), p. 1.

10. *Trevelyan*, pp. 4–9.

11. Ibid., p. 65.

12. Anon [W. E. Gladstone], review of Sir George Otto Trevelyan, *Life and Letters of Lord Macaulay*, *Quarterly Review*, cxlii (1876), p. 2.

13. RBM, *Life and Letters of Thomas Cromwell* (2 vols., Oxford, 1902), vol. i, p. iv; *Harvard University Gazette*, Memorial Minute of RBM, 20 November 1945. RBM's fondness for Oxford is well displayed in his reviews of C. E. Mallet, *A History of the University of Oxford* (2 vols., London, 1924), *AHR*, xxx (1926), pp. 109–11; and of C. E. Mallet, *A History of the University of Oxford*, vol. iii (London, 1928), *AHR*, xxxiii (1927–8), pp. 908–9.

14. Harvard University MSS, HUC 8903, 138, 'History and Government and Economics', course catalogue, 1903–4, p. 17; Merriman MSS, GMT to RBM, 20 December 1925; 2 May 1935; *The Times*, 14 June 1935; *Boston Herald*, 8 September 1945; RBM, 'Some Notes on the Treatment of English Catholics in the Reign of Elizabeth', *AHR*, xi (1907–8), pp. 480–500. See also RBM's many reviews of works on the sixteenth and seventeenth century, including: A. F. Pollard, *Thomas Cranmer and the English Reformation, 1489–1556* (London, 1904), *AHR*, x (1904–5), pp. 861–3; A. D. Innes, *England Under the Tudors* (London, 1905); A. F. Pollard, *Henry VIII* (London, 1905), *AHR*, xi (1905–6), pp. 648–51; H. A. L. Fisher, *The History of England from the Accession of Henry VII to the Death of Henry VIII, 1485–1547* (London, 1906), *AHR*, xiii (1907–8), pp. 334–7; A. F. Pollard, *The History of England from the Accession of Edward VI to the Death of*

Elizabeth (1547–1603) (London, 1910), *AHR*, xvi (1910–11), pp. 600–602; J. Gardiner, *Lollardy and the Reformation in England: an Historical Survey*, vol. iii (London, 1911), *AHR*, xvii (1911–12), pp. 366–7; E. P. Cheyney, *A History of England from the Defeat of the Armada to the Death of Elizabeth*, vol. i (London, 1914), *AHR*, xix (1913–14), pp. 883–5.

15. Nevins MSS, GMT to Nevins, 23 February 148; Jones MSS, GMT to Mary Cadwalader Jones, 25 April 1915; *Trevelyan*, pp. 6, 189.

16. Bryant MSS, GMT to Bryant, 10 April 1936; Notestein MSS, GMT to Notestein, 25 February 1931; Merriman MSS, GMT to RBM, 11 September 1934; GMT's address 'History and Literature' was first given to the Anglo-American Conference of Historians in London in July 1923, and was subsequently published in *History*, ix (1924–5), pp. 81–91, and with modifications in the *Yale Review*, new series, xiv (1924–5), pp. 109–25. For the correspondence about this, see *Yale Review* MSS, GMT to Wilbur Cross, 13, 21 March, 3 May and 18 September 1924.

17. Obituary notice of RBM in *AHR*, li (1945–6), pp. 413–14; P. Novick, *That Noble Dream: The 'Objectivity Question' and the American Historical Profession* (Cambridge, 1988), pp. 44–5; RBM, entry on William Prescott in *Dictionary of American Biography*, vol. xv (New York, 1935), p. 199; Finlay, 'Merriman', p. 2; RBM, *Suleiman the Magnificent, 1520–1566* (Cambridge, Mass., 1944), p. vi; J. H. Elliott, *Imperial Spain, 1469–1716* (London, 1963), p. 383; *Trevelyan*, pp. 183–4.

18. Ibid., pp. 66–7, 149.

19. Ibid., pp. 95, 105–19.

20. RBM, *Cromwell*, vol. i, pp. 308–9; RBM, *Six Contemporaneous Revolutions* (Glasgow, 1937), p. 17. Not surprisingly, RBM's 'deliberately [*sic*] cold and hostile picture' of Cromwell did not commend itself to G. R. Elton, who was never at ease with patrician Whig historians. See G. R. Elton: *The Tudor Revolution in Government* (Cambridge, 1953), pp. 1, 6; *Policy and Police: The Enforcement of the Reformation in the Age of Thomas Cromwell* (Cambridge, 1972), pp. 3, 327–9, 386, 391; and *Reform and Renewal: Thomas Cromwell and the Common Weal* (Cambridge, 1973), p. 39. See also B. W. Beckingsale, *Thomas Cromwell: Tudor Minister* (London, 1978), pp. 144–5.

21. See, for instance, RBM's blistering review of M. Haile, *The Life of Reginald Pole* (New York, 1910), *AHR*, xvi (1910–11), pp. 382–3, which he claimed added 'one more to the already long list of recent attempts to disseminate and popularize the Roman Catholic view of the great figures of the Reformation . . . like most of the species to which it belongs, [it] does not deserve to be treated as serious history'. See also his dismissal for its 'ignorance and credulity . . . preposterous incompetence' of the Catholic William T. Walsh's biography of *Philip II* (New York, 1937), *AHR*, xliv (1938–9), pp. 342–4, and the ensuing, no-less vitriolic correspondence between the author and the reviewer: *AHR*, xlv (1939–40), pp. 265–7. For the background, see Novick, *Noble Dream*, p. 203; P. Allitt, *Catholic Converts: British and American Intellectuals Turn to Rome* (Ithaca, 1997), pp. 244–5.

22. RBM, *The Rise of the Spanish Empire in the Old World and the New*, vol. i, *The Middle Ages* (New York, 1918), pp. xii, 3–4, 39–41; and vol. iv, *Philip the Prudent* (New York, 1934), esp. pp. 671–3, 679–80. See also his review of J. H. Parry, *The*

Spanish Theory of Empire in the Sixteenth Century (Cambridge, 1940), *AHR*, xlvi (1940–41), p. 453. The first volume of *Spanish Empire* was dedicated to the 'honoured memory' of Prescott. For RBM's place in this historical tradition, see R. L. Kagan, 'Prescott's Paradigm: American Historical Scholarship and the Decline of Spain', *AHR*, ci (1996), pp. 423–46, though the author perhaps underestimates RBM's adherence to Prescott's views.

23. Merriman MSS, GMT to RBM, 20 December 1925, 11 September 1934, 8 December 1938.

24. Merriman MSS, Dorothea Merriman to 'Beloved Family', 16 August 1929; RBM to 'Dearest Mother', 18 August 1929. For RBM's connections with the Massachusetts Historical Society, see L. L. Tucker, *The Massachusetts Historical Society: A Bicentennial History, 1791–1991* (Boston, 1995), pp. 377, 512, 540–41, 544.

25. *Trevelyan*, pp. 6–7, 19–26, 130–40, 160–67, 175–9.

26. This was distinctly unusual: FDR did not welcome historians into his administration with the enthusiasm that John F. Kennedy would later show for Arthur M. Schlesinger, jr. See H. Feis, 'Some Notes on Historical Record-keeping, the Role of Historians, and the Influence of Historical Memories During the Era of the Second World War', in F. L. Loewenheim (ed.), *The Historian and the Diplomat: The Role of History and Historians in American Foreign Policy* (New York, 1967), pp. 91–3.

27. F. Friedel, *Franklin D. Roosevelt: The Apprenticeship* (Boston, 1952), pp. 60–61; K. S. Davis, *FDR: The Beckoning of Destiny, 1882–1928* (New York, 1971), pp. 138–40; Harvard University MSS, UA III 15.75.10, FDR Undergraduate Record Card, 1901–3; *New York Times*, 8 September 1945; information kindly supplied by Mrs Helen Merriman Fernald in a letter to the author, 28 January 1998.

28. *New York Herald Tribune*, 8 September 1945. Snatches of the FDR–RBM correspondence are reprinted in *F.D.R. His Personal Letters, 1905–1928*, vol. i (New York, 1950), pp. 50–51, 55–6. See also Roosevelt MSS, President's Personal Files, PPF 962, FDR to RBM, 14 November 1933; RBM to FDR, 10 November 1933, 29 March, 3 October, 10 October 1934, 30 October 1935.

29. *Trevelyan*, pp. 85, 127–9, 133–4.

30. Ibid., pp. 126, 166–7. See also WSC to GMT, 3 January 1935, printed in *CV* v, part ii, pp. 984–5.

31. RBM, 'The Monroe Doctrine – Its Past and Present Status', *The Political Quarterly*, no. vii (1916), pp. 17–40; *New York Herald Tribune*, 8 September 1945.

32. J. T. McGreevy, 'Thinking on One's Own: Catholicism and the American Intellectual Imagination, 1928–1960', *Journal of American History*, lxxxiv (1987), pp. 108–9. For hints as to RBM's attitude to Mussolini's Italy and Hitler's Germany, see his *Six Contemporaneous Revolutions* (Oxford, 1938), pp. 215–17; also his reviews of C. Fatta, *Il regno di Enrico VIII d'Inghilterra secondo I documenti contemporanei* (2 vols., Florence 1938), *AHR*, xliv (1938–9), pp. 964–5; and of F. Hartlub, *Don Juan d'Austria und die Schlacht bei Lepanto* (Berlin, 1940), *AHR*, xlvi (1940–41), pp. 712–13.

33. Information kindly supplied by Arthur M. Schlesinger, jr., in a letter to the author, 15 January 1998. For his own subsequent account of this episode, see

A. M. Schlesinger, jr., *A Life in the Twentieth Century*, vol. i, *Innocent Beginnings, 1917–1950* (Boston, 2000), pp. 196–7.

34. Merriman MSS, GMT to RBM, 28 January 1939.

35. Roosevelt MSS, President's Secretary's File 46, Great Britain 1939, RBM to FDR, 10 February 1939.

36. There are three copies of this biography in the FDR Library, one bearing the president's signature with '1937' under it, the other two apparently being gifts to him in 1938. Information kindly supplied by Raymond Teichman, Supervisory Archivist, Hyde Park Presidential Library, in a letter to the author, 4 February 1998.

37. Merriman MSS, FDR to RBM, 15 February 1939.

38. Roosevelt MSS, President's Secretary's File, Great Britain 1939, RBM to FDR, 17 February 1939.

39. PRO FO 794/18, RBM to GMT, 17 February 1939.

40. Merriman MSS, GMT to RBM, 25 February 1939.

41. PRO FO 794/18, GMT to Halifax, 25 February 1939.

42. PRO FO 794/18, Vyvyan to Strang, 4 March 1939; *Trinity College Annual Record* (1991–2), pp. 56–8.

43. J. R. M. Butler, *Lord Lothian* (London, 1960), pp. 216–17, 222–9.

44. Reynolds: 'FDR on the British', pp. 106–10; and *Lothian and Anglo-American Relations*, pp. 6–8.

45. J. Harvey (ed.), *The Diplomatic Diaries of Oliver Harvey* (London, 1970), pp. 258–9, 274; D. Dilks (ed.), *The Diaries of Sir Alexander Cadogan, OM, 1938–1945* (London, 1971), pp. 78, 82–3, 90, 130, 154.

46. Reynolds, *Lothian and Anglo-American Relations*, p. 7. FDR made the same points to Harold Ickes at about this time: Harold L. Ickes, *The Secret Diary of Harold L. Ickes*, vol. ii, *The Inside Struggle, 1936–1939* (New York, 1954), pp. 571–2.

47. A. Roberts, *'The Holy Fox': A Biography of Lord Halifax* (London, 1991), pp. 139–42; Harvey, *Diplomatic Diaries*, pp. 255–8, 260–61; Reynolds, *Anglo-American Alliance*, pp. 39–40; PRO FO 794/18, GMT to Halifax, 25 February 1939.

48. *Trevelyan*, pp. 16, 134–6, 167–74.

49. *St. Louis Dispatch*, 16 May 1940; *Boston Herald*, 8 October 1941. See also *F.D.R. His Personal Letters, 1928–1945*, vol. ii (New York, 1950), p. 1028.

50. Merriman MSS, GMT to Dorothea Merriman, 9 October 1946.

51. RBM, review of J. Gardiner, *Lollardy and the Reformation in England: an Historical Survey*, vol. iv (London, 1913), *AHR*, xix (1913–14), p. 602.

9 Tradition:
Gilbert and Sullivan as a 'National Institution'

1. This essay originated as a lecture, given at a symposium on 'Gilbert and Sullivan: A Window on the Victorian World', held at the Pierpont Morgan Library in New York on 16 and 17 November 1989, and was subsequently published, in a revised and augmented form, in the *New York Review of Books*, 7 March 1991, pp. 38–43.

In its final version, it appeared in R. Porter (ed.), *Myths of the English* (Oxford, 1992), pp. 12–30. I am most grateful to Mr Frederic Woodbridge Wilson, the Curator of the Gilbert and Sullivan Collection at the Morgan Library, for his expert help and encouragement.

2. C. Brahms, *Gilbert and Sullivan: Lost Chords and Discords* (London, 1975), p. 123; L. Baily, *Gilbert and Sullivan and Their World* (London, 1973), p. 104.

3. H. Pearson, *Gilbert: His Life and Strife* (London, 1957), p. 128.

4. C. Hibbert, *Gilbert, Sullivan and their Victorian World* (New York, 1976), p. 279.

5. For the essential background, see G. Rowell, *Theatre in the Age of Irving* (Oxford, 1981), chs. 1, 2, 4; M. R. Booth, 'The Metropolis on Stage', in H. J. Dyos and M. Wolff (eds.), *The Victorian City: Images and Realities* (2 vols., London, 1973), vol. i, pp. 211–26.

6. R. Traubner, *Operetta: A Theatrical History* (New York, 1989), pp. 11–13, 19, 36–40, 113–18; C. Hayter, *Gilbert and Sullivan* (New York, 1987), pp. 24–42.

7. For the relation between Gilbert's early work and the Savoy Operas, see J. Stedman, *Gilbert Before Sullivan* (Chicago, 1967), pp. 1–52.

8. J. Stedman, 'From Dame to Woman: W. S. Gilbert and Theatrical Transvestism', *Victorian Studies*, xiv (1970), pp. 27–46.

9. G. Smith, *The Savoy Operas: A New Guide to Gilbert and Sullivan* (London, 1983), p. 39.

10. Smith, *Savoy Operas*, pp. 48–9.

11. Hibbert, *Gilbert, Sullivan and their Victorian World*, p. 152.

12. Rowell, *Theatre in the Age of Irving*, p. 88.

13. Baily, *Gilbert and Sullivan*, p. 92.

14. Traubner, *Operetta*, pp. 187, 195–201.

15. A. Hyman, *Sullivan and his Satellites: A Survey of English Operetta, 1860–1914* (London, 1978), p. 116.

16. For the general background, see N. Stone, *Europe Transformed, 1878–1919* (London, 1983), pp. 13–73; E. J. Hobsbawm, *The Age of Empire, 1875–1914* (London, 1987), esp. chs. 2–7.

17. For two pioneering discussions, see: I. Bradley, 'Gilbert and Sullivan and the Victorian Age', *History Today*, vol. 31, no. 9 (1981), pp. 17–20; E. M. Sigsworth, 'W. S. Gilbert ... The Wisest Fool', in idem (ed.), *In Search of Victorian Values: Aspects of Nineteenth-Century Thought and Society* (London, 1988), pp. 179–94.

18. E. P. Lawrence, ' "The Happy Land": W. S. Gilbert as Political Satirist', *Victorian Studies*, xv (1971), pp. 180–83.

19. D. Cannadine, 'The Context, Performance and Meaning of Ritual: The British Monarchy and the "Invention of Tradition", *c.* 1820–1977', in E. J. Hobsbawm and T. Ranger (eds.), *The Invention of Tradition* (Cambridge, 1983), pp. 108–38.

20. Baily, *Gilbert and Sullivan*, p. 100.

21. F. M. L. Thompson, *English Landed Society in the Nineteenth Century* (London, 1963), pp. 305–8; D. Cannadine, *The Decline and Fall of the British Aristocracy* (London, 1990), pp. 406–17.

22. P. M. Kennedy, *The Rise and Fall of British Naval Mastery* (London, 1976), pp. 177–9.

23. B. Bond, 'Recruiting the Victorian Army, 1870–92', *Victorian Studies*, v (1962), pp. 331–2.

24. A. Goodman, *Gilbert and Sullivan at Law* (London, 1983), pp. 178–94.

25. D. Duman, *The English and Colonial Bars in the Nineteenth Century* (London, 1983), pp. 55–70.

26. R. D. Storch, 'The "Plague of the Blue Locusts": Political Reform and Popular Resistance in Northern England, 1840–1857', *International Review of Social History*, xx (1975), pp. 61–90; J. E. King, '"We Could Eat the Police!": Popular, Violence in the North Lancashire Cotton Strike of 1878', *Victorian Studies*, xxviii (1985), pp. 439, 468–71.

27. See W. J. Fishman, *East End* (London, 1988); J. R. Walkowitz, 'Jack the Ripper and the Myth of Male Violence', *Feminist Studies*, viii (1982), pp. 542–74.

28. R. Allen (ed.), *The First Night Gilbert and Sullivan* (London, 1975), pp. 203–4, 413.

29. P. M. Kennedy, 'Continuity and Discontinuity in British Imperialism, 1875–1914', in C. C. Eldridge (ed.), *British Imperialism in the Nineteenth Century* (London, 1985), pp. 32–3.

30. Hayter, *Gilbert and Sullivan*, pp. 45, 118–19.

31. Pearson, *Gilbert*, p. 229.

32. *The Times*, 13 September 1948.

33. R. Wilson and F. Lloyd, *Gilbert and Sullivan: The D'Oyly Carte Years* (London, 1984), pp. 90, 121–8.

34. Hibbert, *Gilbert, Sullivan and their Victorian World*, p. 272.

35. E. J. Hobsbawm, 'Introduction: Inventing Traditions' and 'Mass Producing Traditions: Europe, 1870–1914', in Hobsbawm and Ranger, *Invention of Tradition*, pp. 1–14, 263–308.

36. R. Rhodes James (ed.), *'Chips': The Diaries of Sir Henry Channon* (London, 1967), p. 470.

37. Cannadine, *Decline and Fall*, pp. 48–54, 417–20, 458–71.

38. For the influence of Gilbert and Sullivan on Wodehouse and Coward, see: S. Morley, *A Talent to Amuse: A Biography of Noël Coward* (revised edn, Harmondsworth, 1974), pp. 4, 9, 28; B. Green, *P. G. Wodehouse: A Literary Biography* (London, 1981), pp. 13, 18–19, 26, 49, 95–8.

39. C. F. Behrman, *Victorian Myths of the Sea* (Athens, Ohio, 1977), pp. 104–7.

40. V. A. C. Gatrell, 'The Decline of Theft and Violence in Victorian and Edwardian England', in V. A. C. Gatrell, B. Lenman and G. Parker (eds.), *Crime and the Law: The Social History of Crime in Western Europe since 1500* (London, 1980), pp. 240–41, 280–86, 290–93.

41. G. Best, 'The Making of the English Working Classes', *Historical Journal*, viii (1965), p. 278.

42. L. Ayre, *The Gilbert and Sullivan Companion* (New York, 1972), p. 207.

43. Brahms, *Gilbert and Sullivan*, p. 14.

44. Wilson and Lloyd, *Gilbert and Sullivan*, p. 208.

45. *The Times*, 3 May 1985.

46. A. Jacobs, *Arthur Sullivan: A Victorian Musician* (Oxford, 1984).

47. D. Eden, *Gilbert and Sullivan: The Creative Conflict* (London, 1986).

48. S. Banfield, *Sondheim's Broadway Musicals* (Ann Arbor, 1993), pp. 83, 213, 223, 251–3, 276.

10 Conservation:
The National Trust and the National Heritage

1. I am most grateful to Samantha Wyndham, the National Trust's Centenary Research Assistant, for her prompt and expert help, without which this essay could not have been written. I must also thank Margaret Willes and Merlin Waterson for their advice and encouragement. In fairness to them, I should add that the views expressed in this essay are entirely my own, and that no attempt has been made by anyone at the National Trust to influence them.

2. R. Fedden, *The Continuing Purpose: A History of the National Trust, Its Aims and Work* (London, 1968); J. Gaze, *Figures in a Landscape: A History of the National Trust* (London, 1988); J. Jenkins and P. James, *From Acorn to Oak Tree: The Growth of the National Trust, 1895–1994* (London, 1994); M. Waterson, *The National Trust: the first hundred years* (London, 1994).

3. For other accounts which take a broader perspective, see: R. Hewison, *The Heritage Industry: Britain in a Climate of Decline* (London, 1987), pp. 51–72; T. C. Smout, 'The Highlands and the Roots of Green Consciousness, 1750–1990', *Proceedings of the British Academy*, lxxvi (1991), pp. 237–63; P. Mandler, 'Politics and the English Landscape Since the First World War', *Huntington Library Quarterly*, lv (1992), pp. 459–76.

4. C. P. Snow, *The Masters* (London, 1951), p. 349; D. Cannadine, 'The Context, Performance and Meaning of Ritual: The British Monarchy and the "Invention of Tradition", *c.* 1820–1977', in E. Hobsbawm and T. Ranger (eds.), *The Invention of Tradition* (Cambridge, 1983), pp. 108–38. See also chapter 9.

5. D. Watkin, *The Rise of Architectural History* (London, 1980), pp. 94–5.

6. D. Cannadine, *The Decline and Fall of the British Aristocracy* (1990), pp. 447–55.

7. D. Cannadine, 'The Present and the Past in the British Industrial Revolution, 1880–1980', *Past & Present*, no. 103 (1984), pp. 133–42.

8. M. J. Wiener, *English Culture and the Decline of the Industrial Spirit, 1850–1980* (Harmondsworth, 1992), pp. 37–40, 46–63; J. Marsh, *Back to the Land: The Pastoral Impulse in England from 1880 to 1914* (Cambridge, 1982), *passim*.

9. R. Williams, *The Country and the City* (London, 1973), p. 248; G. Cavaliero, *The Rural Tradition in the English Novel, 1900–1939* (London, 1977), pp. 1–13; A. Howkins, 'The Discovery of Rural England', in R. Colls and P. Dodd (eds.), *Englishness: Politics and Culture* (London, 1986), pp. 62–88.

10. A. Offer, *Property and Politics, 1870–1914: Landownership, Law, Ideology and Urban Development in England* (Cambridge, 1981), pp. 328–49.

11. G. Murphy, *Founders of the National Trust* (London, 1987), is the only group biography.

12. Murphy, *Founders of the National Trust*, p. 98; Canon Rawnsley, 'A National

Benefactor – Sir Robert Hunter', *Cornhill Magazine*, new series, xxxvi (1914), p. 239.

13. H. D. Rawnsley, 'The National Trust', *Cornhill Magazine*, new series, ii (1897), pp. 245–9; E. Rawnsley, *Canon Rawnsley: An Account of His Life* (London, 1923), pp. 107–16, 220–29; E. P. Thompson, *Customs in Common* (London, 1991), pp. 121–6; Lord Eversley, *Commons, Forests and Footpaths* (1910), *passim*; Marsh, *Back to the Land*, pp. 39–59; O. Hill, *Our Common Land* (1877), pp. 1–17, 105–51, 175–206; O. Hill, 'Natural Beauty as a National Asset', *Nineteenth Century*, lviii (1905), pp. 935–41; E. M. Bell, *Octavia Hill: A Biography* (London, 1942), pp. 141–55, 220–39; W. T. Hill, *Octavia Hill: Pioneer of the National Trust and Housing Reform* (London, 1956), pp. 98–108, 125–33, 144–72.

14. *The Times*, 28 June 1906, 30 November 1907; Hewison, *Heritage*, p. 57.

15. H. D. Rawnsley, *A Nation's Heritage* (London, 1920) gives an account of the Trust's holdings immediately after the First World War.

16. J. Lowerson, 'Battles for the Countryside', in F. Gloversmith (ed.), *Class, Culture and Social Change: A New View of the 1930s* (London, 1980), pp. 258–80.

17. Wiener, *English Culture*, pp. 100–110; J. R. Vincent (ed.), *The Crawford Papers* (Manchester, 1984), pp. 2–3, 521, 541.

18. J. Sheial, *Rural Conservation in Inter-War Britain* (London, 1981), *passim*; D. N. Jeans, 'Planning and the Myth of the English Countryside in the Inter-War Period', *Rural History*, i (1990), pp. 249–64; Wiener, *English Culture*, pp. 72–7; A. Potts, ' "Constable Country" Between the Wars', in R. Samuel (ed.), *Patriotism: The Making and Un-Making of British National Identity* (3 vols., London, 1989), vol. iii, pp. 160–86.

19. Cavaliero, *Rural Tradition*, pp. 133–46; and see ch. 7.

20. J. Bailey, *A Question of Taste* (London, 1926), p. 1. See also J. Bailey, *Some Political Ideas and Persons* (London, 1921), *passim*.

21. Trevelyan, pp. 151–67.

22. S. Bailey (ed.), *John Bailey, 1864–1931: Letters and Diaries* (1935), pp. 12–13, 39; O. Brett, *A Defence of Liberty* (1920), pp. 34, 38, 43, 46–7.

23. GMT, *Must England's Beauty Perish?* (1926), pp. 9, 14, 18–20; GMT, *The Calls and Claims of Natural Beauty* (London, 1931), reprinted in *An Autobiography and Other Essays* (London, 1949), pp. 101, 106.

24. *The Times*, 12 June 1923, 24 August 1925, 4 September 1930, 28 February 1935.

25. Trevelyan, pp. 167–77; GMT, 'Fifty Years of the National Trust', *Country Life*, 12 January 1945, pp. 62–4.

26. *The Times*, 30 July 1945, 2 July 1946, 30 October 1946, 19 December 1946, 17 November 1947, 12 November 1949.

27. Bailey, *Bailey*, p. 69.

28. H. Newby, *Country Life: A Social History of Rural England* (London, 1987), pp. 174–9; Weiner, *English Culture*, pp. 118–26; H. Dalton, *Practical Socialism for Britain* (London, 1935), p. 292; B. Pimlott, *Hugh Dalton* (London, 1985), pp. 455–6.

29. J. R. M. Butler, *Lord Lothian* (London, 1960), pp. 144–58; M. Drury, 'The

Early Years of the Country Houses Scheme', *The National Trust Magazine* (Autumn 1987), pp. 31–4; *The Times*, 11 January 1939, 1 March 1939, 18 May 1939.

30. J. Lees-Milne, *People and Places: Country House Donors and the National Trust* (London, 1992), pp. 1–18.

31. Cannadine, *Decline and Fall*, pp. 626–33, 639–45.

32. *The Times*, 13 October 1951, 20 September 1952, 11 October 1952, 13 November 1953.

33. See H. Nicolson's articles on the Trust in the *Spectator*, 16 June 1944, 15 August 1947, 2 July 1948, 18 November 1949.

34. N. Nicolson (ed.), *Vita and Harold: The Letters of V. Sackville-West and Harold Nicolson, 1910–1962* (London, 1992), p. 405.

35. D. Cannadine, *Aspects of Aristocracy: Grandeur and Decline in Modern Britain* (London, 1994), pp. 231–7.

36. J. Lees-Milne: *Another Self* (London, 1970), pp. 53–4, 95–7, 120–21; *Ancestral Voices* (London, 1975), pp. 170, 185, 187, 214, 225; *Prophesying Peace* (London, 1977), pp. 85, 105, 109, 176, 209; *Caves of Ice* (London, 1983), pp. 36, 53, 167, 172; and *Midway on the Waves* (London, 1985), pp. 23, 39, 117, 199.

37. Eversley, *Commons, Forests and Footpaths*, pp. 115–17.

38. *The National Trust and the Preservation of Country Houses* (London, 1947), p. 3.

39. St John Gore, Forward to G. Jackson-Stops (ed.), *National Trust Studies* (London, 1980), p. 6.

40. *The Times*, 16 October 1948, 15 September 1953, 20 October 1954, 25 May 1956, 11 April 1957, 11 October 1958.

41. R. H. S. Crossman, *The Diaries of a Cabinet Minister*, vol. i, *Minister of Housing, 1964–66* (London, 1975), pp. 205, 345, 540–41.

42. Newby, *Country Life*, pp. 229–37; K. V. Thomas, *Man and the Natural World: Changing Attitudes in England, 1500–1800* (London, 1983), pp. 13–16, 300–303.

43. P. Wright, *On Living in an Old Country: The National Trust in Contemporary Britain* (London, 1985), pp. 162–9.

44. Cannadine, *Decline and Fall*, p. 653; A. Jones, *Britain's Heritage: the Creation of the National Heritage Memorial Fund* (London, 1985), *passim*.

45. Cannadine, *Decline and Fall*, pp. 650–52; *The Times*, 20 September 1962.

46. *The Times*, 15 October 1963.

47. *The Times*, 15 October 1960, 12 October and 11 November 1964, 21 April 1970.

48. *The Times*, 28 November 1966, 19 January, 13 February, 23 March, 5 May and 2 November 1967; R. H. S. Crossman, *The Diaries of a Cabinet Minister*, vol. ii, *Lord President of the Council and Leader of the House of Commons, 1966–68* (London, 1976), p. 458.

49. *The Times*, 17 January 1969, 7 October 1969; National Trust, *Report by the Council's Advisory Committee on the Trust's Constitution, Organisation and Responsibilities* (London, 1969); Lord Benson, *Accounting for Life* (London, 1989), pp. 147–9.

50. Cannadine, *Decline and Fall*, pp. 653–5.

51. G. Jackson-Stops (ed.), *The Treasure Houses of Britain: Five Hundred Years of Private Patronage and Collecting* (London, 1984), *passim*; D. Cannadine, *The Pleasures of the Past* (London, 1989), pp. 256–71; Lees-Milne, *People and Places*, pp. 219–21; *The Times*, 23 October 1992.

52. M. Waterson, *The Servants' Hall: A Domestic History of Erddig* (London, 1980), pp. 206–28; J. Cornforth, 'John Fowler', in G. Jackson-Stops (ed.), *National Trust Studies* (London, 1978), pp. 39–49; *The Times*, 19 June 1988.

53. *The Times*, 18 July 1933.

54. *The Times*, 18 December 1982, 29 and 31 October 1988, 23 June 1989, 18 March 1992.

11 Sentiment:
Noël Coward's Patriotic Ardour

1. The most important sources for this chapter are Coward's own works: the *Plays* (*PP* i–vi), the *Diaries*, the *Lyrics*, the *Verse* and the *Autobiography*. To these should be added his *Middle East Diary* (London, 1944) and his novel, *Pomp and Circumstance* (London, 1960). Essential material is also to be found in J. Lahr, *Coward the Playwright* (London, 1982); S. Morley, *A Talent to Amuse: A Biography of Noël Coward* (revised edn, Harmondsworth, 1974); C. Lesley, *The Life of Noël Coward* (1976); and P. Hoare, *Noël Coward: A Biography* (London, 1995). The dates given in the text after the first mention of Coward's major works refer to the year of composition.

2. *PP* iv, p. 352; Hoare, *Coward: A Biography*, pp. 295, 467.

3. *PP* iv, p. viii; Morley, *Talent to Amuse*, pp. 184, 379; Lesley, *Life of Noël Coward*, pp. 122. 141.

4. Morley, *Talent to Amuse*, p. 378.

5. Hoare, *Coward: A Biography*, pp. 44, 52.

6. *Autobiography*, pp. 56, 63, 72; *Lyrics*, p. 3; Morley, *Talent to Amuse*, p. 49; Lesley, *Life of Noël Coward*, p. 41; Lahr, *Coward the Playwright*, pp. 94–5; Hoare, *Coward: A Biography*, pp. 217–20.

7. D. Dromgoole, 'The Damien Hirst of his day', *Sunday Times, Culture*, 20 May 2001, pp. 14–15.

8. *PP* i, pp. 480, 521; Hoare, *Coward: A Biography*, pp. 199–200.

9. Lahr, *Coward the Playwright*, pp. 2, 31, 40–42; Morley, *Talent to Amuse*, p. 93.

10. Hoare, *Coward: A Biography*, pp. 135, 158, 292; *Diaries*, p. 259; *Autobiography*, p. 251.

11. D. Cannadine, *The Decline and Fall of the British Aristocracy* (London, 1990), p. 381.

12. *Diaries*, pp. 290–92; Hoare, *Coward: A Biography*, p. 402.

13. *Autobiography*, pp. 12–13; Morley, *Talent to Amuse*, p. 10; Hoare, *Coward: A Biography*, pp. 17–18.

14. *Autobiography*, p. 5; Hoare, *Coward: A Biography*, pp. 1–6.

15. Lahr, *Coward the Playwright*, pp. 58–9; Hoare, *Coward: A Biography*, pp. 505–6.

16. *PP* iii, pp. 28–9; Hoare, *Coward: A Biography*, pp. 122–3, 164.

17. Morley, *Talent to Amuse*, p. 164; Hoare, *Coward: A Biography*, pp. 276–7. For Coward's tribute to the *Daily Mail* ('Tory truths and Labour lies') see *Verse*, pp. 82–3.

18. *Verse*, p. 107; *Diaries*, p. 350.

19. Coward, *Middle East Diary*, p. 30; *Lyrics*, p. 287; *Diaries*, pp. 280, 657; Hoare, *Coward: A Biography*, pp. 36–7, 80–81.

20. Lesley, *Life of Noël Coward*, p. 53; Hoare, *Coward: A Biography*, pp. 33–7; Lahr, *Coward the Playwright*, p. 103; G. Brandreth, 'The Tory camp', *Sunday Telegraph*, Review, 24 June 2001, p. 1.

21. A. Roberts, *'The Holy Fox': A Biography of Lord Halifax* (London, 1991), p. 305.

22. See especially Coward's introductions to *PP* i–vi; Hoare, *Coward: A Biography*, pp. 255–6.

23. *PP* i, p. 73.

24. *Lyrics*, p. 113; Hoare, *Coward: A Biography*, pp. 231–6.

25. *Autobiography*, pp. 240–42; Lahr, *Coward the Playwright*, pp. 98–99.

26. *Autobiography*, pp. 251–2.

27. Ibid., pp. 212–27; Lesley, *Life of Noël Coward*, p. 149.

28. *Autobiography*, p. 264.

29. Ibid., pp. 218–20; *Diaries*, p. 191; Morley, *Talent to Amuse*, pp. 167, 239; Lesley, *Life of Noël Coward*, pp. 131, 159, 162, 166.

30. *Autobiography*, pp. 322–3, 480–81; Hoare, *Coward: A Biography*, pp. 247, 252.

31. *Diaries*, p. 346; *Verse*, pp. 162–82.

32. *Verse*, p. x.

33. *Lyrics*, pp. 103, 122–3.

34. Ibid., pp. 107–8, 124, 188–91; Hoare, *Coward: A Biography*, pp. 284–5.

35. *PP* iv, pp. 3, 76, 156; *Lyrics*, pp. 169–70.

36. *PP* iv, pp. 475–6, 480, 497, 512–13.

37. Ibid., p. xv; Lahr, *Coward the Playwright*, pp. 104–8; Hoare, *Coward: A Biography*, pp. 300–301.

38. *PP* iv, pp. 553–4.

39. *Autobiography*, p. 412.

40. Ibid., p. 378.

41. Morley, *Talent to Amuse*, p. 276.

42. *Autobiography*, pp. 325–6; Hoare, *Coward: A Biography*, pp. 298–9.

43. *Autobiography*, p. 417.

44. *Lyrics*, pp. 268–70; Morley, *Talent to Amuse*, pp. 268–9.

45. *Lyrics*, pp. 271–4.

46. *Autobiography*, p. 356.

47. Ibid., pp. 402, 404, 448, 449, 462, 463, 480, 489, 491.

48. Ibid., pp. 463–4.

49. *Lyrics*, pp. 211–13.

50. *Autobiography*, pp. 409–10; N. Coward, *Star Quality* (London, 1951), pp. 49–96.

51. *Diaries*, pp. 11–13, 42; Morley, *Talent to Amuse*, p. 212; Hoare, *Coward: A Biography*, pp. 313–17, 338–9.

52. Morley, *Talent to Amuse*, p. 294; Lesley, *Life of Noël Coward*, p. 216.

53. *Autobiography*, p. 421; *Diaries*, pp. 7, 22.

54. Lahr, *Coward the Playwright*, pp. 112–13.

55. *Diaries*, p. 16.

56. Coward, *Middle East Diary*, p. 16; Morley, *Talent to Amuse*, pp. 270–77.

57. Lesley, *Life of Noël Coward*, pp. 215–16, 221, 225; Hoare, *Coward: A Biography*, pp. 365–6.

58. *Diaries*, p. 29.

59. *Autobiography*, p. 459; *Diaries*, pp. 23, 58–9.

60. *PP* v, p. 340.

61. *Diaries*, pp. 119, 134–6, 145–7, 150, 257.

62. Ibid., pp. 92, 209. See also ch. 8.

63. Ibid., pp. 10–11, 49, 324–5.

64. Ibid., pp. 4, 19, 31, 35.

65. Ibid., p. 132; *Autobiography*, p. 417; Lesley, *Life of Noël Coward*, p. 124.

66. *Lyrics*, pp. 228–30, 332–4, 343–6.

67. *Diaries*, pp. 44, 49, 56, 249–50; Lesley, *Life of Noël Coward*, p. 242.

68. *PP* v, pp. 48, 67; *Lyrics*, pp. 242–4, 247; *Diaries*, pp. 70–72, 77.

69. *PP* v, p. 246; *Diaries*, p. 66.

70. *PP* v, pp. 208–12.

71. *Diaries*, p. 92; *Lyrics*, pp. 299, 320–22.

72. Ibid., p. 312.

73. *Autobiography*, p. 310.

74. *PP* v, pp. 296, 371; Lahr, *Coward the Playwright*, pp. 132–5.

75. *PP* v, pp. xvi–xvii; *Diaries*, p. 367.

76. *PP* v, pp. 377, 419–20.

77. *Diaries*, p. 125; *PP* vi, pp. 117, 129.

78. *PP* vi, pp. 138, 140; *Diaries*, pp. 127, 329.

79. *Diaries*, pp. 348–9.

80. *Diaries*, pp. 350, 431, 436, 444, 591; Hoare, *Coward: A Biography*, p. 434.

81. *Diaries*, pp. 294–6; *Lyrics*, p. 291.

82. *Diaries*, pp. 107–8, 382, 389; Lesley, *Life of Noël Coward*, pp. 261, 265.

83. *Diaries*, pp. 263–7.

84. Ibid., pp. 296, 342; Hoare, *Coward: A Biography*, p. 447.

85. *Diaries*, p. 293.

86. Coward, *Pomp and Circumstance*, pp. 86–7, 92–4.

87. M. Amory (ed.), *The Letters of Ann Fleming* (London, 1985), pp. 106–7; *Diaries*, pp. 79, 96, 159, 173, 181–2, 189, 222–3, 357, 437–8; Lesley, *Life of Noël Coward*, p. 402.

88. *Diaries*, p. 593.

89. *Lyrics*, pp. 397–9.

90. Morley, *Talent to Amuse*, pp. 362–3.

91. *Verse*, p. 19; *Diaries*, pp. 531, 635, 637; Hoare, *Coward: A Biography*, p. 481.

92. *Diaries*, pp. 543–4.

93. *Verse*, pp. 151–2.

94. *Diaries*, pp. 341, 463–4. For these articles, see the *Sunday Times, Magazine*, 15 January 1961, p. 23; 22 January, p. 23; 29 January, p. 24.

95. Lahr, *Coward the Playwright*, pp. 137–9; Hoare, *Coward: A Biography*, pp. 465–7.

96. Hoare, *Coward: A Biography*, pp. 422–4.

97. *Diaries*, pp. 405, 434, 447–8, 461, 484; Lahr, *Coward the Playwright*, pp. 143–53.

98. *Diaries*, p. 629; Lahr, *Coward the Playwright*, pp. 154–60; Hoare, *Coward: A Biography*, pp. 494–8.

99. *Diaries*, pp. 335, 456; N. Coward, *Bon Voyage* (London, 1968), pp. 56, 86.

100. *Diaries*, pp. 535, 610–13, 614–15, 662–3.

101. Ibid., pp. 335, 538; *Verse*, p. 28.

102. *PP* vi, p. 499; *Diaries*, pp. 354, 525.

103. Lahr, *Coward the Playwright*, p. 171, note 6; Hoare, *Coward: A Biography*, p. 513.

104. *Diaries*, pp. 634, 673, 679.

105. Ibid., p. 555.

106. Ibid., pp. 600–601, 624; Hoare, *Coward: A Biography*, p. 510.

12 Fantasy:
Ian Fleming and the Realities of Escapism

1. R. Usborne, *Clubland Heroes* (London, 1953), pp. 3–4, 15–16.

2. N. Annan, *Our Age* (New York, 1990), p. 239.

3. The complete list of Bond books, all first published by Jonathan Cape, London, is as follows: *Casino Royale* (1953); *Live and Let Die* (1954); *Moonraker* (1955); *Diamonds Are Forever* (1956); *From Russia With Love* (1957); *Dr No* (1958); *Goldfinger* (1959); *For Your Eyes Only* (1960) (short stories); *Thunderball* (1961); *The Spy Who Loved Me* (1962); *On Her Majesty's Secret Service* (1963); *You Only Live Twice* (1964); *The Man with the Golden Gun* (1965); *Octopussy* (1966) (an incomplete volume of short stories). Because there have been so many subsequent editions and reprintings of the Bond books, I have only given references for the most extended quotations, which are to the chapter (or short story) rather than the page. Fleming's most important (and revealing) works of non-fiction were: *The Diamond Smugglers* (London, 1957); *Thrilling Cities* (London, 1963); 'If I Were Prime Minister', *Spectator*, 9 October 1959, pp. 466–7. For a full bibliography, see I. Campbell, *Ian Fleming: A Catalogue of a Collection* (Liverpool, 1978).

4. S. Raven, 'The Natural Man', *Spectator*, 28 October 1966, p. 552. For one series of contemporary reactions, see R. Hart-Davis (ed.), *The Lyttelton Hart-Davis Letters*

(6 vols., London, 1978–84), vol. ii, pp. 58–9, 61, 78, 80–81, 89–92, 94; vol. iii, pp. 46, 49; vol. iv, pp. 156, 158; vol. v, pp. 33, 59; vol. vi, pp. 27–30.

5. Two important works on nations 'in decline' are: P. Burke, 'Tradition and Experience: The Idea of Decline from Bruni to Gibbon', *Daedalus*, no. 105 (1976), pp. 137–52; and J. H. Elliott, *Spain and its World, 1500–1700* (London, 1989), pp. 215–61. For the broader perspective on British 'decline', see chapter 2. The best contemporary evocations of Fleming's (and Bond's) Britain are: A. Sampson: *Anatomy of Britain* (London, 1962); *Anatomy of Britain Today* (London 1965); and *New Anatomy of Britain* (London, 1971); B. Levin, *The Pendulum Years: Britain and the 'Sixties* (London, 1972). For the fullest historical account, see A. Marwick, *The Sixties* (Oxford, 1998).

6. J. Morris, *Farewell the Trumpets: An Imperial Retreat* (Harmondsworth, 1978), pp. 545–7; J. Dimbleby, *Richard Dimbleby* (London, 1977), pp. 370–75; Levin, *Pendulum Years*, pp. 399–411.

7. B. R. Tomlinson, 'The Contraction of England: National Decline and the Loss of Empire', *Journal of Imperial and Commonwealth History*, xi (1982), pp. 58–72; D. A. Low, *The Contraction of England* (Cambridge, 1985). See also ch. 2.

8. The following section draws extensively on: J. Pearson, *The Life of Ian Fleming* (London, 1966); K. Amis in *DNB, 1961–70* (Oxford, 1981), pp. 365–6; A. Lycett, *Ian Fleming* (London, 1996); D. Hart-Davis, *Peter Fleming: A Biography* (London, 1974); R. Hart-Davis, in *DNB, 1971–80* (Oxford, 1986), pp. 321–2; K. Fleming, *Celia Johnson* (London, 1992); F. Fleming, *Amaryllis Fleming* (London, 1993).

9. L. J. Colley, *Britons: Forging the Nation, 1707–1837* (London, 1992), p. 132. For the Scots in the British Empire, see: R. A. Cage (ed.), *The Scots Abroad: Labour, Capital, Enterprise, 1750–1914* (London, 1985); T. M. Devine (ed.), *Scottish Emigration and Scottish Society* (Edinburgh, 1992); G. T. Stewart, *Jute and Empire: The Calcutta Jute Wallahs and the Landscapes of Empire* (Manchester, 1998); J. M. Mac-Kenzie: 'Essay and Review: On Scotland and the Empire', *International History Review*, xv (1993), pp. 714–39; and 'Empire and National Identities: The Case of Scotland', *Transactions of the Royal Historical Society*, 6th Series, viii (1998), pp. 215–31.

10. *Burke's Landed Gentry* (London, 1952 edn), p. 870; D. Kynaston, *The City of London*, vol. i, *A World of Its Own, 1815–1890* (London, 1994), p. 409; vol. ii, *Golden Years, 1890–1914* (London, 1995), p. 317; Y. Cassis, 'The Emergence of a New Financial Institution: Investment Trusts in Britain, 1870–1914', in J. J. van Helten and Y. Cassis (eds.), *Capitalism in a Mature Economy: Financial Institutions, Capital Exports and British Industry, 1870–1939* (Aldershot, 1990), pp. 140–42. For the concept of 'gentlemanly capitalism', see P. J. Cain and A. G. Hopkins, *British Imperialism*, vol. i, *Innovation and Expansion, 1688–1914*; vol. ii, *Crisis and Deconstruction, 1914–1990* (London, 1993).

11. F. W. S. Craig, *British Parliamentary Election Results, 1885–1918* (2nd edn, Dartmouth, 1989), p. 370.

12. M. Holroyd, *Augustus John*, vol. ii, *The Years of Experience* (London, 1975), pp. 90–93.

13. *DNB, 1961–70*, p. 366; D. Kynaston, *The City of London*, vol. iii, *Illusions of Gold, 1914–1945* (London, 1999), pp. 300–301.

14. C. Andrew, *Secret Service: The Making of the British Intelligence Community* (London, 1985), pp. 455–6.

15. W. Plomer, 'Ian Fleming Remembered', *Encounter*, January 1965, p. 64.

16. IF, *Thrilling Cities*, pp. 18–20.

17. M. Amory (ed.), *The Letters of Ann Fleming* (London, 1985), pp. 43–4, 170, 215–16, 398–9; N. Henderson, *Old Friends and Modern Instances* (London, 2000), p. 121.

18. B. Brivati, *Hugh Gaitskell* (London, 1997), pp. 242–6.

19. Pearson, *Fleming*, pp. 20, 198–9.

20. I. F. Clarke, *Voices Prophesying War* (Oxford, 1992), pp. 93–130; J. Meisel, 'The Germans are Coming! British Fiction of a German Invasion, 1871–1913', *War, Literature and the Arts*, ii (1990), pp. 41–77.

21. Andrew, *Secret Service*, pp. 34–48; C. Wilson, *Snobbery with Violence: Crime Stories and their Audience* (London, 1971), pp. 242, 250.

22. G. Himmelfarb, *Victorian Minds* (New York, 1970), p. 252.

23. IF, *Casino Royale*, ch. 10.

24. K. Amis, *The James Bond Dossier* (London, 1965), p. 42.

25. Himmelfarb, *Victorian Minds*, p. 250.

26. D. Cannadine, *History in Our Time* (London, 1998), p. 241.

27. Himmelfarb, *Victorian Minds*, pp. 271–2.

28. Amis, *Bond Dossier*, p. 86; M. Richler, *Shovelling Trouble* (London, 1973), pp. 62–6.

29. IF, *For Your Eyes Only*, 'For Your Eyes Only'.

30. IF, *You Only Live Twice*, ch. 21.

31. IF, *Moonraker*, ch. 16.

32. Pearson, *Fleming*, p. 18; IF, 'If I Were Prime Minister', p. 466.

33. Amis, *Bond Dossier*, p. 95.

34. IF, *On Her Majesty's Secret Service*, chs. 20, 21.

35. IF, *Thunderball*, ch. 15.

36. Pearson, *Fleming*, pp. 27, 38, 65.

37. IF, *Thrilling Cities*, pp. 85, 90; IF, 'If I Were Prime Minister', p. 466.

38. IF, *Thunderball*, ch. 2.

39. IF, *Thrilling Cities*, p. 122.

40. S. Raven, 'Amis and the Eggheads', *Spectator*, 28 May 1965, p. 694.

41. IF, *Live and Let Die*, ch. 17.

42. Pearson, *Fleming*, pp. 82, 109.

43. IF, *Live and Let Die*, ch. 14.

44. IF, *Diamonds Are Forever*, ch. 21.

45. IF, *Dr No*, chs. 12, 20.

46. Amis, *Bond Dossier*, p. 47.

47. IF, *Casino Royale*, chs. 3, 15.

48. P. Howarth, *'Play Up and Play the Game': The Heroes of Popular Fiction* (London, 1973), p. 175.

49. Amis, *Bond Dossier*, pp. 51–3, 57–61.

50. Raven, 'Amis and the Eggheads', p. 694.

51. IF, *Live and Let Die*, ch. 17.

52. IF, *Dr No*, ch. 7.

53. A. S. Boyd, *The Devil with James Bond* (London, 1966), pp. 41, 48–9; IF, '007 and Me', in S. Lane (ed.), *For Bond Lovers Only* (London, 1965), p. 16.

54. Pearson, *Fleming*, pp. 64, 327; Plomer, 'Ian Fleming Remembered', p. 65.

55. IF, *Thrilling Cities*, pp. 85–6.

56. For Fleming's most outspoken contemporary critics, see: Paul Johnson, 'Sex, Snobbery and Sadism', *New Statesman*, 5 April 1958, pp. 430–43; Bernard Bergonzi, 'The Case of Mr Fleming', *Twentieth Century*, March 1958, pp. 220–28; J. Price, 'Our Man in the Torture Chamber', *London Magazine*, March 1962, pp. 67–70; L. M. Starkey, *James Bond: His World of Values* (1966); Richler, *Shovelling Trouble*, pp. 55–83.

57. Bergonzi, 'Case of Mr Fleming', p. 221.

58. Ibid., p. 222; Levin, *Pendulum Years*, p. 91.

59. Pearson, *Fleming*, p. 57; IF, 'If I Were Prime Minister', pp. 466–7.

60. IF, *Thrilling Cities*, pp. 33, 37, 58, 129.

61. Pearson, *Fleming*, pp. 80–81; Price, 'Our Man in the Torture Chamber', p. 70.

62. Ibid., p. 69.

63. IF, *Moonraker*, ch. 5.

64. Amory, *Letters of Ann Fleming*, p. 382, note 5.

65. Johnson, 'Sex, Snobbery and Sadism', p. 430; Starkey, *James Bond: His World of Values*, p. 8.

66. Richler, *Shovelling Trouble*, p. 60.

67. IF, *Thunderball*, ch. 14.

68. IF, *From Russia with Love*, ch. 5.

69. IF, *Thrilling Cities*, p. 122.

70. IF, *For Your Eyes Only*, 'The Hildebrand Rarity'.

71. IF, *You Only Live Twice*, chs. 3, 5.

72. IF, *The Man with the Golden Gun*, ch. 4.

73. IF, *You Only Live Twice*, ch. 8.

74. Price, 'Our Man in the Torture Chamber', p. 69.

75. P. Augar, *The Death of Gentlemanly Capitalism* (Harmondsworth, 2000), pp. 65–9, 191–2, 197–8, 288–9, 315, 327; D. Kynaston, *The City of London*, vol. iv, *A Club No More, 1945–2000* (London, 2000), p. 782.

76. Annan, *Our Age*, pp. 237–9. Fleming, uncharacteristically, mentions the drabness, despair, squalor and greyness of secret service life in *The Diamond Smugglers*, p. 41.

77. Brivati, *Gaitskell*, pp. 242–3.

78. For a full account of the films, see L. Pfeiffer and D. Worrall, *The Essential Bond: The Authorized Guide to the World of 007* (2nd edn, London, 2000).

79. Marwick, *The Sixties*, p. 471.

Index